To Dad
From Nicki
Christmas 1993

MFK FISHER

Serve It Forth

NORTH POINT PRESS
San Francisco 1989

Copyright © 1937 by M. F. K. Fisher
Printed in the United States of America

LIBRARY OF CONGRESS CATALOGING-IN-PUBLICATION DATA
Fisher, M. F. K. (Mary Frances Kennedy), 1908–
    Serve it forth / M. F. K. Fisher.
        p.   cm.
    Originally published: New York: Harper, 1937.
    ISBN 0-86547-369-2
    1. Gastronomy.   2. Food.   3. Dinners and dining.   I. Title.
II. Title: Serve it forth.
TX631.F53 1989
641'.01'3—dc19   88-37227

For R.B.K. and E.O.H.K.

Contents

"Of course," concluded Robert Kilburn Root, sitting crosslegged and contemplating his *Shashlik*— "of course if this book is well larded with anecdotes, it will of necessity be short."

Serve
It Forth

To Begin

There are two kinds of books about eating: those that try to imitate Brillat-Savarin's, and those that try not to. The first substitute whimsy for his wit, and dull reminiscences for his delightful anecdotes. The second are gross where he would be delicate, and choose blunt statistics rather than his piercing observations.

And books about what to eat: they too are twins from one source, the first written recipes in our world. They are stodgy, matter-of-fact, covered very practically with washable cloth or gravy-coloured paper, beginning with measurements and food values and ending with sections on the care of invalids—oddly enough for books so concerned with hygiene! They are usually German, or English or American.

Or, on the other hand, they are short, bound impractically in creamy paper or chintz, illustrated by woodcutters à la mode. They begin with witty philosophizing on the pleasures of the table, and end with a suggested menu for an intimate dinner given to seven gentlemen who know his wife, by a wealthy old banker who feels horns pricking up gently from his bald skull. These books are usually French. They are much more entertaining, if less useful, than their phlegmatic twins.

To make one into two yet again, there are two painful variants of one most interesting subject: those who eat. The first, foisted upon us at least semiannually by enthusiastic publishers, is listed under *Memoirs* in book catalogues. Its pages totter and crumple under a weight of well-known names, and from each chapter rises a reek, a heady stench of truffles, Château Yquem, and quails *financière*. You sit, pompously nonchalant, on a balcony at Monte Carlo, tête-à-tête with three princes, a millionaire, and the lovely toast of London, God bless her! Or, in a Georgian dining room filled with quietly munching Cabinet ministers, you exchange quips which grow by repetition into fin de siècle epigrams. It is all very enervating—and it sells well, they say.

Its partner, that other kind of book about people who eat, is at times even more objectionable. It is usually written by two self-styled gourmets, or three. It shows pictures of its authors standing beside a quaint old inn near Oxford or a quaint old inn near Cannes. It discusses seriously and with firm authority the problem of Bordeaux *versus* Burgundies or when to drink Barsac, and settles with a fine confidence all questions of vintage, pourboires, and the barbaric horrors of the cocktail. It is perhaps needless to say that its authors are young and full of intellectual fun and frolic, and that they are making a gastronomic tour on bicycles.

Now I am going to write a book. It will be about eating and about what to eat and about people who eat. And I shall do gymnastics by trying to fall between these three fires, or by straddling them all.

The first, that great ghost born in Belley who ate like a fat parson and wrote consummately on eating with delicate art, I shall very humbly recognize.

The second—was it a Sicilian cooking for Cæsar or a Norman chef in old England who first wrote our plans for dishes, or was it perhaps a round monk in Touraine?—the second I shall avoid. Recipes in my book will be there like birds in a tree—if there is a comfortable branch.

The third I can most easily miss. I am not old and famous, with friends whose names sound like the guest lists of all the diplomatic receptions held in all the world capitals since 1872. Nor am I young and intellectually gastronomic on a bicycle.

So my book, hopefully evading each of the three fires, will be singed by all. Brillat-Savarin will haunt it, and very probably show himself in an inevitable aphorism. *The Settlement Cook Book* and Paul Reboux will peer shyly and with little recognition at their ancestors *The Harleian Manuscript* and Mrs. Glasse and Carême and Roselli. And people I know will talk a little and eat more, not with prime ministers in Geneva, perhaps, nor with munitions-makers at Menton. But they are really very nice people, most of them.

I serve it forth.

When a Man
Is Small

When a man is small, he loves and hates food with a ferocity which soon dims. At six years old his very bowels will heave when such a dish as creamed carrots or cold tapioca appears before him. His throat will close, and spots of nausea and rage swim in his vision. It is hard, later, to remember why, but at the time there is no pose in his disgust. He cannot eat; he says, "To hell with it!"

In the same way, some foods are utterly delicious, and he thinks of them and tastes them with a sensuous passion which too often disappears completely with the years.

Perhaps there are little chocolate cookies as a special treat, two apiece. He eats his, all two, with an intense but delicate avidity. His small sister Judy puts one of hers in her pocket, the smug thing. But Aunt Gwen takes a bite from each of her cookies and gives what is left of one to Judy, what is left of the other to him. She is quite calm about it.

He looks at her with dreadful wonder. How can she bear to do it? He could not, *could* not have given more than a crumb of his cooky to anyone. Perhaps even a crumb would be too big.

Aunt Gwen is wonderful; she is brave and superhuman. He feels a little dizzy as he looks at the bitten cooky in his hand. How could she do it?

By the time a man is ten or twelve he has forgotten most of his young passions. He is hungry and he wants to be full. It is very simple.

A few more years and he is at his life's peak of energy. His body is electric with young muscle, young blood, a newfound manhood, an awakening mind. Strangely enough, it is now that he whips himself up to greater speed. He drinks strong raw spirits and countless cups of coffee, hot and black. He devours such mild aphrodisiacs as chili, tamales, and rare beef drowned in bottled sauces. He pours salt and pepper over everything except desserts.

At this age, eighteen or nineteen, gastronomic perceptions are nonexistent, or at the most naïve. I remember that when I was a college freshman my nearest approach to *la gourmandise* was a midnight visit to *Henry's*, the old *Henry's* on Hollywood Boulevard which all the world said that Charlie Chaplin owned secretly.

There I would call for the head waiter, which probably awed my escort almost as much as I hoped it would. The waiter, a kindly soul except on Saturday nights, played up to me beautifully, and together we ordered a large pot of coffee and a German pancake with hot applesauce and sweet butter. ("Salted butter ruins the flavor," I would add in a nonchalant aside to my Tommy or Jimmy.)

When the pancake appeared, after an impressive wait, it was big as a tabletop, with curled edges. Two waitresses fussed over it, while people stared at us and I made sure that the applesauce was spread on *after* the melted butter, and that plenty of lemon juice and cinnamon were sprinkled about.

I always looked away while the monstrous thing was rolled:

the waitresses were too nervous and stuck out their tongues. And I cannot remember ever finishing even my half of the pancake, when it was sliced and powdered and laid before me. Nor can I imagine ordering one now.

It is, however, these innocent experiments with food, mixed though they may be with snobbishness and "showing off," that indicate what kind of older person a young one may become. And he had two choices, the two oft-quoted oft-abused alternatives of eating to live and of living to eat.

Any normal man must nourish his body by means of food put into it through the mouth. This process takes time, quite apart from the lengthy preparations and digestions that accompany it.

Between the ages of twenty and fifty, John Doe spends some twenty thousand hours chewing and swallowing food, more than eight hundred days and nights of steady eating. The mere contemplation of this fact is upsetting enough!

To some men it is actively revolting. They devise means of accomplishing the required nourishments of their bodies by pills of condensed victuals and easily swallowed draughts which equal, they are told, the food value of a beefsteak or a vegetable stew.

To others, the stunning realization of how much time is needed to feed themselves is accepted more philosophically. They agree with La Rochefoucauld's aphorism: To eat is a necessity, but to eat intelligently is an art.

Critics of the resulting scheme of life are easily led to accuse its practicants of substituting a less pleasant word for "intelligent." So, indeed, do many of us. We sink too easily into stupid and overfed sensuality, our bodies thickening even more quickly than our minds. We sharpen one sense at the cost of losing many others, and call ourselves epicures, forgetting that Epicurus himself employed the same adjective as La Rochefoucauld when he advocated our finding an agreeable use for our faculties in "the intelligent enjoyment of the pleasures of the table."

Whichever school a man may adhere to, the protestant or the philosophical, he continues to eat through the middle years of life with increasing interest. He grows more conscious of his body as it becomes less tolerant.

No longer can he dine heavily at untoward hours, filling his stomach with the adolescent excitations of hot sauces and stodgy pastries—no longer, that is, with impunity. No more can he say with any truth: "Oh, I can eat anything. I can drink without showing it. I am made of iron."

He is confused by strange aches and rumblings, and shudders at the thought of being forced by old age to return to the pap and pabulum of his infancy.

Most of us, unhappily, shudder and ache and rumble as secretly as possible, seeming to feel disgrace in what is but one of the common phenomena of age: the general slowing of all physical processes. For years we hide or ignore our bodily protests and hasten our own dyspeptic doom by trying to eat and drink as we did when we were twenty.

When we are past fifty, especially if we have kept up this pathetic pose of youth-at-table, we begin to grow fat. It is then that even the blindest of us should beware. Unfortunately, however, we are too used to seeing other people turn heavy in their fifties: we accept paunches and double chins as a necessary part of growing old.

Instead, we should realize this final protest of an overstuffed system, and ease our body's last years by lightening its burden. We should eat sparingly.

It is here that gastronomy, or an equivalent, can play its most comforting rôle. Even in crude form the desire for a special taste or sensation has often helped an old man more than his critical family can know. They may call him heartless; he in his turn may as logically be acting with good sense, like the ancient sailor whose much-loved son was lost at sea. When at last some one mustered courage to tell the father this tragic news, the old man looked at him coldly for a minute, glanced out the window at the blown sea, and then snapped: "Dad blast it, where's my dish of tea? I want my tea!"

For many old people, eating is the only pleasure left, as were the "endless dishes" and "unceasing cups of wine" to the aged Ulysses. And between gobbling down an indistinguishable mess of heavy meat and bread, or savouring a delicate broiled trout or an aspic full of subtle vegetable flavours, how few of us would choose the distressful insomnia that follows the first for the light easy rest of the second?

But men are thoughtless and they are habit-followers. They have eaten meat and starches for years: they see no reason for stopping when they are old, even when they think enough to realize that every function of their bodies is carried on more slowly and with more effort than ever before.

They go on whipping up their blood with "well-done" roasts, which travel haltingly through the system to the final colonic decay that makes one of the great foes of senescence— constipation.

They are floated to their coffins on a river of "stimulating" infusions of beef extract and iron, usually fed to them surreptitiously by well-meaning daughters.

They plump out their poor sagging paunches for years with the puffed richness of such "nourishing" desserts as the typical English sweet which a friend described to me: "cake soaked with bad port, smothered in boiled custard stained a purple-brown with blackberry juice, which is in turn top-layered with warm ill-beaten white of egg tinted fuchsia pink, the whole garnished with small dirty-brown buttons of granite that are reported by us hardier Britons to be macaroons. This particular foul concoction is called 'Queen o' Puddings'!"

No wonder old people are dubbed "quaintly crabbed and testy" by sentimental novelists, and "plain hell to live with" by their less idealistic offspring!

But we must grow old, and we must eat. It seems far from unreasonable, once these facts are accepted, for a man to set himself the pleasant task of educating his palate so that he can do the former not grudgingly and in spite of the latter, but easily and agreeably because of it.

Talleyrand said that two things are essential in life: to give good dinners and to keep on fair terms with women. As the years pass and fires cool, it can become unimportant to stay always on fair terms either with women or one's fellows, but a wide and sensitive appreciation of fine flavours can still abide with us, to warm our hearts.

Greek Honey
and the Hon-Zo

3000 B.C.–100 A.D.
Egypt, the Orient, and Greece

Twenty-eight hundred years before Jesus broke bread for his children, a wise emperor in China thought of his. Shennung was his name, and before he died he had compiled a great cookbook, the *Hon-Zo*. In forty-seven centuries we have not learned much more about food than it can tell.

While Shennung's millions died and lived, humans all over this world were eating according to their fashions, but principally because they had to. From the north still came a faint snarl of hungry blond men gnashing at raw meat, and an occasional whiff of carrion, that sweet wild sickening smell. But all around the Mediterranean and to the east, a ring of good things was sprouting. Gradually fig trees were planted, and then grapes, and wheat grew because men made it. New pleasures were born for the warm brown people.

In Egypt they ate quite simply. Everyday bread was made from *spelt*, the dried pounded centers of the sacred lotus plants, and for feasts fine wheaten flour in loaves. They caught fish and spread them in the sun to dry, thick with salt.

All the Egyptians ate leeks and onions with some impunity, but tried to hide their passion for garlic from the priests, who most fastidiously denounced it as an unclean abomination.

Ox meat was roasted or boiled, but many kinds of little birds, and even quails and ducks, were salted and eaten raw. And melons in increasing variety made fine the poorest fare, with grapes and figs and dates, and barley beer, and sweet wine in great pottery vases glazed with blue.

Honey from the richly flowered delta had already in those far days been changed into a hundred kinds of sweetmeats, or baked into the breads, or simmered with the flesh of melons and fruits to make the same heavy voluptuous confitures that travellers eat today in Alexandria.

Then, as now, the Egyptians were temperate and frugal, but always hospitable. They welcomed strangers as well as kin to their meals, where men and women ate together, and where, for the most part, the lowest *fellahin* and members of the royal family ate much the same simple food.

It was in the tools for eating, and the dining rooms, that caste difference most clearly showed itself. The peasants and the artisans used pottery, glazed blue or red, perhaps, but always simple, and they sat on benches in their low mud houses.

The palaces of the wealthy people, the nobles and scientists, were airy and beautiful, surrounded by pools and arboured gardens, and built with carved painted columns to hold the canopies that made their walls.

Everywhere, on the stone pillars and the embroidered linens, and in the faïence, and the gold that was "plentiful as dust," the sacred lotus and the date frond curved and lifted.

At feasts guests sat upon wooden armchairs, heavily inlaid with gold and stones, and made more comfortable by soft cushions of leather and silky Egyptian linen. They ate from delicate spoons of carved wood or ivory, and drank from lotus-cups of blue glaze or, later, of iridescent glass. Bowls, no matter how simple their contents, were of the common gold, or rarer silver, or the most valuable bronze.

Unlike the Greeks and Romans, who barred women from all banqueting, and only invited the hetæræ to come in with the final wines for philosophic dalliance, the Egyptians dined easily together. While the lords and ladies tarried over their cool courses of melons and sweet wine, dancers entertained them with slow gay rhythms, or more highly educated singers, usually women, chanted to the ancient plaintive sounds of lutes and pipes.

At more vulgar feasts, girls or young men in female dress performed much the same obscene dances that can still be seen in Cairo or any Egyptian port, but they were rare. In general, the amusement of the Nile people was like their nourishment— delicate, fresh, wholesome.

While the Greeks across the sea were still free of any Egyptian finesse, and lived simply on boiled fish and black broth, with "running, fatigue, hunger, and thirst" for seasoning, things to eastward had taken quite a different turn. There natural indolence and sensuality, and enormous wealth, and climate, and viciousness bred with years of intermarriage, made feasting the chiefest recreation of the nobles.

It is hard to find what the poor people ate, but easy to imagine. Their time was too full to make food anything but a necessity, or something seen on the king's board as fantastic and intangible as the mounds of caviar in a Hollywood movie.

They heard and saw strange things, but dully. They saw Xerxes ruin two cities for a single feast, and heard how Belshazzar of Babylon caused a most luxurious banquet to be spread for all his thousand wives and concubines, with music and revelry and the rarest foods.

They whispered with passive amazement after Darius finished one of his famous saturnalia. They knew that King Solomon kept twelve stewards for his table, and that eleven of them travelled constantly, spying out new wines and the strangest viands.

And for many years they remembered Ahasuerus' carnival. It lasted fourscore and one hundred days. Fine folk from all that part of the world came to it and for seven days at the end of it came all the king's subjects, both great and small. They slept on mammoth gold and silver pillows laid on beds of black marble and yellow and scarlet and white stone. All the pillars were of marble, too, and from their silver rings hung purple and linen cords to hold up the white and green and blue tent-walls. And every man could drink his fill of the king's own wine, in a golden goblet different from any other's.

Whispers and odours and the tantalizing noises of banqueting floated swiftly westward. Greece heard and smelled and was fascinated. Gastronomy nourished itself on rumour, and from the Spartan black broth was born a refined and decadent philosophy of eating.

In their love for fresh vegetables and native fruits, however, the Greeks kept their cuisine basically simple. Honey they used for all sweetening, leaving the cane sugar brought from China to the medicine-makers. Chestnuts were roasted, as they had been for centuries, and eaten after meals with dried fruits.

But now delicate little cakes of sesame and honey were served at the same time, and cities became rivals in varying their shapes and flavours. Athens grew famous for its fine breads and honey-biscuits, and villages waxed haughty over cheeses whose special tastes they had tried to disguise only a few years before.

Locusts were still roasted a light golden hue, and meats spitted over coals, but with a new, investigating fervour. Peacocks were served in their feathers. Pork, long the favourite viand, was found to have over fifty different flavours!

And fish, that long-known flesh for soups and stews, emerged from monotony with a whole complex science of its own. Sole was the king of all the dishes, but almost every swimming creature was cooked at one time or another.

The Greeks drank their own wines, and those not naturally sweet they flavoured to cloying heaviness with honey and aromatic herbs and spices. Their *hippocras*, which was just such a syrupy punch, became after several centuries the favourite drink of France's fourteenth Louis.

As the art of eating grew in Greece, men began to write about it. Artemidorus Aristophanius left recipes, some of them very strange to us and as often generous of good suggestions. More than one modern cook has tried his method of using sour young grapes instead of vinegar, and has been well pleased.

Athenæus, too, gave in his *Banquet of the Learned* several good ideas to present-day chefs. His recipes, however, are more literary than practical—or even appealing. Few of us save the most precious would enjoy his voluptuous dish of bird brains, eggs, wine, and spices, pounded with very fragrant roses and cooked in oil. When the cover was lifted from this dish, its sweet excessive perfume, diffused throughout the supper-room, made all the guests drop their eyelids with pleasure. And one of them quoted poetry.

It was Athenæus who wrote sternly of the duties of a good cook. For the most part the Greeks were not unusually gifted in cookery. Housewives managed to provide plain, wholesome food for their establishments, and for special occasions imitated the aristocrats and called in professional chefs. Of these, Sicilians were the most famous. Their services were rented at enormous fees, and they were recognized as an important part of the increasingly complex Greek culture.

Dinners grew daily more luxurious, with menus to be read first by the guests, who no longer sat in chairs except at the houses of such ascetic hosts as Socrates. Instead they lay on soft couches brought from sensual Asia, and fed themselves languidly with perfumed fingers.

Great men grew concerned over their tables, and literary gourmets became didactic. Athenæus was their leader.

A good cook, he said, must know the time and the place for supper. That in itself is obvious enough, but further he must ascertain who are the guests, and who the entertainers! He must know what fish to buy, as well as where to buy it. And, most demanding requisite of all, "his mind must comprehend all facts and circumstances."

Another Greek writer (was it Nicomachus?) was even more unrelenting. Any cook, according to him, can take a piece of meat that some one else has bought, and dress it up tolerably well. A perfect cook, however, is quite a different thing. He must be a thorough master of many admirable arts—first of all a smattering of painting, and then others in their due importance. It is easy to see why good cooks were so sought after in Athens!

And it is equally easy to understand that, with such niceties considered necessary, rebellion might fume in some minds and stomachs. The good Archestratus, traveller and gourmet, wrote final quiet damnation of all ornate trickeries of the kitchen when he said:

> Many are the ways, and many the recipes
> For dressing a hare, but this is best of all:
> To place before a set of hungry guests
> A slice of roasted meat fresh from the spit,
> Hot, seasoned only with plain simple salt,
> Not too much done. And do you not be vexed,
> At seeing blood fresh trickling from the meat,

But eat it eagerly. All other ways
Are quite superfluous, such as when cooks pour
A lot of sticky clammy sauce upon it.

The restrained fury of that last sentence betrays Archestratus as the universal martyr, ageless and omnipresent, to centuries of over-seasoned sauces and ridiculous conceits of flavour. His is a mutual bond with us all.

The Curious Nose

Central heating, French rubber goods, and cookbooks are three amazing proofs of man's ingenuity in transforming necessity into art, and, of these, cookbooks are perhaps most lastingly delightful. Many an old belly has been warmed by the reading of them, and for one secret from them, steaming ruddy brown on plate, how many youthful pleasures have been counted well lost!

However, cooking in itself is, for most women, a question less of vocation than of necessity. They are not called to the kitchen by the divine inner voice of a Vatel or an Escoffier. Rather are they lured there, willy-nilly, by the piping of their husbands' empty stomachs.

They cook doggedly, desperately, more often than not with a cumulative if uninspired skill. Occasionally one gathers about herself a local renown for tarts or bonbons or meat pies. More rarely she builds up a reputation for epicurean appreciation— this last with the help of an ample purse, of course, and a good cook in her kitchen. Finally she writes a cookbook, and often it is a good one, in spite of Dr. Sam'l Johnson's dictum that such a thing is impossible from any female. It is eminently practical, like Mrs. Simon Kander's perennial volume which points "the

way to a man's heart" between its oilclothed boards. Or it is
very faintly literary and much more expensive to follow, compiled, say, by Mrs. William Vaughan Moody or the delightful
author of *La Cuisine de Madame*.

Definitely in the limbo, or to be passed by quickly with a
shudder of recognition, are cooking-school manuals and those
hideous pamphlets sold by ladies' aid societies in small towns.
The former are dangerously perfect, and if followed with the
care their editors advise, would reduce all cooking to a standard
of horrible monotony. The latter, whose broken covers and
limp yellow pages clutter every Ameri͟ ͟ cookbook shelf of
decent age, are utterly usele͟s͟ ͟ ͟ ͟ ͟ know some of the
women whose prize ͟ ͟ ͟ ͟ ͟ ͟ ͟em. Then, if you
are feeling il͟l ͟ ͟ ͟ ͟ ͟ ͟ ͟ t Mrs. Sophia Ja-
mison's ͟ ͟ ͟ ͟ ͟ ͟ ͟ ͟ ͟ Cousin Annie
Fink's littl͟ ͟ ͟ ͟ ͟ ͟ ͟ ͟ ͟mallows into
the——

But if yo͟u͟ ͟ ͟ ͟ ͟ ͟ ͟ thinking of
food at all. Cl͟ ͟ ͟ ͟ ͟ ͟ ͟ ͟ ͟ the window, or
keep it for a c͟ ͟ ͟ ͟ ͟ ͟ ͟ur eyes from the baleful
hygienic correc͟ ͟ ͟ ͟ ͟ol manuals. There are good cookbooks to read tha͟ ͟ ͟her women have written.

One of the best-known collections of recipes of the last century was *Common Sense in the Household: A Manual of Practical
Housewifery*.

It was the kind of cookbook that, always suitably inscribed,
young husbands gave to wives, and older brothers to their mar-
riageable sisters. My grandmother's copy, the small green edition of 1873, is very spotted and yellow now, but on the flyleaf
are still legible her name and her brother's, with his formal order
in quotation marks—"Improve each shining hour."

Common Sense was made by Marion Harland, a kindly, sensible woman if her book is true indication. She wrote of everything, almost, that might puzzle a student of "housewifery."

[handwritten note:] I have the 1906 edition of Marion Harlands cook book. Compared to what MFK Fisher quotes, it does

In her index, neatly alphabetical, she lists all the plain tricks like Bread, Ice Cream, Pork, Puddings. But there are others less usual and equally difficult to manage: Catsups, Clean-to-etc., Corn-bread in the C's; farther down Familiar Talk and Fritters; Nursery—the, Pancakes, Pickles; in the S's Sauces, Servants, Shellfish, Sick-room, and Soaps and Soups and Sundries, with Tarts to follow.

Towards the close of the century, Marion Harland's sensible attitude was weakened slightly, perhaps by too many decades of adoring disciples. She permitted several Queen Anne editions of her eminently Mary Anne masterpiece to be sold to fin de siècle brides. One, lavishly larded with instructive photographs, illustrates the correct way to serve dinner rolls, each tied with satin ribbon and a red, red rose!

But by 1900 the good lady must have felt very tired. It is in the earlier editions that we find her at her best, the American housewife of the nineteenth century. There her prose is straightforward, occasionally anecdotal, with short bits of Dickens stuck in like raisins in a bun.

She herself was probably a teetotaller, but with motherly tolerance she gives recipes for homemade drinks, always ending them with some such comment as the one for Cranberry Wine: "This is said to be very good for scrofula."

At the end of a recipe for Preserved Green Corn she writes, with the determined optimism of a good hausfrau, "Green corn is difficult to can, but I *know* it will keep if put up in this way. . . . Should the top layer be musty, dig lower still, and you will probably be rewarded for the search."

Her cautiousness, a self-protective virtue, is very obvious. She never commits herself on the outcome of a recipe, unless it is in the following safe statement: "Any cook with a moderate degree of judgment and experience can undertake it with a reasonable expectation of success"!

About some things, however, she allows herself to grow

heated. Read in her introduction to Pork. "We feed the hog with the off-scourings of house, garden, and table; bed him in mire, and swell him with acetous fermentation, not to say active decomposition, and then abuse him for what we have made him—Let us treat Bristles well—I do not say philosophically, but sensibly and kindly."

And sensible and kind she remains, although in her directions for Roast Pig she betrays some of that tenderness for sucklings which is even more noticeable in large men. My father, for instance, who flees sentimentality like the black pox, confesses that one of the loveliest things he has ever seen was—not a sunrise, not a sweet lass naked—was a litter of new piglets, pink and dainty. And in Roast Pig, Marion Harland stops her measurements of salt and dripping long enough to write: "If your pig is large, you can cut off his head and split him down the back before sending to table. Do this with a sharp knife, and lay the backs together. But it is a pity! I have before me now the vision of a pig I once saw served whole on the table of a friend, that forbids me ever to mutilate the innocent before the guests have a chance to feast their eyes upon the goodly picture. He was done to a turn—a rich even brown, without a seam or crack from head to tail, and he knelt in a bed of deep green parsley, alternately with branches of whitish-green celery tops (the inner and tender leaves); a garland of the same was about his neck, and in his mouth was a tuft of white cauliflower surrounded by a setting of curled parsley. Very simple, you see; but I never beheld a more ornamental roast."

Other women as good and wise as Marion Harland have written books on cookery, and long before her, too. In England Mrs. Ellet, Mrs. Rundel, and many another wrote standard handbooks of the early nineteenth and eighteenth centuries, and Mrs. Glasse's classic collection, *The Art of Cookery Made Plain and Easy*, certainly helped as many housewives as it hindered with its syllabubs and "Darling Dainties."

But in 1754 household cookery was so much the rage that even Mrs. Glasse's book had a greater public than it deserved. Cookbooks had freed themselves from the French that was thought necessary to all recipes until well into the seventeenth century, and a veritable rash of such collections broke out.

Some of them were good. Many of them were pompous, quite impractical. Often they were written by men in female fashion, signed or left cravenly anonymous.

It was Gervaise Markham who wrote what will probably remain the most thorough English treatise on the subject. His book, the thinly veiled copy of several less popular works like *The Widdowes Treasure,* which was published in 1625, itself had hundreds of imitators after its publication in London in 1675. They had little left to say; Markham's title page proves that:

> The English housewife; containing the inward and outward Vertues which ought to be in a Compleat Woman; as to her skill in Physick, Chirurgery, Cookery, Extraction of Oyls, Banquetting stuff, Ordering of great Feasts, Preserving of all sorts of Wides, conceited Secrets, Distillations, Perfumes, Ordering of Wool, Hemp, Flax: Making Cloth and Dying; the Knowledge of Dayries: Office of Malting; of Oats, their excellent uses in Families: of Brewing, Baking, and all other things belonging to an household.—A Work generally approved, and now the Eighth time much augmented, Purged, and made most profitable and necessary for all men, and the general good of this Nation.

Of the housewife herself, Markham decided thus: "First she must be cleanly both in garment and body, she must have a quick eye, a curious nose, a perfect taste, and ready ear (she must not be butterfingered, sweet-toothed, nor faint-hearted); for the first will let everything fall; the second will consume what it should increase; and the last will lose time with too much niceness."

Markham's dicta increase in amusing pomposity, and at the same pace seem almost revolutionary, when we remember that only a few years before he uttered them, Ladies kept clear of the kitchen. Women cooked, but Ladies never.

They knew well enough the polite usages of knives and fingers at table, but how that table was loaded was not for their wits to ponder on.

One brave tutor had suggested, years before, that the ladies of at least the lower upper classes might profit by some knowledge of cookery, but his counsel went unheeded.

"The daughters of Knights, Judges, Physicians, or others of similar conditions," he said, "had better learn the art of cooking, though possibly circumstances will not call upon them to put it into practice."

It took three hundred years for Barberino's advice to become acceptable. Then it was a man again, all-knowing Markham, who made it stylish. And since that day he and all his followers, both male and female, have instructed the world's woman in what she rarely escapes and sometimes never learns, *Common Sense in the Household*.

Let the Sky
Rain Potatoes

The Merry Wives of Windsor

There are two questions which can easily be asked about a potato: What is it, and Why is it?

Both these questions are irritating to a true amateur. The answers to the first are self-evident: a potato is a food, delicious, nourishing, and so on. The second question is perhaps too impertinent even to be answered, although many a weary housewife has felt like shouting it to the high heavens if her family has chanced to be the kind that takes for granted the daily appearance of this ubiquitous vegetable.

A dictionary will say that a potato is a farinaceous tuber used for food. An encyclopædia will cover eight or nine large pages with a sad analysis of its origins, modes of cultivation, and diseases, some of which are enough in themselves to discourage any potato enthusiast who might read them carefully.

Between these two extremes of definition is a story interesting even to one who is not overly fond of potatoes as a food. There are romance and colour and the fine sound of brave names in its telling.

In Peru, the Spanish found *papas* growing in the early 1500s, and the monk Hieronymus Cardán took them back with him to his own people. The Italians liked them, and then the Belgians.

About that time, Sir Walter Raleigh found a potato in the American South, and carried it back to his estate near Cork. Some say it was a yam he had, thought strongly aphrodisiac by the Elizabethans. Some say it was a white potato. A German statue thanks Raleigh for bringing it to Europe. On the other hand, the Spanish claim recognition for its European introduction.

No matter what its origin, eat it, eat it, urged the British Royal Society. But for many decades its cultivation made but little progress.

By the time it had become important as a food, especially for poor people, its diseases also had matured, and in 1846 potato blight sent thousands of hungry Irishmen to their graves, or to America.

Warts and scabs and rusts and rots did their work, too, and men worked hard to breed new varieties of potatoes before newer plagues seized them. Great Scott, the Boston Comrade, Magnum Bonum, Rhoderick Dhu and Up-to-Date, Ninety-fold: these and many hundreds more filled pots around the world, and still do.

But no matter the name; a spud's a spud, and by any other name it would still be starchy, and covered with dusty cork for skin, and, what's worse, taken for granted on every blond-head's table.

If the men are darker, it is pastes in slender strings they'll eat, or tubes, always farinaceous, as the dictionary says; but more often on Anglo-Saxon fare the potato takes place before any foreign macaroni or spaghetti.

It is hard sometimes to say why. A potato is good when it is cooked correctly. Baked slowly, with its skin rubbed first in a buttery hand, or boiled in its jacket and then "shook," it is delicious. Salt and pepper are almost always necessary to its hot moist-dusty flavour. Alone, or with a fat jug of rich cool milk or a chunk of fresh Gruyère, it fills the stomach and the soul with a satisfaction not too easy to attain.

In general, however, a potato is a poor thing, poorly treated. More often than not it is cooked in so unthinking and ignorant a manner as to make one feel that it has never before been encountered in the kitchen, as when avocados were sent to the Cornish Mousehole by a lady who heard months later that their suave thick meat had been thrown away and the stones boiled and boiled to no avail.

"Never have I tasted such a poor, flaccid, grey sad mixture of a mess," says my mother when she tells of the potatoes served in Ireland. And who would contradict her who has ever seen the baked-or-boiled in a London Lyons or an A.B.C.?

The Irish prefer them, evidently, to starvation, and the English, too. And in midwestern Europe, in a part where dumplings grow on every kitchen range, there are great cannon balls of them, pernicious as any shrapnel to a foreign palate, but swallowed like feathery eggwhites by the natives.

They are served with goose at Christmas, and all around the year. They are the size of a toddling child's round head. They are grey, and exceedingly heavy. They are made painstakingly of grated raw potato, moulded, then boiled, then added to by moulding, then boiled again. Layer after layer is pressed on, cooked, and cooled, and finally the whole sodden pockmarked mass is bounced in bubbling goose broth until time to heave it to the platter.

Forks may bend against its iron-like curves, stomachs may curdle in a hundred gastric revolutions; a potato dumpling is more adamantine. It survives, and is served to ever-renewing decades of hungry yodelling mouths.

In itself, this always fresh desire for starch, for the potato, is important. No matter what its form, nor its national disguise, the appetite for it is there, impervious to the mandates of dictators or any other blight.

Perhaps its most insidious manifestation is that Anglo-Saxons take it for granted. A meal for them includes potatoes in some form; it always has, therefore it always will. And no revolt, no smouldering rebellion of the meal-planner, can change this smug acceptance.

Most important, however, is the potato's function as a gastronomic complement. It is this that should be considered, to rob it of its dangerous monotony, and clothe it with the changing mysterious garment of adaptability.

Although few realize it, to be complementary is in itself a compliment. It is a subtle pleasure, like the small exaltation of a beautiful dark woman who finds herself unexpectedly in the company of an equally beautiful blonde. It is what a great chef meant once when he repulsed a consolation.

He was a Frenchman, summoned to London when King Edward VII found that his subjects resented his dining more in Paris than at home.

This great cook one day prepared a dish of soles in such a manner that the guests at Edward's table waited assuredly for a kingly compliment. He was summoned. Their mouths hung open in sated expectation.

"The Château Yquem," said Edward VII, "was excellent."

Later the master chef shrugged, a nonchalance denied by every muscle in his pleased face.

"How could my dish have had a greater compliment?" he demanded, calmly. "His Majesty knows, as I do, that when a dish is perfect, as was my sole tonight, the wine is good. If the dish is lower than perfection, the wine, lacking its complement, tastes weak and poor. So—you see?"

Although there are few ways of preparing potatoes to make them approach the perfection of a royal plate of fish, and none I know of to make them worth the compliment of a bottle of Château Yquem, they in their own way are superlative complements. And it is thus, as I have said, that they should be treated.

If, French fried, they make a grilled sirloin of beef taste richer; if, mashed and whipped with fresh cream and salty butter, they bridge the deadly gap between a ragoût and a salad; if, baked and pinched open and bulging with mealy snowiness, they offset the fat spiced flavour of a pile of sausages—then and then alone should they be served.

Then they are dignified. Then they are worthy of a high place, not debased to the deadly rank of daily acceptance. Then they are a gastronomic pleasure, not merely "tubers used for food."

Borderland

Almost every person has something secret he likes to eat. He is downright furtive about it usually, or mentions it only in a kind of conscious self-amusement, as one who admits too quickly, "It is rather strange, yes—and I'll laugh with you."

Do you remember how Claudine used to crouch by the fire, turning a hatpin just fast enough to keep the toasting nubbin of chocolate from dripping off? Sometimes she did it on a hairpin over a candle. But candles have a fat taste that would taint the burnt chocolate, so clean and blunt and hot. It would be like drinking a Martini from silver.

Hard bitter chocolate is best, in a lump not bigger than a big raisin. It matters very little about the shape, for if you're nimble enough you'll keep it rolling hot on the pin, as shapely as an opium bead.

When it is round and bubbling and giving out a dark blue smell, it is done. Then, without some blowing all about, you'll burn your tongue. But it is delicious.

However, it is not my secret delight. Mine seems to me less decadent than Claudine's, somehow. Perhaps I am mistaken. I remember that Al looked at me very strangely when he first saw the little sections lying on the radiator.

That February in Strasbourg was too cold for us. Out on the Boulevard de l'Orangerie, in a cramped dirty apartment across from the sad zoo half full of animals and birds frozen too stiff even to make smells, we grew quite morbid.

Finally we counted all our money, decided we could not possibly afford to move, and next day went bag and baggage to the most expensive pension in the city.

It was wonderful—big room, windows, clean white billows of curtain, central heating. We basked like lizards. Finally Al went back to work, but I could not bear to walk into the bitter blowing streets from our warm room.

It was then that I discovered how to eat little dried sections of tangerine. My pleasure in them is subtle and voluptuous and quite inexplicable. I can only write how they are prepared.

In the morning, in the soft sultry chamber, sit in the window peeling tangerines, three or four. Peel them gently; do not bruise them, as you watch soldiers pour past and past the corner and over the canal towards the watched Rhine. Separate each plump little pregnant crescent. If you find the Kiss, the secret section, save it for Al.

Listen to the chambermaid thumping up the pillows, and murmur encouragement to her thick Alsatian tales of *l'intérieur*. That is Paris, the interior, Paris or anywhere west of Strasbourg or maybe the Vosges. While she mutters of seduction and French bicyclists who ride more than wheels, tear delicately from the soft pile of sections each velvet string. You know those white pulpy strings that hold tangerines into their skins? Tear them off. Be careful.

Take yesterday's paper (when we were in Strasbourg *L'Ami du Peuple* was best, because when it got hot the ink stayed on it) and spread it on top of the radiator. The maid has gone, of course—it might be hard to ignore her belligerent Alsatian glare of astonishment.

After you have put the pieces of tangerine on the paper on the hot radiator, it is best to forget about them. Al comes home, you go to a long noon dinner in the brown dining room, afterwards maybe you have a little nip of *quetsch* from the bottle on the armoire. Finally he goes. Of course you are sorry, but——

On the radiator the sections of tangerine have grown even plumper, hot and full. You carry them to the window, pull it open, and leave them for a few minutes on the packed snow of the sill. They are ready.

All afternoon you can sit, then, looking down on the corner. Afternoon papers are delivered to the kiosk. Children come home from school just as three lovely whores mince smartly into the pension's chic tearoom. A basketful of Dutch tulips stations itself by the tram-stop, ready to tempt tired clerks at six o'clock. Finally the soldiers stump back from the Rhine. It is dark.

The sections of tangerine are gone, and I cannot tell you why they are so magical. Perhaps it is that little shell, thin as one layer of enamel on a Chinese bowl, that crackles so tinily, so ultimately under your teeth. Or the rush of cold pulp just after it. Or the perfume. I cannot tell.

There must be some one, though, who knows what I mean. Probably everyone does, because of his own secret eatings.

Garum

100 A.D.–400 A.D.
Rome

While Greece exchanged black broth and its accompanying simplicity for that more complex kitchen science nurtured by her new esthetes, Rome shadowed her some years behind, mimicking with fantastic exaggeration each of her calm inevitable developments.

For her Spartan pottage, Romans had a gruel of lentils. They too ate chestnuts and cheeses and fruits and green vegetables, with honey to sweeten and wine to gladden. Then when refinement, sure arbiter of a decadent civilization, crept into the Grecian cuisine, her tardy shadow Rome leaped feverishly in a grotesque and fascinating imitation.

As had happened in Greece, towns and villages vied for culinary honours. Certain cakes, cheeses of a special smell, and even fish from a named lake or river began to cause small feuds among the gourmets. Gradually shadow out-leaped self, and in their furious delicacy of palate and heavy-handed subtlety of selection the wealthy Romans left Greeks far behind.

Are *pâtés de foie gras* better made from cygnets than from

milk-white geese? Of course! Not at all! Well, perhaps if the geese are nourished solely on green figs—But on the other hand, a diet of almonds——

Senators cut important electors in the streets; sons quarrelled with fathers, boys with their tutors. Even the philosophers considered such questions weightily, and uttered decisions which had but temporary effect.

When Cleopatra melted her pearl and six million sesterces into the world's most expensive recipe, she set a tantalizingly high mark. Until Rome fell, gourmets tried to outdo her. Undoubtedly the results were more palatable—but never more costly.

Rigid snobbism precluded all but the most extravagant citizens, and thus most plutocratic, from the inner circles of fine eating.

Juvenal drew the portrait of all Roman bon vivants when he wrote of one of the greatest, the general Lucullus:

> Stretched on the unsocial couch, he rolls his eyes
> O'er many an orb of matchless form and size,
> Selects the fairest to receive his plate,
> And at one meal devours a whole estate.

Lucullus, perhaps the truest epicure as we now think of one, was undoubtedly the most refined. He set the pace. Other Romans, like Trimalchio's vulgar prototype, might give banquets whose success depended upon the leaping of three naked virgins from a great crusted tart. It was Lucullus who gave his carefully chosen guests the exquisite compliment of letting them watch their next course die!

Mullets bred in the mountain lake he had transplanted to his estates, or trout brought living from one certain stream in all Italy, expired slowly in beautiful glass jars placed before the diners. Each throe was judged. Lucky the guest whose dying fish

leaped highest and longest! The flavour would be unforgettable.

It was Lucullus who sorted his friends into different rooms,
rather like the various restaurants in a large German railroad station. In some rooms, a meal cost only one or two hundred dollars for each person. Decoration there was relatively simple.
More expensive surroundings showed that here Lucullus spent
more on his food.

And finally, in the Apollo Room, where only his very intimate or important guests were invited, he spent one thousand
dollars for each person.

Here he entertained most frequently, with the most precious
foods laid upon tables now solid ivory, now silver or carved tor-
toise shell. For ordinary guests goblets of inlaid gold did well
enough, but in the Apollo Room glasses hollowed from great
gems were used with nonchalance.

Other men blinked at their own banquet bills, or complained
bitterly, like Julius Cæsar when he found he had spent five millions sterling, one Roman summer, on suppers for his friends—
and on barley water mixed with wine, for his favourite charger
to drink from a golden trough!

Sometimes there was a suicide, nor was it from remorse for
unpaid debts. Apicius, when he found he had squandered over
a million pounds on banquets, and had but a tenth of that sum
left, died as exquisitely as one of the mullets he had watched.

As Rome festered and decayed, the fever for fine eating
mounted. What had been precious became vicious. Mark Antony's largesse of a town of thirty-five thousand souls for his
chef's fine paste of flamingo brains changed to Heliogabalus'
trick of fattening his prized conger eels on living slave-meat.

As much money was spent on perfumes as on food. It was the
usual thing now to have rare aromatic essences blown into the
air between the twenty-four courses of daily banquets, as in

Nero's famous Domus Aurea, from whose revolving walls flowers and sweet distillations showered down upon the guests.

Indeed, such strange behaviour was necessary. Satiety, that monster behind pleasure, breathed into the stuffed bellies of the Romans. Excitants to their palates were prerequisite—those palates by now so ill-treated that some of the gourmets were forced to wear little tongue gloves to protect their delicate taste-glands from all but the most exotic flavours.

And where could they find new foods? They searched desperately. They had eaten every fish in the earth's waters, except Triton's sacred dolphin and perhaps a mermaid. They had sucked the bones of every bird and birdling in—But wait!

"Send hunters to Lydia," Heliogabalus ordered, "and pay two hundred gold pieces to the one who brings us back a Phœnix!"

But none came.

The fretful ruler tried colours. Perhaps they might whip up his dulled taste. For awhile Roman tables bloomed with shades as violent but not so harmless as those in a modern seed-catalogue. They soon faded.

Les Tables Volantes, which Louis XV of France proudly called his own invention, rose first for Heliogabalus. Laden with dishes resolutely emptied, these tables sank, to the strains of young boys' voices, into the marble floor. New perfumes from Araby spiced the air. Strange dances, increasingly erotic, occupied the dulled eyes of the diners. Then the beautiful boys raised their voices in mock amazement, and fell squealing back. From the floor lifted boards new-decked, like the Phœnix the king yearned for—each time with new plumes.

As the feasts grew longer and more extravagant, the guests lost gradually those stately good manners they had aped from the earlier Greek gourmands. Licence of the senses begot loose behaviour.

If the goblets seemed too small, or the wine-supply stingy or of poor vintage, banqueters howled until they were satisfied. If the dishes displeased them, they hurled food and vessel against a pillar or a serving-man. The host apologized.

Emetics were served with the beginning courses of any longer dinner—as they had been indeed in Greece, because of the difficulty of digestion in the reclining position assumed on the banqueting-couches. Now, however, the Romans found the capacity of their sated stomachs infinitely enlarged by the trick. By the time one dish appeared, its predecessor was well out of the way. Twice as much could be eaten!

This wholesale catharsis necessitated certain architectural changes. And suddenly these changes, luxurious privies to begin with, were metamorphosed once more. *Vomitoria* came into being.

They had a fine name, like a California real estate development. Little boys still hear it with fascination and disgust, in first-year Latin. Girls still invent other verbs, to avoid its nauseous root. Only one ever used it in public with the proper reverence: Colette, when she described an *éclair si vomiteusement chocolateux*.

Romans, however, their minds less on future derivatives of the word than on their next course, used their *vomitoria* with appreciation.

Their insides heaved too often. Quacks and honest physickers could not help. Rome grew dyspeptic, and heard clearly old Seneca's wry comment, "Are you astonished at the innumerable diseases?—Count the number of our cooks!"

We are inclined to agree with him. One course of a Roman meal would lay us very low, probably, and strip our palates for many days of even the crudest perceptions of flavour.

Look for a minute, hand over nose and a piece of ice on tongue, at the recipe for *garum*:

> Place in a vessel all the insides of fish, both large fish and small. Salt them well. Expose them to the air until they are completely putrid. In a short time a liquid is produced. Drain this off.

And "this" is *garum*, most highly prized and used of all seasonings. In Cochin-China there is something like it, in these days, called *nuocman*—and of course we have our English meat sauces.

Romans, though, used *garum* not as a condiment in itself, but combined with a startling variety of spices. Dill, anise, hyssop, thyme; pennyroyal and rue; cummin, poppy seed, shallots and onions and garlic and leeks—almost every known savour except our parsley, which they wore in garlands on their heads, made the simplest banquet dish a mess of inextricable flavours.

Inextricable to us, that is. It is doubtful if even a professional taster, today, would be able to describe the sauce Apicius recommends for a boiled chicken:

> Put the following ingredients into a mortar: anise-seed, dried mint, and lazar root which is a kind of asafœtida; cover them all with vinegar. Add dates and pour in garum and oil and a small quantity of mustard-seeds. Reduce all to a proper thickness with red wine warmed, and then pour this same over your chicken.

"The chicken," Apicius adds as an afterthought, "should of course be boiled previously in strong anise-seed water."

To cool your enraged palate after this strange dish you would most probably be served a goblet of red wine mixed with spices and sea water.

Then, while pretty slave children imitated worn-out lechers for your eyes' amusement, you would pretend to eat hungrily at a bowl of red mullet seasoned with pepper, rue, onion, dates, mustard, and the flesh of a sea-hedgehog pounded to a jelly.

With this, a fine cup of *vin rosé*, thickened to syrup with honey, myrrh, and spikenard. And after this, a piglet, soaked in——

A good old Roman custom—*vomitoria!*

Fifty Million Snails

I have eaten several strange things since I was twelve, and I shall be glad to taste broiled locusts and swallow a live fish. But unless I change very much, I shall never be able to eat a slug. My stomach jumps alarmingly at the thought of it.

I have tried to be callous about slugs. I have tried to picture the beauty of their primeval movements before a fast camera, and I have forced myself to read in the *Encylopædia Britannica* the harmless ingredients of their oozy bodies. Nothing helps. I have a horror, deep in my marrow, of everything about them. Slugs are awful, slugs are things from the edges of insanity, and I am afraid of slugs and all their attributes.

But I like snails. Most people like snails.

Once in Dijon I was very dizzy for two days because I ate so many that inside me they changed into old rubber boiled in garlic. I still like them; and in France people eat some fifty million every year.

On a bush they are beautiful, unless you are the gardener who planted the bush. They are beautiful on plates, too, each one in its little dent, shell full of hot green butter like a magic cup.

In Burgundy they are most beautiful, piled in baskets in the stores, the shells one of the most luminous gentle browns in the world, like the hair of a Leonardo Virgin. The round holes are filled very full and smooth with the butter, cold now, firm, and a tender green.

One shop in Dijon sold nothing else, and the window, banked firm against the glass with the finest samples, had from a distance the texture of a heavy glimmering silk. When the door opened, you could taste that peculiar smell of cold cooked snails, not quite like garlic, not quite like rubber tires.

Once I saw a woman eat seven dozen. It was *chez Crespin*, so she had already eaten more than that many oysters. She turned a purplish red. I have often wondered about her.

We lived for two years or so with the Rigagniers in Dijon. The grandfather, Papazi, lived with them too—or did we all live with Papazi?

He was a militant old fellow who mourned lustily every 14th of July that he had been too young to see battle in '71, too old in '14. Instead, he had become one of the most famous candy makers in all the provinces. Retired from bonbon service, he kept his palate agile by cooking fine dishes for his grandchildren.

And thanks to him, the three of them, in spite of a shared age of less than thirty-five, were seasoned gourmets all. It was very amusing to see Plume, the little boy like a monkey, taste a sauce with the slow tongue-rollings of an old Parisian epicure. The others were just as reverently fussy. Every meal *chez* Rigagnier smacked somewhat of professional gastronomy.

Each spring we were worked subtly and completely into a frenzy for snails by Papazi's sure suggestion. As soon as burgeons darkened the bare branches he began speculating mildly on the possible time for the annual snail hunt.

The weeks went by and leaves burst out on all the trees, and

Papazi brought little twigs to the table and rubbed them between his thick dexterous fingers.

"Quite crisp," he would remark, ruminatively. "Yes, I really do think, in fact I am almost sure, that the snails this year will be finer, sweeter, plumper, truly more delicious than ever before."

He looked calmly at his delighted listeners.

The children were almost beside themselves.

"When can we go, Papazi? How about next Sunday? How about tomorrow? Will we get enough?"

"Calm yourselves, my dears! This excitement will ruin the taste of your mother's delicious *quenelles*!"

Plume and Doudouce subsided like pricked popovers, and Dédé smacked his lips more loudly than ever over a fresh bite, to show his mature appreciation. Papazi ate silently for a minute.

"No, not next Sunday," he continued, finally. "Not next Sunday, but perhaps the Sunday after. That is," he added, hastily, before the children could open their mouths to shout great glee, "*if* the day is fine, and *if* the snails have fed well enough, and *if* there are not too many noxious weeds for them to ruin themselves on, this year! And of course, after we have gathered them, something may happen to spoil them. It is a long and difficult business, the preparing of snails!"

The first time I heard Papazi say this I was fool enough to demand, "Why not buy them, then, all ready to eat?"

There was a shocked silence. The children stared at me. Papazi grew pink and haughty. Finally his daughter rebuked me, very gently:

"Oh, but Madame! Nobody can prepare snails like Papazi. These store snails are good, yes—but to fix them as my father does is an art! It is an achievement!"

I never acted so thoughtlessly again, but we were glad when

the hunting-time came to end, we hoped, the daily speculations.

That nightfall we returned from the woods, with most of our snails unescaped from the sacks we carried them in. It had been a pleasant day.

The next morning we noticed a large packing box in the courtyard. It was covered with a sheet of glass, and on the glass were glued the bottoms of what seemed a thousand snails, warming themselves upside down.

At night it was still there, and the next day.

"They must purify themselves," Papazi explained. "They must get rid of any poisonous food in them. They must, you might say, starve to death!"

"How long will it be, then?"

"A few days—a week, perhaps: these are very sturdy snails."

Indeed they were. For a day or two more they stayed, bottoms up, on the glass. Then they began to drop off. Nights were punctuated by the thumps of snails fainting in their little Black Hole. We lost sleep, feeling very sick for them, waiting for the hunger swoon to overcome another and another.

Every morning we counted the survivors, and hoped they would loosen their hold before dark, and let us sleep.

At last Papazi began his work, most of which I missed watching. There were parboilings to get the emaciated little creatures from their shells, and individual operations to remove their less delectable portions. There were endless scrubbings of each lovely shell, with little curved brushes made especially in Paris. Then the cadavers were tucked into their coffins again, and Papazi and Madame Rigagnier made an extra trip to market for the parsley, the garlic, and the sweet butter.

The last scene I caught through the dining room door: Plume and Doudouce bent gravely over a lighted table, pouring the hot sauce into each up-ended snail shell. Their hands trembled very slightly, and Plume's tongue stuck out.

And when we finally ate them, *les escargots d'or*, sizzling hot and delicately pungent on our little curved forks, it was clear that "store snails" were only for those unhappy people who did not live with Papazi—or those fools too impatient to wait for his slow perfection.

That was quite awhile ago. I had forgotten about snails, almost. Then, last month, I heard that a woman in our town was raising them. She had contracted to send them to good restaurants, at a very stiff figure. It seems they were blooded stock!

Last weekend she went away, and left all her animals in the charge of our friend Eric. He had just read all about snail culture in a magazine.

"You simply feed them cornmeal," he explained, easily. "It makes them plump—gives the meat a delightful flavor, too!"

But the snails grew too plump, and then too fat, and then they blew up, all in a few hours! Eric is devastated, and the restaurants threaten to sue for broken contracts.

Perhaps it is better to buy store snails, after all. There are few Papazis, and almost as few recipes, if you can find any escargots alive and edible, which seems doubtful. However, here is one set of directions, from *Le Menagier de Paris*:

Snails, which are called escargots, should be caught in the morning. Take the young small snails, those that have black shells, from the vines or elder trees; then wash them in so much water that they throw up no more scum; then wash them once in salt and vinegar, and set them to stew in water. Then you must pick these snails out of the shell at the point of a needle or a pin; and then you must take off their tail, which is black, for that is their turd; and then wash them and put them to stew and boil them in water; and then take them out and put them in a dish to be eaten with bread. And also some say that they are better fried in oil and onion or some other liquid, after they have been cooked as above said; and they are eaten with spice and are for rich people.

This recipe differs quite plainly from Papazi's method, but of course it is older. *Le Menagier de Paris* was first published about 1394.

A POSTSCRIPT ABOUT SNAILS

This made Dillwyn remember more. In a letter he wrote:

In Hyère, in the middle of summer, I closed the latticed shutters of my room to keep out the dry, blistering sun, but it got through the chinks of the shutters and marked the dusty carpet with a row of white-hot blades. Naked on the bed, I sweated and dozed and imagined myself going to hell in the tropics.

Once I could not stand the feeling of being cooped up, and went for a walk in the middle of the day. The hotel force watched me go, shrugging shoulders and tapping foreheads. *Fou!*—he walks himself in the sun.

Queer world I walked into! The sun made me squint as one squints walking out of a dark theatre into the bright of day. The heat was something more than heat: it had the dry hurting feeling that radiates from an electric grill.

Outside of the town there were trees and bushes, vines and grass—but every leaf, blade, stem was coated with plaster-white dust, a dust that night dews had turned to fast-clinging stucco.

The scorching earth hurt my feet through the thick soles of my shoes.

I marvelled that men and women would work out in the open under such conditions. There they were, the peasants harvesting grapes for wine, bending under the weight of filled baskets. They were brown as wood. Even the children looked old.

The incredible sun was in the middle of the sky. The workers in the vineyards stopped to rest and eat. They burned a
stretch of grass at the edge of the vineyards along the road-
side, and from the black ashes gathered in their hats the snails
that had been roasted in the flames. Into cups, carried at their
belts, they squeezed with their two hands the juice of half-
rotted grapes. It tasted much like wine; it was not wasting the
good grapes.

Roasted snails! Raw wine!

I noticed that they crossed themselves before eating, gratefully.

Meals for Me

"When shall we live, if not now?" asked Seneca before a table laid for his pleasure and his friends'. It is a question whose answer is almost too easily precluded. When indeed? We are alive, and now. When else live, and how more pleasantly than supping with sweet comrades?

Perhaps Landor, a little later, meant more than he said (but more than Seneca?) when he decided, "I shall dine late, but the dining room will be well lighted, the guests few and selected."

Whatever his imputations, his tastes are mine. I too dine late by preference, and I too like my room clear and beautiful, and above all, my guests very few and even more selected.

It is true that in the beginnings of all cultures meals were served early in the day, as indeed they are now among simple folk. A banquet at noon leaves long waking-hours for digestion, conversation, and the easing and refilling of the body. It is practical, and early Greeks and Romans, as well as modern peasants, have appreciated the double festival of a day spent far from the fields before tables tottering under the rare dishes of a marriage or a birthday.

Not until ancient men leave their pastures and their vineyards for the vitiated air of cities; not until they stretch days longer with the false light of burning wax or electricity, and then sleep wastefully in artificial darkness when the sun is high; not until they have grown far away from simplicity do they leave their daytime feastings.

Then, as in old Rome and our own towns, we dine later. For us it is a comparatively recent progression; as few years ago as the early eighteenth century Alexander Pope stabbed scornful couplets at the dissolute Londoners who put off banqueting until well past three o'clock.

We soon grow used to the slow signs of corruption, so surrounded by them are we. In the beginning of the nineteenth century we dined at six, and today a good meal is wasted on most people unless the sun has long set.

What is more tedious for us than an early supper? It thrusts itself into the gathering speed of a day's life like a stick into the spokes of a turning wheel. It forces a pause, a stop, which acts as a kind of disequilibrium to the fine balance of the remaining hours of consciousness.

If the days are short, an early evening meal seems to cut them in two, leaving the second part hanging lifeless on the hardly realized beginning. And if the days are long, they are made twice as monotonously hot by the tired interruption of cooked food.

An early evening meal—a long evening. A long evening—what to do with it? There is a fairly good play, a passable movie, a game of bridge—surely *some* way to kill a few hours.

But an evening killed is murder of a kind, criminal like any disease, and like disease a thorough-going crime. If Time, so fleeting, must like humans die, let it be filled with good food and good talk, and then embalmed in the perfumes of conviviality.

Let us kill it in slow parley, over the leisured savourings of fare both simple and elaborate, in the tempered colour of a room lighted softly, clearly, by living fire of wax or oil or wood, or by the most artful disguises of electricity.

Let the death chamber itself be airy, intimate, free of thick odours and the sensual distraction of high colour. It should be warmed by a fire in winter, cool with moving air in summer; and in summer too the soft comfortable rugs should be taken away, leaving the shadows of chair legs spidering, reflecting, into the polished floor.

The chair should be comfortable, not low and soft enough to slow digestion, as did the Roman couches, not hard as Cornish rocks, but well fitted to the average body. The best I ever sat in were wide, generous, solid, with high backs, made of ash, brought from England and polished in a log cabin long before they ever set leg on a hardwood floor.

The table should be ample, and above all solid, with no squeaks and shiverings. Plates, too, should be large, and the silver heavy rather than light, with smooth simple lines to it. Plain linen, ample as the table, plain colours in the flowers and the fruits, glasses no more ornamented than the bubbles they imitate—all should be simple, and adequate as the food and drink served there.

The guests, "few and selected," are most important to Landor and to me, as they were to Archestratus long ago. He wrote, in a fragment of his lost poem on "Gastronomy":

> I write these precepts for immortal Greece,
> That round a table delicately spread,
> Or three, or four, may sit in choice repast,
> Or five at most. Who otherwise shall dine,
> Are like a troop marauding for their prey.

I would add one more person to his dictum, though, and say that six can dine well at a table. More, even one or two, are dangerous, and beyond ten deadly.

What is worse than the rigid right-left conversational etiquette of a formal banquet, unless it be the forced jollity of an annual feast of some modern "service" club, thick with the noise of too many people eating too much food cooked in too large quantities? In either case there is more than a faint likeness to Archestratus' "troop marauding for their prey."

Too few of us, perhaps, feel that the breaking of bread, the sharing of salt, the common dipping into one bowl, mean more than satisfaction of a need. We make such primal things as casual as tunes heard over a radio, forgetting the mystery and strength in both.

Very simple men still know that if you injure the food another leaves, you can thus injure him. The bones from his plate, the rice from his bowl, can be moulded into a little figurine, and then decay will eat into his own flesh as into the mannequin's. Or poison can be dropped into the bowl.

But it is obvious that none who plans to harm a man through food will himself partake of that same food. Thus, there is honour and sanctity in eating together, when you are simple.

So it should be now, although we have civilised ourselves away from the first rules of life. Sharing our meals should be a joyful and a trustful act, rather than the cursory fulfillment of our social obligations.

I know one man, however, the opposite of what I mean, who has so simplified his concept of human hunger and its quelling that he considers the act of taking food as necessary and intimate as any other function, like defecation or sexual play, and no more to be shared with several other beings. For him it is disgusting to eat even with his dear friends.

His viewpoint is exaggerated, and to my mind unhealthy. For me, there is no more agreeable relaxation than a quiet sharing of food with my few friends. My only approximation of his feeling is the irritation and revolt that rise in me at the thought of obligatory feeding with unknown or uncongenial people.

To such a lewd exhibition I should prefer Plato's solitary bowl of olives, but for neither of these would I forego a slow meal with three or four—or six at most, sitting in "choice repast."

What six persons may consider choice is delicate to decide. Six tastes, six appetites, must be known, and fused by one memory and one skill into a mutually exciting whole. Old preferences must be converted into new. New flavours must be linked with old.

From this fusion should result meals as stimulating to the tongue as to the gastric fluids, meals to be remembered with pleasure, evocative of future delights.

And to concoct such meals and serve them is one of the most satisfying of all civilised amenities, I think. Nothing is much sweeter than the sincere gratification—and admiration—of a friend.

When Horace succoured a storm-bound traveller, he fed him a good chicken, a fat kid roasted, grapes, figs and nuts, and sweet Roman wine.

When we went to sup with Nell Coover, the small old etcher, often hungry in her rooms filled with Whistler's cushions and Heppelwhite's beautiful chairs and cupboards, she gave us a strange lovely salad of sea mosses and jewelled ice plants from the cliffs, and a bowl of green wild spinach. It was all she had, but it was served forth with no apology, nor did it need one. Our eyes and our stomachs were pleased, and Miss Coover too, I think, sure in the pleasure of well-treated guests.

For my own meals I like simplicity above all. I like newness in what I serve, perhaps because any interest I may thus stir in my fellow diners is indirect flattery of myself. I like leisure.

I like a mutual ease. For this reason I prefer not to have among my guests two people or more, of any sex, who are in the first wild tremours of love. It is better to invite them after their new passion has settled, has solidified into a quieter reciprocity of emotions. (It is also a waste of good food, to serve it to new lovers.)

I do not agree with the Greeks and Romans that women should be reserved for the end of a meal and served with the final wines and music, nor do I think that Frenchman was right who stated that there are no blue eyes, no curls and dimpled shoulders, which can replace for a true gourmet the charms of a black truffle.

It is, though, very dull to be at a table with dull people, no matter what their sex.

Dining partners, regardless of gender, social standing, or the years they've lived, should be chosen for their ability to eat—and drink!—with the right mixture of abandon and restraint. They should enjoy food, and look upon its preparation and its degustation as one of the human arts. They should relish the accompanying drinks, whether they be ale from a bottle on a hillside or the ripe bouquet of a Chambertin 1919 in a great crystal globe on finest damask.

And above all, friends should possess the rare gift of sitting. They should be able, no, eager, to sit for hours—three, four, six—over a meal of soup and wine and cheese, as well as one of twenty fabulous courses.

Then, with good friends of such attributes, and good food on the board, and good wine in the pitcher, we may well ask, When shall we live if not now?

Dark Ages and
the Men of God

1000 A.D.–1400 A.D.
Europe

The decline of Rome, that "period of insatiable voracity and the peacock's plume," came to its sure end. Rome fell.

Then the Dark Ages cast their mysterious silent gloom over all the arts of Europe. Gastronomy, with the others, dwindled, tottered, tapered into ignorance. Men ate in those countries, certainly: porridge for the lowly, roast meats for the rich. But as far as we know, they did not care.

Food was only a necessity again, like sleep and sweating. There were no more investigating palates, no more keen nostrils trembling with sensuous fine delight at the perfume of a cold melon drenched with wine, or the heady aroma of a succulent piglet, well basted with its own juices and stuffed full of chestnuts and green almonds. *La gourmandise* was dead.

No, not quite. A faint light still glowed, a little flame in the darkness, well hidden behind holiness and the convent walls.

The good monks, never more wisely, remembered the spiritual importance of physical well-being.

Helped by a hundred fast days, whose strict observance would have reduced every priest in Europe to a stringy skeleton, the plump brothers spent much time and thought on making delicious dishes appear frugal.

The best ecclesiastical brains on the continent studied the egg, and discovered the formulae for making it appear on Lenten boards as a rose, a cabbage, or a roasted duck. And roasted ducks, and kids and pigs and even tender bulls, were made to look like nothing that ever breathed and walked about under the All-Seeing Eye. Juices dripped from every convent spit, and were metamorphosed into the best of all disguises, sauces infinitely elaborate.

So abstinence begot kitchen trickery, and good eating survived with holy blessings through the Dark Ages.

I Arise Resigned

Roasted hares, though eaten, are thought to nourish melancholie.

Elizabethan cookbook

I

Sabri, the homesick Turkish lawyer, invited us for tea. We drank too much of it, and ate, ravenously or discreetly, according to our nationalities, at a large cake like a macaroon. Sabri had made it, and he told us how.

"Cook finest vermicelli thoroughly," he instructed, a cold polite smile on his face and his eyes very warm and melancholy. "Then when it is done spread it in a large shallow baking dish and drip honey and sweet oil upon it until the dish brims.

"Throw slivers of pistachio nuts upon it, as many as you like—I like very many. And then bake it slowly. It will shrivel down to a brown crusty cake with a moist inside, like the one you did not eat much of."

"Sabri, it's—we——"

"I know. It's too sweet for you, eh, Al?"

"Yes. It makes every tooth in my head quiver like a stricken doe."

Sabri almost smiled.

"For myself," he remarked, distantly, "it is barely sweet. And these icings and bonbons you eat! They are tasteless as dust to a Turk.

"Of course, in our world, the Near East, we like anything with starch in it, too. There is a good reason." He looked glumly and perhaps a little maliciously at me.

"Yes, a very good reason—for us, that is. We Easterners eat viscous, sticky foods to make ourselves more virile!

"Perhaps that's what ails us," he added, austerely. Then he grinned, and broke the last chunk of cake in his fat, too-sensitive hands. "Young men try to increase what they have; old men look for what they've passed by—but is it only in Turkey?"

II

No. Cooks, even before Anthippus', were turning their tricks to physical excitation. His, in ancient Athens, boasted of such skill:

> Insensible the palate of old age,
> More difficult than the soft lips of youth
> To move, I put much mustard in their dish;
> With quickening sauces make their stupor keen,
> And lash the lazy blood that creeps within.

It was Louis the Fourteenth, however, tired and honing for lost pleasure, whose senile throat was first cheered by the hot pungency of a cordial. He took slow sips of the new liquor, distilled for him at some thoughtful courtier's command, and from that day his temper was sweeter and his old body less obviously damned. Cordials comforted him.

In his land, then, and on the globe everywhere for many centuries, sweet distillations and the sharp taste of spiced vinegars have warmed old men and young, in the armchair or the marriage bed. Bowls of meat, soaked for days in cordials and hot condiments (Cold pudding settles one's love, says an old English proverb!), are still served at wedding feasts in distant European villages.

And then there are truffles, those mysterious growths which spring seedless and rootless from the oaky soil, which may or may not be as good as they are rare and dear, and which even Brillat-Savarin names aphrodisiac.

People tell me that only virgins have the true nose for truffle-hunting: virgin sows, virgin bitches. I cannot vouch for this, as I have never hunted truffles—but I do know a man who once saw the last human hunter in all the Périgord country.

Franz Mayen is the man. He has Napoleon's rippled lips, the vaguely authentic mannerisms of an important *agent provocateur*, and a friend named Buô Dinh Ngo who is the son of an Annamite official.

It was one of the many nights in Strasbourg when Mayen, Buô Dinh, Al, and I sat comfortably filled with fine food. We had eaten a *pâté de foie gras en brioche* (which at the time made me think of Carême's dictum, "To become a perfect cook, one must first be a distinguished pastry-maker." This plate is, however, more of a tour de force than a true delicacy, for the unctuous salve of a good Strasbourg pâté is not well complemented by the short and sweet flavour of brioche. Dry toast with a pâté moulded in wine aspic is certainly more fortunate a combination. But—) we had dined marvellously well on a *pâté de foie gras en brioche* among other things, and now we sat complacently at our ease.

Buô Dinh crouched behind a huge cigar and fingered a jade bead in his pocket. Al and I shared a glass of Alsatian *quetschwasser*, harsh and clear. Franz Mayen, very sardonic and entertaining, peered at us and talked ceaselessly, as always.

"Yes," he was saying, "I have seen the last virgin woman

truffle-hunter in all France! I am probably—no, certainly—unique, for I was but five or six when it happened, and a little boy among old men. It was a secret hunt——"

"By moonlight, of course?" one of us enquired, smoothly.

"Ah no!" Mayen was unruffled as a bowl of cream. "Naturally it was held in the white sunlight of the south—a van Gogh sun, a French Midi sun. And we had gathered secretly because the Church was opposed to women truffle-hunters. The idea of an old virgin sniffing over the hills, with a pack of men hot at her heels—it is disgusting to the Church, it is—you understand me?—pagan!

"So this was to be the last hunt, with the only woman left alive who had the truffle nose. She was old, very old, and she was—yes, unquestionably—she was a virgin! And, *mon Dieu, mon Dieu,* but what a nose! It was long, most pointed, red at the tip. It quivered.

"We started off at a hill far from the church, I lagging behind on my little legs, but very curious. We walked until I was panting.

"The old maid went ahead. Finally she stopped. She lifted her formidable nose, red and quivering, into the hot air. We all watched.

"Then she was off, and it was hard to follow her, I can tell you. She ran like a demented soul straight through the underbrush, over ditches, up a steep hill. There she stopped, in a barren clearing around an old oak tree.

"She pointed to the ground at her feet. The men dug with their blunt forks. Sure enough, truffles! She started away, stopped suddenly and pointed down. More truffles! And all the time she was trembling and sniffing like a sick dog.

"Finally she stood still, and her nose grew pale. She stopped shivering, and looked very old and weary. The hunt was over.

"When we got home, the best truffles were sent to Lyons,

and the rest we chopped up and cooked with eggs into a kind of omelette."

Mayen pulled at his cigarette, and added disgustedly: "Of course it is too bad! My one chance to eat enough truffles to see if they really are exciting—and I was only six!"

"But is that all true, Franz, about the old woman? Are you telling the truth? Is he, Buô Dinh?"

But Franz was calling for more *quetsch*, and when we looked at the little Indo-Chinese he relit his cigar and hummed a phrase or two of the "Marseillaise."

III

"You may serve me with two roast pigeons for dinner," said the old Maréchal de Mouchy when he returned home from his best friend's funeral. "I have noticed that after eating a brace of pigeons I arise from the table feeling much more resigned."

Oddly enough, it was not until the eighteenth century that Europeans became conscious of the subtle relations between the soul, on whose existence they spent so much thought, and the human stomach, on whose subsistence they spent even more time.

Then, although the king, Louis XVI, paid small attention to any food so long as it filled him without too much discomfort, his courtiers followed the example of such staunch gentlemen as Mouchy, and enquired into many pseudo-magical refinements of eating.

Many of their remedies for lovesickness, melancholy, and the like, were unproved fantasy. Most of them, arrived at with the usual scientific air of discovery, were nostrums older than the altars of Greece. Warm milk soothes jaded nerves, and brings slumber to the insomniac: no new thing this, although the sated Frenchmen seized with surprise on its ancient simplicity, and on many another like it.

They experimented with strange brews, and although most psychic cures may have been due more to the powers of suggestion than to a mixture of wild herbs, fermentation also helped to warm their tired bodies and thus cheer their souls.

Since the earliest days of what is called civilization men have drunk wines made from the juice of grapes or apples or berries; juice which has been "spoiled," had its sugar changed into alcohol and carbon dioxide by a natural process.

Men have been made foolish, or vicious, or even lifeless, by the fumes of wine, but more often they have been succoured. Gaiety and love have seemed easier to attain, and with wine have flowed the wit of great men and the beauty of women. They are resigned; life has been made acceptable.

Death, too, appears less fearful if a man meets it warmed and relaxed by some spiritous cup. Indeed, so often have dying souls been helped to their fate by a last drink that it is the signal for mourning cards to be printed when the doctor prescribes champagne for his patient. Poor uncle is as good as dead—let him die happy, with all he can drink for once in his life!

And men to be killed for crimes they may have committed are often thus mercifully treated, as much, probably, to salve the punisher's conscience as to ease the victim's fears. For them, however, a harsher opiate is needed, brandy or rum.

There is a recipe in one of Paul Reboux's entertaining cookbooks which explains this custom of prelethal drinking not too inappropriately. He is discussing the preparation of a rabbit for execution.

"Many people," he says, "whose stomachs are more demanding than their hearts are tender, raise rabbits only to eat them.

"This is in itself an act of human energy which I would not know how to accomplish. Intimate family life with a rabbit, strengthened by our daily relations, would make me no more capable of devouring my little animal than I would be of eating one of my friends.

"However, if your sense of realism be strong enough, and if you want your rabbit to be even better than your neighbour's, take care to nourish it——"

Monsieur Reboux tells with his own detached care the schedule for feeding: warm milk while the beastie is still nursing from its mother, tender lettuce and meadow salads as it grows older, a few succulent carrots and grains of corn. And herbs, of course, to perfume its flesh before it is cooked rather than after.

It will enjoy leek soup, he advises, and rich hot potato broth with bread. And even, on Sundays, a little bowl of café au lait!

"Finally, the day of the execution, give him a glass of good marc to drink. Rum, although traditional for such occasions, will render him even more careless of his fate. After this, you will without scruple be able to give to his little neck the final and decisive blow. Your rabbit will already be in such a state of anæsthesia that nothing can matter to him.

"Thus you are assured of having given him a beautiful life, and a beautiful death!"

In Sinistra Parte,
Johannus Baptista

1100 A.D.–1450 A.D.
England

In England, things had stayed fairly simple. Barbaric snarlings and pouncings had, of course, been curbed to that state of repressed ferocity which even now marks the hungry Britisher at table. The Romans had come and gone, leaving more roads than recipes.

Druidic laws laid strict taboos on certain foods: hares, poultry, fish. Oil and lard were much preferred to cow's butter. Mortars were busy in every house and hovel, replacing the greater part of all our kitchen paraphernalia. Unleavened cakes of oat or wheaten flour, and the ubiquitous stew, were common fare in all the island's homes.

Things had stayed fairly simple.

Then a vision of the Holy Sepulcher, raped by the foul infidel, flashed over western Europe. England followed, mighty and beautiful. Her bravest soldiers, her wiliest dreamers, the sturdiest folk from all her fields went southward and eastward in those stupendous migrations called the Crusades. Gain and the Holy Grail!

Many of the Englishmen died, in battles or storms or in the heathen's tents. Some of them stayed on in the strange lands, took wives, and raised tall blue-eyed sons with dark skins. A few of them went back to England.

They brought rich brocaded silks in many colours, and jewels, and strange heavy perfumes. These were for their women. Also for the women, they said, were the spices in boxes and sacks—and to please the women, nothing more, they showed how to blend seven powders into a hot paste on meat and eggs, or throw magical pinches of this and that into the daily soup, and so transform it that it steamed like incense.

Then, while their wives watched with polite curiosity, the generous Crusaders ate heartily. Their eyes watered with nostalgic delight.

They taught the spicy secrets to underlings. Apprentices were initiated slowly, and rivalries sprang up between the kitchen staffs of different English castles, which were matched only during the French eighteenth century.

Finally a cookbook was written; then several appeared in the libraries of great houses. We can read one of them (with some stumbling, it is true) in what are known now as *The Harleian Ms. 279*.

In these we see how much men could hold, seven hundred years ago. Purveyance lists, made for every visit of a ruler or nobleman, show us incredible pages of supplies. This is only a part of the poultry listed for one of Richard's weekends in 1387:

> Fifty swans, a hundred and ten geese, fifty capons "of hie grece" and eight dozen other capons, sixty dozen hens, five herons, six kids and seven dozen rabbits (strange place here

for such lively fourlegged wingless little beasts!), five dozen pullets for jelly and some eleven dozen to roast, a hundred dozen peacocks, twenty dozen cranes and curlews, and "wilde fowle ynogh."

Besides the strange meats of crane and peacock and swan, seal was very popular, and whale and porpoise made any meal delicious. Marrow and almond milk were used in almost every recipe, whether with fish, meat, or dainty custard. Puddings of swans' and capons' necks, little birds and oxen salted whole, sweet soups of cinnamon and rose water with the roasts—it all sounds strange now. In as many centuries, our American salads of marshmallow and pink jelly, and our chocolate sodas, will undoubtedly seem even queerer.

Wines, especially a thin red Gascon mixed with honey and spices and called *claré*, were drunk indiscriminately with all foods. More often they were poured over game and puddings and soups.

But Englishmen, even then, drank ale with greater ease, and used it, moreover, in many of their dishes. They soured it in the sun for vinegar; they soaked fish in it as a preservative, and put it in many sauces. Best of all, they quaffed cock-ale, a spiced brew in which one lusty rooster had ended his days and lain for many more.

"To make Cock Ale," instructs one ancient recipe reprinted in 1736 in Smith's *Compleat Housewife*, "take ten gallons of ale and a large cock, the older the better. Parboil the cock, flea him, and stamp him in a stone mortar until his bones are broken. You must craw and gut him when you flea him. Put him into two quarts of sack, and put to it 3 pounds of raisins of the sun stoned, some blades of mace, and a few cloves.

"Put all these into a canvas bag, and a little while before you find the ale has done working, put the ale and bag together into a vessel. In a week or 9 days' time bottle it up, fill the bottles but just above the necks, and leave the same to ripen as other ale."

Recipes in *The Harleian* cookbook are vaguer than this bizarre proof of British strength. In only one or two of them are definite measurements given. "Take sugar enough," says one direction. "Take clean fresh brawn," says another, "and seethe it, but not enough." No step-by-step procedure for young brides here! It is rather the terse understatement of one expert to another.

The directions for thickening sauces and soups leave even more to the reader's foreknowledge. "Let it not be too thick nor too thin, but as *potage* should be . . . make it somewhat running and somewhat standing."

The old cook's English is very pleasant to read. He describes the making of a sauce: "Boil it, and when it cometh on high, ally it and set it a-down—and look that you stir it well!" And for pie shells to fill with meat and birds, he says—most aptly!—"Take and make fair little coffins——"

Meals were hearty then, as well as plentiful. The several main dishes of a course were bound together with a froth, a fluff, of what were called *light plates*. A typical one directs: "Mince pork and dates, add egg yolks and green cheese and ginger and cannel, mix all, and bake with a covering of hard-baked yolks." This hors d'œuvre would, no doubt, keep the diners occupied until some real food came their way, something to sink their teeth into!

Here, then, is a recipe for Beef y-Stewed:

Take fair beef of the ribs of the forequarters, and smite a fair piece, and wash the beef into a fair pot. Then take the water that the beef was soaking in, and strain it through a strainer, and seethe the same water and beef in a pot and let them boil together. Then take cannel, cloves, mace, grains of parise, quibibes, and onions minced, parsley and sage, and cast thereto and let them boil together. And then take a loaf of bread, and steep it with broth and vinegar, and then draw it through a strainer, and let it be still; and when it is near enough, cast the liquor thereto, but not too much; and then let boil and cast saffron thereto, a quantity. Then take salt and vinegar, and cast thereto, and look that it be poignant enough, and serve forth.

As a decoration for this stew, primroses might be tossed upon it, less beautifully than yellow melon flowers upon the roasted duck of China, but with the same desire.

Flowers were often used thus by the Middle English, sometimes most fortunately. What could be more ludicrously lovely than a tiny crackled piglet all garlanded with lilies and wild daffodils? Or a baked swan in its feathers, with roses on its proud reptilian head?

The three main courses of a banquet were heralded by spectacular puddings and tarts called *warners*. These, more often than not, were eaten in spite of the silk, wire, wood, gilt, and feathers that decorated them.

The biggest set pieces marking the end of each course, however, were seldom eaten. Instead, after the guest of honour had duly inspected them, they were paraded slowly around the banquet hall, sometimes carried on long stretchers by the strongest servants and sometimes wheeled cumbersomely on carts.

Subtleties they were called, and in no uncertain style they indicated the character or activities of the honoured diner.

A Templar home from Jerusalem saw sugar heretics bowed down before a Holy Sepulcher of paste and cake, with a Red Sea of jelly shimmering near it.

A sporting nobleman recognized his own hunting party, reduced to candy, galloping across a custard moor.

When John Stafford was made Archbishop of Canterbury toward the middle of the fifteenth century, he nodded with benign pleasure at the three subtleties composed for him. First he saw Saint Andrew, sitting on a high altar of state, with beams of gold; before him kneeling, John Stafford himself in his pontifical robes, with his crozier crouched behind him, coped.

Then after dishes of crane and venison and many other meats and birds and finally fish and fruit and a great tart, the second subtlety appeared. It was the Trinity showing a Son of gold, with a crucifix in His hand. Saint Thomas sat on one side, Saint Austin on the other, and John Stafford knelt again, still in his bishop's robes. Behind him was his crozier, coped with the arms of Rochester. Behind the crozier, on one side, knelt a black monk of Christ's Church, and on the other the Abbot of Saint Austin's.

The third course came to its end, after fourteen separate dishes. The last great subtlety was trundled before the banqueters, and a clerk described it:

A godhede in a son of gold glorified above, in the son the holy giste voluptable. Seint Thomas kneling a-for him, with ye poynt of a swerd in his hede, & a Mitre there-uppon, crowning s. T. in dextera parte, Maria tenens mitram; in sinistra parte, Johannus Baptista; et in iiij partibus, iiij Angeli incensantes.

And with this the banquet ended.

Pity the Blind
in Palate

Frederick the Great used to make his own coffee, with much to-do and fuss. For water he used champagne. Then, to make the flavour stronger, he stirred in powdered mustard.

Now to me it seems improbable that Frederick truly liked this brew. I suspect him of bravado. Or perhaps he was taste-blind.

Almost all people are born unconscious of the nuances of flavour. Many die so. Some of these unfortunates are physically deformed, and remain all their lives as truly taste-blind as their brother sufferers are blind to colour. Others never taste because they are stupid, or, more often, because they have never been taught to search for differentiations of flavour.

They like hot coffee, a fried steak with plenty of salt and pepper and meat sauce upon it, a piece of apple pie and a chunk of cheese. They like the feeling of a full stomach. They resemble those myriad souls who say, "I don't know anything about music, but I love a good rousing military band."

Let the listener to Sousa hear much music. Let him talk to other music listeners. Let him read about music makers.

He will discover the strange note of the oboe, recognize the French horn's convolutions. Schubert will sing sweetly in his head, and Beethoven sweep through his heart. Then one day he will cry. "Bach! By God, I can hear him! I can hear!"

That happens to the taste-blind in just some such way. He eats apple pie, good or bad, because he has always eaten it. Then one day he sees a man turn his back upon the cardboard crust and sodden half-cooked fruit, and eat instead some crisp crackers with his cheese, a crisp apple peeled and sliced ruminatively after the crackers and the yellow cheese. The man looks as if he knew something pleasant, a secret from the taste-blind.

"I believe I'll try that. It is—yes, it is good. I wonder——"

And the man who was taste-blind begins to think about eating. Perhaps he talks a little, or reads. All he really need do is experiment.

He discovers that cream is good in coffee in the morning, but that after dinner black coffee is better. He looks for the first time at soup, and pushes it away if it is too pale, too thick or thin.

Potatoes become more to him than the inevitable companion of meat, and he finds unsuspected tastes in the vegetables he has been gulping since his infancy.

He is pleased. He is awakened. At last he can taste, discovering in his own good time what Brillat-Savarin tabulated so methodically as the three sensations: (1) direct, on the tongue; (2) complete, when the food passes over the tongue and is swallowed; and most enjoyable of all (3) reflection—that is, judgment passed by the soul on the impressions which have been transmitted to it by the tongue.

Yes, he can taste at last, and life itself has for him more flavour, more zest.

Of all the present nations, France has the simplest school of cooking, in spite of the complicated subtleties of her great chefs—simplest in the sense of primitive and natural. Herbs, much sweet butter, cream, and long heating in pots of earthenware give the Gallic cuisine its characteristic flavours, and the juices from boiled and roasted meats are the base of almost every one of its sauces.

It has been said that the foundation of all of French cookery is butter, as that of the Italian is olive oil, German lard, and Russian sour cream. In the same way water or drippings may be designated, unfortunately, as the basis of the English cuisine, and perhaps the flavour from innumerable tin cans, of American!

France today possesses what is probably the most intelligent collective palate. I do not mean that her crudest ragamuffin can name each nuance in *Fruits aux Sept Liqueurs*, or give the year of a vintage wine from its bouquet. Indeed, there are many Frenchmen as callous to the harmonies of taste as any American hotdog-gobbler or English connoisseur of teashop Cornish pasties.

In general, though, France eats more consciously, more intelligently, than any other nation. It may be quails *financière*, or it may be a stew concocted from the rabbit that Papa Jacques caught yesterday under the hedge. Whichever France eats, she does it with a pleasure, an open-eyed delight quite foreign to most people.

The quails are an artful lure to the most refined of palates, and the rabbit stew, steaming, aromatic, is made just as tempting with an onion or two, pepper freshly ground, a little bacon, and a dash of cheap pure wine.

In Paris the gourmets eat with quiet deliberation, rolling each mouthful slowly toward their gullets. In Jacques' little cottage three or four friends inhale the stew's rich fumes, and eat it down like the hungry workingmen they are. In Paris and in the village there is a gusto, a frank sensuous realization of food, that is pitifully unsuspected in, say, the college boarding house or corner café of an American town.

In America we eat, collectively, with a glum urge for food to fill us. We are ignorant of flavour. We are as a nation taste-blind.

Cautiously we blink at a faint glimmer in the gloom. It seems, just now, that we have become conscious of a few subtleties. There is a faddish demand for roomy salad bowls, for pepper mills, which may bring permanent light to our national palate. Already an occasional shamefaced protest is heard against calling a California wine "dry" Sauterne, or a mild titter over some such synthetic gastronomy as prompted an advertisement saying, "This is a vintage year for maple syrup."

These feeble but encouraging signs must survive as best they may, however, while ten million men rush every noontime for their ham-on-white and cherry coke. Those ten million men may die taste-blind as well as stomach-ulcered, unless they are shocked into recognition of their own powers of enjoyment.

It might be good if you could go to them, quietly, and say, "Please, sir, stop a minute and listen to me. Can you imagine eating bananas and Limburger cheese together? You have never thought about it? Then think. Taste them separately in your mind, the banana, the Limburger. Taste them together. Ah! It is horrible? Then how about mutton chops with shrimp sauce? And try herring soup with strawberry jam, or chocolate with red wine."

Some of those ten million men would listen. Some of them would eat with their minds for the first time. You would be a missionary, bringing flavour and light to the taste-blind.

And that is a destiny not too despicable.

A Pigges
Pettie Toes

Elizabethan England

Even in the lusty days of Elizabeth's long reign, when England's blood ran, perhaps, at its fastest and finest, there were melancholy observers of what seemed signs of weakening in the nation's appetite.

Who could tell where things would end, when already the most reputable of rich merchants were copying an effeminate Italian mannerism, and carrying their silver and gold forks about with them instead of eating with their fingers and knives as good Englishmen had been glad to do for centuries?

And the ladies, lying in bed until six o'clock in the morning! When they arose, they breakfasted like babies, thinking they could start the day decently on a pot of ale and but one meager pound of bacon.

The Queen, God be thanked, paid no attention to the new-style finicking, and made her first meal of the day light but sustaining: butter, bread (brown, to stay in the stomach longer and more wholesomely than white), a stew of mutton, a joint of beef, one of veal, some rabbits in a pie, chickens, and fruits, with beer and wine to wash all down in really hygienic fashion.

It is true that Elizabeth could more easily command a full breakfast than most of her subjects, even in that prosperous age. They lived in simpler style, and made their dinners the day's biggest meal. They dined early, at about eleven in the morning, and unless guests had been invited their meals were much like the diet list of one well-to-do London bachelor who, on May 11, 1589, was served in his lodgings in Warwick Lane with the following plain fare:

A pece of bief	xviijd.
A loyne of veale	ijs.
2 chickens	xiiijd.
Orenges	ijd.
For dressings ye veale & chickens & sauce	xijd.

For supper that same day the gentleman ate more lightly, as was the general custom:

A shoulder of mutton	xvjd.
2 rabbettes	xd.
For dressinge ye mutton, rabbettes & a	
pigges pettie toes	viijd.
Colde bief	xiijd.
Cheese	ijd.

But even a bachelor grows tired of the purely animal pleasure of eating, and wishes occasionally to change it by conversation with his friends into the even more purely human pleasure of gastronomy. So, on June 20th of the same year, the Elizabethan Londoner invited a few cronies to dine with him. His cook spared no pennies, and served forth a very agreeable dinner:

Butter	iiijd.
A pece of bief	xiiijd.

A legg of mutton	xviijd.
A loyne of veale	xiipd.
2 pecks of pescodes	viijd.
3 rabbettes	ijs.
A quart of creame	vjd.
3 quarts of strawberies	xvjd.
2 li. of cheries	xxd.
Di: li. of muske confectes	xd.
Di: li. of violett confectes	xjd.
Orenges	iijd.
2 lemans	vjd.
Bred	viijd.
Beare	ixd.

Either this gentleman was a moderate drinker, or his cook did not follow the usual rule of adding beverage prices to the daily lists. There are few such entries: an occasional pint of claret or Rhenish, and sometimes beer for dinner.

In most establishments, however, enormous quantities of wines were drunk on ordinary days as well as festivals, and this in spite of the rising prices, which had jumped from the penny-a-gallon of two hundred years before, to an average of one shilling twopence for the same quantity in 1590.

Sack, alicant, claret, muscadine, Rhenish, and a port-like charneco, brown bastard, cider: all these were drunk as well as ales and beers, and most of them were mixed, according to the host's taste, with sugar, hot spices, and even the prized seasoning ambergris.

Queen Bess herself called mead her favourite tipple, and wherever she went had jugs of it carried with her, in case what was provided by her subjects was not spiced to her taste. And indeed, it was a difficult task to add to each brew of honey and water the same amount of herbs and lemon peel and ground spices, although from there on the procedure was the same for the Queen and the kitchen maid: three months in the keg and six weeks in the bottles before the sweet heady stuff could be drunk.

Perhaps such cloying wines made palates insensible to unsweetened fare; perhaps the great quantities of meat that were eaten made Elizabethan stomachs demand more stimulus. Whatever the reason, Englishmen then, as now, sucked greedily on candies, and counted as a failure any feast whose table did not include large bowls of "sugared meats" and sweet Naples biscuits, and marchpane, with eringo the candied root of sea holly, and kissing comfits to end the meal and sweeten the hot breath.

Even when we know that it was the fashion, in Elizabeth's days, to serve much more food for each course than could possibly be eaten—a fashion always coexistent with periods of prosperity—it is hard not to feel that the social observers were probably too pessimistic. Granted that appetites had dwindled from earlier Gargantuan size, that forks were turning the Britishers into a race of "foppish fursifers," that men ate like women and women like lazy infants. We cannot but be thankful that we are spared the critical eye of such carpers, as we sit down to our balanced lunches of orange juice and salad, free perhaps from the gout and dropsy that stood like evil fiends behind every dining-bench in old England.

But are we so thankful that we are free also from fine furious Elizabethan life?

The Standing
and the Waiting

It was at the top of the stairs that I first felt something wrong.
Until then all had been as I last knew it: the archway, the irregular honey-coloured courtyard, the rounded trees in tubs. The
stairs, too, were the same, bending round and back over themselves in several shallow flights; and at the top was the familiar
glass box with trout, a plate of mushrooms, and some steaks
laid carelessly across the cold-pipes that made its bottom.

We looked for a moment into the box, Chexbres with the
hurried, timid appraisal of a man who is in a strange place and
conscious of being watched for his reactions to it by another
person to whom it is familiar, I with the proud worry of a
woman who fears she has too much boasted.

Would the dishes be as exciting, as satisfying? Would the
wine still be the best wine? And I, would I be accepted, a loving
admirer, or would I now be long forgotten?

Well, the glass box was the same. Chexbres flipped me a
quick smile of reassurance. We went along the ugly tiled corridor, past the water closets where I felt a sudden hilarious memory of my mother's consternation when she had first entered

them and found them full of men all chatting, easing themselves, belching appreciatively.

I started to tell Chexbres of her face, puckered in an effort to look broad-minded. We turned the first abrupt corner of the hall, the corner where the kitchens started.

One of the doors opened. A rat-like boy darted out, ducking his head and grinning shyly as he passed us. I refused to look at Chexbres, for I knew that he had smelled, as I had, as alas! I had, that faint trail of bad air following after the scullion like the silver of a snail, bad air rising noxiously from the hidden dirty corners of the kitchens.

I finished the story of my mother's dauntless face, as we hurried on down the long dim corridor.

"There are two dining rooms for the *pensionnaires*," I chattered foolishly, "and the *pensionnaires* are everybody—like the mayor and the rich brothel-keepers and carpenters and Chinese students.

"And here is Ribaudot's office."

I was trying to sound casual, but I felt very nervous. Oh, to have talked so much of the restaurant, to have boasted! And then that little ominous whiff! Or had Chexbres noticed it?

I tapped nonchalantly on the half-open glass door of the small, incredibly disordered room.

"Come in, then!" The voice was cross and muffled.

We pushed into the office. By the dim window two cooks in very tall hats sat with their bare arms leaning on a table covered with empty dishes. A cradled bottle lay in front of them. They smiled impersonally.

Ribaudot stood clumsily with one leg still half under the table, his hands leaning on his tall desk.

"Come in, come in," he said, more pleasantly. He wiped his mouth, and peered politely at us.

"How do you do—good afternoon, Monsieur Ribaudot. I

am sure you don't remember me: Madame Fischer, who used so often to dine here? I used to come here with——"

"Oh, of course! Why of course!" He smiled warmly, but I could see that he did not remember. I shrugged inside, and while I introduced Chexbres as a fervent student of gastronomy, and we all chattered and assured each other of remembrance and good will, I looked for change.

If the whiff, the faint bad trail, had caught Ribaudot, it was not yet evident. His office was filled with the conglomerate cooling odours of a good meal, and he himself with the first leisurely torpor of perfect digestion. Yes, of course he looked older, perhaps thinner, uncombed as ever, though, and still modestly sure of being a great *restaurateur*.

"And Charles, little Charles?" I asked, suddenly.

Several looks crossed in the air. Chexbres looked at me, warmly, smiling at my nostalgic probings and at what I had told him of the waiter Charles. I looked first at Chexbres, thanking him for recognizing the name, and assuring him that even if Charles were long dead, he had still been the ultimate, the impeccable peak of all waiters. Then I saw Ribaudot look swiftly at the two silent cooks and they at him, a look—a look—I felt very sad and puzzled.

Ribaudot interrupted me.

"The little Charles?" he asked, blandly. "Ah, you remember the little old Charles?" His voice was noncommittal. "But certainly he is here. We will call him."

Through my halfhearted protestations he walked majestically the three paces to the door, and disappeared. The air was still full of crossed meaningful looks. I wondered very much, and watched Chexbres' impassive interest in the framed diplomas on the walls. I tried to feel impassive, too.

Chexbres turned. Charles stood in the doorway, breathing

quickly, a rumpled napkin over one arm. Oh, I had forgotten how small—but hadn't he been fatter? Yes, old, the little *old* Charles.

I went quickly toward him, watching his pouchy face lighten quickly from peevish bewilderment to pleasure.

"Howdedo, Charles. I don't know if you remember ——"

"O my God! Oh, pardon, pardon, but it is the little American student, the little lady!"

Behind me, Chexbres laughed to hear me called little as I peered down on Charles, he up at me, timidly still, but recognizing me.

"And you, Madame? And how long is it? And you, are you well? Has it been two years? *Six?* Impossible! But it is good, pardon me for saying so, but it is good to see you!"

He stopped suddenly, looking confusedly at the two silent cooks, and then at Ribaudot. He seemed to shrink even smaller.

"Monsieur Ribaudot," I said, "would it be possible to command a dinner for this evening, and ask for the services of Charles?"

"But certainly, certainly!" He pulled a pad of paper toward him, and started to make squiggles on it.

"Until eight tonight, then, Charles. And the old table in the corner—was it Number Four?"

I turned to Ribaudot again. He seemed to know me at last, and to be trying to comfort me, to soften life for me. And all the time we discussed food so pleasantly I wondered at Charles' quick, poignant, wet look of—of gratitude—as he hurried back to his work.

I felt sad, but said nothing to Chexbres. Instead, we talked of Burgundian architecture, not even mentioning the Burgundian meal we had so long planned.

At eight o'clock the small dining room was full, except for

our waiting table. As we sat down I saw in one easy glance that the people were no different after six years. There was the old woman with a dog and a dancing boy on her way to Cannes, and the table of American schoolteachers eating from a guidebook. And there were the two big young Englishmen in brown and grey, looking embarrassed before their larks on toast.

At the table under the mirror sat a college professor; the College Professor, twirling a glass of Corton, the pedagogic connoisseur, sipping alone in solemn appreciation, sure that his accent was as refined as his taste.

There were two tables of French people, gay and hungry. I remembered that their faces would grow red, later on.

A Chinese eating truffled pâté in a trance of philosophical nausea, two Lesbians drinking Vichy, three silent *pensionnaires*, a priest—the hard white lights burned down on all of us, the mirror reflected our monotonous gestures, the grey walls picked out our pale natures and the warmth of colour and odour and taste before us on the white tables.

"This is a good room," Chexbres murmured, lowering his eyelids and straightening a straight fork. "I like small rooms. Small rooms, for eating—or mountainsides."

"Good evening! Ah, 'sieur-'dame, you are here!"

Charles stood by the table, breathing fast. His minute moustache was newly stiff with wax, and his hair was plastered in a thin replica of the debonair curlicues he used to wear. He beamed anxiously at us.

"Does—is everything as you wished?"

"Everything is perfect, Charles!" I wondered if my voice were too fervent. "Now we will start with a little glass of Dubonnet, please."

When he had gone, Chexbres said: "You are known, my dear! You should be much flattered—or I for being with you."

He smiled, the sweet-tongued self-mocker, at me and at the

table, and I looked with less haste at the tall crystal tulips to hold wine, at the napkins folded like pheasants, at the inky menu big as a newspaper, and our own little typewritten one on top of it, at the flowers———

Flowers *chez* Ribaudot, Ribaudot who hated any foreign odours near his plates? Never before—no, we were the only diners with flowers on our table.

On the little serving-board beside us, Charles fussed clumsily with a new bottle of Dubonnet. Finally it was open. He poured it with a misjudged flourish. Purple spread on the cloth. I looked quickly, without meaning to, at Chexbres, but he was watching the quiet colour in his glass. Perhaps he had not seen, had not realized, the fumblings of my perfect waiter?

He raised his *apéritif.* His eyes were wide and candid.

"I drink to our pasts—to yours and mine. And to ours. The wine is strong. Time is strong, too." He bowed slightly. "I grow solemn—or sententious."

I laughed at him. "I'm not afraid of time."

"Don't boast."

"I'm not boasting. Really, I'm glad six years—oh, it's too complicated. But this tastes good. I'm hungry."

"And this will be a good meal, worth waiting even longer than six years for. Do you know," he asked naïvely, "that I've never before had a menu written just for me? It's very exciting."

I felt my self-confidence sweep back, as he meant it to.

"And flowers," he went on. "I've had flowers on my table, but never the only ones, in a room of such important people."

We looked vaguely, amicably, at the stiff little bouquet, mimosa and a purplish rosebud and a short twig of cypress.

Charles steamed beside us, with a tall pitcher of soup. While he served it, it spilled from the trembling cups into the saucers. I felt a flash of intense irritation: wet saucers, God! how they irritate me! I looked straight into his eyes.

They were not wet and grateful now. They were desperate eyes, bloodshot, frantic, desperate. I cringed away.

"Oh, Chexbres," I whispered, "don't mind the spilling! Don't! It's that he's nervous. His hand's shaking because of that, I know."

You are lying to save your own boastful face, too, I said inside. You know Charles is drunk. Yes, Charles, the perfect waiter, spilling soup and drunk, and it hurts your pride.

"Maybe his feet hurt him," I went on very fast. "I know you hate soup in saucers. But you know I've heard that waiters do stranger things than most criminals, simply because their feet hurt."

"Yes, I'm sure," Chexbres agreed, vaguely. "This is really delicious, my dear.

"You know," he said, in a suddenly direct voice, "I can't understand why most people are put off at first by the coloured tiles on the roofs of Burgundy. It seems to me they're a definite outcropping of the plebeian in architecture, like the frescoes of Swiss interiors during the same period."

For a moment I felt rebuffed. But almost at once I knew he was right. Six years—six hundred years . . . architecture was better.

We talked, and well, and all the dinner was most excellent, and the wine was like music on our tongues. Time was forgotten, and its signals, too. But I noticed, with a kind of fifth eye, that Charles' hand grew steady, and his own eye clear, until by the end of the meal I dared preen myself upon his delicate sure touch.

"Have you ever seen that better done?" I asked Chexbres.

"No. No, he is wonderful. He is an artist."

We watched as in a blissful dream the small fat hands moving like magic among bottles and small bowls and spoons and plates, stirring, pouring, turning the pan over the flame just so, just so, with the face bent keen and intent above.

"It's like a brain operation," Chexbres said, "—the hard light, the excitement, the great surgeon. Thank you for bringing me here. It's worth——"

It was done. We tasted. We nodded silently, and smiled at Charles, and he looked almost like the old Charles again, very self-sure. I felt happy.

After coffee, I laughed to think of us sitting there almost the last, and at what I was going to do.

"Chexbres, you think I've shown off, but that was only the beginning! Now I really do show off, and all for your benefit."

We smiled at each other, very effortless and calm.

"Charles," I called, warning Chexbres quickly, "You have never tasted the local *marc*, remember!

"Charles, what do you think has been the sad experience— but first, are we keeping you too late?"

I waved my hand at the now empty room, dim in every corner but ours, and at a scullery boy scrubbing the hall. I felt expansive, warm from the wine, at ease in Time.

"Oh, but what an idea!" Charles exploded. "Excuse me for chiding you, Madame, but what an idea! Madame, you must know that for you to have another good meal *chez* Ribaudot, and go away remembering it and me, I would gladly stay here until morning—no, until tomorrow night, by God!"

Chexbres and I bowed courteously. Charles did, too.

"And the sad experience, Madame?"

"Oh, thank you for recalling me. I had almost forgotten. Charles, last night we had a stroke of luck that was unfortunate—I should say almost desolating. I, who wished to introduce our good friend Monsieur Chexbres to the famous *marc* of Burgundy, was served with a glass of some strange liquid—

thank God I had the good sense to taste it before letting Monsieur come near it!—some strange liquid, pale, cut, rank, which could never——"

"Ah, but I know! I know where!" Charles beamed, flourishing his napkin with glee.

"Oh, but naturally I would not be so indiscreet as to mention the name of the miserable restaurant," I protested, rhetorically. I glanced at Chexbres exultantly: the scene was beautiful.

"No need, no need, Madame! A restaurant serving the good *marc* so insultingly, and to you, a connoisseur" (here I bowed graciously) "and to this poor gentleman a sure amateur having his first taste" (here Chexbres lowered his eyes modestly)— "ah, such poisonous conduct, my God! could only be at" (and here Charles leaned very close to us in the empty room and hissed) "could only be at *La Tour*!"

He stood off, triumphant. I pressed a little line into the table-cloth with my thumb nail, smirking, murmuring, "Of course I say nothing, no names!" in complete agreement. I could feel Chexbres' appreciation all around me.

"But, *but* 'dame, we must rectify that infected, that—pardon me—that stinking behaviour!"

I sighed faintly. It had worked!

"Yes, my idea, too. But no ordinary *marc*, Charles, no liqueur served on anyone's order. This must be——"

"Yes, very special," he finished for me. "Trust me, Madame. It may take a few extra minutes. A little more *filtre*, perhaps, while I am gone?"

Chexbres and I sat wordless, looking mildly and somnolently at each other. We sipped at the bitter black coffee. A rickety old ventilator whirred in the ceiling, and the boy cleaning the hall bumped his bucket against the tiles. Lights went out, except over our table.

Charles tiptoed back, wheezing, but his face full of life. He held a filthy old green bottle, not picturesquely crusted, but filthy. Silently he poured a little dark brown liquid into a large glass. He swirled it round. Chexbres reached for it.

"Permit me, sir," Charles halted him, "permit me to suggest that Madame taste it."

I winked slightly at Chexbres, and took up the glass. I tried to look like a connoisseur, a little pompous probably. I sipped, and then I could only look beatifically delighted, for it was the cleanest, smoothest distillation that I had ever met.

"Ah!"

Charles sighed. I had told him. He poured the glass almost half full, at least twice as full as he should have, and with a jubilant look disappeared into the wet dark hall.

"Chexbres, now *I* shall be solemn. But I have never been served such *marc*! Not even Ribaudot would serve that to his best friends, to anyone less than the mayor or maybe the Holy Ghost. Where did Charles get it?"

Chexbres let it run under his tongue, and sat nodding ecstatically at me. I could almost see it seeping through his head, in and around in a hot tonic tide, and then down his throat.

"Dear sweet gentle Jesus!" he remarked, softly.

"Oh, I'm glad we came, Chexbres. After all, I mean."

We both drank at the one glass, and talked peacefully under the one white light. Finally the *marc* was gone. Charles appeared, carrying the filthy bottle.

"Oh, no more, no more! Really, we couldn't——"

He stopped very still, and looked at me.

"Madame, you must drink one glass. Please!" he said, in a quiet voice, almost muttering. "Please drink this glass from me. It is I, Charles, who offer it to you and to Monsieur Chexbres."

"But—it is so late, and—" The thought of swallowing one more mouthful closed my throat, almost.

"I have said I would stay until tomorrow for you. I would stay until the end of the world, truly." He looked at me calmly, standing between us and the dark doorway. Beyond him I could see nothing, and there was not a sound anywhere, except the three of us breathing rather cautiously.

"Thank you," Chexbres said, warmly. "Madame was afraid only of detaining you too long, Charles. Otherwise we could sit forever, too, drinking this miraculous liqueur."

He held out the glass. With a hand steady as oak, Charles poured it to the brim, a good half-pint of strong *marc*.

"Thank you, Charles," I said. "I want never to leave, here where I have so often been happy. It may be six years again. Will you prepare the bill, please?"

We knew we must drink it all. It was like smouldering fire, wonderful still, but hard now to swallow. We sat without moving, conscious suddenly of exhaustion, and of being perhaps too full of food, with all the heady wine-life gone out of us.

Charles came back, with the little sheet of flimsy paper on a plate. I wondered about the tip: in a way I felt like not leaving one, because he seemed more than a waiter now. But when he brought back change, I left it all on the plate.

"Thank you, Madame," he said, and did not pick it up. He stood watching us sip resolutely at the *marc*. Finally I looked up at him.

"Madame, thank you, thank you for coming again."

I wanted not to be personal, so I said, "But why not? All people who love good food come to Ribaudot's again."

"Yes," he stuttered slightly, "but—pardon me—but I mean thank you for asking for me. You don't know——"

"Oh, Charles, it is we who are fortunate, to have your services." I felt very polished and diplomatic, but at the same time sincere, sincere as hell under the weariness and all the *marc*.

"No, no—I mean, you will never know what it meant, tonight, to have you ask for me, little old Charles. And now, good evening."

Chexbres asked, quickly, "But we will pass this way again, and soon we hope, and then of course ——?"

"Ah, who knows?" Charles raised his eyebrows toward his thinning curlicue of hair, restrained a gesture to stroke his little whiff of moustache, smiled debonairly at us, and disappeared finally into the black corridor.

"I thought he said he would wait until tomorrow night," I murmured, flippantly. Then I felt rather ashamed, and apologized. "He'll probably be waiting at the end of the hall, the top of the stairs, to help us with our coats."

Chexbres said nothing, but slowly drank down the rest of the *marc.*

The chairs squawked wildly as we stood up. The sound was almost good in that silent room.

In the corridor we saw a dim light, and as we went by Ribaudot's office, his silhouette was sharp against the frosted glass, bent over his high desk.

"I know where the coats are," I whispered, and we tiptoed down the hall.

"Is it Madame Fischer?" His voice came muffled through the door. He opened it, blinking at us, with his hair mussed.

"Oh, I'm sorry! I do hope we haven't kept you," I said, in confusion.

He looked very tenderly at us. "No. And have you dined well? I am glad. I have your coats in here."

We stood awkwardly in the doorway while he crossed the little room to the table where the two cooks had sat in the afternoon. Our coats were piled on it, to one side, and a stiff ugly bouquet of mimosa and two purplish rosebuds and a twig of cypress stood by them. I looked dully at it, wishing I were home in bed, very tired.

"It was good of you to remember Ribaudot," he said.

"It was very natural. Who does not?"

"Ah, things nowadays—the affairs—" but he bowed, acceptance calm on his face.

"And the poor old Charles. It was especially good for him. I see you and I shared the honour of flowers from him." He looked impersonally at the ugly bouquet. "Yes, I fired Charles today, just before your first visit. He is on his way to the South by now.

"Permit me to help you with your scarf. It was sad—a fine waiter once, a brave little man always—but what will you do? Everything changes. Everything passes.

"Good night. Good night, sir, and Madame, and thank you. And good-bye."

"Au revoir, we hope," I called as we walked away from him towards the dark.

"Who knows?" He shrugged, and closed the glass door.

In the long hall corruption hung faint and weakly foul on the still air. The stairs were deep, with the empty glass box like a dark ice cube, and we breathed freely once out in the courtyard.

It was filled with moonlight. The trees in tubs were black, and through the archway the tower of the palace gleamed and glowed against the black sky.

Chexbres took my hand gently, and pointed to the roofs, coloured tiles, Burgundian, drained of their colour now, but plainly patterned. I began to cry.

Catherine's Lonesome Cooks

1533 A.D.–1810 A.D.
France

Until well into the sixteenth century French cooking developed little. Lordly kitchens aped the British in the length, breadth, and depth of their enormous meals.

Restaurants there were none, unless you could so name that redoubtable hostelry *La Tour d'Argent*, old then, older today. Now it serves *crêpes Suzette* and *canards pur-sang*, but in 1533 it was still dishing forth such favourites of the Middle Ages as dormouse pasty and a mixed pie of snake, porpoise, swan, and plum-stuffed crane.

It was that year that Fate and Pope Clement VII changed the table manners of Europe. The Holy Father, probably conscious less of the gastronomic importance of his act than of its political results, married off his niece Catherine de Medici to France's young Henry.

And Catherine took her cooks to France with her. They were probably the first great *chefs de cuisine* in that land, and galling though the fact may be to those Frenchmen who mix patriotism with their love of fine food, they were Italians every one.

Paris seemed harsh and boorish to the lonesome Florentines. They moped for the gay lightness of their own banquet halls. There ladies and gentlemen were taught *The Fifty Courtesies of the Table* as soon as they were old enough to eat at all. Here in Paris many people still laughed jeeringly at "those Italian neatnesses called forks," and gulped down great chunks of strongly seasoned meats from their knife-ends or their greasy fingers.

Catherine's cooks shuddered, and conferred together in low voices.

It was not long before they acted. Their innovation burst like a bomb over all the noble tables of Paris. Sherbets appeared! In every shape and colour, with flavours as clear and subtle as summer flowers, sherbets were set before the startled Frenchmen by the Queen's wily chefs.

Roughened tongues were made smooth, and hot throats cooled; palates, long calloused by the indiscriminate spicings of the dark centuries, slowly grew keen and sensitive.

The chefs chuckled. These Frenchmen might be able, in good time, to appreciate their Italian sauces and their tarts and soups. In good time!

By the beginning of the next century the French palate had indeed grown much more sophisticated, and some knowledge of culinary tricks was a necessary part of any worldling's education. Louis XIII, it is true, became his own cook less for pleasure than because of his inherited fear of being poisoned. His court, however, led by Richelieu's careful genius, developed a passionate interest in cookery.

It became smart to cook the main dish of a supper oneself. Kitchens, suddenly invaded by guests in elaborate costumes and dainty shoes, were the centre of attention. They bloomed with new pots, crest-emblazoned: A hundred impractical inventions of the amateur chefs for turning spits and whipping cream were discreetly ignored by harassed cooks, who worked as expertly as ever in this new shade.

Kitchen gardens, as well, grew very amusingly under the ecstatic gushings of court ladies and the silent care of gardeners, and a bouquet of lettuces and shallots was as chic as lilies.

The greatest men in all France became authors of strange poems on food and stranger recipes, which were greeted with peals of respectful laughter. Some of them, like Cardinal Richelieu's invention of a sauce made with eggs and oil which he called *maionnaise*, are as familiar a part of our diet today as almond milk and brawn were in 1600.

The next Louis, the fourteenth, and the fifteenth who was his great-grandson, were less timid than the king who feared poison. They loved good food as they loved war and fine buildings and beautiful women, with a boundless and intelligent zest.

Kitchens and kitchen gardens were just as fashionable under their energetic reigns, but it now became even more stylish to own a famous chef. Great men stooped to the most childish tricks to win a rival's cook or steward, and recipes were guarded like coronation jewels.

Diplomats and nobles were proud to give their revered family names to a new sauce or a bonbon, or share kudos with the chef who so honoured them. Soubise sauce, so subtly oniony, and béchamel, that lifesaver of *la haute cuisine*, are only two of the innumerable recipes that have come to us from the snobbish palates of the French eighteenth century.

Great chefs were its oracles, and wrote serious treatises on the arts of carving and serving, or the complexities of gastronomic etiquette. The Prince de Condé's chef, Vatel, who committed suicide when fish he had ordered for a dinner arrived too late to be served, gave some indication of his own seriousness as well as his art's, in the essay *L'Escuyer Tranchant*.

"A carver," he dictates in one section, "should be scrupulous in his deportment; his carriage should be grave and dignified, his appearance cheerful; his eye serene, his head erect and well combed, abstaining as much as possible from sneezing, yawning, or twisting his mouth, speaking very little and directly, without being too near or too far from the table."

Oddly enough, Vatel's disciples earned their princely pay as much from those glamorous women kept by the diplomats as from the great men themselves. The pleasures of the table had become so important, by the time Madame du Barry and la Pompadour reigned over France, that no intelligent courtesan could afford to be without a fine chef. Dining eclipsed its old companion lovemaking, and many a beautiful *fille* was coveted more for her chef's skill with omelette than for her own artful thighs.

Waning passions, Louis the King's and Louis the fat silk merchant's, were fanned by the invention of a thousand new recipes. It was this, most probably, that started the extravagant fad for turkeys stuffed with truffles.

French interest in anything from the American Colonies ran high, and such dishes as Indian corn pudding and wild roasted turkey made any table smart. Prices for them ran into several figures—almost as expensive as truffles. It took a woman of unlimited income and capricious brain to combine the two whims of the moment, and serve a turkey stuffed with truffles to her admirers.

Immediately a rage for the crazy dish swept Paris. First the demimonde and then the court devoured it, with only slight qualms at its exorbitant cost.

Then, in an epidemic frenzy, the middle classes, the little shopkeepers, the laundresses and coachmen were seized with a mad appetite for *dinde truffée*. Truffles became so scarce that they were escorted through the city with armed guards, and men ruined themselves in order to prove their social stability by serving one stuffed turkey.

Only the courtesans and the great lords could afford the dish. They soon tired of it. In a few months Paris had forgotten it, except in the bankruptcy courts.

Under Louis XVI, gastronomy continued its somewhat debauched course. Louis himself was a plain man, more interested in locks and musical timepieces than in the intricacies of sauce-making. His simplicity, though, may have had its own subtle influence on the reigning vogue of the court, for under his poor giddy queen the pastoral life was lived most artificially.

Marie Antoinette and all her ladies became, for several hours of every sunny day, milkmaids more exquisite than ever spaded dung in any truthful farmyard. Gowned in picturesque and very flattering costumes, they sat on ivory stools to milk their perfumed animals, and churned at little silver churns until their arms grew tired.

A dainty pat of butter made by a noble lady's own hands, with the print of a strawberry leaf upon its smooth fresh bottom, was a love token almost more desired than kisses, and deserved at least a folk song in reply, or a country dance written for four partners.

Finally milk itself, so embarrassingly natural, was decided to be worthy of a true gourmet's attentions if it came from the hands of an aristocratic milkmaid. To add to the taste, so pure, so chastely sweet, the more promiscuous ladies gave special drinking cups to their courtiers. Made of the finest porcelain from impressions taken at the height of their owners' loveliness, each cup mirrored the curves of a woman's breast, wanton, fragile, evanescent.

Napoleon broke like a bull into this china shop. But then the Revolution had already scattered the aristocrats, demoralized the servants, and wiped out the depraved etiquette of court life. The Little Corporal brought with him another world of pretentious newly-rich, sharp-witted and vulgar. Paris blazed with jewels and affectations, all awkwardly displayed.

Napoleon himself was a bad eater. He gobbled. He had little patience with the long silences and deliberate smackings of his gourmand friends, although he tried at times to imitate them.

Once, in a sorry effort to pretend that he really cared a tinker's dam about such things as eggs, he insisted that he could flip an omelette better than his lady ever could. It landed on the floor.

For days he was morose, hearing in his head the muffled snickers of Josephine and his agile courtiers. He really preferred scrambling treaties, anyway, and men, and boundary lines.

Two Birds
Without a Branch

Apparently the chief purpose for stating intentions in an introduction is to have something later for contradiction and denial.
Herewith I give you two recipes, for no reason at all unless it
could be because I said that such a thing would never happen.

We knew a woman who sold real estate in a small beach col-
ony. She had a face like a brick wall, and a desire, some sixty
years old and still undaunted, to play ingenue rôles on Broad-
way. Her past was cautiously shaded.

We said we were going to live in France.

She said, "Where?"

We said, "Here, there—maybe Dijon——"

Suddenly her face was blasted. "Oh, Dijon!"

She put her hands up to her eyes and wept, and then cried
fiercely: "The smell of it! The smell of Dijon gingerbread!
When you are there smell it for me!"

So we did.

We smelled Dijon mustard, especially at the corner where
Grey-Poupon flaunts little pots of it. We smelled Dijon cassis in
the autumn, and stained our mouths with its metallic purple.
But all year and everywhere we smelled the Dijon gingerbread,

that *pain d'épice* which came perhaps from Asia with a tired Crusader.

Its flat strange odour, honey, cow dung, clove, something unnamable but unmistakable, blew over all the town. Into the theatre sometimes would swim a little cloud of it, or quickly through a café grey with smoke. In churches it went for one triumphant minute far above the incense.

At art school, where tiny Yencesse tried to convince the hungriest students that medal-making was a great career, and fed them secretly whether they agreed or not, altar smoke crept through from the cathedral on one side, and from the other the smell of *pain d'épice* baking in a little factory. It was a smell as thick as a flannel curtain.

This is the Dijon recipe, without, of course, the mysterious quality that makes each little gingerbread shop bake loaves quite different from any others:

Take two pounds of old black honey, the older and blacker the better, and heat it gently. When it has become a thin liquid, stir it very slowly and thoroughly into two pounds of the finest bread flour, of which about one-third is rye.

Put this hot paste away in a cold place. It must stay there for at least eight days, but in Dijon, where *pain d'épice* is best, it ripens in the cold for several months or even years!

Wait as long as you can, anyway. Then put it in a bowl and add six egg yolks, one level teaspoon of carbonate of soda, and three teaspoons of bicarbonate of soda.

Next comes the seasoning—and it is there, I think, that lies the magic. Try these the first time, before you begin your own experimenting: some pinches of anise, a teaspoon of dry mustard, and the zest of a large lemon.

Now beat it for a painfully long time. Put it in a buttered mould or pan and bake in a moderate oven for one hour—or less if you have divided this measure into more than one pan.

In Dijon little gingerbread orange slices are stuffed with marmalade and glazed, or great square loaves are sliced several times and spread with apricot jam before they are put together again. Or currants and candied fruits are baked in the loaves. Or they are left plain, to be sliced very thin and be spread with sweet butter for tea.

Whatever you do with your *pain d'épice*, you should put it away in waxed paper and an airtight box. It will taste even better in two months or three.

The next recipe is very exciting, like finding a diamond on the garden path. For this recipe has never yet been printed nor even told, though a marshal of France begged for it, long ago.

How it comes to be here is a story in which duplicity plays a minute but important part. I prefer to forget it, and comfort myself with the surety of my friend's benign forgiveness.

I translate literally from his handwriting, a trifle shaky but still delicately ornate, in purple ink:

Diplomate au Kirsch
A la manière de PAPAZI *Confiseur-licencié ès . . . bec*

For eight or ten people.

Cut eight small dry sponge biscuits into half-inch cubes. Into slightly smaller cubes cut a scant half-pound of fruits candied in syrup.

Soak the fruits in kirschwasser *for thirty minutes. Drain them, and moisten the biscuit cubes with the same* kirsch.

Whip three cups of cream which is sweet and very cold. *When it is whipped, season it with powdered sugar and add a little vanilla flavour.*

Put the whipped cream, the biscuits, and the candied fruits into a mould and mix them well. Cover the mould with a sheet of white paper and seal with its cover. (Be careful to butter the lip of the mould under the paper, so that salt will not make itself a part of the composition.)

Then put the mould for two hours into ice finely chopped and very salty—about two pounds of salt to ten of ice.

The liquid Cream to Pour
Over the Diplomate when
It is Taken from the Mould
Just Before Serving.

Into a double-boiler stir one full cup of milk, two egg yolks, one-fourth cup of powdered sugar, and one teaspoon of fine flour.

See that the mixture does not boil, and when it thickens take it from the stove. Then perfume it amply with kirsch.

Let it get very cold (either on the window-sill in winter or in summer in the ice chest), and pour it over the Diplomate and serve at once.

And be lifted, willy-nilly, to heavenly levels, for never was there a dessert more delicate, more fragrant, more sophisticated and naïve. In my mind I call it *L'Ingénue Libertine,* and already I regret having told its secret.

The Pale
Yellow Glove

Once at least in the life of every human, whether he be brute or trembling daffodil, comes a moment of complete gastronomic satisfaction.

It is, I am sure, as much a matter of spirit as of body. Everything is right; nothing jars. There is a kind of harmony, with every sensation and emotion melted into one chord of well-being.

Oddly enough, it is hard for people to describe these moments. They have sunk beatifically into the past, or have been ignored or forgotten in the harsh rush of the present. Sometimes they are too keen to be bandied in conversation, too delicate to be pinioned by our insufficient mouthings.

Occasionally, in a moment of wide-flung inebriation or the taut introspection of search for things past, a person hits upon his peak of gastronomic emotion. He remembers it with shock, almost, and with a nostalgic clarity that calls tears to his inward-looking eyes.

If you can surprise him at such quick times, and make him talk, you are more than fortunate. It is as tricky a business as to watch a bird of paradise at play.

Two or three times I have been successful. Of course there were a few other times when I have almost felt so, but then I had asked. And if you ask people, they search their memories, and occasionally produce a sad shadow of the spontaneity you desire, a pale image of the vivid shaking recollection that should have sprung forth unaware.

I remember once I asked a beautiful flat-faced actress with golden hair and skin. She spoke vaguely and with a kind of embarrassment of two steaks that she had stolen from a rich woman's dog, and broiled over a driftwood fire, and shared on the Cape Cod beach with a hungry stonecutter.

Two or three people, when I've prodded them, have mumbled of apples: biting into them, feeling the cold juice flow into the mouth corners, hearing the snap of skin and pulp.

But the spontaneous revelations are rare. They must, from what I have discovered, be inspired by wine or high emotional pressure. They are thus doubly poignant.

I

Miss Lyse was an English teacher in a middle-sized town in Bavaria. She had been one ever since her militantly British mother had brought her there, some sixty years before. She would be one until she died, helped always and in spite of her dwindling powers of instruction by the impatiently thoughtful families whose parents and grandparents had recited the verb TO BE at her virginal knee.

It was easy to see that she had once been very lovely. Even now her small dark-eyed head rose above its lumpy old body like the dream of a swan, or a piece of Chinese crystal.

It was hard to see why she had not long since married some member of the aristocratic families with whom she lived; hard, that is, until you heard her describe—so lovingly, too—her genteel Tartar of a mother, who on her deathbed had made Lyse swear never, *never* to forget her English accent. And now, with this old maid who for more than half a century had spent all her days with the fine flower of Germany, her soft flat voice was as British as a currant bun; her intonation so carefully preserved marked her anywhere as a "Miss," never a *Fräulein*, and her German was half English, her English very German.

She was garrulous, with the embarrassingly naïve language of an aged person who has spent all her life explaining things simply to children who might have listened better had the explanations been complex.

She talked with a vivacity which had long since ceased to be affected, and was now as much a part of her as her jet brooch of the young Queen Victoria, or her lace fichu that had been admired (on another's shoulder) by Franz Josef.

"Once, my dears," she told us on a chill October afternoon when even shawls laid along the window ledges could not keep cold drafts from shushing into her high attic room, "once I stood so close to the great Sadi Carnot that to touch him I would have been able! Yes, then I was that near!

"That was the summer after we went to Garmisch, to the *Schloss* of my little pupils—you remember?"

She peered merrily at us, and we nodded recognition to a season dead some forty years before we were conceived. We poured another glass of sherry for her, the sherry we had brought to warm her bones while we were far from her and Bavaria.

(And here it is perhaps significant to say that all old pupils treated Miss Lyse thus, feeling a kind of guilty neglect if they did not often go to her stuffy pleasant garret with wine, a cold chicken, even a pat of sweet butter. I am sure that we kept her alive for years in this compulsive, desultory way——)

"Yes, that was *such* a nice summer! The trees in full bloom early were, and everybody said that *never* had there been so many forest flowers. I remember the *Graf* himself said that to me, one morning on the stairs!"

She coloured delicately, and raised her young dark eyes above the rim of her glass. "I used to wear flowers in my hair— it was black then—except at dinner, of course, when I was invited down to dine with the family if they needed an extra one at table.

"But there was one thing about that summer—when was it, in 'sixty-eight?" She looked sharply at our blank faces, as if she had a good mind to rap our knuckles for inattention, and then laughed. "What does it matter? It was several years ago, yes? A beautiful summer.

"My dear blessed mother was with me, in the village near the *Schloss*—I had not been long away from England, and she watched over me—and one day, one day we had a picnic, a real English tea in the forest! It was lovely!

"My mother, a sweet young Russian girl who taught also at the *Schloss*, and——"

Suddenly she put down her glass, giggled, and peeked naughtily at us between her knobby, loose-skinned fingers.

"Now you must never tell, never!" She looked stern for a second, and then giggled again. "It was very daring, but my dear mother was there and Tanya, and—three—young— gentlemen—from—the *Schloss*!

"*Yes*, my dears! We all went on the picnic, Tanya and the three young gentlemen (*so* handsome were they), and myself, and of course my dear good mamma to see that everything was proper.

"*Well*," and she settled herself back in her chair as we filled her glass again, "we went far into the woods, with a servant to carry the tea-basket. We came to a stream, such a small sweet brooklet was it, with flowers and watercress on its borders.

"My mother sat down, and whilst the servant built a little blaze yet, she got out her silver teapot, which had gone to India twelve times with her. It was a pretty teapot.

"We gathered watercress. One of the young gentlemen—what *was* his name, now?—got his gloves quite wet. They were pale yellow gloves, of the thinnest kid, and from München, too.

"Then my dear mamma boiled water from the little brook, the most sparkling water I have ever seen, and when it just began to bubble she poured it over the tea, and then we drank. And, my dears, I never, *never* have such tea tasted!"

Miss Lyse looked at us almost sombrely. We felt very young and serious as we watched her raise her glass slowly to her lips and then set it down again.

"No, it was tea like no tea before—or since. I have often boiled the water from brooklets, and poured it over the same brand of tea, *and* in my dear mother's silver teapot that to India twelve times went. But that tea, that summer afternoon near Garmisch, with dear mamma and Tanya and the three young gentlemen—and the little flowers, and I remember the poor yellow gloves——"

Miss Lyse was silent. She sipped slowly, and her eyes looked far back, like the picture of Albrecht Dürer's mother.

"Thank God in heaven," she concluded, emphatically, "that my poor departed mother watched over me, or I should not be where I am! That tea, so clear, so piquant like fine *Liebfraumilch*——"

II

Occasionally I hear from Al a dreamy, half-coherent reference to one day when he went to a small restaurant in Paris, and sat alone before an iced silver bowl of wood strawberries, spooning them up all coated with the fine effervescence of a bottle of champagne.

That must have been a good day, like the far September Wednesday in 1819 when John Keats wrote to his friend:

Talking of Pleasure, this moment I was writing with one hand, and with the other holding to my Mouth a Nectarine—good God how fine. It went down soft pulpy, slushy, oozy—all its delicious embonpoint melted down my throat like a large beatified Strawberry. I shall certainly breed.

III

Sometimes it is hard to say, even from remembrance, just what magic chord has sounded for you with the right blending of time, space, and the physical sensation of eating. On a hot day it is easiest to think back to such things as silver-green mint juleps, or the smooth golden taste of cold papaya on a freighter near Guatemala, or crisp lettuce anywhere.

On a cold day such things as hot baked potatoes, all sprinkled over with fresh-ground pepper and sweet butter, or creamy tomato soup with a faint smell of cinnamon to it, or rare steaming beef, pink and succulent: these are the things that flow first into our remembrance on cold days.

There is one time, though, one souvenir of eating, that I can keep with impunity throughout all seasonal changes. Perhaps I remember it oftener in winter, but that does not affect its poignancy.

When I belonged to the Alpine Club of the Côte d'Or, I felt rather lost. The robust elderly members were more than courteous to me; the walks were energetic but agreeable; the carefully planned feasts at little village inns were masterpieces, even though each day's march was so routed that the most difficult part of it came after the many courses and as many wines of the dinner.

Still, I felt rather lonesome, "foreign," until one bitter February Sunday when we stood panting on a hill near Les Laumes-Alésia. The earth was hard as granite beneath me, and air drawn into my tired lungs felt like heavy fire before it thawed. I broke a twig clumsily between my mittened fingers.

"Here!" a voice said, roughly. I looked with surprise at the old general, who stood, shaggy and immense, beside me. He had never done more than bow to me, and listen now and then with a face of stony suffering to my accent, which always grew ten times as thick when he was near. What did he want now?

"Here! Try some of this, young lady!" And he held out a piece of chocolate, pale brown with cold. I smiled and took it, resolving to say as little as possible.

He cleared his throat grumpily and shifted his eyes to the far thunderous horizon.

In my mouth the chocolate broke at first like gravel into many separate, disagreeable bits. I began to wonder if I could swallow them. Then they grew soft, and melted voluptuously into a warm stream down my throat.

The little doctor came bustling up, his proudly displayed alpenstock tucked under one short arm.

"Here! Wait, wait!" he cried. "Never eat chocolate without bread, young lady! Very bad for the interior, very bad. My General, you are remiss!"

The soldier peered down at him like a horse looking at a cheeky little dog, and then rumbled, "Give us some, then, old fellow. Trade two pieces (and big ones, mind) for some of our chocolate?"

And in two minutes my mouth was full of fresh bread, and melting chocolate, and as we sat gingerly, the three of us, on the frozen hill, looking down into the valley where Vercingetorix had fought so splendidly, we peered shyly and silently at each other and smiled and chewed at one of the most satisfying things I have ever eaten. I thought vaguely of the metamorphosis of wine and bread——

The Brothers

Once there were two brothers. They were twins, but their nine closed months were all they had in common.

One brother, the elder by some minutes, was a big fellow, red-faced and hairy. He spent all his days afield and swiftly grew into a great hunter, and at night he made into savoury stews the day's killing. His father loved the stews and his elder son who made them.

The younger brother was his mother's love. In him she admired her own sly, clever ways. He stayed by her side and learned from her to make lentil pottage, which he could sell each day, and profitably, to the workers.

One day the hunting was very bad, and the sun too hot. Then chill came suddenly into the darkening air, and the older brother, still far afield and very tired, turned empty-handed homeward. No fine stew tonight to cheer him and to warm his old man's innards! Afterwards no rest by the fire for the two of them! He sighed and longed to be home, full and warm.

The younger brother sat by a great pot of his steaming soup, with hard sour bread in a pile beside him. The day was almost over, with no more labourers to buy food from him. But he sat on, quiet and sure, waiting for what he knew must happen sometime, and perhaps today.

Suddenly his toes curled under him with scorn and fear, for he saw his elder brother. The great lazy spendthrift lout! He smiled and waited.

And you know what happened. Jacob was the little crafty fellow who sold lentil soup, and Esau was the hungry man who gave his birthright for a bowl of it. And Jacob's mother Rebekah was, like many women, a good cook and a good teacher of cookery for one purpose or another, but never for pleasure. She taught her dear son to be the father of all (almost all) *restaurateurs*.

Her other son she never understood, nor his father Isaac neither, for they would spend all day catching a deer, simply that they might cook it and eat it and then lie by the fire and talk about it. They may have been the first gastronomers.

Set Piece for
a Fishing Party

1810 A.D.–1900 A.D.
France

The twentieth century may yet be remembered as one of monstrous mass-feeding. Certainly the nineteenth will never be forgotten for its great contribution to gastronomy—the restaurants.

After the Revolution, Paris found itself practically kitchenless. Scullions had fled, or fought for their new estate; great chefs had scuttled to safety with their masters; most important, the money that had bought rare wines and strange exotic dishes was gone now from the hands that had known so well how to spend it.

Paris recovered quickly enough. Her citizens, uncomfortably Republican and somewhat more affluent than before, cast about restlessly for a new, a significant diversion.

It was not hard to find. Word was noised abroad that in the cellar of Number So-and-so, Rue Such-and-such, the ex-chef, Jean Durand, was cooking again.

What! Durand, the inventor of *petits pois aux noisettes grillées*, the great Durand who for twenty years had made famous the table of the ex-Marquise Sainte-Nitouche, ex-mistress of the even more ex-Duke Volte-face? But certainly not that Durand who once corrected Citizeness Marie Antoinette for adding mustard to a salad dressing before she had put in the salt? Impossible!

But—but can anyone go to Number So-and-so, Rue Such-and-such? Hah! Then I, Jacques Maillot, and I, Pierre Doudet, shall order the ex-chef of the ex-marquise to prepare a good dinner. It is expensive? Pouf! It is certainly worth the pleasure of eating what the damned aristos used to!

Thus Parisian restaurants blossomed from a few dark corners. Their trembling chefs, not long out of hiding, grew confident—and rich. They gathered round them enough of the old guard of pastry cooks, roasters, and *sommeliers* to keep things moving, and soon had more apprentices than they needed. Their furtive restaurants moved into fine quarters, and quickly became those boulevard palaces of fat gourmets, twinkling mirrors, pink plush, and belles, that Zola and Maupassant knew so well for us.

Fine food, once the privilege of the moneyed aristocracy, was now at the summons of any man with enough silver and manners to go to a good restaurant.

As the century rolled forward, and Jacques and Pierre flourished, the palaces grew more glittering, and their patrons more extravagant and gouty. But new blood, vulgar as it could be at times, brought freshness and vigour to the somewhat depleted art of eating. Vim and zest chased out the satiety which had become almost synonymous with pleasure under the several Louis. People ate enormously, with a lusty bourgeois delight born of strong constitutions and palates untouched by preciosity.

The fine art of eating was not wholly a thing of the stomach, however. Great minds considered it. As early as the 1820's, the learned Doctor Villermet presented a short but important paper to the Academy of Science. In it he proved conclusively that gourmands live longest and in the best health!

Nor is only their physical state influenced by gastronomy. Even the modern critic, in discussing that bon vivant Dumas, observes that "his marked intellectual superiority over his son may be readily attributed to his greater knowledge of dining." *Le Grand Dictionnaire de Cuisine* helps prove it.

Indeed, the obsession for fine eating that swept over Europe, and especially France, during the nineteenth century, had a strange and wonderful influence on the literature of that world.

Grimod de la Reynière, who wrote *Le Manuel des Amphi-tryons* in 1808, and edited the great *Almanach des Gourmands*; Carême, who cooked for the princes of six countries and Baron Rothschild, and wrote books on everything from the maker of picturesque pastry to the history of ancient kitchens; Alexandre Dumas—all these skilled artists and many another lived then in the respect and admiration which were their due.

Strangely enough, the greatest of them was probably the least known, was in fact scoffed at by the Paris exquisites as a rough mannered provincial. Brillat-Savarin lived quietly and very pleasantly, ate with a refined and prejudiced palate, thought for many years, and a few months before his death in 1828 published *La Physiologie du Goût*.

This work, a masterpiece of clarity and charm in any subject, is still without peer among books on eating. It is difficult to write about physical pleasures without being either coarse or over-delicate, vaguely sentimental or dry and scientific. *The Physiology of Taste* is none of these. It is as near perfection as we yet know it, and a constant wonder. The temptation to quote from its clear, pungent prose is hard to resist. Infinitely better, however, is the companionship of the book itself, for there is no superfluous word in it, no dull page.

While Brillat-Savarin finished his unobtrusive days in Paris and Belley, speculating with deliberate wisdom on the problems of transcendental gastronomy, Europe went mad over the art of dining.

Never have Continental restaurants been so crowded, unless perhaps it was during the First World War. The atmosphere differed, however, almost as much as the costumes.

In 1914–1918 women wore tight sheaths of glittering cloth over their slender bodies, and helped all the sad young men to be gay and gather rosebuds. In the nineteenth century women were fuller, softer, smoother. They dined opulently at all the best tables of every good restaurant in Paris, and knew to perfection the whims and dislikes of their fastidious gentlemen.

Foyot's, the *Café de Paris*, the *Brasserie Universelle*—there were a hundred temples of fine food, some chic for a moment, some apparently eternal in their devotion to *la gourmandise*.

Their chefs, seldom as coveted by princes as the great Carême, rejoiced nevertheless in as respectfully adoring a public as any royal offspring.

Their smallest triumphs were town gossip before the last bite was swallowed, and their most insignificant utterances were lapped up by such hungry brains as Dumas' and Maupassant's, to appear later in solemn or witty conversation.

It was toward the end of the First Empire that Brillat-Savarin and Carême, by persuasive argument, substituted the "made dish" for masses of roast meat, piled high on a platter and held clumsily erect by skewers. That modern gourmet, Paul Reboux (whose witty essay on gastronomy in a reputable encyclopædia is, tactlessly enough, flanked by a large and greyly horrible photograph of a gastric ulcer!), remarks that "these enormous, barbaric accumulations of food were yet another

Bastille which the French Revolution overthrew." And for a few years, at least, they gave the Parisians almost as much to think about.

Meats, fruits, vegetables, wines, were combined and cooked and served in a thousand new ways. Flavours and aromas never dreamed of ran and rose from the exciting dishes. Gradually their appearance grew more rigidly ornate, and their construction more difficult. Finally the most complicated of these "made dishes" were classed by themselves, and *pièces montées* came into being.

Pièces montées were to Frenchmen of the last century what modern-art exhibits and automobile shows and fan dances are to John Doe today. Public contests were held, schools were founded to teach worthy chefs how to construct the sacred tricks, great artists drew designs, and solemn tomes were written on the art.

The Romans had pies which spilled out dancing dwarfs, or let fly up a flock of blackbirds and white doves. Later, in England, ponderous subtleties set all the banqueters guessing on full stomachs. It was in France, though, the brilliant vital France of the last century, that these inventions reached their peak of artistry and popularity.

Every good restaurant had its special department from which a *pièce montée* could be commanded for any kind of festivity, christening party or wake. If the prices were too high, there was the neighbourhood bakeshop, where even the apprentice could turn out a passable sugar dove rising from a nest of mocha and pistachio cream.

Of all the real artists of the set piece, Carême was certainly the greatest. He had an uncanny ability to use pastry and sugar, and a mighty respect for them both. In one of his books he announces quite seriously:

The Fine Arts are five in number: Painting, Music, Sculpture, Poetry, and Architecture—whereof the principal branch is confectionery.

As the vogue for set pieces increased, he combined this reverential talent with all his others to produce amazing structures, dreamlike, fantastic. His disciples exaggerated his strange juxtapositions and his mixtures of irony and beauty. Finally, as with every school of art headed by one man, cheap imitators crept after him with their coarsening touch, and by the end of the century set pieces had become almost ridiculous, a synonym for the pretentious vulgarity of new-rich entertainment.

It is in Carême's own book on the subject, *Le Pâtissier Pittoresque*, or in the several other volumes of this period, that we must look to see *pièces montées* at their best. There countless engravings, as well as the restrained rhetoric of the prose, make very clear the incredible delicacy and variety of these strange dishes which cost thousands of francs and were seldom eaten.

One little engraving is very pleasant to remember. It shows a *pièce* which stands probably four or five feet high. A froth of green foliage forms its base—leaves of mashed potato as delicate as ever grew from pastry tube. From that a Doric column, garlanded with pale full-blown flowers of lobster meat, diminishes twice.

At the top, on a pedestal edged with little shells and shrimpy rosebuds, is a pool of the clearest blue-green sugar, crystallized. And from it, with only the ankles of his tail held in the crystal, curves a fresh plump fish, every scale gleaming, his eyes popping with satiric amusement, and a beautiful umbrella of spun sugar held over his head by one sturdy fin!

Above the engraving runs the legend, in that somewhat smudgy printing of the 1830's: *A Culinary Fantasy—the Cautious Carp*.

On Dining
Alone

Lucullus, the Roman host whose dinners are still talked about for their elaborate menus and their fabulous cost, grew tired one day of dining with other men.

He ordered a meal for one person. When it was served to him, he was conscious of a certain slackness: the wine was perhaps a shade too cold, and the sauce for the carp, which certainly was less succulent than usual, lacked that tang for which his chef was justly famed.

Lucullus frowned and summoned the majordomo.

"Perhaps, perhaps," that official agreed, with a flood of respectful salutations. "We thought that there was no need to prepare a fine banquet for my lord alone——"

"It is precisely when I am alone," the great gourmet answered, icily, "that you require to pay special attention to the dinner. At such times, you must remember, Lucullus dines with Lucullus."

At such times few men realize that they are dining with themselves. In fact, they try to forget that rather frightening truth. They read the newspaper or turn on the radio if they are at home. More often they flee from themselves to friend-filled clubs, or to the noisiest nearest restaurant, where other lone humans eat crowded together in a hungry, ugly mob and take digestive pills between their hurried courses.

It is a pity. An occasional meal with himself is very good for Mr. Doe. It gives him time to look about him; quiet in which to savour his present mouthful; opportunity to broil his steak a new way or try again those dishes his wife hates.

He need not take it too seriously, however. Old Thomas Walker, The Original, whose preoccupation with the fine points of dining approached pomposity at times, declared himself thus on the problem:

> When dining alone is necessary, the mind should be disposed to cheerfulness by a previous interval of relaxation from whatever has seriously occupied the attention, and by directing it to some agreeable object.

The "interval of relaxation" might well be used for broiling a tender filet, although I doubt if Mr. Walker meant just that; and there could be no more "agreeable object" toward which to direct attention than a fine little bottle of red wine from the Côte d'Or. There with a leaf or two of salad and some crusty sourdough bread, Lucullus has a meal fit even for Lucullus.

An Englishman, however, and an earl at that, once mapped out a slightly more complicated menu.

> "A good soup," he said, "a small turbot, a neck of venison, ducklings with green peas or chicken with asparagus, and an apricot tart—it is a dinner for an emperor."

Perhaps he was right. Louis XIV of France, who always dined alone at one o'clock, ate several soups, three solid courses, and then a dessert.

He also ate only from a square table, and was served by nobles of his court, both facts probably influencing his digestion to a certain extent. (Many people enjoy good food only to the sound of soft music, or in a room with black walls. My mother cannot swallow if a cat is near her. Hunger, I observe, is not a part of these equations.)

I have known two people who understood, and probably without one thought about it, why Lucullus dined with Lucullus. One was an old man, the other a girl sixteen and usually inarticulate.

Biddy was tall and quiet, with magnificent brown eyes and the stiff awkwardness of a new-hatched butterfly. She lived in a kind of doze, seemingly placid, lethargic, docilely stubborn.

One day she took her week's allowance and moved tranquilly and relentlessly towards the tram, muttering of errands and birthdays and such. To her mother's puzzled questions she smiled reassurance, vague but firm.

Late that afternoon she came back.

She brought no birthday presents nor evidences of errands done, but one rather spotted paper bag, from which she drew a long brown cut of *apfelstrudel* for her mother. She was vaguer than usual, but seemed to be unharmed—and the *strudel* was delicious.

Later I saw Biddy. We were talking of restaurants. I saw her eyes flash suddenly when I mentioned Spring Street in Los Angeles, where, one man said, the best and worst food in seven states can be found in less than as many blocks.

"I hear you went to town last Saturday," I said, feeling like Sherlock Holmes and Tom the Peeper. "What did you do?"

Biddy looked quickly at me, and then smiled rather sheepishly.

"Spring Street, eh? Where did you go?"

"Well—I went to *Katie Levey's*. And why haven't you told me how good it is? And the people!"

"Lots of Austrian Jews, I suppose?"

"Naturally, in a kosher restaurant run by a Viennese! Of course," she added, carelessly, "Jews are the best indication of good food in a place."

I nodded recognition to one of her mother's favourite remarks, and asked, "But what did you do from eleven to three? You can't eat lunch for four hours."

Biddy answered me somewhat scornfully: "I ate breakfast, not lunch, and certainly I ate it for four hours: they understand things like that in a decent restaurant. I drank coffee, with lots of hot milk in it, and ate Viennese tarts and—and things."

"Things meaning salami and sweet pickles?"

"Mhm."

She looked dreamily past me. I said nothing, and finally she went on: "I sat by the cake counter and watched people in the mirror. They were so queer—so *pleasant* at eleven when everybody else in town was rushing around—and especially down there on Spring. And they spoke every language and dipped their tarts in their coffee-glasses.

"Yes," Biddy exclaimed, "my coffee was in a glass! It was wonderful!"

Her face was vivid, and in her dark eyes was a quiet awareness I had never seen before. She concluded, almost fiercely: "Four hours I sat there, watching them dip their bread in coffee-glasses, and thinking. And I'll do it again! It was—it was just what I needed."

Biddy breakfasted with Biddy, and saw in a mirror clearly, for the first of many times.

The other one who understood was an old man. I never knew who he was. Whenever we went to *Victor Hugo's* he was there, at a quiet corner table. He was dressed carefully in rather old-fashioned dinner clothes, with his feet in tiny twinkling pumps, like a doll's.

He ate little, and drank a half-bottle of wine with his meat. For dessert he went through a never-varying formula with the intensity and detachment of a high priest.

An avocado was brought to him, cradled in a napkin. He felt of it delicately, smelled it, usually nodded yes. It was cut in two with a silver knife. Then he himself detached the stone-skin from each half, placed one part of the fruit gently on a large plate before him, and sent the other back to the kitchen.

Powdered sugar was brought, and the old man pressed it into the hollow of the fruit. He spent some time over this, making it firm and even.

Next the *sommelier* appeared with a pear-shaped bottle of clear Russian *kümmel*. He poured a generous liqueur-glass of it, waited for the old man's sniff of approval, and went away.

Drop by drop the *kümmel* disappeared into the moon of white sugar, very slowly, very patiently. Very delicately it was stirred and pressed down and stirred again.

Finally the old man ate a small spoonful of the smooth green fruit-flesh, then another. Sometimes he stopped, sometimes he finished it. Then he drank a mouthful of coffee and left.

I have not yet tested his strange dish. I have never been able to construct its flavours for my mind's palate with any clearness. But very clear in my memory is the expression on the old man's face. He was happy as Biddy was happy with her coffee in a glass and her mirror. He was at peace, and aware—aware that Lucullus dined with Lucullus for a reason.

Sing of Dinner
in a Dish

More than six per cent of the inmates of San Quentin give their previous occupation as cook (labourers form the largest group and cooks the second largest); but male cooks compose less than two-tenths of one per cent of the total U.S. population, according to the 1930 census.

I would like to know to what type of crime cooks are peculiarly given. I have heard it said by men who have been much up and down the world that cooks as a class are irascible men, with the instincts of dictators. It is an interesting speculation: does the profession attract men of a certain character, or are nerves and tempers shattered by the life they lead? Or does the emotional effect result from a physical deterioration of stomach and liver through too much tasting of their own cooking?

Just what, in brief, is the moral hazard involved in being a cook?

We Who Are About to Die, DAVID LAMSON

"Always have a Chinese cook," said the woman who had followed her sailor seven times round the globe, and settled at last inside the Golden Gate. "Yes, always have a Chinese cook—and never go into the kitchen!"

Is this foul slander, or the cool tongue of wisdom? When on the bottom of a casserole doth grimed grease hiss, is ignorance bliss? Probably.

Surely I have eaten many a tart that felt the floor before it felt my plate, and more than a hundred bowls of soup whose temperature was tested, consciously or not, by a fat thumb. I have even pushed dead flies to one side of an omelette or ragoût, and eaten to the last bite undaunted. I have not really minded, inside of me, because what I ate was good, and I do not think that good food can come from a bad kitchen.

It can come from a cluttered kitchen piled with used dishes, redolent with the escaped smells of garlic, vanilla, and wine-vinegar, a kitchen steamy and full of rattle and clash.

Madame Rigagnier's is like that—a dark cabinet not nine feet square, its walls banked with copper pots and pans, and a pump for water outside the door. And from that little hole, which would make an American shudder with disgust, she turns out daily two of the finest meals I've yet eaten.

Or good food can come from a gigantic factory of fine dishes, such as Arnold Bennett describes so well in a book he wrote about grand hotels.

But good food can never come from a bad kitchen. A bad kitchen is what it is for two reasons: either nobody cares whether it produces decent victuals, or it is filthy. And if it is filthy, it is, says Webster, defiled with filth; foul; impure; obscene; unclean; squalid; and above all nasty.

I know one like that. It is the back side of a kosher restaurant. In the window are pans of strudel and *auf-lauf* and rice *kugel*, which look good. Furthermore, the prices are low and the tables are crowded—favourable signs, surely. Perhaps this is one of those rare little places that lurk in big towns like pearls in the sea.

We go in. There is a great clatter. Nobody notices us. All the tables are occupied, and we push toward the end of the long room. The last table is freed by two silent men, and a large waitress slaps at it with a cloth. She looks at us dully with monkey eyes, and hurries away.

We slide our legs under the slimy tabletop. A pandemonium of cries and crashes swells in my ears whenever a waitress goes through the swinging doors beside me. I see Al, who faces it, peering with a strange expression, which he masks politely as I look at him.

My purse slips to the floor, and when I touch it again it is stuck all over one side with crumbs and nastiness.

I forget what we order. Whatever it is, we do not eat it. By now I too have peered through the swinging door, and I too have stiffened my face into politeness. We sit silently, watching with every pore, for this is a unique (Please God, unique!) experience, and we shall miss none of it by maiden squeamishness.

The kitchen is small and overcrowded and hot, as is Madame Rigagnier's—and our own. There the comparison ends.

The floor, slick and black, is uneven where dishtowels and utensils have been half-swallowed in its eternal ooze. Water from the grease-ridged sink runs over it in iridescent trickles, and crusts of bread and slippery wilted lettuce scraps lie everywhere, never too trodden for the rats of dawn.

Up from the floor and in and down from the foul walls and ceiling seeps a smell more evil and obscene than Mr. Webster dreamed of. It is acrid and heavy, a slippery, dark grey smell, like the piled-up excrement of a million ducks.

Waitresses go in and out with the look of women who have been so nauseated for so long that it can never matter any more. Fortunately, we do not see the faces of the two cooks.

They are men, evidently, wearing old tennis shoes, trousers, oily grey underwear, and bandannas knotted around their heads.

They yell at each other and at the waitresses, and the waitresses yell frantically back at them, and nobody ever yells at the strange brown man who walks among them.

He carries trays of soiled dishes, sometimes on his head, and sometimes not, from the front of the restaurant to the kitchen. He might be a Filipino, but more probably he is a last Hawaiian or Tahitian. He looks like the pictures we see of those fading races of the world.

His body is good, with no bones holding it up, but not soft, either, and his hair is fine and purple above his dark face.

He moves like a wave, steadily and impersonally. Other people are shoved and pushed, but as he walks through the restaurant, balancing his body easily under the tray, he is never touched.

There is no sign that he sees or hears. His face is expressionless and his eyes are contracted and dull. He seldom moves them, and when they light on my face he does not see me, as I do not see one telephone pole among all the other poles from a train window.

He is full of drugs, or hypnotized; he is mad; he is transcendental, taboo.

We begin to feel uneasy, and go away, turning as we pass the street window for one more puzzled look at the false *apfelstrudel* lying there.

The air tastes like mead in our throats.

And the cleanest kitchen? That was at Beaune, in Burgundy, in the *Hospice* where the old and the poor and the fatherless have for centuries been fed by the sale of some of the finest wines of the Côte d'Or.

A black Virgin looks down upon the blue-curtained beds of

the Convalescent Hall; exquisite faïence jars hold medicines in the pharmacy; and in the kitchen the biggest, brightest copper kettles anywhere glow like moons on the dim walls.

That great room is warm and pungent in winter, and in summer cool and sweet as a well. It is spacious. Cupboards as big as pantries, and tables like ballroom floors, are easy in it. Ranges stretch for yards, with innumerable rounds for pots to rest on, and across the yawning hearths are spits sturdy for whole oxen and slender for the lark.

It smells good. It smells pure and kindly, like linen bleaching on a highland meadow. Herbs hang in bunches near the ceiling, and fume from a simmering pot or wooden chopping bowl. Clean cloths dry by a stove, and hang, cheerily checkered, from shelf and window ledge. Above all, there is the smell of cleanliness. The stone floors, the walls and shelves and all the wood, the kettles and the pokers and the smallest pewter spoon, are clean with the devout scourings of not one century, but five.

That is indeed a good kitchen, in the *Hospice*. Simple food comes from it, gruel and stews for the very young, the weak, and the old, all good because of the kitchen.

It is a pleasant pastime to think of what might be a good kitchen for yourself. Just now it is very smart, too. Women's magazines flash with brilliant colour photos of dreamlike rooms where glass walls and metal sinks compete with electric dishwashers and mixers of cake for the fascinated reader's favour.

Washable chintz curtains wave in the controlled breeze. Ivy grows around the telephone table, where an easy chair, a radio, and an alarmingly narrow cook-book shelf promise relaxation to the American *hausfrau*.

For myself, I should like a kitchen with some of these magic things, but none of the conscious design, the June-bride's-first-little-home look about it.

When I think of all the kitchens I have seen, there is not one I would willingly accept unchanged. Some are cool in summer but too big, or snug for winter but inconveniently small. Almost all are cluttered with things that I would never need to use, or are too dark or too airless.

The kitchen in the Ducal Palace in Dijon was certainly sensible, built as it was like one great oven, with its whole roof the dwindling chimney for eight fires, its four sides and ample floor the interior of a stove capable of satisfying the hunger of even such great trenchermen as the old Burgundians.

For me, however, such stretched proportions would have to be carved down to a ridiculous smallness, and the picture of myself simmering alongside my five-pound roast of beef in a miniature ducal kitchen is almost insulting to the good mediæval architect who built for Philip the Hardy in the fourteenth century.

The first kitchen I ever had of my own was above a cake shop in the working quarter of a small French city. It was perhaps five feet long, and certainly not more than three feet wide.

Its floor of uneven baked tiles was scoured to a mellow pinkness. There were two weak shelves, slanting toward the floor. A two-burner gas plate on a tottering wooden table was the stove. To stand at it I had to keep the door open into the other room. That was all right: the door had been stuck open for several decades.

I had four plates, four goblets, and some three or four or five pans and casseroles.

But I made very good things to eat in that kitchen, and I have always felt that this was partly so because one end of it, from side to side and from ceiling almost to floor, was a window.

It was a sparkling window of many-paned glass, a window curtained briefly with two silly little dabs of cheap net, a window split down the middle ready to fling open as wide as those windows can be flung, wider really than any others.

It looked over treetops into the square where gibbets and then a guillotine once stood, where wandering circus families set up their gas flares for a night or two by the busy fountain and the *pissoir*, where people moved and talked incessantly above the high wail of a café phonograph playing ten thousand times the record of Josephine Baker's *"J'ai Deux Amours."*

All the noises flowed in and out the window of the tiny kitchen, gay and sombre and mysterious and always real, and I may be too sentimental in thinking that they helped me cook some good dishes—but I doubt it.

There is a Basque kitchen I once heard of that has very pleasant things about it, too. One wall of the stone-built room is packed with straw, all of it, solidly. Its surface is clipped to a neat smoothness. Then, the first cold night of autumn, the straw wall is lit from the bottom, and so cleverly has it been laid that the whole room blazes with a slow steady warmth until late spring comes. Ashes sift down all winter to the hot bed on the floor, where three-legged gipsy pots send out the heady odours of Basque stews; and no lamps are ever needed.

Of course this kitchen, obviously, is meant for long hard winters, and how intelligent and beautiful an arrangement it is! For me—no, it would not be practical. I should like to spend a time in it, though. The air would be strong, no doubt, but warm and hearty on a cold night.

The problem of an ideal kitchen grows more complex as I ponder on it. There are many small things I am sure about: no shelf papers; no sharp edges or protruding hooks or wires; no ruffled curtains; and no cheap-coloured stove, mauve or green or opalescent like a modern toilet seat.

Instead of these things I would have smooth shelves of some

material like ebony or structural glass, shelves open or protected by sliding transparent doors. I would have curved and rounded edges, even to the floor, for the sake of cleanliness, and because I hate the decayed colours of a bruise.

Instead of curtains I would have Venetian blinds, of four different colours for the seasons of the year. They would be, somehow, on the outside of the glass.

And the stove would be black, with copper and earthenware utensils to put on it. It would be a wood stove, or perhaps (of this I am doubtful, unless I am the charwoman and janitor as well as the cook) electrical with place for a charcoal grill.

There are other things, too, that would be very pleasant, like a little side-kitchen in which to make the ices and salads and tarts that should not be near the heat and high flavour of roasting meats, and racks let down from the ceiling for the pots and skillets to lie on, and a radio or an automatic phonograph to make dull tasks agreeable. I would want the sinks and the tabletops made to my own height, too, and not for some mythical short-legged cook.

All these, though, are relatively unimportant. There are only three things I need, to make my kitchen a pleasant one as long as it is clean.

First, I need space enough to get a good simple meal for six people. More of either would be wasteful as well as dangerously dull.

Then, I need a window or two, for clear air and a sight of things growing.

Most of all I need to be let alone. I need peace.

From there—from there, on the sill of my wide window, the plan is yours. It will include an herb-bed surely, and a brick courtyard for summer suppers. And an apple orchard perhaps? A far sea view?

Shell Shock and
Richard the Third

1900 A.D. ——
Europe and America

When humans are not especially hungry they love to play tricks with their palates. That was why Nicodemus, king of Babylon, chuckled and smacked his lips over his chef's dish of anchovies, which, it was disclosed, were really turnips disguised most artfully with oil and spice and poppy seeds.

For the same reason Petronius Arbiter's plump citizen could afford to boast:

> Only command him, and my cook will make you a fish out of the pig's chitterlings, a wood-pigeon out of the lard, a turtledove out of the gammox, and a hen out of the shoulder!

But all that is for play. It is different when men are hungry. Then in Alaskan snowfields they simmer old shoes for soup, and when they eat it they call it soup made from shoes, quite simply. Or, in Paris during the siege of the 1870's, scrambled rats and potted poodledog meat were delicacies candidly desired by the most fastidious of gourmets.

During the First World War, there were not even rats enough, in some parts of those countries which the more optimistic of modern historians call defeated. Their natives ate wood pulp in their cereals and chocolate, nut shells in their coffee, and Fuller's earth (when they were lucky) in their sugar. They were grateful, and when the war ended they were still very hungry, with distended stomachs and dulled palates.

All over Europe gastronomy lay in a kind of coma, shell-shocked. The great chefs of *avant-guerre* were dead, or senile, or seemingly apathetic. The young apprentices, those boys who had learned so painstakingly how to glaze and stir and test in famous kitchens, lay in the earth now, or wandered restlessly.

By the 1920's, things had revived to some extent, especially in Paris. Hordes of refugees had flocked there, bringing strange tantalizing dishes from their own countries.

Americans, too, chased from their land by a political experiment which for a time reduced good native gastronomy to an equation of raw alcohol and five-cent candybars, marched like an innocent and enthusiastic army on Parisian restaurants.

Skullduggery was inevitable. Much bad food, much impure wine, was swallowed in honourable surroundings. Several of the old guard of mastercooks, recovered now from their apathy, retreated in disgust to England or Long Island. A few worked doggedly and with increasing affluence in Paris and Berlin and Vienna and Rome.

Gastronomy seemed normal again, as normal as the rest of the arts. Painting, it is true, was undergoing a series of -isms reminiscent of the whims of a pregnant woman. Architecture tiptoed gingerly toward steel-and-glass construction, and sculptors and writers used tin cans, matches, and dream sequences with symbolic seriousness.

This same symbolism increased in importance gastronomically. Academicians as well as dieticians pondered long on possible food combinations, both hygienic and esoteric.

Finally, as late as 1931, the peak of this new kind of eating was reached by an eminent figure, Signor Marinetti of the Italian Academy.

His proposals, based on the theory that the future will need birdmen, light and keen, rather than our present stodgy bodies, received much publicity. Most of it was decidedly jeering. And it is true that some of his ideas, such as one advising the use of concentrated food pills in order to give men more time for the enjoyment of fine food, sound slightly silly. Many of them do not.

He wishes to take the first step in preparing for "an existence that will be more aerial and rapid" by abolishing flour pastes from diet. No more spaghetti, no more macaroni, no more of those viscous white masses that French children call *semoule* and Americans gulp down as breakfast food! That sounds practical, especially if one has ever watched little porkers being fattened with great troughs of steaming mush.

Further, the Italian prophet would abolish the very common delusion that weight and volume are factors in the appreciation of food. His preoccupation with this proves that many men, and some of them true lovers of fine eating, still measure their satisfaction by the tightness of their belts.

Marinetti also wishes to abolish traditional condiments. In their place he would revive such ancient excitants as perfumes to be blown into the air between courses. To anyone, however, who has tried to find the bouquet of a fine wine in the same room with highly-scented flowers or women, or has pretended to be able to taste a *pâté de foie gras* between puffs on a Turkish cigarette, this idea is somewhat ridiculous.

The next step in the forming of the future race is the abolition of routine, daily mediocre monotony. Marinetti is surely not the first who has pondered this, nor is Yuan Mei, the Chinese who wrote so beautifully of fine and simple foods. "Into no department of life," said he, "should indifference be allowed to creep—into none less than into the domain of cookery."

In modern families especially is this a very important problem. It is likely that more neurasthenics and downright homicidal maniacs have been formed by roast-on-Sunday, fish-on-Friday, than by any other social custom. And the same room for every meal, with the same pictures on the walls! Very dangerous.

Certain plates can be just as virulently monotonous. Baked potatoes, no matter how hot and flaky, become almost nauseating the seven-hundredth time they are served pinched open, with paprika and butter on the scar. They form a pattern with steak; then there are patterns of pork-and-applesauce, lamb-and-peas-with-mint-sauce, yams-and-sausage—all very good, all hideously familiar.

Here, according to Marinetti, is the solution: Show various dishes between courses (some to be eaten and some not), as did Robert May, who in his *Accomplisht Cook* laments in 1610 the fast-disappearing English custom of making dishes to arouse and startle the diners, as well as feed them. By doing this, say both men, you will excite curiosity, surprise, and the imagination.

And tint your potatoes blue or rose or green! How do you know that you will not like them? Put new names on old dishes. Be stimulating!

For instance, ask your artist friends to design some such plate as this one made for the academician by his futuristic *confrère* Prampolini:

Equator Plus North Pole
Equatorial ring of hard-boiled egg yolks stuck here and there with bits of orange. In centre a white-of-egg cone crowned by truffles cut in the shape of airplanes.

That should at least rout dull monotony at a luncheon table!

Paul Reboux, whose view of modern gastronomy is equally sceptical but more humorous, has attacked the same problem of routine. In an aside on salads, he remarks:

You need to have the soul of a rabbit to eat lettuce as it is usually served—green leaves slightly lubricated with oil and flavoured with vinegar. A salad is only a background; it needs embroidering. To give character to a lettuce salad, cut up slivers of orange rind as small as pine needles, and sprinkle them over the salad. If you want something still more entertaining for your guests, cut up a carrot into equally small slips. This will at once arouse the attention of any gourmet. Which is orange and which is carrot? he will wonder. How does the Orange come to have a taste of Carrot, and the Carrot a flavour of Orange? You will have given him a real gastronomic entertainment.

Another recipe which seems preoccupied with the routing of monotony from the table (and this time the king's, no less) gives a plan for a most amazing dish.

"Take a capon and a little pig," it instructs, "and smite them in the waist. Sew the hind part of one on the fore quarters of the other, and stuff, and roast, and serve them forth."

It was an unknown cook some six hundred years ago, his art-istry marked down in *The Harleian Manuscript 279* by a careful clerk, who seems to have been bothered even then by Marinet-ti's problem.

Does this mean that Richard the Third and Cæsar and Ahas-uerus had their own *Equator Plus North Poles*?

The Social Status
of a Vegetable

Although we had walked into the little Swiss village restaurant without warning, an almost too elaborate meal appeared for us in the warm empty room, hardly giving us time to finish our small glasses of thick piny bitters.

We were hungry. The climb had been steep, through bare vineyards and meadows yellow with late primroses. We ate the plate of sliced sausages, and then the tureen of thick potato soup, without much speaking. We hardly blinked at the platter of fried eggs—ten of them for only three people!—with dark pink ham curling all around like little clouds.

We reached for more bread, sighed, and pulled off coats. The wine was light and appetizing.

Mrs. Davidson's old face looked fresher now. She straightened her shoulders, and settled her hat with a slightly coquettish movement of gnarled arms. For a wonder, she had eaten without mention of her self-styled "bird-like" appetite, with no apology for the natural hunger which she usually felt to be coarse and carnal. (Or so at least we had gathered from her many bored, sad smiles at any admission on our parts that we did like to eat.)

Now, when I realized that she was at last on the point of recognizing the existence of such low lust in herself, I rushed to forestall her with instinctive perversity.

"That was good," I said. "But I'm still hungry."

At once I was sorry, ashamed of myself. Mrs. Davidson looked cut into, and then settled her small handsome old face in its usual lines of refined disapproval. I had destroyed a rare human moment in her stiff life.

"So far, the meal, if you could really call such an impromptu thing a meal, has been quite passable," she admitted. "This inn, for such a small and unattractive village, seems respectable enough."

My nephew pulled the cork from another bottle, filled her glass, and quietly put more bread by her plate.

"I think it's awfully decent of you to come here while we eat," he told her, his face smooth and innocent.

She looked flattered, and finished the bread without noticing it.

The waitress, fat and silent, staggered in under a tray, her knees bending slightly outwards with its weight. She put down a great plate of steaks, with potatoes heaped like swollen hay at each end. We looked feebly at it, feeling appetite sag out of us suddenly.

Another platter thumped down at the other side of the table, a platter mounded high with purple-red ringed with dark green.

"What—*what* is that beautiful food?" Mrs. Davidson demanded, and then quickly mended her enthusiasm, with her eyes still sparkling hungrily. "I mean, beautiful as far as food could be."

My own appetite revived a little as I answered: "That's a ring of spinach around chopped red cabbage, probably cooked with ham juice."

At the word spinach her face clouded, but when I mentioned cabbage a look of complete and horrified disgust settled like a cloud. She pushed back her chair.

"Cabbage!" Her tone was incredulous.

"Why not?" James asked, mildly. "Cabbage is the staff of life in many countries. You ought to know, Mrs. Davidson. Weren't you raised on a farm?"

Her mouth settled grimly.

"As *you* know," she remarked in an icy voice, with her face gradually looking very old and discontented again, "there are many kinds of farms. My home was *not* a collection of peasants. Nor did we eat such—such peasant things as this."

"But haven't you ever tasted cabbage, then, Mrs. Davidson?" I asked.

"Never!" she answered proudly, emphatically.

"This is delicious steak." It was a diplomatic interruption. I looked gratefully at James. He grinned almost imperceptibly, and went on, "Just let me slide a little sliver on your plate, Mrs. Davidson, and you try to nibble at it while we eat. It will do you good."

He cut off the better portion of a generous slice of beef and put it on her well-emptied plate. She looked pleased, as she always did when reference was made to her delicacy, and only shuddered perfunctorily when we served ourselves with the vegetable.

As the steak disappeared, I watched her long old earlobes pinken. I remembered what an endocrinologist had told me once, that after rare beef and wine, when the lobes turned red, was the time to ask favours or tell bad news. I led the conversation back to the table, and then plunged brusquely.

"Why do you really dislike cabbage, Mrs. Davidson?"

She looked surprised, and put down the last bite from her bowl of brandied plums.

"Why does anyone dislike it? Surely you don't believe that I think your eating it is anything more than a pose?" She smiled knowingly at my nephew and me. He laughed.

"But we *do* like it, really. In our homes we cook it, and eat it, too, not for health, not for pretence. We like it."

"Yes, I remember my husband used to say that same sort of thing. But he never got it! No fear! It was the night I finally accepted him that I understood why my family had never had it in the house."

We waited silently. James filled her glass again.

"We missed the last train, and couldn't find a cab, and of course Mr. Davidson, who thought he knew everything, wandered down the wrong street. And there, in that dark wet town, lost, cold, miserable——"

"Oh, night of rapture, when I was yours!" James murmured.

"——cold, miserable, we were suddenly almost overcome by a ghastly odour!"

I repressed my instinctive desire to use the word "stink" and asked maliciously, "A perfume, or a smell?"

"A dreadful *odour*," she corrected me, with an acidulous smile at my coarseness. "It was so terrible that I was almost swooning. I pressed my muff against my face, and we stumbled on, gasping.

"When finally I could control myself enough to speak, I murmured, 'What was it? What was that gas?' My husband hurried me along, and I will say he did his best to apologize for what he had done—and well he should have!—by saying, 'It was cabbage, cooking.'

"'*Oh!*' I cried. 'Oh, we're in the *slums*!'

"So you see what a terrible memory of it all I have kept. Is it any wonder that I shudder when I see it or have it near me? Those horrible slums! Its *odour*!"

We looked blankly at her. Then I asked, "But do you smell it now? Did it bother you on the table?"

Mrs. Davidson stared peevishly at me, and said to James, "Well, if you two have finished your food, I should like to go."

Then, as we walked down the stairs to the crooked narrow street, I thanked her for the pleasant meal. She almost smiled, and said, grudgingly, "It was, I admit, not bad—for the slums."

It is constantly surprising, this vegetable snobbism. It is almost universal.

My mother, who was raised in a country too crowded with Swedish immigrants, shudders at turnips, which they seem to have lived on. And yet there she ate, week in and week out, corn meal mush and molasses, a dish synonymous to many Americans with poor trash of the pariah-ridden South.

And my grandmother—I remember hearing her dismiss some unfortunate person as a vulgar climber by saying, quietly, "Oh, Mrs. Zubzub is the kind of woman who serves artichokes!"

Of course, to a child reared within smelling distance, almost, of the fog-green fields of those thistly flowers, such damnation was quite meaningless; but I suppose that to a Midwestern woman of the last century it meant much.

Just a few years ago, the same class consciousness was apparent in a small college in Illinois, where students whispered and drew away from me after I had innocently introduced a box of avocados from my father's ranch into a dormitory "feast." From that unfortunate night, I was labelled a stuck-up snob.

The first time, though, that I ever felt surprise at the social position of a vegetable, was when I was a lower-classman in a boarding school. Like most Western private schools, it was filled largely with out-of-state children whose families wintered in California, and the daughters of local newly-rich.

Pretension and snobbishness flourished among these oddly segregated adolescents, and nowhere could such stiff cautious conventionality be found as in their classrooms, their teas, their sternly pro-British hockey matches.

One girl, from Englewood in New Jersey or maybe Tuxedo Park, was the recognized leader of the Easterners, the "bloods." She was more dashing than the rest; she used with impressive imitation her mother's high whinnying gush of poise and good breeding. She set the pace, and with a certain surety, too, for such an unsure age as sixteen. She was daring.

The reason I know she was daring, even so long ago, is that I can still hear her making a stupendous statement. That takes courage at any time, but when you are young, and bewildered behind your affectation of poise, and surrounded by other puzzled children who watch avidly for one wrong move, it is as impressive as a parade with trumpets.

We were waiting for the lunch bell. Probably we were grumbling about the food, which was unusually good for such an institution, but, like all food cooked *en masse*, dull. Our bodies clamoured for it, our tongues rebelled.

The girl from Englewood or Tuxedo Park spoke out, her hard voice clear, affectedly drawling to hide her own consciousness of daring. She must have known that what she said, even while aping her mother's social sureness, was very radical to the children round her, the children fed from kitchens of the *haute bourgeoisie* and in luxurious hotels. It was rather like announcing, at a small débutante ball in Georgia, "Of course, *I* prefer to dance with Negroes."

"I know it's terribly, terribly silly of me," she said, with all she could summon of maternally gracious veneer, "but of course I was brought up near Pennsylvania, and the customs there are so quaint, and I know you'll all be terribly, terribly shocked, but I *love*, I *adore* wieners and sauerkraut!"

Yes, it was surprising then and still is. All round are signs of it, everywhere, little trickles of snobbish judgment, always changing, ever present.

In France old Crainquebille sold leeks from a cart, leeks called "the asparagus of the poor." Now asparagus sells for the asking, almost, in California markets, and broccoli, that strong age-old green, leaps from its lowly pot to the *Ritz's* copper saucepan.

Who determines, and for what strange reasons, the social status of a vegetable?

César

For one reason or another it is thought advisable to change the names of real people when you write about them. I can do that sometimes, but not now. And of course there is no reason why I should. César is very real: he lives more surely than most men; and if he does read about himself in any book, which is doubtful, he will at the most be amused.

I cannot remember how we first met him. He was the butcher in a village of fishermen. We were foreigners, who stayed in the village several weeks. It is probably strange that we knew César so well, and he us.

The women of the village hated him and were afraid of him, but, "All I do is reach through my window at night," said César, "and there's a fine piece of woman waiting for me in the dark street. Any time, every night, I pluck them in."

The women hated him for two reasons. He had been very cruel to his termagant wife. She fled from him finally, and the two sons with her, after a fight between them and their father.

They were very strong men, all three, and when they were angry they swelled with muscle and spleen. César chased them out, all howling maledictions.

Later one of the sons crept back and stabbed at his father, but César broke the dagger between his fists and gave the pieces to his son's mistress, one night after he had plucked her through his window.

But it was sorrow for the poor wife, even if she was a foul-mouthed shrew, that made the village women hate César. That was the first reason. The second was that the men in the village loved César more than they did their women or their sons or even their boats.

They loved him for a thousand reasons and one reason. César was all that every man wants secretly to be: strong, brave; foul, cruel, reckless; desired by women and potent as a goat; tender and very sweet with children; feared by the priest, respected by the mayor; utterly selfish and as generous as a prince; gay. César was man. Man noble and monstrous again after so many centuries.

Once a week, two or three times a week, we'd walk down the one street, after noon dinner. All the boats beached on one side of us, all the doorsteps empty on the other, desertion would lie like dust in the air, with here and there a woman peering sourly from a dark room.

Madame Revenusso or Madame Médin, maybe, would call sullenly that César was looking for Monsieur Fischer.

Al's face would flash with joy, like a torch or a trumpet call. He'd hurry away. I'd go home alone, understanding some of the village women's jealous anger.

César's meat shop was behind the chapel, in a dirty alley. It was seldom peopled: women would buy no cuts from him, the devil, and even if they had wanted to, he was always saving the best for himself. Probably he ran the shop because it was an easy way to have good meat ready to hand.

Back of the store, there was one large room. It was dark, spotless, full of clean cold air from stone walls and floor, and almost bare. Under the lone window was César's big bed, very conveniently arranged for his carnal nocturnes. A wide ledge jutted from two walls, wide enough to sit on or lie on. There were one or two chairs on the scrubbed tiles of the floor, nuisances to stumble over in the room's darkness.

In the centre was the heart, the yolk, the altar, the great stone fireplace flat and high as a table, with an iron top for pots and a grill. And the whole ceiling of the room was its chimney, rising to a point and a far hole above the fire, like an ancient ducal kitchen.

It was there, to that big dark room, that the men would come, usually in the afternoon. I never saw them there, nor the room, either, but I know they came to it as quickly as they could, very joyfully. César would say "Come!" and they would hurry.

On the stove there was always something steaming in a great black pot—a stew of tiny opaque whitebait, or tripe jugged in sour white wine, or succulent scraps whose origin César leeringly would not tell.

Piled on a chair, or on the floor near the stove, were steaks as thick as your fist, or four or five lamb's legs, or a kid ready to broil. On the stone ledge were two kegs of wine, or three, or bottles never counted.

The fire was hot, the steam rose toward the roof.

César stood taller and broader than any other man before his stove, stirring, basting, smelling. His voice was mightier.

"Drink!" he cried out. "Drink, eat!" And he roared with joy.

In the other houses women snapped at their children or perked their heads towards the chapel alley. When they heard songs and wild laughter, or more alarming silence, they sighed and looked black. If there'd only been bad strumpets there behind the butcher shop, they would have comprehended, but just men—it was unnatural.

If their husbands came home before dark, they would not eat fish soup and bread with the children. If they came too late for that, they leaped fiercely and silently on the sleeping women, or stood for a long time looking through the shutters at the sea, their faces very gentle and intent.

The women hated César.

The mornings after, they cackled maliciously when his shop stayed closed until noon, and when he finally opened its wide door, they looked sideways at his tired thick face.

"M'sieur César appears ill today," they would greet him, oil-ily.

"Ill? My God, no, dear Madame Dirtypot! Two quarts of purgative water is all I need—or three. And I'd advise the same for your husband—but in proportion, in proportion, my good Mrs. Soilskirt. I'd say a half-glass. More would tear his vitals clean off, with more loss to you than to him, eh, Madame Foul-face?"

César's eyes, almost shut, gleamed wickedly, and he hoisted up his big sagging belly with lewd relish.

Then his face cleared. A young woman came towards him, with a warm little naked child on one arm. César called her.

"Célestine! How goes it with your new rascal?"

He paid no attention to her stiff mouth and forehead, but looked lovingly at the tiny brown baby she had.

"Oh, he is a beauty, but a beauty, so strong and straight! Cé-lestine, you've done a fine job here. That's right, girl—smile. César is your good friend, really. And this child! He is a grand fellow, I tell you. Here, come to me, you little beautiful limb of the devil!"

César stood in the strong white sunlight, his two bottles of physic forgotten. The naked baby in his arms grinned up at him candidly while he murmured to it. He turned it across his arm, and ran his huge hand over its firm little bottom.

"My God!" he exclaimed, suddenly, "what delicious, truly what a delicious morsel that would be, broiled!"

With an outraged squawk Célestine tore her baby from him

and scuttled away. César yelled with laughter, belched might-
ily, and went toward his shop, his physic under his arms.

Whenever a strange creature came up in the nets, some sea
beast's child or watery vegetable, the fishermen carried it to
César.

He'd poke it, smell it, inevitably taste it. If he spat it out,
they'd nod wisely. Poison! If he gulped it down alive, or cooked
it up into a queer stew, they'd talk for days, admiringly. Brave
man, to eat a mass of purple jelly with a little green-toothed
mouth in its middle!

But do you remember, and their eyes would glisten with
amazed delight, do you remember the time the crocodile died at
the big zoo in the city, and César was called to skin it, and
brought himself back a fine thick steak from it? Ah, do you remember?

The time came for us to go. We asked César to come to our
house to eat a last supper.

I felt awkward, because I was a woman—but there was no
other place for me to eat. César felt awkward for the same reason.

He came with a coat on, and a pink shirt, and silently handed
me a massive filet of beef. I left the room with it, and heard him
talking to Al, but when I came back he stopped.

The meal was strained at the beginning, but we had plenty of
good wine, and the meat was the best I have ever tasted.

César put down his knife and fork.

"She likes it, she likes good food!" he said, wonderingly, to
Al. "She cannot be a real woman!"

After that things were very pleasant. He took off his coat,
and we ate and drank and talked, all a good deal.

"I hear you are married," César remarked. "It is a filthy lie,
naturally?"

"But of course we are married," Al protested. "We have been married for several years."

César peered incredulously at us, and then laughed.

"Ridiculous! And why? Children, you are not married, I say—because marriage is a rotten business, and you are not rotten." He spat neatly over his huge pink shoulder. "If you were married, Alfred, Alfred-the-Penguin, my Al, would not be a real man, happy. And he is. And you," he glared at me, "would not be sitting knowing good meat between your teeth. And you are.

"Therefore, my two peculiar little foreign children, you are not married! No, you are brother and sister, living in sinful glory!"

He laughed until the whole room shook, and tipped a full bottle of wine down his throat.

"I shall die soon," he said, "and when I die, every man in the village will laugh for many days. Do you know why? Because they'll have all my wine to drink, barrels and casks of it, to drink to my commands, and they'll all try to drink as I would, as I've taught them.

"Yes, they'll drink for me, to float my soul to Purgatory. And the biggest cask of wine will be my coffin. My friends know. They'll put me in it and bury me deep, and they and all the women, too, will weep."

He was silent for a minute, and then roared another laugh.

"And grapes will grow up from me," he cried, "and by God, what wine I'll make!"

Al and I looked and recognized there a ghost with us, another Man from whose dead heart had sprung a vine. Was he César, was César that dim great figure who heard of Pan's death and cried tears as big as ostrich eggs?

We parted merrily, with no farewells.

About a year later, a shabby post card came from the village on the Mediterranean coast. It was stiffly pencilled.

"My friends in Sinful Glory, plant a tree somewhere for César."

Since then we have planted many, almost all for him.

To End

We lived, once, above a little pastry shop which called itself "At the Sign of the Fin Gourmet." It sold probably the worst apricot tarts that ever sogged and stuck in throat.

"*N'est pas gourmand qui veut,*" said Brillat-Savarin. The aphorism is, as I predicted at the first, inevitable. Truly a man is not a gourmand, much less a *fin gourmet*, by wishing to be so.

Design by David Bullen
Typeset in Mergenthaler Bembo
by Wilsted & Taylor
Printed by Malloy Lithographing
on acid-free paper

PRAISE FOR

Beautiful Ruins

"A high-wire feat of bravura storytelling. . . . The surprising and witty novel of social criticism that flows away from its lush, romantic opening offers so much more than just entertainment. [It] stirs the heart and amuses as it also rescues us from the all-too-human pain that is the motor of this complex and ever-evolving novel. . . . You're going to love this book."
— Helen Schulman, *New York Times Book Review*

"A literary miracle. . . . A sweeping stunner of a narrative. . . . The entire novel is a kaleidoscopic collection of 'beautiful ruins,' both architectural and human. This novel is a standout not just because of the inventiveness of its plot, but also because of its language."
— Maureen Corrigan, NPR's *Fresh Air*

"Audacious . . . weds the grand dramatic impulses of the cinematic blockbuster to the psychological interiority of high literary art. The result is a page-turner that doubles as an elegant meditation on fame, desire, duty, and fate. . . . Walter has planted himself firmly in the first rank of American authors. He has crafted a novel with pathos, piercing wit, and, most important, the generous soul of a literary classic. . . . *Beautiful Ruins* will endure."
— Steve Almond, *Boston Globe*

"A lyrical, heartbreaking, and funny novel [that] ends with a twelve-page bolt of brilliance, a perceptive, moving, and altogether superb piece of writing. Walter closes the deal with such command that you begin to wonder why up till now he's not often been mentioned as one of the best novelists around. *Beautiful Ruins* might just correct that oversight."
— Kevin Canfield, *Kansas City Star*

"A near-perfect rendezvous. . . . A novel whose decade- and continent-hopping ingenuity expertly scratches the seasonal itch for both literary depth and dazzle. That Walter is able to juggle his sprawling cast—including one legendary real-life movie star—and hopscotching timelines is an impressive novelistic trick. But it's the beating heart in *Ruins* that makes it beautiful. A-."

—*Entertainment Weekly*

"Parts of *Beautiful Ruins* are darkly bitter and others are flush with a sincere romanticism. It's a novel about the possibility of achieving art in popular culture, and love in a world where people don't hesitate to use each other mercilessly. . . . [*Beautiful Ruins*] exhilarates with its breadth. Pasquale's decency, Deane's ruthlessness, the former starlet's weariness, the D-girl's disgust, and the screenwriter's flickering optimism—each is presented as legitimate in its own way."

—Laura Miller, *Salon*

"Ambitious . . . [with] an ensemble of memorable characters. . . . Beneath Walter's black comic's mask beats the brain of an ethical philosopher and the heart of a romantic."

—Mary Ann Gwinn, *Seattle Times*

"[Walter] is a genius of the modern American moment. . . . As always in Walter, there's a lot to laugh at amid the tragedy, and a lot to think about. . . . You're gonna have fun with this novel."

—Susan Balée, *Philadelphia Inquirer*

"Deeply romantic, [with] vividly etched characters. . . . A monument to crazy love."

—Janet Maslin, *New York Times*

"Poignant, comical, and marvelous . . . a mix of satire and love story."

—Tom Nolan, *San Francisco Chronicle*

"Energetic, entrancing. . . . Walter's turns of phrase are as brilliant as his plot twists."

—*People*

"Wonderfully sprawling. . . . Walter vividly draws a world both tender and cutthroat, where ambition battles reality, daydreams fight doldrums and sometimes win. His novel is cinematic, taking on the soft-focus glow of golden-era Hollywood, so that his images become indelible flickers on a big screen, staying with us forever, somehow larger than life."
—Royal Young, *Interview*

"A marvel, an absolute gem. . . . Surprises abound but Walter keeps his plot tethered to reality, resonating and reverberating and building to a conclusion that is as satisfying as it is gratifying."
—Nina Sankovitch, *Huffington Post*

"Superb. . . . Walter makes each character memorable. . . . The verve and enthusiasm of this novel, from its let's-go-everywhere structure to the comedy in the marrow of its sentences, are wholly life-affirming."
—Mark Athitakis, *Minneapolis Star Tribune*

"Walter is a prodigiously gifted writer. His sentences nearly sing. . . . What unfolds is ambitious, and a lesser writer could never have engineered such masterful jumps through time."
—Christopher Bollen, *Los Angeles Review of Books*

"A great read [and] a beautiful novel. . . . *Beautiful Ruins* shows novelists how it is done."
—Anne Trubek, *Cleveland Plain Dealer*

"A witty, sharply observant writer. . . . Walter's having so much fun with this stuff, it becomes infectious."
—Jeff Baker, *The Oregonian*

"*Beautiful Ruins* has a quality of spectacle, the epic journey of people who enthrall us with personalities that are bigger than reality. But because Spokane-based author Jess Walter knows his way around a novel (*The Zero* and, most notably, *The Financial Lives of the Poets*), his extravaganza teeters atop a bedrock of hard reality, speaking uncomfortable truths about the frail, often narcissistic nature of identity. . . . What pulls us back into the book's core is the characters' earnest search for real happiness, an intrepid desire to embrace 'the sweet lovely mess that is life.'"

—Margaret Gunning, *Vancouver Sun*

"Perfectly executed. . . . Walter tells his story elegantly [with] precise brushstrokes, echoing the appropriate rhythm of each location. . . . A spectacular story of love, frustration, selfish intent, and the patience of the human heart." —Melody Datz, *The Stranger* (Seattle)

"Majestic. . . . Alternately poignant and laugh-out-loud funny. . . . A delicious summer read."   —Matt Buckingham, *Willamette Week*

"The bestselling author of *The Financial Lives of the Poets* has written another winner, a clever, quirky, sun-drenched blockbuster about the lives of Hollywood glitterati in the 1960s—and then what happens fifty years later. Remarkably touching and full of surprises, this novel of love and greed will stick with you long after the makeup has come off."   —Emily Temple, *Flavorwire*

"Gloriously and darkly funny. . . . Coming to understand what's going on in *Beautiful Ruins* brings the thrill of epiphany. Walter's sardonic wit and mischievous intelligence shine out to the very end."

—Katherine A. Powers, *Christian Science Monitor*

"So effortlessly engrossing that its considerable technical accomplishments take a backseat to its more conventional charms. . . . A great novel."   —*Portland Mercury*

"Hilarious and compelling."   —*Esquire*

"Irresistible."   —*O, The Oprah Magazine*

"A beautiful story."   —*Hollywood Reporter*

"A brilliant, madcap meditation on fate. . . . Walter's prose is a joy—funny, brash, witty, and rich, with ironic twists. He's taken all of the tricks of the postmodern novel and scoured out the cynicism, making for a novel that's life-affirming but never saccharine."

—*Kirkus Reviews* (starred review)

"So appealing we'd be idiots not to buy it. . . . A novel shot in sparkly Technicolor."   —*Booklist* (starred review)

"Walter's newest book will have readers . . . marveling at his imagination and spot-on characters. . . . Not to be missed."

—*Library Journal* (starred review)

"Why mince words? *Beautiful Ruins* is an absolute masterpiece."

—Richard Russo, author of *Empire Falls*

"This is a blockbuster, with romance, majesty, comedy, smarts, and a cast of thousands." —Daniel Handler, author of *Why We Broke Up*

"Nothing less than brilliant, a tour de force that crosses decades, continents, and genres to powerful and often hilarious effect."

—Ben Fountain, author of *Billy Lynn's Long Halftime Walk*

"Characters so exhilaratingly human that you want to break out into cheers and sobs. . . . To be untouched by *Beautiful Ruins* might well be like having no inner life at all."

—Rebecca Newberger Goldstein, author of
Thirty-Six Arguments for the Existence of God

Beautiful Ruins

ALSO BY JESS WALTER

FICTION

We Live in Water: Stories

The Financial Lives of the Poets

The Zero

Citizen Vince

Land of the Blind

Over Tumbled Graves

NONFICTION

Ruby Ridge

Beautiful Ruins

a Novel

Jess Walter

HARPER ◗ PERENNIAL

NEW YORK • LONDON • TORONTO • SYDNEY • NEW DELHI • AUCKLAND

HARPER PERENNIAL

A hardcover edition of this book was published in 2012 by HarperCollins Publishers.

P.S.™ is a trademark of HarperCollins Publishers.

FIRST HARPER PERENNIAL EDITION PUBLISHED 2013.

Designed by Michael P. Correy

Map illustrated by Shawn E. Davis

Library of Congress Cataloging-in-Publication Data has been applied for.

ISBN 978-0-06-192817-8 (pbk.)

13 14 15 16 17   OV/RRD   10 9 8 7 6 5 4 3 2 1

To Anne, Brooklyn, Ava, and Alec

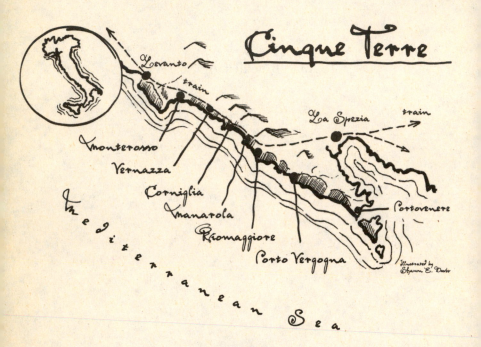

The ancient Romans built their greatest
masterpieces of architecture for wild beasts to fight in.

—*Voltaire,* The Complete Letters

Cleopatra: I will not have love as my master.
Marc Antony: Then you will not have love.

—*from the 1963 disaster film* Cleopatra

[Dick] Cavett's four great interviews with Richard Burton
were done in 1980. . . . Burton, fifty-four at the time, and
already a beautiful ruin, was mesmerizing.

—*"Talk Story" by Louis Menand,* The New Yorker, *November 22, 2010*

1

The Dying Actress

April 1962
Porto Vergogna, Italy

The dying actress arrived in his village the only way one could come directly—in a boat that motored into the cove, lurched past the rock jetty, and bumped against the end of the pier. She wavered a moment in the boat's stern, then extended a slender hand to grip the mahogany railing; with the other, she pressed a wide-brimmed hat against her head. All around her, shards of sunlight broke on the flickering waves.

Twenty meters away, Pasquale Tursi watched the arrival of the woman as if in a dream. Or rather, he would think later, a dream's opposite: a burst of clarity after a lifetime of sleep. Pasquale straightened and stopped what he was doing, what he was usually doing that spring, trying to construct a beach below his family's empty *pensione*. Chest-deep in the cold Ligurian Sea, Pasquale was tossing rocks the size of cats in an attempt to fortify the breakwater, to keep the waves from hauling away his little mound of construction sand. Pasquale's "beach" was only as wide as two fishing boats, and the ground beneath his dusting of sand was scalloped rock, but it was the closest thing to a flat piece of shoreline in the entire village: a rumor of a town that had ironically—or perhaps hopefully—been designated *Porto* despite the fact that the only boats to come in and out regularly belonged to the village's handful of sardine and anchovy fishermen. The rest of the name, *Vergogna*, meant shame, and was a remnant from the founding of the village in the seventeenth century as a place for sailors and fishers to find women of . . . a certain moral and commercial flexibility.

On the day he first saw the lovely American, Pasquale was chest-deep in daydreams as well, imagining grubby little Porto Vergogna as an emergent resort town, and himself as a sophisticated businessman of the 1960s, a man of infinite possibility at the dawn of a glorious modernity. Everywhere he saw signs of *il boom*—the surge in wealth and literacy that was transforming Italy. Why not here? He'd recently come home from four years in bustling Florence, returning to the tiny backward village of his youth imagining that he brought vital news of the world out there—a glittering era of shiny *macchine*, of televisions and telephones, of double martinis and women in slender pants, of the kind of world that had seemed to exist before only in the cinema.

Porto Vergogna was a tight cluster of a dozen old whitewashed houses, an abandoned chapel, and the town's only commercial interest—the tiny hotel and café owned by Pasquale's family—all huddled like a herd of sleeping goats in a crease in the sheer cliffs. Behind the village, the rocks rose six hundred feet to a wall of black, striated mountains. Below it, the sea settled in a rocky, shrimp-curled cove, from which the fishermen put in and out every day. Isolated by the cliffs behind and the sea in front, the village had never been accessible by car or cart, and so the streets, such as they were, consisted of a few narrow pathways between the houses—brick-lined roads skinnier than sidewalks, plunging alleys and rising staircases so narrow that unless one was standing in the piazza San Pietro, the little town square, it was possible anywhere in the village to reach out and touch walls on either side.

In this way, remote Porto Vergogna was not so different from the quaint cliff-side towns of the Cinque Terre to the north, except that it was smaller, more remote, and not as picturesque. In fact, the hoteliers and restaurateurs to the north had their own pet name for the tiny village pinched into the vertical cliff seam: *culo di baldracca*—the whore's crack. Yet despite his neighbors' disdain, Pasquale had come to believe, as his father had, that Porto Vergogna could some-day flourish like the rest of the Levante, the coastline south of Genoa that included the Cinque Terre, or even the larger tourist cities on the Ponente—Portofino and the sophisticated Italian Riviera. The rare foreign tourists who boated or hiked into Porto Vergogna tended to be lost French or Swiss, but Pasquale held out hope the 1960s would bring a flood of Americans, led by the *bravissimo* U.S. president, John Kennedy, and his wife, Jacqueline. And yet, if his village had any chance of becoming the *destinazione turistica primaria* he dreamed of, Pasquale knew it would need to attract such vacationers, and to do that, it would need—first of all—a beach.

And so Pasquale stood half-submerged, holding a big rock beneath his chin as the red mahogany boat bobbed into his cove. His old friend Orenzio was piloting it for the wealthy vintner and hotelier Gualfredo, who ran the tourism south of Genoa but whose fancy ten-meter sport boat rarely came to Porto Vergogna. Pasquale watched the boat settle in its chop, and could think of nothing to do but call out, "Orenzio!" His friend was confused by the greeting; they had been friends since they were twelve, but they were not yellers, he and Pasquale, more . . . acknowledgers, lip-raisers, eyebrow-tippers. Orenzio nodded back grimly. He was serious when he had tourists in his boat, especially Americans. "They are serious people, Americans," Orenzio had explained to Pasquale once. "Even more suspicious than Germans. If you smile too much, Americans assume you're stealing from them." Today Orenzio was especially dour-faced, shooting a glance toward the woman in the back of his boat, her long tan coat pulled tight around her thin waist, her floppy hat covering most of her face.

Then the woman said something quietly to Orenzio, and it carried across the water. Gibberish, Pasquale thought at first, until he recognized it as English—American, in fact: "Pardon me, what is that man doing?"

Pasquale knew his friend was insecure about his limited English and tended to answer questions in that awful language as tersely as possible. Orenzio glanced over at Pasquale, holding a big rock for the breakwater he was building, and attempted the English word for *spiaggia*—beach—saying with a hint of impatience: "Bitch." The woman cocked her head as if she hadn't heard right. Pasquale tried to help, muttering that the bitch was for the tourists, *"per i turisti."* But the beautiful American didn't seem to hear.

It was an inheritance from his father, Pasquale's dream of tourism. Carlo Tursi had spent the last decade of his life trying to get the five larger villages of the Cinque Terre to accept Porto Vergogna as the sixth in the string. ("How much nicer," he used to say, *"Sei Terre,* the six lands. Cinque Terre is so hard on tourists' tongues.") But tiny Porto Vergogna lacked the charm and political pull of its five larger neighbors. So while the five were connected by telephone lines and eventually by a tunneled rail line and swelled with seasonal tourists and their money, the sixth atrophied like an extra finger. Carlo's other fruitless ambition had been to get those vital rail lines tunneled another kilometer, to link Porto Vergogna to the larger cliff-side towns. But this never happened, and since the nearest road cut behind the terraced vineyards that backed the Cinque Terre cliffs, Porto Vergogna remained cut off, alone in its wrinkle in the black, ribbed rocks, only the sea in front and steep foot-trails descending the cliffs behind.

On the day the luminous American arrived, Pasquale's father had been dead for eight months. Carlo's passing had been quick and quiet, a vessel bursting in his brain while he read one of his beloved newspapers. Over and over Pasquale replayed his father's last ten minutes: he sipped an espresso, dragged a cigarette, laughed at an item in the Milan newspaper (Pasquale's mother saved the page but never found anything funny in it), and then slumped forward as if he were napping. Pasquale was at the University of Florence when he got news of his father's death. After the funeral, he begged his elderly mother to move to Florence, but the very idea scandalized her. "What kind of wife would I be if I left your father simply because he is dead?" It left no question—at least in Pasquale's mind—that he must come home and care for his frail mother.

So Pasquale moved back into his old room in the hotel. And perhaps it was guilt over having dismissed his father's ideas when he was younger, but Pasquale could suddenly see it—his family's small inn—through newly inherited eyes. Yes, this town could become a new kind of Italian resort—an American getaway, parasols on the rocky shore, camera shutters snapping, Kennedys everywhere! And if there was a measure of self-interest in turning the empty *pensione* into a world-class resort, so be it: the old hotel was his only inheritance, the sole familial advantage in a culture that required it.

The hotel was comprised of a *trattoria*—a three-table café—a kitchen and two small apartments on the first floor, and the six rooms of the old brothel above it. With the hotel came the responsibility of caring for its only regular tenants, *le due streghe*, as the fishermen called them, the two witches: Pasquale's crippled mother, Antonia, and her wire-haired sister, Valeria, the ogre who did most of the cooking when she wasn't yelling at the lazy fishermen and the rare guest who stumbled in.

Pasquale was nothing if not tolerant, and he abided the eccentricities of his melodramatic *mamma* and his crazy *zia* just as he put up with the crude fishermen—each morning skidding their *peschereccio* down to the shoreline and pushing out into the sea, the small wooden shells rocking on the waves like dirty salad bowls, thrumming with the *bup-bup* of their smoking outboards. Each day the fishermen netted just enough anchovies, sardines, and sea bass to sell to the markets and restaurants to the south, before coming back to drink grappa and smoke the bitter cigarettes they rolled themselves. His father had always taken great pains to separate himself and his son—descendants, Carlo claimed, of an esteemed Florentine merchant class—from these coarse fishermen. "Look at them," he would say to Pasquale from behind one of the many newspapers that arrived weekly on the mail boat. "In a more civilized time, they would have been our servants."

Having lost two older sons in the war, Carlo wasn't about to let his youngest son work on the fishing boats, or in the canneries in La Spezia, or in the terraced vineyards, or in the marble quarries in the Apennines, or anywhere else a young man might learn some valuable skill and shake the feeling that he was soft and out of place in the hard world. Instead, Carlo and Antonia—already forty when Pasquale was born—raised Pasquale like a secret between them, and it was only after some pleading that his aging parents had even allowed him to go to university in Florence.

When Pasquale returned after his father's death, the fishermen were unsure what to think of him. At first, they attributed his strange behavior—always reading, talking to himself, measuring things, dumping bags of construction sand on the rocks and raking it like a vain man combing his last wisps of hair—to grief. They strung their nets and they watched the slender twenty-one-year-old rearrange rocks in hopes of keeping storms from hauling away his beach, and their eyes dewed over with memories of the empty dreams of their own dead fathers. But soon the fishermen began to miss the good-natured ribbing they'd always given Carlo Tursi.

Finally, after watching Pasquale work on his beach for a few weeks, the fishermen could stand it no longer. One day, Tommaso the Elder tossed the young man a matchbox and called out, "Here's a chair for your tiny beach, Pasquale!" After weeks of unnatural kindness, the gentle mockery was a relief, the bursting of storm clouds above the village. Life was back to normal. "Pasquale, I saw part of your beach yesterday at Lerici. Shall I take the rest of the sand up there or will you wait for the current to deliver it?"

But a beach was something the fishermen could at least understand; after all, there were beaches in Monterosso al Mare and in the Riviera towns to the north, where the town's fishermen sold the bulk of their catches. When Pasquale announced his intention to carve a tennis court into a cluster of boulders in the cliffs, however, the fishermen declared Pasquale even more unhinged than his father. "The boy has lost his sense," they said from the small piazza as they hand-rolled cigarettes and watched Pasquale scamper over the boulders marking the boundaries of his future tennis court with string. "It's a family of *pazzi*. Soon he'll be talking to cats." With nothing but steep cliff faces to work with, Pasquale knew that a golf course was out of the question. But there was a natural shelf of three boulders near his hotel, and if he could level the tops and cantilever the rest, he thought he could build forms and pour enough concrete to connect the boulders into a flat rectangle and create—like a vision rising out of the rocky cliffs—a tennis court, announcing to visitors arriving by sea that they had come upon a first-class resort. He could close his eyes and see it: men in clean white pants lobbing balls back and forth on a stunning court projecting out from the cliffs, a glorious shelf twenty meters above the shoreline, women in dresses and summer hats sipping drinks beneath nearby parasols. So he chipped away with a pick and chisels and hammers, hoping to prepare a large enough space for a tennis court. He raked his dusting of sand. He tossed rocks in the sea. He endured the teasing of the fishermen. He peeked in on his dying mother. And he waited—as he always had—for life to come and find him.

For eight months after his father's death, this was the sum of Pasquale Tursi's life. And if he wasn't entirely happy, he wasn't unhappy, either. Rather, he found himself inhabiting the vast, empty plateau where most people live, between boredom and contentment.

And perhaps this is where he would have always lived had not the beautiful American arrived on this cool, sunny afternoon, Pasquale standing chest-deep in the water twenty meters away, watching the mahogany boat come to rest against the wooden bollards of the pier, the woman standing in the stern, gentle wind ruffling the sea around her.

She was impossibly thin, and yet amply curved, the beautiful American. From Pasquale's vantage in the sea—sun flickering behind her, wind snapping her wheat-blond hair—it was as if she were another species, taller and more ethereal than any woman he'd ever seen. Orenzio offered her a hand, and after a moment of hesitation she took it. He helped her from his boat onto the narrow pier.

"Thank you," came an uncertain voice from beneath the hat, and then, *"Grazie,"* the Italian word breathy and unpracticed. She took her first step toward the village, seemed to stagger a moment, and then regained her balance. It was then that she pulled the hat off to get a look at the village, and Pasquale saw her full features and was mildly surprised the beautiful American wasn't ... well ... more beautiful.

Oh, she was striking, certainly, but not in the way he'd expected. First, she was as tall as Pasquale, nearly six feet. And from where he stood, weren't her features a bit too much for such a narrow face—plunging jawline so pronounced, mouth so full, eyes so round and open that she seemed startled? And could a woman be *too* thin, so that her curves seemed sudden, alarming? Her long hair was pulled back into a ponytail and her skin was lightly tanned, drawn tight over features that were somehow at once too sharp and too soft—nose too delicate for such a chin, for such high cheeks, for those big dark eyes. No, he thought, while she was striking, this was no great beauty.

But then she turned directly to him, and the disparate features of her drastic face came together as a single, perfect thing, and Pasquale recalled from his studies how some buildings in Florence could disappoint from various angles and yet always presented well in relief, always photographed well; that the various vantages were made to be composed; and so, too, he thought, some people. Then she smiled, and in that instant, if such a thing were possible, Pasquale fell in love, and he would remain in love for the rest of his life—not so much with the woman, whom he didn't even know, but with the moment.

He dropped the rock he was holding.

She glanced away—right, then left, then right again—as if looking for the rest of the village. Pasquale flushed over what she must be seeing: a dozen or so drab stone houses, some of them abandoned, clinging like barnacles to the cliff seam. Feral cats poked around the small piazza, but otherwise all was quiet, the fishermen out in their boats for the day. Pasquale sensed such disappointment when people hiked in accidentally or arrived by boat through a mistake in cartography or language, people who believed they were being taken to the charming tourist towns of Porto*venere* or Porto*fino* only to find themselves in the *brutto* fishing village of Porto Vergogna.

"I'm sorry," the beautiful American said in English, turning back to Orenzio. "Should I help with the bags? Or is it part of . . . I mean . . . I don't know what has been paid for and what hasn't."

Done with devilish English after that "beach" business, Orenzio merely shrugged. Short, jug-eared, and dull-eyed, he carried himself in a manner that often suggested brain damage to tourists, who were so impressed by this slack-eyed simpleton's ability to operate a motorboat that they tipped him lavishly. Orenzio, in turn, surmised that the duller he behaved, and the less English he mastered, the more he would be paid. So he stared and blinked stupidly.

"Should I get my own luggage, then?" the woman asked again, patiently, a little helplessly.

"*Bagagli, Orenzio,*" Pasquale called to his friend, and then it dawned on Pasquale: this woman was checking into *his* hotel! Pasquale started wading over to the pier, licking his lips in preparation for speaking unpracticed English. "Please," he said to the woman, his tongue like a hunk of gristle in his mouth, "I have honor and Orenzio for carry you bag. Go upon Ad-e-quate View Hotel." The comment appeared to confuse the American, but Pasquale didn't notice. He wanted to end with a flourish and tried to think of the proper word to call her (*Madam?*) but he longed for something better. He had never really mastered English, but he'd studied enough to have a healthy fear of its random severity, the senseless brutality of its conjugations; it was unpredictable, like a cross-bred dog. His earliest education in the language had come from the only American to ever stay in the hotel, a writer who came to Italy each spring to chip away at his life's work—an epic novel about his experiences in World War II. Pasquale tried to imagine what the tall, dashing writer might say to this woman, but he couldn't think of the right words and he wondered if there was an English equivalent for the Italian staple *bella*: beautiful. He took a stab: "Please. Come. Beautiful America."

She stared at him for just a moment—the longest moment of his life to that point—then smiled and looked down demurely. "Thank you. Is this your hotel?"

Pasquale finished sloshing through the water and arrived at the pier. He pulled himself up, shaking the water from his pant legs, and tried to present himself, every bit the dashing hotelier. "Yes. Is my hotel." Pasquale pointed to the small, hand-lettered sign on the left side of the piazza. "Please."

"And . . . you have a room reserved for us?"

"Oh yes. Many is room. All is room for you. Yes."

She looked at the sign, and then at Pasquale again. The warm gust was back and it roused the escaped hairs from her ponytail into streamers around her face. She smiled at the puddle dripping off his thin frame, then looked up into his sea-blue eyes and said, "You have lovely eyes." Then she replaced the hat on her head and started making her way toward the small piazza and the center of what little town lay before her.

Porto Vergogna had never had *un liceo*—a high school—and so Pasquale had boated to La Spezia for secondary school. This was where he'd met Orenzio, who became his first real friend. They were tossed together by default: the shy son of the old hotelier and the short, jug-eared wharf boy. Pasquale had even stayed sometimes with Orenzio's family during the winter weeks, when the passage was difficult. The winter before Pasquale left for Florence, he and Orenzio had invented a game that they played over glasses of Swiss beer. They would sit across from each other at the docks in La Spezia and fire offenses back and forth until they either ran out of words or started repeating themselves, at which point the loser would have to drain the pint before him. Now, as he hoisted the American's bags, Orenzio leaned over to Pasquale and played a dry version of the game. "What did she say, nut-smeller?"

"She loves my eyes," Pasquale said, missing his cue.

"Come on, ass-handler," Orenzio said. "She said nothing like this."

"No, she did. She is in love with my eyes."

"You are a liar, Pasqo, and an admirer of boys' noodles."

"It is true."

"That you love boys' noodles?"

"No. She said that about my eyes."

"You are a fellater of goats. The woman is a cinema star."

"I think so, too," Pasquale said.

"No, stupid, she really is a performer of the cinema. She is with the American company working on the film in Rome."

"What film?"

"*Cleopatra*. Don't you read the newspapers, shit-smoker?"

Pasquale looked back at the American actress, who was climbing the steps to the village. "But she's too fair-skinned to play Cleopatra."

"The whore and husband-thief Elizabeth Taylor is Cleopatra," Orenzio said. "This is another player in the film. Do you really not read the newspapers, bung-slopper?"

"Which role is she?"

"How should I know? There must be many roles."

"What's her name?" Pasquale asked.

Orenzio handed over the typed instructions he'd been given. The paper included the woman's name, said that she should be taken to the hotel in Porto Vergogna, and that the bill should be sent to the man who had arranged her trip, Michael Deane, at the Grand Hotel in Rome. The single sheet of paper said that this Michael Deane was a "special production assistant" for "20th Century Fox Pictures." And the woman's name—

"Dee . . . Moray," Pasquale read aloud. It wasn't familiar, but there were so many American movie stars—Rock Hudsons, Marilyn Monroes, John Waynes—and just when he thought he knew them all, some new one became famous, almost as if there were a factory in America manufacturing these huge movie-screen faces. Pasquale looked back up to where she was already making her way up the steps of the cliff seam and into the waiting village. "Dee Moray," he said again.

Orenzio looked over his shoulder at the paper. "Dee Moray," Orenzio said. There was something intriguing in the name and neither man could stop saying it. "Dee Moray," Orenzio said again.

"She is sick," Orenzio said to Pasquale.

"With what?"

"How would I know this? The man just said she was sick."

"Is it serious?"

"I don't know this, either." And then, as if winding down, as if even he were losing interest in their old game, Orenzio added another insult, *un mangiaculo*—"one who eats ass."

Pasquale watched as Dee Moray moved toward his hotel, taking small steps along the stone pathway. "She can't be too sick," he said. "She's beautiful."

"But not like Sophia Loren," Orenzio said. "Or the Marilyn Monroe." It had been their other pastime the winter before, going to the cinema and rating the women they saw.

"No, I think she has a more intelligent beauty . . . like Anouk Aimée."

"She is so skinny," Orenzio said. "And she's no Claudia Cardinale."

"No," Pasquale had to agree. Claudia Cardinale was perfection. "I think it is not so common, though, her face."

The point had become too fine for Orenzio. "I could bring a three-legged dog into this town, Pasqo, and you would fall in love with it."

That's when Pasquale became worried. "Orenzio, did she intend to come here?"

Orenzio smacked the page in Pasquale's hand. "This American, Deane, who drove her to La Spezia? I explained to him that no one comes here. I asked if he meant Portofino or Portovenere. He asked what Porto Vergogna was like, and I said there was nothing here but a hotel. He asked if the town was quiet. I said to him only death is quieter, and he said, 'Then that is the place.'"

Pasquale smiled at his friend. "Thank you, Orenzio."

"Fellater of goats," Orenzio said quietly.

"You already said that one," Pasquale said.

Orenzio mimed finishing a beer.

Then they both looked toward the cliff side, forty meters uphill, where the first American guest since the death of his father stood regarding the front door of his hotel. Here is the future, thought Pasquale.

Dee Moray stopped and looked back down at them. She shook out her ponytail and her sun-bleached hair snapped and danced around her face as she took in the sea from the village square. Then she looked at the sign and cocked her head, as if trying to understand the words:

THE HOTEL ADEQUATE VIEW

And then the future tucked her floppy hat under her arm, pushed open the door, ducked, and went in.

After she disappeared inside the hotel, Pasquale entertained the unwieldy thought that he'd somehow summoned her, that after years of living in this place, after months of grief and loneliness and waiting for Americans, he'd created this woman from old bits of cinema and books, from the lost artifacts and ruins of his dreams, from his epic, enduring solitude. He glanced over at Orenzio, who was carrying *someone's* bags, and the whole world suddenly seemed so unlikely, our time in it so brief and dreamlike. He'd never felt such a detached, existential sensation, such terrifying freedom—it was as if he were hovering above the village, above his own body—and it thrilled him in a way that he could never have explained.

"Dee Moray," Pasquale Tursi said, suddenly, aloud, breaking the spell of his thoughts. Orenzio looked over. Then Pasquale turned his back and said the name again, to himself this time, in something less than a whisper, embarrassed by the hopeful breath that formed those words. Life, he thought, is a blatant act of imagination.

2

The Last Pitch

Recently
Hollywood, California

Before sunrise—before Guatemalan gardeners in dirty dinged lawn trucks, before Caribbeans come to cook, clean, and clothe, before Montessori, Pilates, and Coffee Bean, before Benzes and BMWs nose onto palmed streets and the blue-toothed sharks resume their endless business—*the gentrification of the American mind*—there are the sprinklers: rising from the ground to spit-spray the northwest corner of Greater Los Angeles, airport to the hills, downtown to the beaches, the slumbering rubble of the entertainment regime.

In Santa Monica, they call to Claire Silver in the predawn quiet of her condo—*psst hey*—her curly red hair splayed out on the pillow like a suicide. They whisper again—*psst hey*—and Claire's eyelids flutter; she inhales, orients, glances over at the marbled shoulder of her boyfriend, sprawled asleep on his 70 percent of the king-size. Daryl often cracks the bedroom window behind their bed when he comes in late, and Claire wakes like this—*psst hey*—to water spritzing the rock garden outside. She's asked the condo manager why it's necessary to water a bed of rocks every day at five A.M. (or at all, for that matter), but of course sprinklers are not the real issue.

Claire wakes jonesing for data; she fumbles on the crowded bedside table for her BlackBerry, takes a digital hit. Fourteen e-mails, six tweets, five friend requests, three texts, and her calendar—life in

a palm. General stuff, too: Friday, sixty-six degrees on the way to
seventy-four. Five phone calls scheduled today. Six pitch meetings.
Then, amid the info dump she sees a life-changing e-mail, from
affinity@arc.net. She opens it.

Dear Claire,

*Thanks again for your patience during this long process. Both
Bryan and I were very impressed by your credentials and your
interview and we'd like to meet you to talk more. Would you be
available for coffee this morning?*

Sincerely,
James Pierce
Museum of American Screen Culture

Claire sits up. Holy shit. They're going to offer her the job. Or
are they? *Talk more?* They've already interviewed her twice; what
can they possibly need to talk about? Is this it? Is today the day she
gets to quit her dream job?

Claire is chief development assistant for the legendary film producer Michael Deane. The title's phony—her job's all assisting, no
developing, and she's nobody's chief. She tends Michael's whims.
Answers his calls and e-mails, goes for his sandwiches and coffee.
And mostly she reads for him: great herds of scripts and synopses,
one-sheets and treatments—a stampede of material going nowhere.

She'd hoped for so much more when she quit her doctoral film
studies program and went to work for the man who was known in the
seventies and eighties as the "Deane of Hollywood." She'd wanted to
make movies—smart, moving *films.* But when she arrived three years
ago, Michael Deane was in the worst slump of his career, with no
recent credits save the indie zombie bomb *Night Ravagers.* In Claire's
three years, Deane Productions has made no other movies; in fact, its
only production has been a single television program: the hit reality
show and dating Web site Hookbook (Hookbook.net).

And with the monstrous success of that cross-media abomination, movies have become a fading memory at Deane Productions. Instead, Claire's days are spent listening to TV pitches so offensive she fears she's singlehandedly hastening the Apocalypse: *Model Behavior* ("We take seven models and put them in a frat house!") and *Nympho Night* ("We film the dates of people diagnosed with sex addiction!") and *Drunk Midget House* ("See, it's a house . . . full of drunk midgets!").

Michael's constantly urging her to adjust her expectations, to set aside her highbrow pretensions, to accept the culture on its own terms, to expand her notions of what's *good*. "If you want to make art," he's fond of saying, "go get a job at the *Loov-ruh*."

So that's what she did. A month ago, Claire applied for a job she saw posted on a Web site, for "a curator for a new private film museum." And now, almost three weeks after her interview, the crisp businessmen on the museum's board of directors appear to be close to offering her the job.

If it's not a no-brainer, this decision is a quarter-brainer at most: their proposed Museum of American Screen Culture (MASC) will pay better, the hours will be better, and it's certainly a better use of her master's degree from UCLA in Moving Image Archive Studies. More than that, she thinks the job might allow her to feel like she's actually using her brain again.

Michael is dismissive of this intellectual discontent of hers, insisting that she's just paying her dues, that every producer spends a few years in the wilderness—that, in Michael's clipped, inimitable lingo, she must "sift shit for the corn," make her bones with a commercial success or ten so that she can later do the projects she loves. And so she finds herself here, at life's big crossroad: stick it out with this crass career and her unlikely dream of one day making a great film, or take a quiet job cataloguing relics from a time when film actually mattered?

Faced with such decisions (college, boyfriends, grad school), Claire has always been a pro-con lister, a seeker of signs, a dealmaker—and she makes a deal with herself now, or with Fate: *Either a good, viable film idea walks in the door today—or I quit.*

This deal, of course, is rigged. Convinced that the money is all in TV now, Michael hasn't liked a single film pitch, script, or treatment in two years. And everything *she* likes he dismisses as too expensive, too dark, too period, not commercial enough. As if that didn't make the odds long enough, today is Wild Pitch Friday: the last Friday of the month, set aside for off-the-rack pitches from Michael's old cronies and colleagues, from every burned-out, played-out has-been and never-was in town. And on this particular Wild Pitch Friday, both Michael and his producing partner, Danny Roth, have the day off. Today—*psst hey*—she has all these shit pitches to herself.

Claire glances down at Daryl, snoozing in the bed next to her. She twinges guilt for not talking to him about the museum job; this is partly because he's been out late almost every night, partly because they haven't been talking much anyway, partly because she's thinking of quitting him, too.

"So?" she says quietly. Daryl makes a deep-sleep noise—something between a grunt and a peep. "Yeah," she says, "that's what I figured."

She rises and stretches, starts for the bathroom. But on the way she pauses over Daryl's jeans, which sit like a resting dancer on the floor right where he's stepped out of them—*Psst don't,* the sprinklers warn—but what choice does she have, really—a young woman at the crossroads, on the lookout for signs? She bends, picks up the jeans, goes through the pockets: six singles, coins, a book of matches, and . . . ah, here it is:

A punch card for something charmingly called ASSTACULAR: THE SOUTHLAND'S FINEST IN LIVE NUDE ENTERTAINMENT. Daryl's diversion. She turns the card over. Claire doesn't have much of an instinct for the gradations of the adult entertainment industry, but she imagines the employment of punch cards doesn't exactly distinguish ASSTACULAR as the Four Seasons of titty bars. Oh, and look: Daryl is just two punches from a free lap dance. How excellent for him! She leaves the card next to the snoring Daryl, on her pillow, in the indentation left by her head.

Then Claire starts for the bathroom, officially adding Daryl to her deal with Fate, like a hostage (*Bring me a great film idea today or the strip-clubbing boyfriend gets it!*). She pictures the names on her schedule, and wonders if one will magically step up. She imagines them as fixed points on a map: her nine thirty having an egg-white omelet as he goes over his pitch in Culver City, her ten fifteen doing tai chi in Manhattan Beach, her eleven rubbing one off in the shower in Silver Lake. It's liberating to pretend her decision is up to them now, that she's done all she can, and Claire feels almost free, stepping openly, nakedly, into the capricious arms of Destiny—or at least into a hot shower.

And that's when a single wistful thought escapes her otherwise made-up mind: a wish, or maybe a prayer, that amid today's crap she might hear just one . . . decent . . . *pitch*—one idea for a *great film*—so she won't have to quit the only job she's ever wanted in her entire life.

Outside, the sprinklers spit laughter against the rock garden.

Also naked, eight hundred miles away in Beaverton, Oregon, Claire's last appointment of the day, her four P.M., can't decide what to wear. Not quite thirty, Shane Wheeler is tall, lean, and a little feral-looking, narrow face framed by an ocean-chop of brown hair and two table-leg sideburns. For twenty minutes, Shane has been coaxing an outfit from this autumn-leaf pile of discarded clothes: wrinkly polos, quirky secondhand Ts, faux Western button shirts, boot-cut jeans, skinny jeans, torn jeans, slacks, khakis, and cords, none of it quite right for the too-talented-to-care nonchalance he imagines is appropriate for his first-ever Hollywood pitch meeting.

Shane absentmindedly rubs the tattoo on his left forearm, the word *ACT* inked in elaborate gangster calligraphy, a reference to his father's favorite Bible passage and, until recently, Shane's life motto—*Act as if ye have faith and it shall be given to you.*

His was an outlook fed by years of episodic TV, by encouraging teachers and counselors, by science-fair ribbons, participant medals, and soccer and basketball trophies—and, most of all, by two attentive and dutiful parents, who raised their five perfect children with the belief—hell, with the birthright—that as long as they had faith in themselves, they could be anything they wanted to be.

So in high school, Shane acted as if he were a distance runner and lettered twice, acted as if he were an A student and pulled them, acted as if a certain cheerleader was in his wheelhouse and *she asked him* to a dance, acted as if he were a shoo-in for Cal-Berkeley and got in and for Sigma Nu and they pledged him, acted as if he spoke Italian and studied abroad for a year, acted as if he were a writer and got accepted to the University of Arizona's MFA creative writing program, acted as if he were in love and got married.

But recently, fissures have appeared in this philosophy—faith proving to be not nearly enough—and it was in the run-up to his divorce that his soon-to-be ex-wife (*So tired of your shit, Shane . . .*) dropped a bombshell: the Bible phrase he and his father endlessly quoted, "Act as if ye have faith . . . ," never actually *appears* in the Bible. Rather, as far as she could tell, it came from the closing argument given by the Paul Newman character in the film *The Verdict*.

This revelation didn't *cause* Shane's trouble, but the news did seem to explain it somehow. This is what happens when your life is authored not by God but by David Mamet: you can't find a teaching job and your marriage dissolves just as your student loans come due and the project you've worked on for six years, your MFA thesis—a book of linked short stories called *Linked*—is rejected by the literary agent you've secured (Agent: *This book doesn't work.* Shane: *You mean, in your opinion.* Agent: *I mean in English*). Divorced, jobless, and broke, his literary ambition scuttled, Shane saw his decision to become a writer as a six-year detour to nowhere. He was in the first funk of his life, unable to even get out of bed without ACT to spur him on. It fell to his mother to yank him out of it, convincing him to go on antidepressants and hopefully rescuing the blithely confident young man she and his father had raised.

"Look, it's not like we were a religious family anyway. We only went to church on Christmas and Easter. So your dad got that saying from a thirty-year-old movie instead of a two-thousand-year-old book? That doesn't mean it isn't true, does it? In fact, maybe that makes it *more* true."

Inspired by his mother's deep faith *in him*, and by the low dose of selective serotonin reuptake inhibitor he'd recently begun taking, Shane had what could only be described as an epiphany:

Weren't movies his generation's faith anyway—its true religion? Wasn't the theater our temple, the one place we enter separately but emerge from two hours later together, with the same experience, same guided emotions, same moral? A million schools taught ten million curricula, a million churches featured ten thousand sects with a billion sermons—but the same movie showed in every mall in the country. And we all saw it! That summer, the one you'll never forget, every movie house beamed the same set of thematic and narrative images—the same *Avatar*, same *Harry Potter*, same *Fast and the Furious*, flickering pictures stitched in our minds that replaced our own memories, archetypal stories that became our shared history, that taught us what to expect from life, that defined our values. What was that but a religion?

Also, movies paid better than books.

And so Shane decided to take his talents to Hollywood. He started by contacting his old writing professor, Gene Pergo, who had tired of being a teacher and ignored essayist and had written a thriller called *Night Ravagers* (hot-rodding zombies cruise postapocalyptic Los Angeles looking for human survivors to enslave), selling the film rights for more than he'd made in a decade of academia and small-house publishing, and quitting his teaching job midsemester. At the time, Shane was in the second year of his MFA, and Gene's defection was what passed for scandal in the program—faculty and students alike huffing at the way Gene shat all over the cathedral of literature.

Shane tracked Professor Pergo down in LA, where he was adapting the second book of what was now a trilogy—*Night Ravagers 2: Streets of Reckoning (3-D)*. Gene said that in the last two years, he'd heard from "roughly every student and colleague I ever worked with"; those most scandalized by his literary abdication had been the first to call. Gene gave Shane the name of a film agent, Andrew Dunne, and the titles of screenwriting books by Syd Field and Robert McKee, and, best of all, the chapter on pitching from the producer Michael Deane's inspiring autobiography, *The Deane's Way: How I Pitched Modern Hollywood to America and How You Can Pitch Success Into Your Life Too*. It was a line in Deane's book—"In the room the only thing you need to believe is yourself. YOU are your story"—that had Shane recalling his old ACT self-confidence, honing his pitch, looking for apartments in LA, even phoning his old literary agent. (Shane: *I thought you should know, I am officially done with books.* Agent: *I'll inform the Nobel Committee.*)

And today it all pays off, with Shane's first-ever pitch to a Hollywood producer, and not just any producer, but Michael Deane himself—or at least Deane's assistant, Claire Somebody. Today, with Claire Somebody's help, Shane Wheeler takes the first step out of the dank closet of books into the brightly lit ballroom of film—

As soon as he figures out what to wear.

As if on cue, Shane's mother calls down the stairs: "Your dad's ready to take you to the airport." When he doesn't answer, she tries again: "You don't want to be late, honey." Then: "I made French toast." And: "Are you still deciding what to wear?"

"Just a minute!" Shane calls, and in a burst of frustration—mostly with himself—he kicks at the pile of clothes. In the ensuing explosion of fabric, the perfect outfit seems to float in midair: whisker-washed boot-cut denims and a double-yoke Western snap shirt. Perfect with his double-buckle biker boots. Shane dresses quickly, turns to the mirror, and rolls his sleeve so he can just see the right cross of the *T* in his tattoo. "Now," Shane Wheeler says to his dressed self, "let's go pitch a movie."

Claire's Coffee Bean is crowded at seven thirty, every table sporting a sullen white screenwriter in glasses, every pair of glasses aimed at a Mac Pro laptop, every Mac Pro open to a digitized Final Draft script—every table, that is, but the small one in back, where two crisp businessmen in gray suits face an empty chair meant for her.

Claire strides over, her skirt drawing the eyes of the Coffee Bean screenwriters. She hates heels, feels like a shoed horse. She arrives and smiles as they stand. "Hello, James. Hello, Bryan."

They sit and apologize for taking so long to get back to her, but the rest is just as she imagined—*great résumé, wonderful references, impressive interview.* They've met with the full museum planning board, and after much deliberation (they offered it to someone who passed, she figures) they've decided to offer her the job. And with that James nods at Bryan, who slides a manila envelope forward on the little round table. Claire picks up the envelope, opens it a bit, just enough to see the words "Confidentiality Agreement." Before she can go further, James puts out a cautioning hand. "There is one thing you should know before you look at our offer," he says, and for the first time one of them breaks eye contact: Bryan, looking around the room to see who might be listening.

Shit. Claire riffles through worst-case scenarios: *The pay is in cocaine; she has to kill the interim curator first; it's a porn film museum—*

Instead, James says, "Claire, how much do you know about Scientology?"

Ten minutes later—having begged the weekend to think over their generous offer—Claire is driving to work, thinking: This doesn't change anything, does it? Okay, so her dream film museum is a front for a cult—wait, that's not fair. She knows Scientologists and they're no more cultish than the stiff Lutherans on her mother's side or her father's secular Jews. But isn't that how it will be perceived? That she's managing a museum full of the shit Tom Cruise couldn't unload at his garage sale?

James insisted that the museum would have no connection to the church, except to provide initial funding; that the collection would start with the donations of some church members, but the vast majority of the museum would be up to her to build. "This is the church's way of giving back to an industry that nourished our members for years," Bryan said. And they loved her ideas—interactive CG exhibits for kids, a Silent Film vault, a rotating weekly film series, a dedicated film festival each year. She sighs; of all the things they could be, why Scientologists?

Claire mulls as she drives, zombie-like—all basic animal reflex. Her commute to the studio is a second-nature maze of cut-offs and lane changes, shoulders, commuter lanes, residential streets, alleys, bike lanes, and parking lots, devised to get her to the studio each day precisely eighteen minutes after she leaves her condo.

With a nod to the security guard, she drives through the studio gate and parks. She grabs her bag and walks toward the office, even her footfalls deliberating (*quit, stay, quit, stay*). Michael Deane Productions is housed in an old writer's bungalow on the Universal lot, wedged between soundstages, offices, and film sets. Michael doesn't work for the studio anymore, but he made so much money for it in the 1980s and 1990s that they've agreed to keep him around, a scythe on the wall of a tractor plant. The lot office is part of a first-look production deal Michael signed a few years back when he needed cash, giving the studio the first crack at whatever he produced (not much, as it turned out).

Inside the office, Claire turns on the lights, slides behind her desk, and switches on her computer. She goes straight to the Thursday night box-office numbers, early openers, and weekend holdovers, looking for some sign of hope that she might have missed, a last-second break in trend—but the numbers show what they've shown for years: it's all kid stuff, all presold comic-book sequel 3-D CGI crap, all within a range of algorithmic box-office projections based on past-performance-trailer-poster-foreign-market-test-audience reaction. Movies are nothing more than concession-delivery now, ads for new toys, video game launches. Adults will wait three weeks to get a decent film on demand, or they'll watch smart TV—and so what passes for theatrical releases are hopped-up fantasy video games for gonad-swollen boys and their bulimic dates. Film—her first love—is dead.

She can pinpoint the day she fell: 1992, May 14, one A.M., two days before her tenth birthday, when she heard what sounded like laughter in the living room, and came out of her bedroom to find her father crying and nursing a tall glass of something dark, watching an old movie on TV—*C'mere, Punkin*—Claire sitting next to him as they quietly watched the last two-thirds of *Breakfast at Tiffany's*. Claire was amazed at the life she was seeing on that little screen, as if she'd imagined it *without ever knowing*. This was the power of film: it was like déjà vu dreaming. Three weeks later, her father left the family to marry chesty Leslie, the twenty-four-year-old daughter of his former law partner, but in Claire's mind it would always be Holly Golightly who stole her daddy.

We belong to nobody and nobody belongs to us.

She studied film at a small design school, then got her master's at UCLA, and was headed straight into the doctoral program there when two things revealed themselves in rapid succession. First, her father had a minor stroke, giving Claire a glimpse of his mortality and, by extension, her own. And then she had a vision of herself thirty years in the future: a spinster librarian in an apartment full of cats named after New Wave directors. (*Godard, leave Rivette's chew toy alone—*)

Recalling her *Breakfast at Tiffany's* ambition, Claire quit her doctoral program and ventured out of the cloistered academic world to take one shot at *making* films rather than simply studying them.

She started by applying to one of the big talent agencies, the agent who interviewed her barely glancing at her three-page CV before saying, "Claire, do you know what coverage is?" The agent spoke as if Claire were a six-year-old, explaining that Hollywood was "a very busy place," people attended by agents, managers, accountants, and lawyers. Publicists handled images, assistants ran errands, groundskeepers mowed lawns, maids cleaned houses, au pairs raised kids, dog walkers walked dogs. And each day these busy people got stacks of scripts and books and treatments; didn't it make sense that they'd need help with those, too? "Claire," the agent said, "I'm going to let you in on a secret: *No one here reads.*"

Having seen a number of recent movies, Claire didn't think that was a secret.

But she kept that answer to herself and became a coverage reader, writing summaries of books, scripts, and treatments, comparing them with hit movies, grading the characters, dialogue, and commercial potential, allowing agents and their clients to seem as if they'd not only read the material but taken a grad-level seminar on it:

Title: SECOND PERIOD: DEATH
Genre: YOUNG ADULT HORROR
Logline: The Breakfast Club *meets* Nightmare on Elm Street *in* SECOND PERIOD: DEATH, *the story of a group of students who must battle a deranged substitute teacher who may in fact be a vampire . . .*

Then, only three months into the job, Claire was reading a middlebrow bestseller, some big gothic chub of sentimentality, and she got to the ridiculous *deus ex machina* ending (a windstorm dislodges a power pole and an electrical line whips the villain's face) and she just . . . changed it. It was as simple as being in a clothing store, seeing an uneven stack of sweaters, and just straightening them. In her synopsis, she gave the heroine a part in her own rescue and thought nothing more about it.

But two days later, she got a call. "This is Michael Deane," the voice on the other end of the phone said. "Do you know who I am?"

Of course she did, although she was surprised to hear that he was still alive: the man once referred to as "the Deane of Hollywood," a man who'd had a hand in some of the biggest films of the late twentieth century—all those mobsters, monsters, and meet-cute romances—a former studio executive and capital-*P Producer* from an era when that title meant a fit-throwing, career-making, actress-bagging, coke-snorting *player.*

"And you," he said, "are the coverage girl who just fixed the bound pile of shit I paid a hundred K for." And like that, she had a job, on a studio lot of all places, with Michael Deane of all people, as his chief development assistant, personally assigned to help Michael "get my ass back in the game."

At first, she loved her new job. After the slog of grad school, it was thrilling—the meetings, the buzz. Every day, scripts came in, and treatments and books. And the pitches! She loved the pitches—*So there's this guy and he wakes to find that his wife's a vampire*—writers and producers sweeping into the office (bottled water for everyone!) to share their visions—*Over credits we see an alien ship and we cut to this guy, sitting at a computer*—and even after she realized these pitches were going nowhere, Claire still enjoyed them. Pitching was a form unto itself, a kind of existential, present-tense performance art. It didn't matter how old the story was: they'd pitch a film about Napoleon in the present tense, a caveman movie, even the Bible: *So there's this guy, Jesus, and one day he rises from the dead . . . like a zombie—*

Here she was, barely twenty-eight, working on a studio lot, not doing what she'd dreamed, exactly, but doing what people did in this business: taking meetings, reading scripts, and hearing pitches—pretending to like everything while finding myriad reasons to make nothing. And then the worst possible thing happened: success—

She can still hear the pitch: *It's called Hookbook. It's like a video Facebook for hookups. Anyone who posts a video on the site is also auditioning for our TV show. We snatch up the best-looking, horniest people, film their dates, and follow the whole thing: hookups, breakups, weddings. Best of all, it casts itself. We don't pay anyone a cent!*

Michael set up the show at a secondary cable channel, and just like that he had his first hit in a decade, a steaming pile of TV/Web synchronicity that Claire can't bear to watch. Michael Deane was back! And Claire saw why people worked so hard to *not* get things made—because once you did one thing, that became your thing, the only thing you were capable of doing. Now Claire spends her days listening to pitches for *Eat It* (obese people racing to eat huge meals) and *Rich MILF, Poor MILF* (horny middle-aged women set up on dates with horny young men).

It's gotten so bad she's started to actually look forward to Wild Pitch Fridays, the one day she still might listen in on a random pitch for a *film*. Unfortunately, most of these Friday pitches come from Michael's past: people he's met in AA, people he owes favors to, or who owe him favors, people he sees at the club, old golf partners, old coke dealers, women he slept with in the sixties and seventies, men he slept with in the eighties, friends of ex-wives and of his three legitimate children or of his three older, less-than-legitimate ones, his doctor's kid, his gardener's kid, his pool boy's kid, his kid's pool boy.

Take, for instance, Claire's nine thirty: a liver-spotted TV writer who played squash with Michael during the Reagan years and now wants to make a reality show about his grandkids (proudly displaying their pictures on the conference table). "Cute," Claire says, and "Aw," and "How sweet," and "Yes, they do seem to be over-diagnosing autism now."

But Claire can't complain about meetings like this unless she's ready to hear the Michael Deane Loyalty Lecture: how, in this cold town, Michael Deane is a man who never forgets his friends, holding them in tight clench and staring into their eyes: *You know I've always loved your work, (NAME HERE). Come down next Friday and see my girl Claire.* Then Michael takes a business card, signs it, and presses it into the person's hand, and just like that, they're in. People with a signed Michael Deane business card might want tickets to a premiere, or the number of a certain actor, or a signed movie poster, but usually what they want is the same thing everyone here wants—to *pitch*.

To pitch here is to live. People pitch their kids into good schools, pitch offers on houses they can't afford, and when they're caught in the arms of the wrong person, pitch unlikely explanations. Hospitals pitch birthing centers, daycares pitch love, high schools pitch success . . . car dealerships pitch luxury, counselors self-esteem, masseuses happy endings, cemeteries eternal rest . . . It's endless, the pitching—endless, exhilarating, soul-sucking, and as unrelenting as death. As ordinary as morning sprinklers.

A signed Michael Deane business card is a form of currency on this lot—the older the better, in her estimation. When Claire's ten fifteen flashes a card from Michael's days as a studio exec, she hopes for a movie pitch, but the man launches into a reality pitch so awful it might just be brilliant: "*Paranoid Palace*: we take mental patients off their meds, put them in a house with hidden cameras, and fuck with their minds; turn on a light and music comes on, open the refrigerator and the toilet flushes . . ."

And speaking of meds, her eleven thirty seems to have gone off his: Michael Deane's neighbor's son striding in wearing a cape and a chinstrap beard, never making eye contact as he pitches a television miniseries about a fantasy world he's created all in his head ("If I write it down someone will steal it"), called *The Veraglim Quatrology*—*Veraglim* being an alternate universe in the eighth-string dimension, *Quatrology* being "like a trilogy, except with four stories instead of three." As he drones on about the physics of this fantasy world (in Veraglim, there's an invisible king, an ongoing centaur rebellion, and male penises are erect for one week every year), Claire glances down at the buzzing phone in her lap. If she were still in the market for signs, this would be a good one: her career-challenged, strip-clubbing lunk of a boyfriend has just gotten up—at twenty minutes to noon—and texted her this one-word unpunctuated question: *milk*. She pictures Daryl in front of the refrigerator in his underwear, seeing no milk and texting this inane question. Where does he think this extra milk might be? She types back *washing machine*, and while the Veraglim guy drones on about his schizoid fantasy, Claire can't help but wonder if Fate isn't fucking with her now, mocking the deal she made by giving her the worst Wild Pitch Friday in history—maybe the worst day of any kind since eighth grade, when an alarmingly gushy period arrived during a coed PE kickball game and dreamy Marshall Aiken pointed at the blossom on her gym shorts and screamed to the teacher, *Claire's hemorrhaging*—because it's her brain hemorrhaging now, bleeding out all over the conference table as this wing-nut launches into book two of *The Veraglim Quatrology* (*Flandor unsheathes his shadow-saber!*) and another text arrives from Daryl, flashing on the BlackBerry in her lap: *cereal.*

Jet tires chirp, grab the runway, and Shane Wheeler jerks awake and checks his watch. Still good. Yeah, his plane's an hour late, but he's got three hours until his meeting, and he's a mere fourteen miles away now. How long can it take to drive fourteen miles? At the gate he uncoils, deplanes, and makes his way in a dream down the long, tiled airport tunnel, through baggage claim and a revolving door, onto a sunlit curb, jumps a bus to the rental-car center, falls in line with the smiling Disney-bounders (who must've seen the same $24 online rental-car coupon), and when his turn in line comes, slides his license and credit card to the rental clerk. She says his name with such significance ("Shane *Wheeler?*") that for a deluded moment he imagines he's traveled forward in time and fame, and she's somehow heard of him—but of course she's just happy to find his reservation. We live in a world of banal miracles.

"Here for business or pleasure, Mr. Wheeler?"

"Redemption," Shane says.

"Insurance?"

Coverage declined, upgrade shaken off, pricey GPS and refueling options rejected, Shane heads off with a rental agreement, a set of keys, and a map that looks like it was drawn by a ten-year-old on meth. Ensconced in a rented red Kia, Shane slides the driver's seat into the same zip code as the steering wheel, takes a breath, starts the car, and rehearses the first words of his first-ever pitch: *So there's this guy . . .*

An hour later, he's somehow *farther* from his appointment. Shane's Kia is gridlocked and, he thinks, might even be pointed in the wrong direction (the GPS now seeming like a screaming deal). Shane tosses aside the worthless rental-car map and tries Gene

Pergo's cell: voice mail. He tries the agent who set up the meeting, but the agent's assistant says, "Sorry, I don't have Andrew," whatever that means. He begrudgingly tries his mom's cell, then his dad's, and finally, the home number: *Shit, where are they?* The next number that pops into his head is his ex-wife's. Saundra is the last person he wants to call right now—but that's just how desperate he feels.

His name must pop up on her phone still, because her first words are: "Tell me you're calling because you have the rest of the money you owe me."

This is what he hoped to avoid—the whole who-ruined-whose-credit and who-stole-whose-car business that has colored their every conversation for a year. He sighs. "As a matter of fact, I'm in the process of getting your money right now, Saundra."

"You're not giving plasma again?"

"No. I'm in LA, pitching a movie."

She laughs and then realizes he's serious. "Wait. You're writing *a movie* now?"

"No. I'm *pitching* a movie. First you pitch it, then you write it."

"No wonder movies suck," she says. This is classic Saundra: a waitress with a poet's pretensions. They met in Tucson, where she worked at Cup of Heaven, the coffee shop where Shane went to write every morning. He fell for, in order: her legs, her laugh, and the way she idealized writers and was willing to support his work.

For her part—she said at the end—she fell mostly for his bullshit.

"Look," Shane says, "could you just hold the cultural criticism and MapQuest Universal City for me?"

"You seriously have a meeting in Hollywood?"

"Yes," Shane says. "With a big producer on a studio lot."

"What are you wearing?"

He sighs and tells her what Gene Pergo told him, that it doesn't matter what one wears to a pitch meeting (*Unless you own a bullshit-proof suit*).

"I'll bet I know what you're wearing," Saundra says, and proceeds to describe his outfit down to the socks.

Shane is regretting this call. "Just help me figure out where I'm going."

"What's your movie called?"

Shane sighs. He has to remember they're no longer married; her bitter-cool ironic streak has no power over him anymore. *"Donner!"*

Saundra is quiet a moment. But she knows his interests, his reading table obsessions. "You're writing a movie about cannibals?"

"I told you, I'm *pitching* a movie, and it's not about cannibals."

Clearly, the Donner Party could be a tough subject for a film. But pitches are all in *the take*, as Michael Deane wrote in the oft-copied chapter fourteen of his memoir/self-help classic, *The Deane's Way*:

> Ideas are sphincters. Every asshole has one. Your take is what counts. I could walk into Fox today and sell a movie about a restaurant that serves baked monkey balls if I had the right take.

And Shane has the perfect "take." *Donner!* will concern itself not with the classic Donner Party story—all those people stuck at the awful camp, freezing and starving to death and finally eating one another—but with the story of a cabinetmaker in the party, named William Eddy, who leads a group of people, mostly young women, on a harrowing, heroic journey out of the mountains to safety, and then—*attention, third act!*—when he's regained his strength, returns to rescue his wife and kids! As Shane pitched this idea over the phone to the agent Andrew Dunne, he felt himself becoming animated by its power: *It's a story of triumph*, he told the agent, *an epic story of resiliency! Courage! Determination! Love!* That very afternoon the agent set up a meeting with Claire Silver, a development assistant for . . . get this . . . *Michael Deane!*

"Huh," Saundra says when she's heard the whole story. "And you really think you can sell this thing?"

"Yes. I do," Shane says, and he does. It's a key sub-tenet of Shane's movie-inspired ACT-as-if faith in himself: his generation's profound belief in *secular episodic providence*, the idea—honed by decades of entertainment—that after thirty or sixty or one hundred and twenty minutes of complications, things generally work out.

"Okay," Saundra says—still not entirely immune to the undeniable charm of Shane's deluded self-belief—and she gives him the MapQuest instructions. When he thanks her, Saundra says, "Good luck today, Shane."

"Thanks," Shane says. And, as always, his ex-wife's passionless, entirely genuine goodwill leaves him feeling like the loneliest person on the planet.

It's over. What a stupid deal: one day to find a great idea for a film? How many times has Michael told her, *We're not in the film business, we're in the buzz business.* And yes, the day's not quite over, but her two forty-five is picking at an open scab on his forehead while pitching a TV procedural (*So there's this cop*—pick—*a zombie cop*) and Claire feels the loss of something vital in her, the death of some optimism. Her four P.M. looks like a no-show (somebody named Shawn Weller . . .) and when Claire checks her watch—four ten—it is through bleary, sleepy eyes. So that's it. She's done. She won't say anything to Michael about her disillusionment; what would be the point? She'll quietly give two weeks, box up her things, and slink out of this office into a job warehousing souvenirs for the Scientologists.

And what about Daryl? Does she dump him today, too? Can she? She's tried breaking up with him recently, but it never takes. It's like cutting soup—nothing to push against. She'll say, *Daryl, we need to talk,* and he just smiles in that way of his, and they end up having sex. She even suspects it turns him on a little. She'll say, *I'm not sure this is working,* and he'll start taking off his shirt. She'll complain about the strip clubs and he'll just look amused. (Her:

Promise me you won't go again? Him: *I promise I won't make you go.*) He doesn't fight, doesn't lie, doesn't care; the man eats, breathes, screws. How do you disengage from someone who's already so profoundly disengaged?

She met him on what is now looking like the only movie she'll ever work on—*Night Ravagers.* Claire has always been weak for ink, and Daryl, who had a walk-on (lurch-on? stagger-on?) as Zombie #14, had these great ropy, tattooed arms. She'd dated mostly smart, sensitive types (who made her smart sensitivity seem redundant) and a couple of slick industry types (whose ambition was like a second dick). She hadn't yet tried the unemployed-actor type. And wasn't this what she had in mind when she left the cocoon of film school in the first place, tasting the visceral, the worldly? And at first, visceral-worldly was as good as advertised (she recalls wondering: *Was I ever even touched before this?*). Thirty-six hours later, as she lay postcoital in bed with the best-looking guy she's ever slept with (sometimes she just likes to *look* at him), Daryl matter-of-factly admitted that he'd just been tossed out by his girlfriend and had no place to live. Almost three years later, *Night Ravagers* remains Daryl's best acting credit, and Zombie #14 remains a gorgeous lump in her bed.

No, she won't break up with Daryl. Not today. Not after the Scientologists and the proud grandpas, the lunatics, zombie cops, and skin-pickers. She'll give Daryl one more chance, go home, bring him a beer, nestle into his broad, tatted shoulder; together they'll watch the *TeeVee* (he likes those trucks that drive across the ice on the Discovery Channel) and she'll have that tenuous connection to life, at least. No, it's not the stuff of dreams, but it's a perfectly American thing to do, a whole nation of *Night Ravager* zombies racing across the horizon, burning through peak oil to get home and sit dull-eyed, watching *Ice Road Truckers* and *Hookbook* on the fifty-five-inch flat (the *Double Nickel,* as Daryl calls it, the *Sammy Hagar*).

Claire grabs her coat and starts for the door. She pauses, glances back over her shoulder at the office where she thought she might get to make something great—*silly Holly Golightly dream*—and once more checks her watch: 4:17 and counting. Outside, she locks the door behind her, takes a breath, and goes.

The clock in Shane's rented Kia also reads 4:17—he's more than a quarter-hour late, and he's dying. "Shit shit shit!" He pounds the steering wheel. Even after finally getting turned around, he got caught in several traffic snarls and took the wrong exit. By the time he rolls up to the studio gate and the security guard shrugs and informs him that his destiny is at the *other* gate, he is twenty-four minutes late, sweating through his carefully chosen *whatever-clothing*. When he arrives at the proper gate, he's twenty-eight minutes late—thirty when he finally gets his ID back from the second security guard, shakily slaps a parking pass on his dash, and pulls into the lot.

Shane is only two hundred feet away now from Michael Deane's bungalow, but he stumbles out of his car the wrong way, wanders among the big soundstages—it is the cleanest warehouse district in the world—and finally walks in a circle, toward a nest of bungalows and a tram filled with fanny-packed tourists on a studio tour, holding up cameras and cell phones, listening to a microphone-aided guide tell apocryphal stories of bygone magic. The camera-people listen breathlessly, waiting for some connection to their own pasts (*I loved that show!*), and when Shane staggers up to their tram, the star-alert tourists run his disheveled hair, broad sideburns, and thin, frantic features through the thousands of celebrity faces they keep on file—*Is that a Sheen? A Baldwin? A celebrity rehabber?*—and while they can't quite match Shane's oddly appealing features with anyone famous, they take pictures anyway, just in case.

The tour guide chutters into his headset, telling the tram-people in something like English how a certain famous breakup scene from a certain famous television show was famously filmed "right over there," and as Shane approaches, the driver holds up a finger so he can finish his story. Sweating, near tears, in full overheated self-loathing, fighting every urge to call his parents—his ACT resolve now a distant memory—Shane finds himself staring at the tour guide's name tag: ANGEL.

"Excuse me?" Shane says.

Angel covers the headset microphone and says, heavily accented, "Fuck *jou* want?" Angel is roughly his age, so Shane tries for late-twenties camaraderie. "Dude, I'm totally late. Can you help me find Michael Deane's office?"

Something about this question causes another tourist to take Shane's picture. But Angel merely jerks his thumb and drives the tram away, revealing a sign that he was blocking, pointing to a bungalow: MICHAEL DEANE PRODUCTIONS.

Shane looks at his watch. Thirty-six minutes late now. *Shit shit shit.* He runs around the corner and there it is—but blocking the door to the bungalow is an old man with a cane. For a second, Shane thinks it might be Michael Deane himself, even though the agent said Deane wouldn't be at the meeting, that it would just be his development assistant, Claire Something. Anyway, it's not Michael Deane. It's just some old guy, seventy maybe, in a dark gray suit and charcoal fedora, cane draped over his arm, holding a business card. As Shane's feet clack on the pavement, the old man turns and removes his fedora, revealing a shock of slate hair and eyes that are a strange, coral blue.

Shane clears his throat. "Are you going in? 'Cause I . . . I'm very late."

The man holds out a business card: ancient, wrinkled and stained, the type faded. It's from another studio, 20th Century Fox, but the name is right: Michael Deane.

"You're in the right place," Shane says. He presents his own Michael Deane business card—the newer model. "See? He's at *this* studio now."

"Yes, I go this one," says the man, heavily accented, Italian—Shane recognizes it from the year he studied in Florence. He points at the 20th Century Fox card. "They say, go this one." He points to the bungalow. "But . . . is locked."

Shane can't believe it. He steps past the man and tries the door. Yes, locked. Then it's over.

"Pasquale Tursi," says the man, holding out his hand.

Shane shakes it. "Big Loser," he says.

Claire has texted Daryl to ask what he wants for dinner. His answer, *kfc*, is followed by another text: *unrated hookbook*—she's told Daryl that her company is about to stream out an unrated, raunchier version of that show, full of all the nudity and sodden stupidity they couldn't air on regular TV. Fine, she thinks. She'll go back for her company's apocalyptic TV show, then swing through the KFC drive-through, and she'll curl up with Daryl and deal with her life on Monday. She turns her car around, is waved back through security, and parks back in the lot above Michael's bungalow office. She starts back to the office to get the raw DVDs, but when she rounds the path, Claire Silver sees, standing at the door to the bungalow, not one Wild Pitch Friday lost cause . . . but two. She stops, imagines turning around and leaving.

Sometimes she makes a guess about Wild Friday Pitchers, and she does this now: mop-haired sideburns in factory-torn blue jeans and faux Western shirt? *Michael's old coke dealer's son.* And old silver-haired, blue-eyed charcoal suit? This one's tougher. *Some guy Michael met in 1965 while getting rimmed at an orgy at Tony Curtis's house?*

The frantic younger guy sees her approaching. "Are you Claire Silver?"

No, she thinks. "Yes," she says.

"I'm Shane Wheeler, and I am *so* sorry. There was traffic and I got lost and . . . Is there any chance we could still have our meeting?"

She looks helplessly at the older guy, who removes his hat and extends the business card. "Pasquale Tursi," he says. "I am look . . . for . . . Mr. Deane."

Great: two lost causes. A kid who can't find his way around LA, and a time-traveling Italian. Both men stare at her, hold out Michael Deane business cards. She takes the cards. The young guy's card is, predictably, newer. She turns it over. Below Michael's signature is a note from the agent Andrew Dunne. She recently screwed Andrew, not in that she had sex with him—that would be forgivable—but she asked him to hold off circulating a sizzle reel for his client's unscripted fashion show, *If the Shoe Fits*, while Michael considered it; instead, he optioned a competing show, *Shoe Fetish*, which effectively killed Andrew's client's idea. The agent's note reads: "Hope you enjoy!" A payback pitch: Oh, this must be horrible.

The other card is a mystery, the oldest Michael Deane business card she's ever seen, faded and wrinkled, from Michael's *first* studio, 20th Century Fox. It's the job that catches her—publicity? Michael started in publicity? How old is this card?

Honestly, after the day she's had, if Daryl had texted anything other than *kfc* and *unrated hookbook*, she might just have told these two guys the game was up—they'd missed today's charity wagon. But she thinks again about Fate and the deal she made. Who knows? Maybe one of these guys . . . right. She unlocks the door and asks their names again. Sloppy sideburns = Shane. Popping eyes = Pasquale.

"Why don't you both come on back to the conference room," she says.

In the office, they sit beneath posters for Michael's classic movies (*Mind Blow*; *The Love Burglar*). No time for pleasantries; it's the first pitch meeting in history in which no water is proffered. "Mr. Tursi, would you like to go first?"

He looks around, confused. "Mr. Deane . . . is not here?" His accent is heavy, as if he's chewing on each word.

"I'm afraid he's not here today. Are you an old friend of his?"

"I meet him . . ." He stares at the ceiling. "Eh, *nel sessantadue*."

"Nineteen sixty-two," says the young guy. When Claire looks curiously at him, Shane shrugs. "I spent a year studying in Italy."

Claire imagines Michael and this old guy, back in the day, tooling around Rome in a convertible, screwing Italian actresses, drinking grappa. Now Pasquale Tursi looks disoriented. "He say . . . you . . . ever need anything."

"Sure," Claire says. "I promise I'll tell Michael all about your pitch. Why don't you just start at the beginning?"

Pasquale squints as if he doesn't understand. "My English . . . is long time . . ."

"The beginning," Shane tells Pasquale. "*L'inizio.*"

"There's this guy . . ." Claire urges.

"A woman," Pasquale Tursi says. "She come to my village, Porto Vergogna . . . in . . ." He looks over at Shane for help.

"Nineteen sixty-two?" Shane says again.

"Yes. She is . . . beautiful. And I am build . . . eh . . . a beach, yes? And tennis?" He rubs his brow, the story already getting away from him. "She is . . . in the *cinema*?"

"An actress?" Shane Wheeler asks.

"Yes." Pasquale Tursi nods and stares off into space.

Claire checks her watch and does her best to jumpstart his pitch: "So . . . an actress comes to this town and she falls for this guy who's building a beach?"

Pasquale looks back at Claire. "No. For me . . . maybe, yes. E— *l'attimo,* yes?" He looks at Shane for help. "*L'attimo che dura per sempre.*"

"The moment that lasts forever," Shane says quietly.

"Yes," Pasquale says, and nods. "Forever."

Claire feels pinched by those words in such close proximity, *moment* and *forever.* Not exactly KFC and Hookbook. She suddenly feels angry—at her silly ambition and romanticism, at her taste in men, at the loopy Scientologists, at her father for watching that stupid movie and then leaving, at herself for coming back to the office—at herself because she keeps hoping for better. And Michael:

Goddamn Michael and his goddamn job and his goddamn business cards and his goddamn old buzzard friends and the goddamn favors he owes the goddamn people he screwed back when he screwed everything that screwed.

Pasquale Tursi sighs. "She was sick."

Claire flushes with impatience: "With what? Lupus? Psoriasis? Cancer?"

At the word *cancer*, Pasquale looks up suddenly and mutters in Italian, *"Sì. Ma non è così semplice—"*

And that's when the kid Shane interrupts. "Uh, Ms. Silver? I don't think this guy's pitching." And he says to the man, in slow Italian, *"Questo è realmente accaduto? Non in un film?"*

Pasquale nods. *"Sì. Sono qui per trovarla."*

"Yeah, this really happened," Shane tells Claire. He turns back to Pasquale. *"Non l'ha più vista da allora?"* Pasquale shakes his head no, and Shane turns back to Claire again. "He hasn't seen this actress in almost fifty years. He came to find her."

"Come si chiama?" Shane Wheeler asks.

The Italian looks from Claire to Shane and back again. "Dee Moray," he says.

And Claire feels a tug in her chest, some deeper shift, a cracking of her hard-earned cynicism, of this anxious tension she's been fighting. The actress's name means nothing to her, but the old guy seems utterly changed by saying it aloud, as if he hasn't said the name in years. Something about the name affects her, too—a crush of romantic recognition, those words, *moment* and *forever*—as if she can *feel* fifty years of longing in that one name, fifty years of an ache that lies dormant in her, too, maybe lies dormant in everyone until it's cracked open like this—and so weighted is this moment she has to look to the ground or else feel the tears burn her own eyes, and at that moment Claire glances at Shane, and sees that he must feel it, too, the name hanging in the air for just a moment . . . among the three of them . . . and then floating to the floor like a falling leaf, the Italian watching it settle, Claire guessing, hoping, praying the old Italian will say the name once again, more quietly this time—to underline its importance, the way it's so often done in scripts—but he doesn't do this. He just stares at the floor, where the name has fallen, and it occurs to Claire Silver that she's seen too goddamn many movies.

3

The Hotel Adequate View

April 1962
Porto Vergogna, Italy

All day he waited for her to come downstairs, but she spent that first afternoon and evening alone in her room on the third floor. And so Pasquale went about his business, which seemed not like business at all but the random behavior of a lunatic. Still, he didn't know what else to do, so he threw rocks at the breakwater in the cove and he chipped away at his tennis court and he glanced up occasionally at the whitewashed shutters over the windows in her room. In the late afternoon, when the feral cats were sunning themselves on the rocks, a cool spring wind chopped the surface of the sea and Pasquale retreated to the piazza to smoke alone, before the fishermen came to drink. At the Adequate View, there was no noise from upstairs, no sign at all that the beautiful American was even up there, and Pasquale worried again that he had imagined the whole thing—Orenzio's boat lurching into the cove, the tall, slender American walking up the narrow staircase to the best room in the hotel, on the third floor, pushing open the window shutters, breathing in the salty air, pronouncing it "Lovely," Pasquale saying she should let him know if there was anything "upon you are happy to having," and her saying, "Thank you," and pushing the door closed, leaving him to descend the tight, dark staircase alone.

Pasquale was horrified to find that, for dinner, his aunt Valeria was making her signature *ciuppin*, a soup of rockfish, tomatoes, white wine, and olive oil. "You expect me to take your rotten fish-head stew to an American cinema star?"

"She can leave if she doesn't like it," Valeria said. So, at dusk, with the fishermen pulling their boats up into the cove below, Pasquale clicked up the narrow staircase built into the rock wall. He knocked lightly on the third-floor door.

"Yes?" the American called through the door. He heard the bedsprings creak.

Pasquale cleared his throat. "I am sorry for you disturb. You eat antipasti and a soap, yes?"

"Soap?"

Pasquale felt angry that he hadn't talked his aunt out of making the *ciuppin*. "Yes. Is a soap. With fish and *vino*. A fish soap?"

"Oh, *soup*. No. No, thank you. I don't think I can eat anything just yet," she said, her voice muffled through the door. "I don't feel well enough."

"Yes," he said. "I see."

He descended the stairs, saying the word *soup* over and over in his mind. He ate the American's dinner in his own room on the second floor. The *ciuppin* was pretty good. He still got his father's newspapers by mail-boat once a week, and although he didn't study them the way his father had, Pasquale flipped through them, looking for news about the American production of *Cleopatra*. But he found nothing.

Later, he heard clumping around in the *trattoria* and came out, but he knew it wouldn't be Dee Moray; she did not appear to be a clumper. Instead, both tables were full of local fishermen hoping to get a look at the glorious American, their hats on the tables, dirty hair plastered and combed tight to their skulls. Valeria was serving them soup, but the fishermen were really just waiting to talk to Pasquale, since they'd been out in their boats when the American arrived.

"I hear she is two and a half meters tall," said Lugo the Promiscuous War Hero, famous for the dubious claim that he had killed at least one soldier from every major participant in the European theater of World War II. "She is a giant."

"Don't be stupid," Pasquale said as he filled their glasses with wine.

"What is the shape of her breasts?" asked Lugo seriously. "Are they round giants or alert peaks?"

"Let me tell you about American women," said Tommaso the Elder, whose cousin had married an American, making him an expert on American women, along with everything else. "American women cook only one meal a week, but before they marry they perform fellatio. So, as with all life, there is good and there is bad."

"You should eat from a trough like pigs!" Valeria spat from the kitchen.

"Marry me, Valeria!" Tommaso the Elder called back. "I am too old for sex and my hearing will soon be gone. We are made for each other."

The fisherman that Pasquale liked best, thoughtful Tommaso the Communist, was chewing on his pipe. He removed it now to weigh in on the subject. He considered himself something of a film buff and was a fan of Italian neorealism and therefore dismissive of American movies, which he blamed for sparking the dreadful *commedia all'italiana* movement, the antic farces that had replaced the serious existential cinema of the late 1950s. "Listen, Lugo," he said, "if she is an American actress, it means she wears a corset in cowboy films and has talent only for screaming."

"Fine. Let's see those big breasts fill with air when she screams," Lugo said.

"Maybe she will lie naked on Pasquale's beach tomorrow," said Tommaso the Elder, "and we can see for ourselves her giant breasts."

For three hundred years, the fishermen in town had come from a small pool of young men who'd grown up here, fathers handing over their skiffs and eventually their houses to favored sons, usually the eldest, who married the daughters of other fishermen up and down the coast, sometimes bringing them back to Porto Vergogna. Children moved away, but the *villaggio* always maintained a kind of equilibrium and the twenty or so houses stayed full. But after the war, when fishing, like everything else, had become an industry, the family fishermen couldn't compete with the big seiners motoring out of Genoa every week. The restaurants would still buy from a few old fishermen, because tourists liked to see the old men bring in their catches, but this was like working in an amusement park: it wasn't real fishing, and there was no future in it. An entire generation of Porto Vergogna boys had to leave to find work, to La Spezia and Genoa and even farther for jobs in factories and canneries and in the trades. No longer did the favored son want the fishing boat; already six of the houses were empty, boarded, or brought down; more were sure to follow. In February, Tommaso the Communist's last daughter, the unfortunately cross-eyed Ileana, had married a young teacher and moved away to La Spezia, Tommaso sulking for days afterward. And on one of those cool spring mornings, as Pasquale watched the old fishermen scuff and grumble to their boats, it dawned on him: he was the only person under forty left in the whole town.

Pasquale left the fishermen in the *trattoria* to go see his mother, who was in one of her dark periods and had refused to leave her bed for two weeks. When he opened the door, he could see her staring at the ceiling, her wiry gray hair stuck to the pillow behind her, arms crossed over her chest, mouth in the placid death face that she liked to rehearse. "You should get up, Mamma. Come out and eat with us."

"Not today, Pasqo," she rasped. "Today I hope to die." She took a deep breath and opened one eye. "Valeria tells me there is an American in the hotel."

"Yes, Mamma." He checked her bedsores but his aunt had already powdered them.

"A woman?"

"Yes, Mamma."

"Then your father's Americans have finally arrived." She glanced over at the dark window. "He said they would come and here they are. You should marry this woman and go to America to make a proper tennis field."

"No, Mamma. You know I wouldn't—"

"Leave before this place kills you like it killed your father."

"I would never leave you."

"Don't worry about me. I will die soon enough and go to be with your father and with your poor brothers."

"You're not dying," Pasquale said.

"I am already dead inside," she said. "You should push me out into the sea and drown me like that old sick cat of yours."

Pasquale straightened. "You said my cat ran away. While I was at university."

She shot him a glance from the corner of her eye. "It is a saying."

"No. It's not a saying. There is no saying such as that. Did you and Papa drown my cat while I was in Florence?"

"I'm sick, Pasqo! Why do you torment me?"

Pasquale went back to his room. That night he heard footsteps on the third floor as the American went to the bathroom, but the next morning she still hadn't emerged from her room, so he went about his work on the beach. When he returned to the hotel for lunch, his Aunt Valeria said that Dee Moray had come down for an espresso, a piece of torta, and an orange.

"What did she say?" Pasquale asked.

"How would I know? That awful language. Like someone choking on a bone."

Pasquale crept up the stairs and listened at her door, but Dee Moray was quiet.

He went back outside and down to his beach, but it was hard to tell if the currents had taken any more sand away. He climbed up past the hotel onto the boulders where he'd staked out his tennis court. The sun was high over the coast and hidden by wispy clouds, which flattened the sky and made him feel as if he were under glass. He looked down at the stakes that marked his future tennis court and felt ashamed. Even if he *could* build forms high enough to contain the concrete to level his court—six feet high at the edges of the boulders—and managed to cantilever some of the court so that it hung out over the cliff, he would still have to blast away at the cliff side with dynamite to flatten the northeast corner. He wondered if it was possible to have a smaller tennis court. Maybe with smaller rackets?

He had just lit a cigarette to think about it when he saw Oren-zio's mahogany boat round the point up the coast near Vernazza. He watched it angle away from the chop along the shoreline, and he held his breath as it passed Riomaggiore. As it got closer he could see there were two people besides Orenzio in the boat. Were these more Americans coming to his hotel? It was almost too much to hope for. Of course, the boat was likely going past him, to lovely Portovenere, or around the point into La Spezia. But then the boat slowed and curled into his narrow cove.

Pasquale began climbing down from his tennis court, hopping from boulder to boulder. Finally, he walked along the narrow trail down to the shoreline, slowing up when he saw that it wasn't tour-ists in the boat with Orenzio, but two men: Gualfredo the bastard hotelier, and a huge man Pasquale had never seen before. Orenzio tied the boat up and Gualfredo and the big man climbed out.

Gualfredo was all jowls, bald, with a huge brush mustache. The other man, the giant, appeared to be carved from granite. In the boat, Orenzio looked down, as if he couldn't bear to meet Pasquale's eyes.

As Pasquale approached, Gualfredo put his hands out. "So it's true. Carlo Tursi's son returns a man to tend the whore's crack."

Pasquale nodded grimly and formally. "Good day, Signor Gualfredo." He'd never seen the bastard Gualfredo in Porto Ver-gogna before, but the man's story was well known on the coast: his mother had carried on a long affair with a wealthy Milan banker, and to buy her silence the man had given her petty-criminal son interest in hotels in Portovenere, Chiavari, and Monterosso al Mare.

Gualfredo smiled. "You have an American actress in your old whorehouse?"

"Yes," Pasquale said. "We sometimes have American guests."

Gualfredo frowned, his mustache seeming to weigh down his face and his trunk of a neck. He looked over at Orenzio, who pre-tended to be checking the boat motor. "I told Orenzio there must be a mistake. This woman was surely meant to be at my hotel in Portovenere. But he claims that she really wanted to come to this . . ." He looked around. "Village."

"Yes," Pasquale said, "she prefers the quiet."

Gualfredo stepped in closer. "This is not some Swiss farmer on holiday, Pasquale. These Americans expect a level of service you can't provide. Especially the American cinema people. Listen to me: I've been doing this a long time. It would be regrettable if you were to give the Levante a bad reputation."

"We are taking care of her," Pasquale said.

"Then you won't mind if I talk to her, to make sure there wasn't some mistake."

"You can't," Pasquale said, too quickly. "She's sleeping now."

Gualfredo looked back at Orenzio in the boat and then returned his dead eyes to Pasquale. "Or perhaps you are keeping me from her because she has been tricked by two old friends who took advantage of a woman's poor Italian to convince her to come to Porto Vergogna rather than Porto*venere*, as she intended."

Orenzio opened his mouth to object but Pasquale beat him to it. "Of course not. Look, you're welcome to come back later when she is not resting and ask her anything you like, but I won't let you disturb her now. She's sick."

A smile pushed at the ends of Gualfredo's mustache and he gestured at the giant beside him. "Do you know Signor Pelle, of the tourism guild?"

"No." Pasquale tried to meet the big man's eyes but they were tiny pinpoints in the fleshy face. His silver suit coat strained beneath his bulk.

"For a small yearly fee and a reasonable tax, the tourism guild provides benefits for all the legitimate hotels—transportation, advertising, political representation . . ."

"*Sicurezza,*" added Signor Pelle in a bullfrog voice.

"Ah yes, thank you, *Signor Pelle*. Security," said Gualfredo, half of his shrub mustache rising in a smirk. "Protection."

Pasquale knew better than to ask, *Protection from what?* Clearly, Signor Pelle provided protection from Signor Pelle.

"My father never said anything about this tax," Pasquale said, and he got a quick glance of warning from Orenzio. It was something Pasquale was trying to figure out, endemic to doing business in Italy, determining which of the countless shakedowns and corruptions were necessary to pay and which could safely be ignored.

Gualfredo smiled. "Oh, your father paid. A yearly fee and also a small per-night foreign guest fee . . . which we haven't always collected because, frankly, we didn't think there were any foreign guests in the whore's crack." He shrugged. "Ten percent. It's nothing. Most hotels pass the tax on to their guests."

Pasquale cleared his throat. "And if I don't pay?"

This time, Gualfredo did not smile. Orenzio glanced up at Pasquale, another grim look of warning on his face. Pasquale crossed his arms to keep them from shaking. "If you can provide some documentation of this tax, then I will pay it."

Gualfredo was quiet for a long moment. Finally, he laughed and looked around. He said to Pelle, "Signor Tursi would like documentation."

Pelle stepped forward slowly.

"Okay," Pasquale said, angry with himself for caving so quickly. "I don't need documentation." But he wished he'd made the brute Pelle take more than one step. He glanced over his shoulder to make sure the American woman's shutters were closed and that she hadn't witnessed his cowardice. "I'll be back in a moment."

He started back up the crease toward his hotel, face burning. He could never remember feeling more ashamed. His Aunt Valeria was in the kitchen, watching.

"Zia," Pasquale said. "Did my father pay this tax to Gualfredo?"

Valeria, who had never liked Pasquale's father, scoffed. "Of course."

Pasquale counted the money out in his room and started back for the marina, trying to control his anger. Pelle and Gualfredo were facing the sea when he returned, Orenzio sitting in the boat with his arms crossed.

Pasquale's hand shook as he handed over the money. Gualfredo slapped Pasquale's face lightly, as if he were a cute child. "We'll come back later to talk to her. We can figure out the fees and back taxes then."

Pasquale's face reddened again, but he held his tongue. Gualfredo and Pelle climbed in the mahogany boat and Orenzio pushed them off without looking at Pasquale. The boat bobbed in the chop for a moment; then the coughing engine found its voice and the men rumbled back up the coast.

Pasquale sulked on the porch of his hotel. There was a full moon that night and the fishermen were out in their boats, using the extra moonlight to hit the thrashing squall of a spring run. Pasquale leaned out over the wooden railing he'd built, smoking and replaying the ugly business with Gualfredo and the giant Pelle, imagining brave rejoinders (*Take your tax and use your snake's tongue to push it up your big friend's greasy ass, Gualfredo*), when he heard the springs on the door open and close. He glanced over his shoulder, and there she was—the beautiful American. She wore tight black pants and a white sweater. Her hair was down, streaked blond and brown, hanging straight below her shoulders. She was holding something in her hands. Typed pages.

"May I join you?" she asked in English.

"Yes. Is my honor," Pasquale said. "You feel good, no?"

"Better, thank you. I just needed sleep. May I?" She held out her hand and Pasquale wasn't sure at first what she meant. Finally, he fumbled in his trousers for his cigarette box. He opened it and she took out a smoke. Pasquale thanked his hands for their steady obedience as he struck a match and held it out.

"Thank you for speaking English," she said. "My Italian is dreadful." She leaned against the railing, took a long drag and let the smoke out in a sigh. "*Whooooo.* I needed that," she said. She considered the cigarette in her hand. "Strong."

"They are Spanish," Pasquale said, and then there was nothing

else to say. "I must ask: you choose come here, yes, to Porto Vergogna?" he asked finally. "Not to Porto*venere* or Porto*fino*?"

"No, this is the place," she said. "I'm meeting someone here. It
was his idea. He'll be here tomorrow, hopefully. I understand this
town is quiet and . . . discreet?"

Pasquale nodded, said, "Oh, yes," and made a note to try to find
the word *dus-kreet* in his father's English-Italian dictionary. He
hoped it meant romantic.

"Oh. I found this in my room. In the bureau." She handed
Pasquale the neat stack of paper she'd carried down: *The Smile of
Heaven*. It was the first chapter of a novel by the only other American guest who had ever come to the hotel before, the writer Alvis
Bender, who every year lugged in his little typewriter and a stack
of blank carbon paper for two weeks of drinking and occasional
writing. He'd left a carbon of the first chapter for Pasquale and his
father to puzzle over.

"Is the pages of a book," Pasquale said, "by an American,
yes? . . . A writer. He come to the hotel. Every year."

"Do you think he would mind? I didn't bring anything to read
and it looks like all the books you have here are in Italian."

"Is okay, I think, yes."

She took the pages, leafed through them, and set them on the
railing. For the next few minutes they stood quietly, staring out at
the lanterns, whose reflections bobbed together on the sea's surface
like two sets of strung lights.

"It's beautiful," she said.

"Mmm," Pasquale said, but then he remembered Gualfredo
saying the woman was not supposed to be here. "Please," he said,
recalling an old phrase book: "I inquire your accommodation?"
When she said nothing, he added: "You have satisfaction, yes?"

"I have . . . I'm sorry . . . what?"

He licked his lips to give the phrase another try. "I am try to
say—"

She rescued him. "Oh. Satisfaction," she said. "Accommodations. Yes. It's all very nice, Mr. Tursi."

"Please . . . I am, for you, Pasquale."

She smiled. "Okay. Pasquale. And for you I am Dee."

"Dee," Pasquale said, nodding and smiling. It felt forbidden and dizzying just to say her name back to her, and the word escaped from his mouth again. "Dee." And then he knew he had to think of something else to say or he might just stand there all night saying *Dee* over and over. "Your room is close from a toilet, yes, Dee?"

"Very convenient," she said. "Thank you, Pasquale."

"How long will you stay?"

"I . . . I don't know. My friend has some things to finish. He'll arrive hopefully tomorrow, and then we'll decide. Do you need the room for someone else?"

And even though Alvis Bender should be arriving soon, too, Pasquale said, quickly, "Oh, no. Is no one else. All for you."

It was quiet. Cool. The water clucked.

"What exactly are they doing out there?" she asked, pointing with her cigarette at the lights dancing on the water. Beyond the breakwater, the fishermen dangled the lanterns over the sides of their skiffs, fooling the fish into feeding at the fake dawn, and then swung their nets through the water at the thrashing school.

"They are fishing," Pasquale said.

"They fish at night?"

"Sometimes at night. But more in the day." Pasquale made the mistake of staring into those expansive eyes. He'd never seen a face like this, a face that looked so different from every angle, long and equine from the side, open and delicate from the front. He wondered if this was why she was a film actress, this ability to have more than one face. He realized he was staring and had to clear his throat and turn away.

"And the lights?" she asked.

Pasquale glanced out at the water. Now that she mentioned it, this view really was quite striking, the way the fishing lanterns floated above their reflections in the dark sea. "For . . . is . . ." He searched for the words. "Make fish to . . . They . . . uh . . ." He ran into a wall in his mind and mimed a fish swimming up to the surface with his hand. "Go up."

"The light attracts the fish to the surface?"

"Yes," Pasquale said, greatly relieved. "The surface. Yes."

"Well, it's lovely," she said again. From behind them, Pasquale heard a few short words, and then "Shhh" from the window next to the deck, where Pasquale's mother and his aunt would be huddled in the dark, listening to a conversation that neither of them could understand.

A feral cat, the angry black one with the bad eye, stretched near Dee Moray. It hissed when she reached for it and Dee Moray pulled her hand back. Then she stared at the cigarette in her other hand and laughed at something far away.

Pasquale thought she was laughing at his cigarettes.

"They are expensive," he said defensively. "Spanish."

She tossed her hair back. "Oh, no. I've been thinking about how people sit around for years waiting for their lives to begin, right? Like a movie. You know what I mean?"

"Yes," said Pasquale, who had lost the sense of what she was saying after *people sit* but was so taken by the toss of her liquid blond hair and her confidential tone that he would have agreed to having his own fingernails pulled out and fed to him.

She smiled. "I think so, too. I know I felt that way. For years. It was as if I was a character in a movie and the real action was about to start at any minute. But I think some people wait forever, and only at the end of their lives do they realize that their life has happened while they were waiting for it to start. Do you know what I mean, Pasquale?"

He did know what she meant! It was just how he felt—like someone sitting in the cinema waiting for the film to start. "Yes!" he said.

"Right?" she asked, and she laughed. "And when our lives *do* begin? I mean, the exciting part, the action? It's all so fast." Her eyes ran across his face and he flushed. "Maybe you can't even believe it . . . maybe you find yourself on the outside looking in, like watching strangers eat in a nice restaurant?"

Now she'd lost him again. "Yes, yes," he said anyway.

She laughed easily. "I'm so glad you know what I mean. Imagine, for instance, being a small-town actress going out to look for film work and having your first role be in *Cleopatra*? Could you possibly even believe that?"

"Yes," Pasquale answered more assuredly, picking out the word *Cleopatra*.

"Really?" She laughed. "Well, I sure couldn't."

Pasquale grimaced. He'd answered incorrectly. "No," he tried.

"I'm from this small town in Washington." She gestured around with the cigarette again. "Not this small, obviously. But small enough that I was a big deal there. It's embarrassing now. Cheerleader. County Fair Princess." She laughed at herself. "I moved to Seattle after high school to act. Life seemed inevitable, like rising out of water. All I had to do was hold my breath and rise all the way to the surface. To some kind of fame or happiness or . . . I don't know . . ." She looked down. "Something."

But Pasquale was stuck on one word he wasn't sure he'd heard correctly: *princess*? He thought Americans didn't have royalty, but if they did . . . what would that mean to his hotel, to have a princess stay here?

"Everyone was always telling me, 'Go to Hollywood . . . you should be in pictures.' I was acting in community theater and they raised money for me to go. Can you beat that?" She took another drag. "Maybe they wanted to get rid of me." She leaned in, confiding. "I'd had this . . . fling with another actor. He was married. It was stupid."

She stared off, and then laughed. "I've never told anyone this, but I'm two years older than they think I am. The casting guy for *Cleopatra*? I told him I was twenty. But I'm really twenty-two." She thumbed through the typed carbon pages of Alvis Bender's little novel as if the story of her own life were contained in its pages. "I was using a new name anyway, so I thought, Why not pick a new age, too? If you give them your real age, they sit in front of you doing this horrible math, figuring out how long you have left in the business. I couldn't bear it." She shrugged and set the book down again. "Do you think that was wrong?"

He had a fifty-fifty chance of getting this one right. "Yes?"

She seemed disappointed at his answer. "Yeah, I suppose you're right. Something like that always catches up with you. It's the thing I hate most about myself. My vanity. Maybe that's why . . ." She didn't finish the thought. Instead, she took a last drag of her cigarette, dropped the butt to the wooden patio, and ground it with her deck shoe. "You're very easy to talk to, Pasquale," she said.

"Yes, I have pleasure talk to you," he said.

"Me, too. I have pleasure, too." She eased up off of the railing, wrapped her arms around her shoulders, and looked out at the fishing lights again. With her arms around herself, she grew even taller and thinner. She seemed to be contemplating something. And then she said, quietly, "Did they tell you that I'm sick?"

"Yes. My friend Orenzio, he tell me this."

"Did he tell you what's wrong with me?"

"No."

She touched her belly. "You know the word *cancer*?"

"Yes." Unfortunately, he did know this word. *Cancro* in Italian. He stared at his burning cigarette. "Is fine, no? The doctors. They can . . ."

"I don't think so," she answered. "It's a very bad kind. They say they can, but I think they're trying to soften the blow for me. I wanted to tell you to explain that I might seem . . . frank. Do you know this word, *frank*?"

"Sinatra?" Pasquale asked, wondering if this was the man she was waiting for.

She laughed. "No. Well, yes, but it also means . . . direct, honest."

Honest Sinatra.

"When I found out how bad it was . . . I decided that from now on I was just going to say what I think, that I would stop worrying about being polite or imagining what people thought of me. That's a big deal for an actress, refusing to live in the eyes of others. It's nearly impossible. But it's important that I don't waste any more time saying what I don't mean. I hope that's okay with you."

"Yes," Pasquale said, quietly, relieved to see from her reaction that it was the right answer again.

"Good. Then we'll make a deal, you and me. We'll do and say exactly what we mean. And to hell with what anyone thinks about it. If we want to smoke, we'll smoke, if we want to swear, we'll swear. How does that sound?"

"I like very much," Pasquale said.

"Good." Then she leaned down and kissed him on the cheek, and when her lips grazed his stubbly cheek he felt his breath come short and sharp and he found that he was shaking exactly as when Gualfredo had threatened him.

"Good night, Pasquale," she said. She grabbed the lost pages of Alvis Bender's novel and started back for the door, but paused to consider the sign: THE HOTEL ADEQUATE VIEW. "How ever did you come up with the name of the hotel?"

Still stricken by that kiss, unsure how to explain the name, Pasquale simply pointed to the manuscript in her hand. "Him."

She nodded and looked around again at the tiny village, at the rocks and cliffs around them. "Can I ask, Pasquale . . . what it's like, living here?"

And this time he had no hesitation in coming up with the proper English word. "Lonely," Pasquale said.

Pasquale's father, Carlo, came from a long line of restaurateurs in Florence, and he had always assumed that his sons would follow him in the business. But his oldest, the dashing, jet-haired Roberto, dreamed of being a flier, and in the run-up to World War II he had dashed off to join the regia aeronautica. Roberto did indeed get to fly—three times before his rickety Saetta fighter stalled over North Africa and he fell from the sky like a shot bird. Vowing revenge, the Tursis' other son, Guido, volunteered for the infantry, sending Carlo into a despairing rage: "If you truly want vengeance, forget the British and go kill the mechanic who let your brother fly that rusty bucket of shit." But Guido was insistent, and he trucked off with the rest of the Eighth Army's elite expeditionary force, sent by Mussolini as proof that Italy would do its part to help the Nazis invade Russia. (*Bunnies off to eat a black bear*, Carlo said.)

It was while comforting his wife over Roberto's death that the forty-one-year-old Carlo had somehow mustered one last, good seed and passed it on to the thirty-nine-year-old Antonia. At first she disbelieved her condition, then assumed it was temporary (she'd been plagued by miscarriages after her first two). Then, as her belly ballooned, Antonia saw her wartime pregnancy as a sure sign from God that Guido would survive. She named her blue-eyed *bambino miracolo* Pasquale, Italian for Passover, to honor this deal with God—that the plague of violence sweeping the world would pass over the rest of her family.

But Guido died, too, shot through the throat in the icy meat-fields outside Stalingrad in the winter of '42. His parents, now ruined by grief, wanted only to hide from the world, and to protect their miracle boy from such insanity. So Carlo sold his stake in the family business to some cousins and bought the tiny Pensione di San Pietro in the most remote place he could find, Porto Vergogna. And there they hid from the world.

Thankfully, the Tursis had saved most of the money from selling their Florence holdings, because the hotel did very little business. Confused Italians and other Europeans occasionally wandered in, and the little three-table *trattoria* was a gathering place for the dwindling fishing families of Porto Vergogna, but months could pass between real guests. Then, in the spring of 1952, a water taxi drifted into the cove, and from it stepped a tall, neatly handsome young American with a narrow mustache and slicked brown hair. The man clearly had been drinking, and smoked a thin cigar as he stepped onto the pier with his one suitcase and a portable typewriter. He looked around at the village, scratched his head, and said, in surprisingly fluid Italian, "*Qualcuno sembra aver rubato la tua città*"—Someone seems to have stolen your town. He introduced himself to the Tursis as "Alvis Bender, *scrittore fallito ma ubriacone di successo*"—failed writer but successful drunk—and proceeded to hold court on the porch for six hours, drinking wine and talking about politics and history and, finally, about the book he wasn't writing.

Pasquale was eleven, and other than the occasional trip to see family in Florence, all he knew of the world came from books. To meet an actual author was unbelievable. He'd lived entirely in the shelter of his parents in this tiny village, and he was enthralled by the towering, laughing American, who seemed to have been everywhere, to know everything. Pasquale sat at the writer's feet and asked him questions. "What's America like? What is the best kind of automobile? What's it like in an airplane?" And one day: "What is your book about?"

Alvis Bender handed the boy his wineglass. "Fill this up and I'll tell you."

When Pasquale returned with more wine, Alvis reclined and stroked his thin mustache. "My book is about how the whole of human history and advancement has brought us only to the realization that death is life's point, its profound purpose."

Pasquale had heard Alvis make such speeches to his father. "No," he said. "What's it *about*? What *happens*?"

"Right. Market demands a story." Alvis took another drink of wine. "Okay then. Well, my book is about an American who fights in Italy during the war, loses his best friend, and falls out of love with life. The man returns to America, where he hopes to teach English and write a book about his disillusionment. But he only drinks and broods and chases women. He can't write. Perhaps it is his guilt over being alive while his friend died. And guilt is sometimes a kind of envy—his friend left a young son, and when the man goes to visit his friend's son, afterward, he longs to be a noble memory, too, rather than the obscene wreck that he's become. The man loses his teaching job and goes back to his family business, selling cars. He drinks and broods and chases women. He decides the only way he's ever going to write his book and ease his sorrow is to go back to Italy, the place that holds the secret to his sadness, but a place that escapes his powers of description when he isn't there—a dream he can't quite recall. So for two weeks every year, the man goes to Italy to work on his book. But here's the thing, Pasquale—and you can't tell anyone this part, because it's the secret twist—even in Italy, he doesn't really write his book. He drinks. He broods. He chases women. And he talks to a smart boy in a tiny village about the novel he will never write."

It was quiet. Pasquale thought the book sounded boring. "How does it end?"

For a long time, Alvis Bender stared at his glass of wine. "I don't know, Pasquale," he said finally. "How do you think it should end?"

Young Pasquale considered the question. "Well, instead of going back to America during the war, he could go to Germany and try to kill Hitler."

"Ah," Alvis Bender said. "Yes. That is exactly what happens, Pasquale. He gets drunk at a party and everyone warns him not to drive, but he makes a giant scene leaving the party and he jumps in his car and accidentally drives over Hitler."

Pasquale didn't think it should be an accident, Hitler's death. It would take all the suspense out. He offered, helpfully, "Or he could shoot him with a machine gun."

"Even better," Alvis said. "Our hero makes a huge scene leaving the party. Everyone warns him that he's too drunk to operate a machine gun. But he insists and he accidentally shoots Hitler."

When Pasquale thought Bender was making fun of him, he would change the subject. "What is your book called, Alvis?"

"*The Smile of Heaven*," he said. "It's from Shelley." And he did his best to translate: "The whispering waves were half asleep/the clouds were gone to play/And on the woods, and on the deep/the smile of Heaven lay."

Pasquale sat for a while, thinking about the poem. *Le onde andavano sussurrando*—the whispering waves, he knew these. But the title, *The Smile of Heaven—Il sorriso del Paradiso*—seemed wrong to him. He didn't think of heaven as a smiling place. If mortal sinners went to Hell and venal sinners like himself went to Purgatory, then Heaven had to be full of no one but saints, priests, nuns, and baptized babies who died before they had a chance to do anything wrong.

"In your book, why does heaven smile?"

"I don't know." Bender guzzled the wine and handed Pasquale the empty glass again. "Maybe because someone has finally killed that bastard Hitler."

Pasquale stood to get more wine. But he began to worry that Bender wasn't teasing after all. "I don't think Hitler's death should be an accident," Pasquale said.

Alvis smiled wearily at the boy. "Everything is an accident, Pasquale."

During those years, Pasquale couldn't recall Alvis ever writing for more than a few hours; sometimes he wondered if the man ever unpacked his typewriter. But he came back year after year, and finally, in 1958, the year Pasquale left for university, he presented Carlo with the first chapter of his novel. Seven years. One chapter.

Pasquale couldn't understand why Alvis came to Porto Vergogna at all, since he seemed to get so little done. "Of all the places in the world, why do you come here?"

"This coast is a wellspring for writers," Alvis said. "Petrarch invented the sonnet near here. Byron, James, Lawrence—they all came here to write. Boccaccio invented realism here. Shelley drowned near here, a few kilometers from where his wife invented the horror novel."

Pasquale didn't understand what Alvis Bender meant by these writers "inventing." He thought of inventors as men like Marconi, the great Bolognese who'd invented the wireless. Once the first story was told, what was there to invent?

"Excellent question." Since losing his college teaching job, Alvis was always looking for opportunities to lecture, and in the sheltered, teenage Pasquale he found a willing audience. "Imagine truth as a chain of great mountains, their tops way up in the clouds.

Writers explore these truths, always looking out for new paths up these peaks."

"So the stories are paths?" Pasquale asked.

"No," Alvis said. "Stories are bulls. Writers come of age full of vigor, and they feel the need to drive the old stories from the herd. One bull rules the herd awhile but then he loses his vigor and the young bulls take over."

"Stories are bulls?"

"Nope." Alvis Bender took a drink. "Stories are nations, empires. They can last as long as ancient Rome or as short as the Third Reich. Story-nations rise and decline. Governments change, trends rise, and they go on conquering their neighbors. Like the Roman Empire, the epic poem stretched for centuries, as far as the world. The novel rose with the British Empire, but wait . . . what is that rising in America? Film?"

Pasquale grinned. "And if I ask if stories are empires, you'll say—"

"Stories are people. I'm a story, you're a story . . . your father is a story. Our stories go in every direction, but sometimes, if we're lucky, our stories join into one, and for a while, we're less alone."

"But you never answered the question," Pasquale said. "Why you come here."

Bender pondered the wine in his hand. "A writer needs four things to achieve greatness, Pasquale: desire, disappointment, and the sea."

"That's only three."

Alvis finished his wine. "You have to do disappointment twice."

If, in the glow of too much wine, Alvis treated Pasquale like a little brother, Carlo Tursi looked on the American with a similar affection. The two men would sit up drinking late, having parallel conversations, but not exactly listening to each other. As the 1950s unrolled and the ache from the war faded, Carlo began to think like a businessman again, and he shared with Alvis his ideas about bringing tourists to Porto Vergogna—even though Alvis insisted that tourism would ruin the place.

"At one time every town in Italy was surrounded by medieval walls," Alvis lectured. "To this day, nearly every hilltop in Tuscany rises into gray castle walls. In times of danger, peasants took refuge behind these walls, safe from bandits and armies. In most of Europe, the peasant class disappeared thirty, forty years ago, but not in Italy. Finally, after two wars, houses spill into the flats and river valleys outside the city walls. But as the walls come down, so does Italian culture, Carlo. Italy becomes like any other place, overrun with people looking for 'the Italian experience.'"

"Yes," Carlo said. "This is what I want to profit from!"

Alvis pointed to the jagged cliffs above and behind them. "But here, on this coast, your walls were made by God—or volcanoes. You can't tear them down. And you can't build outside them. This town can never be more than a few barnacles on the rocks. But someday, it could be the last Italian place in all of Italy."

"Exactly," Carlo said drunkenly. "Then the tourists will flock here, eh, Roberto?"

It was quiet. Alvis Bender was exactly the age Carlo's oldest son would have been if he hadn't gone down in that tumbling box over North Africa. Carlo sighed, his voice thin and weak. "Pardon me. I meant, of course, to say *Alvis*."

"Yes," Alvis said, and he patted the older man's shoulder.

Many times Pasquale went to bed to the sound of his father and Alvis talking, and woke hours later to find them still on the porch, the writer holding forth on some obscure topic (*And thus the sewer is man's greatest achievement, Carlo, the disposal of shit the apex of all this inventing and fighting and copulating*). But eventually Carlo would turn the conversation back to tourism and ask his one American guest how he might make the Pensione di San Pietro more attractive to Americans.

Alvis Bender indulged these conversations, but usually came around to pleading with Carlo not to change a thing. "This whole coast will be spoiled soon enough. You've got something truly magical here, Carlo. Real isolation. And natural beauty."

"So I will trumpet these things, perhaps with an English name?

How would you say *L'albergo numero uno, tranquillo, con una bella vista del villaggio e delle scogliere?*"

"The Number One Quiet Inn with a Most Beautiful View in the Village of Cliffs," Alvis Bender said. "Nice. Might be a bit long, though. And sentimental."

Carlo asked what he meant by *sentimentale*.

"Words and emotions are simple currencies. If we inflate them, they lose their value, just like money. They begin to mean nothing. Use 'beautiful' to describe a sandwich and the word means nothing. Since the war, there is no more room for inflated language. Words and feelings are small now—clear and precise. Humble like dreams."

Carlo Tursi took this advice to heart. And so, in 1960, while Pasquale was away at college, Alvis Bender came for his yearly visit—he strode up the steps to the hotel and he found Carlo bursting with pride, standing before the baffled fishermen and his new hand-lettered English sign: THE HOTEL ADEQUATE VIEW

"What does it mean?" said one of the fishermen. "Empty whorehouse?"

"*Vista adeguata,*" said Carlo, translating for them.

"What kind of idiot says that the view from his hotel is only adequate?" said the fisherman.

"*Bravo,* Carlo," said Alvis. "It's perfect."

The beautiful American was vomiting. From his dark room Pasquale could hear her retching upstairs. He flipped on the light and pulled his watch off the dresser. It was four in the morning. He dressed quietly and made his way up the dark, narrow stairs. Four steps from the top of the landing he saw her leaning against the bathroom doorway, trying to catch her breath. She wore a thin, white nightgown cut several inches above her knees—her legs so impossibly long and smooth, Pasquale could go no further. She was almost as white as her nightgown.

"I'm sorry, Pasquale," she said. "I woke you."

"No, is fine," he said.

She turned back toward the basin and began to retch again, but there was nothing in her stomach and she doubled over in pain.

Pasquale started up the rest of the stairs but then stopped, remembering how Gualfredo had said Porto Vergogna and the Hotel Adequate View weren't properly equipped for American tourists. "I am send for the doctor," he said.

"No," she said, "I'm okay." But just then she grabbed her side and slumped to the floor. "Oh."

Pasquale helped her back to bed and hurried downstairs and outside. The nearest doctor lived three kilometers down the coast, in Portovenere. He was a kindly old gentleman *dottore*, a widower named Merlonghi who spoke fine English and who came to the cliffside villages once a year to check on the fishermen. Pasquale knew just which fisherman to send for the doctor: Tommaso the Communist, whose wife answered the door and stepped aside. Tommaso pulled on his suspenders and accepted his job with proud formality, removing his cap and saying he wouldn't let Pasquale down.

Pasquale went back into the hotel, where his Aunt Valeria was sitting with Dee Moray in her room, holding her hair as she bent over a large bowl. The two women looked ridiculous next to each other—Dee Moray with her pale, perfect skin, her shimmery blond hair; Valeria sprouting whiskers from that craggy face, her hair a spool of wire. "She needs to drink water so there is something to spit," Valeria said. A glass of water sat on the bedside table, next to the pages of Alvis Bender's book.

Pasquale started to translate what his aunt had said, but Dee Moray seemed to understand the word *acqua*, and she reached for the glass of water and sipped it.

"I'm sorry for all the trouble," she said.

"What does she say?" Valeria asked.

"She is sorry for the trouble."

"Tell her that her tiny bedclothes are a whore's rags," Valeria said. "This is what she should be sorry for, that she tempts my nephew like a whore."

"I'm not going to tell her that!"

"Tell the pig-whore to leave, Pasqo."

"Enough, Zia!"

"God made her sick because He disapproves of cheap whores in tiny bedclothes."

"Be quiet, crazy old woman."

Dee Moray had been watching this exchange. "What is she saying?" she asked.

"Um." Pasquale swallowed. "She is sorry you are sick."

Valeria stuck out her bottom lip, waiting. "You told the whore what I said?"

"Yes," Pasquale told his aunt. "I told her."

The room was quiet. Dee Moray closed her eyes and shook with another wave of nausea, her back bucking as she tried to vomit.

When it had passed, Dee Moray breathed heavily. "Your mother is sweet."

"She is not my mother," Pasquale said in English. "She is my aunt. Zia Valeria."

Valeria watched their faces as they spoke English, and seemed suspicious about hearing her own name. "I hope you're not going to marry this whore, Pasquale."

"Zia—"

"Your mother thinks you are going to marry her."

"Enough, Zia!"

Valeria gently pushed the hair out of the beautiful American's eyes. "What is the matter with her?"

Pasquale said quietly, "*Cancro.*"

Dee Moray didn't look up.

Valeria seemed to think about this. She chewed the inside of her cheek. "Oh," she said finally. "She will be fine. Tell the whore she will be fine."

"I'm not going to tell her that."

"Tell her." Valeria looked at Pasquale seriously. "Tell her that as long as she doesn't leave Porto Vergogna, she will be fine."

Pasquale turned to his aunt. "What are you talking about?"

Valeria handed Dee the glass of water again. "No one dies here.

Babies and old people, yes, but God has never taken a breeding adult from this village. It's an old curse on this place—that the whores would lose many babies but would live to old age with their sins. Once you outgrow childhood in Porto Vergogna, you are doomed to live at least forty years. Go on. Tell her." She tapped the beautiful American's arm and nodded to her.

Dee Moray had been watching the conversation, understanding none of it, but she could tell the old woman was trying to communicate something important. "What is it?" she asked.

"Nothing," Pasquale said. "Talk of witches."

"What?" Dee Moray said. "Tell me. Please."

Pasquale sighed. He rubbed his brow. "She say . . . young people do not die in Porto Vergogna . . . no one die young here." He shrugged and tried to smile away the old woman's crazy superstition. "Is old story . . . *stregoneria* . . . story of witches."

Dee Moray turned and looked full into Valeria's moley, mustachioed face. The old woman nodded and patted Dee's hand. "If you leave this village you will die a whore's death, blind and thirsty, scratching at your dry dead birth hole," Valeria said in Italian.

"Thank you so much," Dee Moray said in English.

Pasquale felt sick.

Valeria bent and spoke sharply to their guest. "*E smettila di mostrare le gambe a mio nipote, puttana.*" And stop showing your legs to my nephew, you whore.

"You, too," Dee Moray said, and squeezed Valeria's hand. "Thank you."

It was another hour before Tommaso the Communist arrived back at the hotel, his boat lurching into the marina. The other fishermen were already out; the sun was rising. Tommaso helped old Dr. Merlonghi onto the pier. In the *trattoria*, Valeria had prepared a hero's meal for Tommaso, who once again removed his cap and was quiet with the importance of his job. But he had worked up an appetite and accepted the meal proudly. The old doctor was wearing a wool coat, but no tie. Tufts of gray hair shot from his ears. He followed Pasquale up the stairs and was out of breath by the time they reached Dee Moray's room on the third floor.

"I'm sorry that I put you to all of this trouble," she said. "I'm actually feeling better now."

The doctor's English was more practiced than Pasquale's. "It is no trouble seeing a pretty young woman." He looked down her throat and listened to her heart with his stethoscope. "Pasquale said you have stomach cancer. When were you diagnosed?"

"Two weeks ago."

"In Rome?"

"Yes."

"They used an endoscope?"

"A what?"

"It is a new instrument. A tube was pushed down the throat to take a photograph of the cancer, yes?"

"I remember the doctor looked down there with a light."

The doctor felt her abdomen.

"I'm supposed to go to Switzerland for treatment. Maybe they're going to do it there, this scope thing. They wanted me to go two days ago, but I came here instead."

"Why?"

She glanced at Pasquale. "I'm meeting a friend here. He picked this place because it's quiet. After that, I might go to Switzerland."

"Might?" The doctor was listening to her chest, poking and prodding. "What is to might? The treatment is in Switzerland, you should go there."

"My mother died of cancer . . ." She paused and cleared her throat. "I was twelve. Breast cancer. It wasn't the disease so much as the treatment that was difficult to watch. I'll never forget. It was . . ." She swallowed and didn't finish. "They cut out her breasts . . . and she died anyway. My dad always said he wished he'd just taken her home and let her sit on our porch . . . enjoy the sunsets."

The doctor let his stethoscope fall. He frowned. "Yes, it can make worse the end, treatment for cancers. It is not easy. But every day is better. In the United States are . . . advances. Radiation. Drugs. It is better now than it was with your mother, yes?"

"And the prognosis for stomach cancer? Has that gotten any better?"

He smiled gently. "Who was your doctor in Rome?"

"Dr. Crane. An American. He worked on the film. I guess he's the best there is."

"Yes." Dr. Merlonghi nodded. "He must be." He put the stethoscope over her stomach and listened. "You went to the doctor complaining of nausea and pain?"

"Yes."

"Pain here?" He put his hand on her chest and Pasquale flinched with jealousy.

She nodded. "Yes, heartburn."

"And . . ."

"Lack of appetite. Fatigue. Body aches. Fluid."

"Yes," the doctor said.

She glanced at Pasquale. "And some other things."

"I see," the doctor said. Then he turned to Pasquale and said in Italian, "Can you wait in the hall a moment, Pasquale?"

He nodded and backed out of the room. Pasquale stood outside in the hallway, on the top step, listening to their hushed voices. A few minutes later, the doctor came out. He looked troubled.

"Is it bad? Is she dying, Doctor?" It would be terrible, Pasquale thought, to have his first American tourist die in the hotel, especially a movie actress. And what if she really was some kind of princess? Then he felt ashamed for having such selfish thoughts. "Should I get her to a bigger city, with proper care?"

"I don't think she's in immediate danger." Dr. Merlonghi seemed distracted. "Who is this man, the one who sent her here, Pasquale?"

Pasquale ran down the stairs and returned with the single sheet of paper that had accompanied Dee Moray.

Dr. Merlonghi read the paper, which had a billing address at the Grand Hotel in Rome, to "20th Century Fox special production assistant Michael Deane." He turned the sheet over and saw there was nothing on the back. Then he looked up. "Do you know how a young woman suffering from stomach cancer would present to a physician, Pasquale?"

"No."

"There would be pain in the esophagus, nausea, lack of appetite, vomiting, perhaps some swelling in the abdomen. As the disease progressed or the cancer spread, other systems would be affected. Bowels. Urinary tract. Kidneys. Even menstruation."

Pasquale shook his head. The poor woman.

"These could be the symptoms of stomach cancer, yes. But here is my problem: what doctor, when encountering such symptoms, would conclude—without endoscopy or biopsy—that the woman has stomach cancer, and not a more common diagnosis?"

"Such as?"

"Such as . . . pregnancy."

"Pregnancy?" Pasquale asked.

The doctor shushed him.

"You think she's . . ."

"I don't know. It would be too early to hear a heartbeat, and her symptoms are severe. But if I was presented with a young female patient complaining of nausea, abdominal swelling, heartburn, and no menstruation . . . well, stomach cancer is extremely rare in young women. Pregnancy . . ." He smiled. "Not so rare."

Pasquale realized they were whispering, even though Dee Moray wouldn't have understood their Italian. "Wait. Are you saying that maybe she doesn't have cancer?"

"I don't know what she has. Certainly there is a family history of cancer. And maybe American doctors have tests that haven't reached us. I'm just telling you that I couldn't determine that someone has cancer based on those symptoms."

"Did you tell her that?"

"No." The doctor seemed distracted. "I told her nothing. After all she has been through I don't want to give her false hope. When this man comes to see her, perhaps you can ask him. This . . ." He looked at the paper again. "Michael Deane."

This was the last thing Pasquale wanted to ask some American movie person.

"One other thing." The doctor put his hand on Pasquale's arm. "Isn't it strange, Pasquale? With this film being made in Rome, that they would send her here?"

"They wanted a quiet place with a view of the sea," Pasquale said. "I asked if they wanted *Venere*, but her paper said Vergogna."

"Yes, of course. I don't mean this isn't a fine place, Pasquale," said Dr. Merlonghi, hearing the defensiveness in Pasquale's voice. "But a town like Sperlonga is almost as quiet, and is on the sea, and is much closer to Rome. So why here?"

Pasquale shrugged. "My aunt says the young never die in Porto Vergogna."

The doctor laughed politely. "You'll know more after this man has visited. If she's still here next week, have Tommaso the Communist bring her to my office."

Pasquale nodded. Then he and the doctor opened the door to Dee Moray's room. She was asleep, that blond hair swirled like butter on the pillow beneath her. She was cradling the big pasta bowl, the carbon-copied pages of Alvis Bender's book on the pillow next to her.

4

The Smile of Heaven

April 1945
Near La Spezia, Italy

By Alvis Bender

Then spring came, and with it, the end of my war. The generals with their grease pencils had invited too many soldiers and they needed something for us to do and so we marched over every last inch of Italy. All that spring we marched, through the chalky coastal flats below the Apennines, and once the way was cleared, up pocked green foothills toward Genoa, into villages crumbled like old cheese, cellars spitting forth grubby thin Italians. Such a horrible formality, the end of a war. We groused at abandoned foxholes and bunkers. We acted for one another's sake as if we wanted a fight. But we secretly rejoiced that the Germans were pulling back faster than we could march, along that wilting front, the Linea Gotica.

I should have been pleased merely to be alive, but I was in the deepest misery of my war, afraid and alone and keenly aware of the barbarism around me. But my real trouble was below me: my feet had turned. My wet, red, sick hooves, my infected, sore feet, had gone over to the other side, traitors to the cause. Before my feet mutinied, I thought primarily about three things during my war: sex, food, and death, and I thought about these every moment that we marched. But by spring, my fantasies had given way entirely to dreams of dry socks. I coveted dry socks. I lusted, pined, hallucinated that after the war I would find myself a nice fat pair of socks and slide my sick feet into them, that I would die an old man with old dry feet.

Each morning, the grease pencil generals caused artillery waves to crash to the north as we marched in our sodden rain gear into a slashing, insistent drizzle. We moved two days behind the forward combat units of the Ninety-second, the Negro Buffalo Soldiers, and two battalions of Japanese Nisei from the internment camps, hard men brought in by the grease pencils to do the heavy fighting on the western edge of the Gothic Line. We were goldbricks, mop-ups, arriving hours or days after the Negro and Japanese soldiers had opened the way, happy beneficiaries of the generals' crude biases. Ours was a recon/intel unit, trained specialists: engineers, carpenters, burial detail, and Italian translators like me and my good friend, Richards. Our marching orders were to come in behind the forward units to the edges of overrun and destroyed villages, help bury the bodies, and hand out candy and smokes in exchange for information from whatever frightened old women and children were left. We were meant to gather from these wraiths intelligence about the fleeing Germans: placement of mines, locations of troops, storage of armaments. Only recently had the grease pencils asked that we also record the names of men who'd escaped the Fascists to fight alongside us, the Communist partisan units in the hills.

"So it's to be the Communists next," grumbled Richards, whose Italian mother had taught him the language as a boy and thus saved him from heavy combat years later. "Why can't they let us finish this war before they start planning the next one?"

Richards and I were older than our platoonmates, he a twenty-three-year-old two-stripe, me a twenty-two-year-old PFC, both of us with some college. In neither appearance nor manner could anyone tell Richards and me apart: I a lanky towhead from Wisconsin, part-owner of my father's automobile dealership, he a lanky towhead from Cedar Falls, Iowa, part-owner with his brothers of an insurance firm. But while I had back home only a string of old girlfriends, a job offer to teach English, and a couple of fat nephews, Richards had a loving wife and son eager to see him again.

In 1944 Italy, no piece of intel was too small for Richards and me. We reported how many loaves of bread the Germans had requisitioned and which blankets the partisans had taken, and I wrote two paragraphs about a poor German soldier with impacted bowels cured by an old witch's palliative of olive oil and ground bonemeal. As dreary as these duties were, we worked hard at them because the alternative was liming and burying corpses.

Clearly, there were larger tactics at play in my war's end (we heard rumors of nightmare camps and of the grease pencils dividing the world in half), but for Richards and me, our war consisted of wet, fretful marches up dirt roads and down hillsides to the edges of bombed-out villages, short bursts of interrogating dead-eyed dirty peasants who begged us for food. The clouds had come in November, and now it was March and it felt like one long rain. We marched that March for the sake of marching, not for any tactical reason, but because a wet army not marching begins to smell like a camp of hobos. The bottom two-thirds of Italy was liberated by then, if by liberated one means ground over by armies that chose only to shell the most beautiful buildings, monuments and churches, as if architecture were the true enemy. Soon the North would be a liberated rubble heap as well. We marched up that boot like a woman rolling up a stocking.

It was during one of these routine sorties that I began to imagine shooting myself. And it was while debating where to put the bullet that I met the girl.

We had hiked up some donkey highway, two tracks in the weeds, villages appearing at the tops of knolls and the bottoms of draws, hungry bug-eyed old women slumped alongside roads, children peering from windows of broken houses like modernist portraits, framed by cracked sashes, waving gray fabric, holding out their hands for chocolate: "Dolci, per favore. Sweeeets, Amer-ee-can?"

A gravel tide had washed over these villages, smashing everything once coming in, again going out. At night we camped on the outskirts of these rutted burgs, in leaning barns, in the carcasses of abandoned farmhouses, in the ruins of old empires. Before crawling in my mummy bag each night, I eased out of my boots, took off my socks and swore at them, pleaded with them and hung them

in desperation from a fence post, a windowsill or
tent strut. Every morning I woke with great optimism, put these dry socks on my dry feet, and
some chemical reaction ensued, turning my feet
into moist, larval creatures that fed on my blood
and bone. Our supply sergeant, an empathetic, fine-
boned young man who Richards believed had his
eye on me ("You know what?" I told Richards, "If
he can fix my feet I'll blow taps on his yacker"),
was constantly getting me new pairs of socks and
foot powders, but the traitorous creatures always
found their way back in. Each morning I sprinkled
powder in my boots, put on new dry socks, felt
better, took a step, and found rapacious leeches
feeding on my toes. They were going to kill me
unless I acted soon.

On the day I met the girl, I had finally had
enough and gotten the nerve to act: AD, accidental discharge, right through one of my rebellious
hooves. I would be sent home to Madison to live
with my parents, a footless invalid listening to
Cubs games on the radio and telling my nephews
an ever-improving story of how I lost my foot (I
stepped on a land mine, saving my platoon-mates).

That day we were to march to a newly liberated
village to interview survivors ("Cand-ee, Amer-
ee-can! Dolci, per favore!"), to ask the peasants
to rat out their Communist grandsons, to inquire
as to whether the routed Germans might have happened to mention, as they ran away, oh, say, where
Hitler was hiding. As we marched toward this little hill town, we passed, just off the road, the
rotting body of a German soldier draped over
some kind of rough, half-finished sawhorse made of
gnarled tree limbs.

This is mostly what we saw of Germans that spring, corpses previously taken out by hardened soldiers or even harder partisans, whose work we superstitiously respected. Not that we were simply tourists ourselves; we'd seen a bit of action. Yes, dear dull nephews, your uncle had issue upon which to fire his .30 caliber in the enemy's direction, little puffs of dirt exploding at the end of my every shot. It's difficult to know how many clods of dirt I hit, but suffice it to say I was deadly to the stuff, dirt's worst enemy. Oh, and we took a bit of fire, too. Earlier that spring we lost two men when German 88-mm cannons hailed the road to Seravezza and three more in a horrific nine-second firefight outside Strettoia. But these were exceptions, frightened bursts of adrenaline-blinding fear. Certainly, I saw valor and heard other soldiers testify to it, but in my war combat was something we tended to come across after the fact, grim puzzles like this one, left as brutal tests of illogic. (Was the German building a sawhorse when his throat was cut? Or was it part of his death, sentenced to have his throat slit across a half-finished sawhorse? Or was it symbolic or cultural, like a knight slung over his horse, or merely coincidental, a sawhorse happening to be where the German fell?) We debated such questions when we encountered these meat puzzles: Who took the head of the partisan sentry? Why was the dead infant buried upside down in a grain bin? Based on smell and insect activity, this German meat puzzle on the sawhorse was two days past decent burial, and we hoped that if we ignored him we wouldn't be ordered by our CO, the gap-toothed idiot Leftenent Bean, to deal with the ripening body.

We were safely past the body and burial detail when I suddenly stopped marching and sent word forward that I would deal with the stewing corpse. I had my reasons, of course. Someone had taken the dead German's boots already, and he'd surely been picked clean of insignia and weaponry and anything else that might make a decent trophy to show to the nephews at Thanksgiving in Rockport ("This is the Hitler battle spoon I took from a murderous Hun I killed using my poor bare feet"), but for some reason this particular dead man still had his socks. And so crazed was I with discomfort that this dead man's socks looked to me like salvation: two clean, tight-woven sheaths that appeared to cover his feet like bedsheets at a four-star hotel. After dozens of pairs of Allied replacement socks courtesy of my empathetic supply sergeant, I had thought I might try my luck with Axis footwear.

"That's sick," Richards said when I told him I was going back for the corpse's socks.

"I'm sick!" I admitted. But before I could move for the dead man's feet, that moron silver bar, Leftenent Bean, came astride and said that a mine-rigged body had been encountered by another platoon, and so our most recent orders were to eschew burial detail. I had to walk away from what appeared to be the warmest, driest, cleanest pair of socks in Europe, to march another two miles in these soggy, spiky beasts in full pupa stage. And that was it. I was done. I said to Richards, "I'm doing it tonight. SIW. I'm blowing off my foot tonight."

Richards had been listening to me gripe for days, and he thought I was all talk, that I could no more shoot myself in the foot than I could levitate. "Don't be stupid," Richards said. "War's over."

That was what was so perfect, I told him. Who would suspect it now? Earlier in my war, a foot-shot might not have been enough to send me home, but now, with the thing winding down, I liked my odds. "I'm going to do it."

Richards indulged me. "Fine. Do it. I hope you bleed to death in the stockade."

"Death would be better than this pain."

"Then forget your foot, shoot yourself in the head."

We'd stopped just short of this village, and decamped in the rubble of an old barn on a vine-covered hillside. Richards and I set up OP on a small ledge that served as our cover. I sat there debating with Richards which part of my foot I should shoot, as easily as a man might talk about where to have lunch, and that's when a scrap-ing came from the road below us. Richards and I looked at one another silently. I grabbed my carbine, pushed up to the ledge, and rolled my sight along the road below us until I landed on the approaching figure of . . .

A girl? No. A woman. Young. Nineteen? Twenty-two? Twenty-three? I couldn't say in the dusky light, only that she was lovely, and that she seemed to be bouncing alone on this narrow dirt road, brown hair swept up and pinned in back, face narrow at the chin, rising over flushed cheeks to a pair of eyes framed by bursts of black lash, like two lines of oil smoke. She was small, but everyone in the bruised shin of Italy was small. She didn't appear to be starving. She wore a wrap over a dress and it pains me to not recall the color of that dress, but I believe it was a faded blue, with yellow sunflowers, though I can't honestly say it was so, only that I remember it that way (and I find it suspicious that every woman in the Europe of my memory, every whore, grandmother, and waif I encountered, wears the same blue dress with yellow sunflowers).

"Halt," Richards called. And I laughed. Here was a vision on a road beneath us and Richards comes up with Halt? Had I my wits beneath me instead of brutalized feet, I'd have steered him to the Bard's more existential Who's there? and we'd have done the whole of Hamlet for her.

"Don't shoot, nice Americans," called the girl from the road, in pristine English. Unsure where this "Halt" had come from, she addressed the trees on both sides, then our small ledge before her. "I am walking to see my mother." She held up her hands and we rose on the hillside above her, rifles still trained. She lowered her hands and said that her name was Maria and that she was from the village just over the hill. Despite a slight accent, her English was better than most of the guys' in our unit. She was smiling. Not until you see a smile like that do you understand how much you've missed it. All I could think about was how long it had been since I'd seen a smiling girl on a country road.

"Road's closed. You'll have to walk around," Richards said, pointing with his rifle back the way she'd come.

"Yes, fine," she said, and asked if the road to the west was open. Richards said it was. "Thank you," she said, and started back up the road. "God bless America."

"Wait," I yelled. "I'll walk you." I took off my wool helmet liner and patted down my hair with spit.

"Don't be an idiot," Richards said.

I turned, tears in my eyes. "Goddamn it, Richards, I am walking this girl home!" Of course, Richards was right. I was being an idiot. Leaving my post was desertion, but at that moment I'd have spent the rest of my war in the stockade to walk six feet with that girl.

"Please, let me go," I said. "I'll give you anything."

"Your Luger," Richards said without hesitation.

I knew this was what Richards would ask for. He coveted that Luger as much as I coveted dry socks. He wanted it as a souvenir for his son. And how could I blame him? I had been thinking of the son I didn't have when I bought the Luger at a little Italian market outside Pietrasanta. With no son back home, I'd figured to show it to my wayward girlfriends and my lousy nephews after too many whiskeys, when I'd pretend not to want to talk about my war, then would pull the rusted Luger from a bureau and tell the lazy shits how I wrestled it from a crazy German who killed six of my men and shot me in the foot. The black-market economy of German war trophies depended on such deception: retreating, starving Germans trading their broken weapons and their identifying insignia to starving Italians for bread, and the starving Italians in turn selling them as trophies to Americans like Richards and me, starved for proof of our heroism.

Sadly, Richards never got to give the Luger to his boy, because six days before we shipped

home, me to listen to Cubs games on the radio,
him to his wife and son, Richards died inglori-
ously of a blood infection he acquired in a field
hospital, after surgery for a ruptured appendix.
I never even got to see him after he went in for
a fever and gut ache, our moron lieutenant simply
informing me that he'd died ("Oh, Bender. Yeah.
Look. Richards is dead"), the last and best of my
friends to go in my war. And if this marks the
end of Richards's war, I offer this epilogue: A
year later I found myself driving through Cedar
Falls, Iowa, parking in front of a bungalow with
an American flag on the brick porch, removing my
cap, and ringing the doorbell. Richards's wife
was a short, boxy thing and I told her the best
lie I could imagine, that his last words had been
her name. And I handed his little boy the box with
my Luger in it, said his daddy had taken it off
a German soldier. And as I looked down on those
ginger cowlicks, I ached for my own son, for the
heir I would never have, for someone to redeem the
life I was already planning to waste. And when
Richards's God-sweet boy asked whether his father
had been "brave at the war," I said, with all hon-
esty, "Your dad was the bravest man I ever knew."

And he was, because on the day I met the girl,
Brave Richards said, "Just go. Keep your Luger.
I'll cover for you. Just tell me all about it af-
terward."

If, in this confession of fear and discomfort
during my war, I have portrayed myself as lacking
in valor, I offer this evidence of my Galahad-
like heart: I had no intention of laying a hand
on that girl. And I needed Richards to know it,
that I risked death and dishonor not to nick my

willy, but simply to walk with a pretty girl on a road at night, to feel that sweet normalcy again.

"Richards," I said. "I'm not gonna touch her."

I think he could see I was telling the truth, because he looked pained. "Then Christ, let me go with her."

I patted his shoulder, grabbed my rifle, and ran down the road to catch her. She was a fast walker, and when I came upon her, she had edged over to the side of the road. Up close, she was older than I'd thought, maybe twenty-five. She took me in warily. I put her at ease with my bilingual charm: "Scusi, bella. Fare una passeggiata, per favore?"

She smiled. "Yes. You may walk with me," she said in English. She slowed and took my arm. "But only if you stop wiping your ass on my language."

Ah. So it was love.

Maria's mother had raised three sons and three daughters in this village. Her father had died early in the war and her brothers had been conscripted at sixteen, fifteen, and the last at twelve, dragged off to dig Italian trenches and, later, German fortifications. She prayed that at least one of her brothers was alive somewhere north of what was left of the Linea Gotica, but she didn't hold out much hope. Maria gave me the quick history of her little village during the war, squeezed like a washcloth of its young men by Mussolini, then squeezed again by the partisans, again by the retreating Germans, until there were no males between the ages of eight and fifty-five, the town bombed, strafed, and picked clean of food and supplies. Maria had studied English at a convent school, and with the invasion found work as a nurse's aide at an

American field hospital. She was gone weeks at a time but always returned to the village to check on her mother and sisters.

"So when this is all finished," I asked, "do you have a nice young man to marry?"

"There was a boy, but I doubt he's alive. No, when this is over I will care for my mother. She is a widow whose three sons were taken from her. When she's gone, maybe I'll get one of you Americans to take me to New York City. I'll live in the Empire State Building, eat ice cream every night in fancy restaurants, and grow fat."

"I can take you to Wisconsin. You can get fat there."

"Ah, Wisconsin," she said, "the cheese and the dairy fields." She waved her hand in front of her face as if Wisconsin lay just beyond the scrub trees alongside the road. "Cows, farms, and Madison, moon over the river, and the college of Badgers. It is cold in the winter but in the summer there are beautiful farm girls with pigtails and red cheeks."

She could do that for any state you named, so many American boys in her hospital had taken time to reminisce about the place they came from, often before they died. "Idaho? The deep lakes and big mountains, endless trees and beautiful farm girls with pigtails and red cheeks."

"No farm girl for me," I said.

"You will find one after the war," she said.

I said that after the war I wanted to write a book.

She cocked her head. "What kind of book?"

"A novel. About all of this. Maybe a funny novel."

She became somber. Writing a book was an important thing to do, she said, not a joke.

"Oh, no," I said, "I don't mean to joke about it. I don't mean that sort of funny."

She asked what other kind of funny there was and I didn't know what to say. We were within sight of her village, a cluster of gray shadows that sat like a cap on the dark hill in front of us.

"The sort of funny that makes you sad, too," I said.

She looked at me curiously and just then, a bird or a bat flushed from the bushes ahead and we both started. I put my arm around Maria's shoulder. And I can't say how it happened, but suddenly we were off the road and I was on my back and she was lying on top of me in a grove of lemon trees, the unripe fruit above me like hanging stones. I kissed her lips and cheeks and neck and she quickly undid my pants and held me between her two hands, stroking me expertly with one soft hand and caressing me with the other, as if she had read some top secret army manual on this maneuver. And she was exceptional at it, far better than I'd ever managed to be, so that in no time I was making snuffling noises and she pressed against me and I smelled lemons and dirt and her, and the world fell away as she shifted her body and aimed me perfectly away from her pretty dress, like a farmwife directing a stream of cow's milk, toward the unripe lemons, all of this happening in less than a minute, without her having to so much as loosen the bow in her hair.

She said: "There you go."

To this day, these three words remain the most

lovely, sad, awful thing I have ever heard. There you go.

I started crying. "What is it?" she said.

"My feet hurt," was all I could manage. But of course I wasn't crying because of my feet. And while I was overcome with gratitude toward Maria, and with regret and nostalgia and relief over being alive this late in my war, I wasn't crying for those reasons, either. I was crying because clearly I wasn't the first brute that Maria had so efficiently and delicately brought to fruition using only her hands.

I was crying because, behind her speed and skill, her mastery of technique, there could only exist an awful history. This was a maneuver learned after encounters with other soldiers, when they pushed her to the ground and she wasn't able to deflect them using only her hands.

There you go.

"Oh Maria . . ." I cried. "I'm sorry." And I was clearly not the first brute to cry in her presence, either, because she knew just what was needed, unbuttoning the top of her blue dress and putting my head between her breasts, whispering, "Shh, Wisconsin, shh," her skin so soft and butter-sweet, so wet with my tears that I cried harder and she said, "Shh, Wisconsin," and I buried my face between those breasts as if her skin were my home, as if Wisconsin lay there, and to this day, it is the greatest place I have ever been, that narrow ribbed valley between those lovely hills. After a moment I stopped crying and managed to regain a bit of dignity, and five minutes later, after I had given her all of my money and cigarettes and pledged my undying love and sworn that I would return, I hobbled shamefully back to my sentry post, insisting to my disappointed, soon-to-be-dead best friend, Richards, that I did nothing more than walk her home.

God, this life is a cold, brittle thing. And yet it's all there is. That night I settled into my mummy bag, no longer myself but a played-out husk, a shell.

Years passed and I found myself still a husk, still in that moment, still in the day my war ended, the day I realized, as all survivors must, that being alive isn't the same thing as living.

There you go.

A year later, after I delivered the Luger to Richards's son, I stopped at a little bar in Cedar Falls and had one of the six million drinks I've had since that day. The barmaid asked what I was doing in town and I told her, "Visiting my boy." Then she asked about my son, that good imaginary boy whose biggest failing was that he didn't exist. I told her that he was a fine kid, and that I was delivering a war souvenir to him. She was intrigued. What was it? she asked. What thing of significance had I brought home from the war for my boy? Socks, I answered.

But in the end, this is what I brought home from my war, this single sad story about how I lived while a better man died. How, beneath a scraggly lemon branch on a little dirt track outside the village of R—, I received a glorious twenty-second hand job from a girl who was desperately trying to avoid being raped by me.

5

A Michael Deane Production

Recently
Hollywood Hills, California

The Deane of Hollywood reclines in silk pajamas on a chaise on his lanai, sipping a Fresca-with-ginseng and looking out over the trees to the glittering lights of Beverly Hills. Open in his lap is a script, the sequel to *Night Ravagers* (*EXT. LOS ANGELES—NIGHT: A black Trans Am speeds past a burning Getty Museum*). His assistant, Claire, has pronounced the script "not even good by crap standards," and while Claire's critical limbo stick is set too high, in this case—given the shrinking margin in movies and the shit business the first *Night Ravagers* did—Michael has to agree.

This is a view he's looked at for twenty years, and yet somehow it seems new to him this late afternoon—the sun sliding over the green-and-glassed hills. Michael sighs with the contentedness of a man back on top. It's remarkable, the difference a year can make. Not long ago, he'd stopped seeing the beauty in this view, in everything. He'd begun to fear that the end had come—not death (Deane men never succumbed before ninety), but something worse: obsolescence. He was in a terrible slump, with nothing resembling a hit in almost a decade, his only recent credit of any kind the first *Night Ravagers*, which was really more of a *dis*credit. He'd also suffered through the debacle surrounding his memoir, when his publisher's lawyers decided the book he wanted to write was "libelous," "self-serving," and "impossible to fact-check," and his editor sent a ghostwriter to turn it into some strange hybrid of autobiography and self-help book.

His run seemingly over, Michael was on his way to being one of those ancients who haunt the dining room at the Riviera Country Club, spooning soup and dithering on about Doris Day and Darryl Zanuck. But it turned out the old Deane magic wasn't quite finished. It's what he loves about this town, and this business: one simple idea, one good pitch, and you're back in. He didn't even entirely understand the pitch that brought him back, this Hookbook (he only pretends to grasp all the computer-bloggy-twitty gewgaw business), but he could tell by the reactions of his producing partner, Danny—and especially his tight-assed, impossible-to-please assistant, Claire—that it was big. So he did what he does best: pitched the shit out of it.

And now Michael Deane is back on every call sheet in town, on every master list for every spec script and sizzle reel. In fact, his biggest problem now is the restrictive life-raft arrangement he made with the studio, giving it a first look at (and a big cut of) whatever he does. Thankfully, his lawyers believe they have a way out of this, too, and Michael has already started looking for office space elsewhere. Just thinking about being out on his own makes him feel thirty again—a tingling excitement in his lap.

Or wait . . . is that the pill he took an hour ago? Ah yes, there it is, kicking in right on schedule: beneath the script, decrepit nerve terminals and endothelial cells release nitric oxide into the corpus cavernosum, which stimulates the synthesis of cyclic GMP, stiffening the well-used smooth muscle cells and flooding the old spongy tissue with blood.

The script rises in his lap like the flag at Iwo Jima.

"Hello there." Michael sets the script on the garden table next to his Fresca, pushes himself up, and starts toward the house for Kathy.

His silk pajama pants straining, Michael shuffles past the gravity pool, the life-size chess board, the koi pond, Kathy's exercise ball and yoga mat, the wrought-iron outdoor Tuscan brunch table.

He spots Wife No. 4 through the open kitchen door, in yoga pants and tight T-shirt. He gets the full protuberant effect of his recent investment in her, the top-of-the-line viscous silicone gel sacs implanted in her retromammary cavities, for minimal capsular contracture and scarring, between breast tissue and pectoralis muscle, replacing the old, slightly drooping silicone sacs.

It's hot.

Kathy's always telling him not to shuffle—*It makes you look a hundred*—and Michael reminds himself to pick up his feet. She's just turned her back to him when he steps through the open slider into the kitchen. "Excuse me, miss," he says to his wife, positioning himself so she can see his pajama tent-pole. "You order the wood pizza?"

But she has those infernal earbuds in and hasn't seen or heard him—or maybe she's just pretending she hasn't. When things were at their worst the last two years, Michael sensed a whiff of condescension from her, a nurse's on-duty patience in her tone. Kathy has reached the magical "half his age" mark—thirty-six to his seventy-two—Michael making a late career of thirtysomething women. It's scandalous when a man his age dips into the twenties, but no one flinches when the woman is in her thirties; here, you could be a hundred, date a thirty-year-old, and still seem respectable. Unfortunately, Kathy is also five inches taller than him, and this is the truly unbridgeable gap; he sometimes gets an unpleasant picture in his mind of their lovemaking, of him scurrying across her hilly landscape like a randy elf.

He comes around the counter and positions himself so she can see the disturbance in his pajama pants. She looks up, then down, then up again. She removes her earbuds. "Hi, honey. What's up?"

Before he can say the obvious, Michael's cell phone vibrates, jumping on the counter between them. Kathy slides the buzzing phone to him, and if not for the chemical help, her lack of interest might endanger Michael's condition.

He checks the number on the phone. Claire? At four forty-five on a Wild Pitch Friday—what could this be? His assistant is whip-smart—and he has the superstitious belief that she might have that rare quality: luck—but she makes life so tough on herself. The girl anguishes over everything, is constantly measuring herself, her expectations, her progress, her sense of worth. It's exhausting. Michael has even become suspicious that she's looking for another job—he has a sixth sense for such things—and this is probably the reason he holds up a finger to Kathy and takes the call.

"What is it, Claire?"

She rambles, chatters, titters. My God, he thinks, this girl, with her unshakable upper-middlebrow taste, her world-weary, faux cynicism. He always warns her about cynicism; it is as thin as an eighty-dollar suit. She's a great reader, but she lacks the cool clarity required for producing. *I don't love it,* she'll say about an idea, as if love had anything to do with it. Michael's producing partner, Danny, calls Claire *the Canary*—as in *coal mine*—and half-jokingly suggests they use her as a reverse barometer: "If the Canary likes it, we pass." For instance, even though she admitted Hookbook was a big idea, she begged him not to produce it. (Claire: *After all the films you've produced, is this really the kind of thing you want to be known for making?* Michael: *Money is the kind of thing I want to be known for making.*)

On the phone, Claire is at her mumbling, apologetic worst, droning on about Wild Pitch Friday, about some old Italian guy and a writer who happens to speak his language, and Michael starts to interrupt, "Claire—" but the girl won't even pause for breath. "Claire—" he says again, but his assistant won't let him in.

"The Italian guy is looking for an old actress, somebody named"—and Claire utters a name that momentarily takes away his breath—"Dee Moray?"

Michael Deane's legs go out from under him. The phone drops from his right hand onto the counter as the fingers on his left hand skitter for purchase; only Kathy's quick reflexes keep him from falling all the way to the floor, from possibly hitting his head on the counter and impaling himself on his erection.

"Michael! Are you okay?" Kathy asks. "Is it another stroke?"

Dee Moray.

So this is what ghosts are like, Michael thinks. Not white cor-poreal figures haunting your dreams, but old names buzzed over cell phones.

He waves his wife off and grabs the phone from the counter. "It's not a stroke, Kathy, let me go." He concentrates on breathing. A man so rarely gets the full sweep of his life. But here is Michael Deane, chemically enhanced erection straining his silk pajamas in the open kitchen of his Hollywood Hills home, holding on to a tiny wireless telephone and speaking across fifty years: "Don't move. I'll be right there."

The first impression one gets of Michael Deane is of a man con-structed of wax, or perhaps prematurely embalmed. After all these years, it may be impossible to trace the sequence of facials, spa treatments, mud baths, cosmetic procedures, lifts and staples, colla-gen implants, outpatient touch-ups, tannings, Botox injections, cyst and growth removals, and stem-cell injections that have caused a seventy-two-year-old man to have the face of a nine-year-old Fili-pino girl.

Suffice it to say that, upon meeting Michael for the first time, many people stare open-mouthed, unable to look away from his glistening, vaguely lifelike face. Sometimes they cock their heads to get a better angle, and Michael mistakes their morbid fascination for attraction, or respect, or surprise that someone his age could look this good, and it is this basic misunderstanding that causes him to be even more aggressive about fighting the aging process. It's not just that he gets younger-looking each year, that's common enough here; it's as if he is somehow transforming himself, evolving into a different being altogether, and this transformation defies any at-tempts to explain it. Trying to picture what Michael Deane looked like as a young man in Italy fifty years ago, based on his appearance now, is like standing on Wall Street trying to understand the topog-raphy of Manhattan Island before the Dutch arrived.

As this strange man shuffles toward him, Shane Wheeler can't quite get his mind around the idea that this lacquered elf is the famous Michael Deane. "Is that—"

"Yes," Claire simply says. "Try not to stare."

But this is like ordering someone to stay dry in a rainstorm. Especially when he shuffle-walks, the contradiction is just too much, as if a boy's face has been grafted onto the body of a dying man. He's dressed strangely, too, in silk pajama pants and a long wool coat that covers most of his torso. If Shane didn't know this was one of the most famous producers in Hollywood, he might go with escaped mental patient.

"Thanks for calling, Claire," Michael Deane says once he's reached them. He points to the door of the bungalow. "The Italian's in there?"

"Yeah," she says, "we told him we'd be right back." Claire has never heard Michael so shaken; she tries to imagine what could have happened between these two to upset Michael this way, to have him call from the car and ask Claire and "the translator" to meet him outside, so he could take a minute before seeing Pasquale.

"After all these years," Michael says. He usually speaks in a clipped hurry, like a forties gangster rushing his lines. But now his voice seems strained, uneasy—although his face remains remarkably neutral, placid.

Claire steps forward, takes Michael's arm.

"Are you okay, Michael?"

"I'm fine." And only then does he look at Shane. "You must be the translator."

"Oh. Well, I studied for a year in Florence, so I do speak a little Italian. But actually I'm a writer. I'm here to pitch a film idea—Shane Wheeler?" There is no recognition on Michael Deane's face that the man is even speaking English. "Anyway, it's a pleasure to meet you, Mr. Deane. I loved your book."

Michael Deane bristles at the mention of his autobiography, which his editor and ghostwriter turned into a how-to-pitch-in-Hollywood primer. He spins back to Claire. "What did the Italian say . . . exactly?"

"Like I told you on the phone," Claire says. "Not much."

Michael Deane looks at Shane again, as if there might be something in the translation that Claire has missed.

"Uh, well," Shane says, glancing at Claire, "he just said that he met you in 1962. And then he told us about this actress who came to his town, Dee—"

Michael holds up his hand to keep Shane from saying the whole name. And he looks back to Claire to pick up, as if, in this verbal relay, he might find some answers.

"At first," Claire says, "I thought he was pitching a story about this actress in Italy. He said she was sick. And I asked with what."

"Cancer," Michael Deane says.

"Yeah, that's what he said."

Michael Deane nods. "Does he want money?"

"He didn't say anything about money. He said he wanted to find this actress."

Michael runs a hand through his postnaturally plugged and woven sandy hair. He nods toward the bungalow. "And he's in there now?"

"Yes, I told him I was going to come get you. Michael, what's this about?"

"About? This is about everything." He looks Claire over, all the way down to her heels. "Do you know what my real talent is, Claire?"

Claire can't imagine a satisfying answer to a question like that, and thankfully Michael doesn't wait for an answer.

"I see what people want. I have a kind of X-ray vision for desire. Ask some guy what he wants to watch on TV and he'll say news. Opera. Foreign films. But put a box in his house and what's he watch? Blow jobs and car crashes. Does that mean the country is full of lying degenerates? No. They want to want news and opera. But it's not what they *want*.

"What I do is look at someone"—he narrows his eyes at Claire's clothing again—"and I see straight to her desire, to what she truly wants. A director won't take a job and insists it isn't about the money, I go get him more money. An actor says he wants to work in the States to be near his family, I get him a job overseas so he can get away from his family. That ability has served me for almost fifty years—"

He doesn't finish. He takes a deep breath in through his nose and smiles at Shane, as if just remembering he was there. "Those stories of people trading their souls . . . you don't really understand them until you get a little older."

Claire is stunned. Michael never reflects like this, never describes himself as "old" or "older." If there is one remarkable thing about Michael, Claire would have said an hour ago, it is that for someone with such a rich history, he never looks back, never mentions the starlets he's had or the movies he's made, never questions himself, never bemoans the changing culture, the death of movies, the sorts of things she and everyone else here whine about constantly. He loves what the culture loves, its sheer speed, its callous promiscuity, its defections and deflections, its level-seeking ability to always go shallower; to him, the culture can do no wrong. Don't ever give in to cynicism, he is always telling her, believe in everything. He is a shark ceaselessly swimming forward into the culture, into the future. And yet here he is now, staring off, as if he's looking directly into the past, a man stricken by something that happened fifty years ago. He takes another deep breath and nods at the bungalow.

"Okay," he says. "I'm ready. Let's go."

Pasquale Tursi narrows his eyes and stares at Michael Deane. Can this possibly be the same man? They are sitting in Michael's office, Michael sliding easily behind his desk, Pasquale and Shane on the couch, Claire in a chair she's dragged in. Michael has kept his heavy coat on, and his face is placid, but he squirms a bit, uncomfortable in his chair.

"Good to see you again, my friend," Michael tells Pasquale, but it comes across as oddly insincere. "It has been a long time."

Pasquale simply nods. Then he turns to Shane and asks quietly: *"Sta male?"*

"No," Shane says, and tries to think of how to tell Pasquale that Michael Deane is not sick but has had numerous procedures and surgeries. *"Molto . . .* uh . . . *ambulatori."*

"What did you tell him?" Michael asks.

"He, uh . . . he said you look good and I just said you take care of yourself."

Michael thanks him, and then asks Shane, "Will you ask if he wants money?"

Pasquale jerks at the word *money*. He looks mildly disgusted. "No. I come . . . to find . . . Dee Moray."

Michael Deane nods, a bit pained. "I have no idea where she is," Michael says. "I'm sorry." Then he looks at Claire, as if for help.

"I Googled her," Claire says. "I tried different spellings, looked at the IMDb listing for *Cleopatra*. There's nothing."

"No," Michael says, chewing his lip. "There wouldn't be. It wasn't her real name." He rubs his lineless face again, considers Pasquale, and turns to Shane. "Please, translate for me. Tell him that I am sorry for the way I behaved back then."

"Lui è dispiaciuto," Shane says.

Pasquale nods slightly, acknowledging the words if not accepting them. Whatever is between these two men, Shane thinks, it runs deep. Then there is a buzzing and Claire brings her cell phone to her ear. She answers it, and says calmly into the device: "You're gonna have to go get your own chicken."

All three men stare at her. She clicks off the call. "Sorry," she says, then opens her mouth to explain but thinks better of it.

Michael looks back to Pasquale and Shane again. "Tell him I'll find her. That it's the least I can do."

"Egli vi aiuterà a . . . um . . . *trovarla."*

Pasquale simply nods again.

"Tell him that I plan to do this right away, that I consider it an honor to be able to help, and a chance for redemption, to complete the circle of this thing that I started so many years ago. And please tell him that I never had any intention of hurting anyone."

Shane rubs his brow, looks from Michael to Claire. "I'm not sure how to . . . I mean . . . Um . . . *Lui vuole fare il bene.*"

"That's it?" Claire says. "He said fifty words. You said, like, four."

Shane feels stung by the criticism. "I told you, I'm not a translator. I don't know how to say all of that; I just said, *He wants to do good now.*"

"No, that's right," Michael says. He looks with admiration at Shane, and for a moment, Shane imagines parlaying this translation job into a screenwriting deal. "That's exactly what I want to do," Michael says. "I want to do *good*. Yes." Then Michael turns to Claire. "This is our number one priority now, Claire."

Shane watches all of this with fascination and disbelief. This morning he was sitting in his parents' basement; now he's in Michael Deane's office (*the* Michael Deane's office!) while the legendary producer barks orders to his development assistant. In the words of the prophet Mamet, *Act as if . . .* Go with it. Be confident and the world responds to your confidence, rewards your faith.

Michael Deane pulls an old Rolodex from a desk drawer and begins spinning it while he talks to Claire. "I'm going to get Emmett Byers to work on this right away. Can you get Mr. Tursi and the translator settled in a hotel?"

"Look," Shane Wheeler says, surprising even himself, "I told you. I'm not a translator. I'm a writer."

They all turn to look at him, and for a moment Shane questions his resolve, recalls the dark period he's just come through. Before that, Shane Wheeler always knew he was headed for great things. Everyone told him so—not just his parents, but strangers, too—and while he didn't exactly tear it up in college and Europe and grad school (all on his parents' dime, as Saundra liked to point out), he never doubted he'd be a success.

But during the collapse of his brief marriage, Saundra (and the crabby marriage counselor who clearly took her side) described a very different pattern: a boy whose parents never said no, who never required him to do chores or to get a job, who stepped in whenever he got into trouble (Exhibit A: the spring-break thing with the police in Mexico), who supported him financially long after they should have. Here he was, almost thirty, and he'd never had a real job. Here he was, seven years out of college, two years out of his master's program, married—and his mother still sent him a monthly clothing allowance? (*She* likes *buying my clothes,* Shane argued. *Isn't it cruel to make her stop?*)

In that doomed final month of the marriage—in what felt like a live autopsy of his manhood—Saundra tried to make him feel "better" by insisting it wasn't entirely his fault; he was part of a ruined generation of young men coddled by their parents—by their mothers especially—raised on unearned self-esteem, in a bubble of overaffection, in a sad incubator of phony achievement.

Men like you never had to fight, so you have no fight in you, she said. *Men like you grow up flaccid and weak,* she said. *Men like you are milk-fed veal.*

And what milk-fed Shane did next only proved her point: after a particularly heated argument, when Saundra went to work, he moved out, taking the car they'd bought together and heading for Costa Rica and a job on a coffee plantation he'd heard about from some friends. But the car died in Mexico, and—broke and carless—Shane made his way back to Portland and moved back in with his parents.

Since then, he's come to regret his behavior and has apologized to Saundra, even sending her the irregular check for her part of the car (birthday money from his grandparents, mostly), and promising that soon he'd pay her back completely.

The most painful thing about Saundra's milk-fed-veal rant (as he's begun to think of it) was not the truth of it, which was undeniable. Yeah, she was right; he could see that. The awful thing is that he didn't see it *before.* As Saundra said with incredulity, *I think you really believe your shit.* And he did. He really believed his own shit. And now, after she'd blown it all up . . . he really didn't.

For the first few months of their divorce, Shane felt empty and alone in his humiliation. Without his old belief in his slow-brewing talents, Shane was rudderless, adrift, and he sank into the depths of depression.

Which is why—he realizes now—he's got to make the most of this second chance, to go out and prove that ACT wasn't simply a motto or a tattoo, a childish delusion, but the truth. He is not milk-fed veal. He is a bull, a man on the come, a winner.

Shane takes a deep breath in the studio bungalow offices of Michael Deane Productions, looks from Claire Silver to Michael Deane and back, and with all the old, Mamet-inspired confidence he can muster, says: "I came here to pitch a movie. And I'm not translating another word until you hear it."

6

The Cave Paintings

April 1962
Porto Vergogna, Italy

The narrow trail was etched into the cliff face like bunting on the side of a wedding cake, a series of switchbacks zigzagging the steep ledge behind the village. Pasquale stepped carefully along the old goat path and continually looked back to make sure Dee was behind him. Near the top, the trail had been washed out by this year's heavy winter rains and Pasquale reached back for Dee's warm hand as the path gave way to bare rock. At the last switchback, an unlikely orange grove had been planted on the cliff side—six gnarled trees, three on each side, tied to the rocks with wire to keep them from blowing over the side. "Is a little more only," Pasquale said.

"I'm fine," she said, and they made their way along the last stretch of trail, the lip of the cliff just over their heads now, Porto Vergogna peeking out from the rocks sixty vertical meters beneath them.

"You feel bad? Stop or go?" Pasquale asked over his shoulder. He was becoming accustomed to speaking English again.

"No, let's keep going. It's nice to be out walking."

Finally, they crested the cliff and stood on the ledge above the village, the drop-off right at their feet—wind ripe, sea pulsing, foam curling on the rocks below.

Dee stood near the edge, so frail that Pasquale had the urge to grab her, to keep her from being blown away by the wind. "It's gorgeous, Pasquale," she said. The sky was hazy-clear beneath a smear of faint cloud, washed-out blue against the darker sea.

On top of the cliffs, trails spiderwebbed the hills. He pointed up one trail to the northwest, up the coast. "This way, Cinque Terre." Then he pointed east, behind them, over the hills toward the bay. "This way, Spezia." Finally, he turned to the south and showed her the trail they were going to take; it carved the hills for another kilometer before dipping back into the craggy, unpopulated valley along the shoreline. "Portovenere this way. Is easy at first, then difficult. Only for goats is trail from Venere."

She followed Pasquale on the easy part, a series of switchbacks up and down the pitched hills. Where they met the sea, the cliffs had been carved by shore break, but here, on top, the terrain was friendlier. Still, a few times, Dee and Pasquale had to reach for scraggly trees and vines to descend the steep hills and climb the sharp creases. At the crest of a rocky knob, Dee paused at the remnants of a stone foundation, Roman ruins rounded by weather and wind until they looked like old teeth.

"What was this?" she asked, pushing brush away from the smoothed stone.

Pasquale shrugged. For a thousand years, armies used these points to look out over the sea; there were so many ruins up here Pasquale hardly noticed them anymore. Sometimes the rubble of these old garrisons gave him a dull sadness. To think that this was all that was left of an empire; what mark could a man like him ever leave? A beach? A cliff-side tennis court?

"Come," he said, "is a little more only."

They walked another fifty meters and Pasquale pointed out where the hillside trail started down the cliffs into Portovenere, still more than a kilometer away. Then, taking Dee by the hand, Pasquale left the trail and scrambled over some boulders, pushed through brush—and they emerged on a point with a stunning view of the coastline in both directions. Dee gasped. "Come," Pasquale said again, and he lowered himself onto a rocky shelf. After a brief hesitation, Dee followed, and they came to what he had wanted to show her—a small concrete dome the same color as the rocks and boulders around it. Only its uniformity and the three long, rectangular machine-gun turret windows gave it away as man-made: a machine-gun pillbox bunker left over from World War II.

Pasquale helped her climb on top of it, the wind dancing in her hair. "This was from the war?" she asked.

"Yes," Pasquale said. "Everywhere still is the war. Was to see ships."

"And was there fighting here?"

"No." Pasquale waved at the cliffs behind them. "Too . . ." He frowned. He wanted to say *lonely* again, but that wasn't quite right. "*Isolato?*" he asked in Italian.

"Isolated?"

"*Sì*, yes." Pasquale smiled. "Only war here is boys play shoot at boats." The concrete for the pillbox had been poured into the boulders behind it, so that it wasn't visible from above and it looked like just another stone from below. Jutting from the brow of the cliff, the bunker had three open horizontal windows—inside was a machine-gun nest with a 280-degree view on the jagged cove of Porto Vergogna to the northwest, and beyond that, the rocky shoreline and the less drastic cliffs behind Riomaggiore, the last village of the Cinque Terre. To the south the mountains receded to the village of Portovenere, and beyond that Palmaria Island. On both sides the sea foamed on the rocky points, and the steep cliffs rose into green bursts of raggedy pine, clusters of fruit trees, and the furrowed beginnings of the Cinque Terre vineyards. Pasquale's father used to say that ancient people believed this coast was the end of the flat world.

"It's wonderful," she said, standing atop the abandoned pillbox.

Pasquale was pleased that she liked it. "Is good place to think, yes?"

She smiled back at him. "And what do you think about up here, Pasquale?"

Such an odd question; what does anyone think about anywhere? When he was a kid he'd imagine the rest of the world up here. Now, mostly, he thought about his first love, Amedea, whom he'd left behind in Florence; he replayed their last day together, and wondered if there was something else he could've said. But occasionally, his thoughts up here were of a different order, thoughts about time and his place in the world—big, quiet thoughts, difficult to speak of in Italian, let alone English. And yet he wanted to try. "I think . . . all people in the world . . . and I am one only, yes?" Pasquale said. "And sometimes I see the moon here . . . yes, is for everyone . . . all people look at one moon. Yes? Here, *Firenze*, America. For all people, all time, same moon, yes?" He saw lovely Amedea, staring at the moon from the narrow window of her family's house in Florence. "Sometimes, this same moon, it is good. But sometimes . . . more sad. Yes?"

She stared at him a moment, as it registered. "Yes," she said finally. "I think so, too." She reached over and squeezed his hand.

He felt drained from trying to speak English, but pleased to have communicated something abstract and personal after two days of *How is room?* and *More soap?*

Dee looked up the coast; Pasquale knew she was watching for Orenzio's boat and he assured her they would be able to see it from up here. She sat, curled up on her knees, staring to the northeast, where the soil was better than in rocky Porto Vergogna and the gradual cliffs were seamed with parallel rows of grapevines.

Pasquale pointed back down toward his village. "Do you see this rock? I am build a tennis court there."

She looked perplexed. "Where?"

"There." They had climbed and gone half a kilometer to the south, and so he could just make out the cluster of boulders beyond the village. "Will be *primo* tennis."

"Wait. You're putting a tennis court . . . on the cliffs?"

"For make my hotel *destinazione primaria*, yes? Very luxury."

"I guess I don't see where you're going to fit a tennis court."

He leaned in closer and extended his arm, and she pressed her cheek against his shoulder to look straight down his arm past his pointing finger, to make sure she was seeing the right place. There was a jolt of electricity in his shoulder, where her cheek touched him, and

Pasquale's breath fell short again. He'd assumed that his romantic education, courtesy of Amedea, had done away with the old nervousness he used to feel around girls, but here he was, shaking like a child.

She was incredulous. "You're building a tennis court there?"

"Yes. I make the rocks . . . flat." He remembered the English word. "*Cantilever*, yes? Will be very famous, best tennis in Levante, *numero uno* court rising from the sea."

"But won't the tennis balls just . . . fly off the edge?"

He looked from her to the boulders and back, wondering if she knew the game. "No. The players hit the ball." He held his two hands apart. "On this side and this side."

"Yeah, but when they miss—"

He just stared at her.

"Have you ever played tennis, Pasquale?"

This was a sore subject, sports. Even though Pasquale was tall for his family, over 1.8 meters, he had played no sports growing up in Porto Vergogna; for a long time this shame was at the front of his insecurities. "I see many pictures," he said, "and I make measure from a book."

"When the player on the sea side misses it . . . won't the balls fly into the sea?"

Pasquale rubbed his jaw and considered it.

She smiled. "Maybe you could put up high fences."

Pasquale stared out at the sea, imagining it covered with bobbing tennis balls. "Yes," he said. "A fence . . . yes. Of course." He was an imbecile.

"I'm sure it will be a wonderful court," she said, and turned back to the sea.

Pasquale looked at Dee's sharp profile, the wind snapping her hair. "The man who comes today, you are in love with him?" He was surprised at himself for asking, and when she turned back Pasquale looked down. "I hope . . . is okay I ask this."

"Oh, of course." She took a deep breath and blew air out. "Unfortunately, I think I am, yes. But I shouldn't be. He's not a good man to fall in love with."

"And . . . he is in love?"

"Oh, yes," she said. "He's in love with himself, too."

It took a second to register, but Pasquale was delighted by her joke. "Ah!" he said. "Very funny."

Another gust riffled Dee's hair and she held it down against her head. "Pasquale, I read the story I found in my room, by the American writer."

"The book . . . is good, yes?" Pasquale's mother had never liked Alvis Bender as much as Pasquale and his father did. If the man was such a brilliant writer, she said, why had he only written one chapter in eight years?

"It's sad," Dee said, and she put her hand on her chest. Pasquale couldn't look away from those lovely fingers splayed out over the tops of Dee Moray's breasts.

"I am sorry," he cleared his throat, "you find this sad story in my hotel."

"Oh, no, it's very good," she said. "It has a kind of hopelessness that made me feel less alone in my own hopelessness. Does that make sense?"

Pasquale nodded unsurely.

"The movie I was working on, *Cleopatra*, it's about how destructive a force love can be. But maybe that's what every story is about." She removed her hand from her chest. "Pasquale, have you ever been in love?"

He felt himself flinch. "Yes."

"What was her name?"

"Amedea," he said, and he wondered how long it had been since he'd said *Amedea* out loud; he was amazed at the power it had, that simple name.

"Do you still love her?"

Of all the difficulties of speaking in another language, this one was the worst. "Yes," Pasquale finally said.

"Why aren't you with her?"

Pasquale exhaled, surprised at the sharpness at the base of his ribs. He finally just said, "Is not simple, no?"

"No," she said, and looked out to a tight roll of white clouds just beginning to pearl on the horizon. "It's not simple."

"Come. One more thing." Pasquale moved to the far corner where the bunker met the jagged boulders of the cliff face. He pulled away branches and pushed rocks aside, revealing a narrow, rectangular hole in the concrete roof. He squeezed in and lowered himself down. Halfway into the pillbox, he looked across its roof to see that Dee still hadn't moved. "Is safe," Pasquale said. "Is okay. Come."

He dropped into the bunker, and a moment later Dee Moray squeezed through the narrow hole and dropped in next to him.

It was dark inside, the air a bit stale, and in the corners they had to stoop a bit to avoid hitting their heads on the concrete ceiling. The only light came from the three gun turrets, which, in the early morning, cast distorted rectangles of light on the pillbox floor. "Look," Pasquale said, and he pulled a matchbox from his pocket, struck a single kitchen match and held it to one of the concrete walls in the back of the bunker.

Dee walked toward the flickering light of the match. The back wall was covered with paintings, five frescoes immaculately painted on the concrete, one after the other, as if it were a crude gallery wall. Pasquale lit another match and handed it to her and she stepped even closer to the wall. The artist had painted what looked like wooden frames around the paintings, too, and even though they had been done on concrete and the paint was faded and cracked, it was clear the artist had real talent. The first was a seascape—the rough coast beneath this very pillbox, the churning waves on the rocks, Porto Vergogna just a cluster of rooftops in the right-hand corner. The next two were official-looking portraits of two very different German soldiers. And finally there were two identical paintings of a single girl. Time and weather had faded the colors to dull versions of some earlier vibrancy, and a stream of water seeping into the bunker had damaged the seascape, while a large crack split one of the soldiers' portraits and a fissure ran through the corner of the first painting of the girl. But otherwise the art was remarkably well-preserved.

"Later, the sun, it come through these windows." Pasquale pointed to the machine-gun slots in the pillbox wall. "Make these paint . . . it seem alive. The girl, she is *molto bella*, yes?"

Dee stared, open-mouthed. "Oh, yes." Her match went out and Pasquale lit another. He put a hand on Dee's shoulder and pointed to the two paintings in the center, the portraits of the two soldiers. "The fishermen say two German soldiers live here in the war, for guard the sea, yes? One, he paint this wall."

She stepped in closer to look at the soldiers' portraits—one a young, chinless boy with his head cocked proudly, looking off to the side, tunic buttoned to his chin; the other a few years older, shirt open, staring straight out from the wall—and even with the paint faded on the concrete, an unmistakable wistful look on his face. "This one was the painter," she said quietly.

Pasquale bent in close. "How do you know this?"

"He just looks like an artist. And he's staring at us. He must've looked in a mirror as he painted his own face."

Dee turned, took a few steps, and looked out the gun turret, to the sea below. Then she turned back to the paintings. "It's amazing, Pasquale. Thank you." She covered her mouth, as if about to cry, and then she turned to him. "Imagine being this artist, creating master-pieces up here . . . that no one will ever see. I think it's kind of sad."

She returned to the painted wall. Pasquale lit another match, handed it to her, and she made her way down the wall again . . . the roiling sea on the rocks, the two soldiers, and finally two paint-ings of the girl—sitting three-quarters sideways, painted from the waist up, two classic portraits. Dee paused over these last paint-ings. Pasquale had always assumed the two portraits of the girl were identical, but Dee said, "Look. This one wasn't quite right. He cor-rected it. From a photograph, I'll bet." Pasquale stepped in beside her. Dee pointed. "In this one, her nose is a little too angled and her eyes dip." Yes, Pasquale could see, she was right.

"He must have loved her very much," she said.

She turned, and in the flickering match light Pasquale thought she might have tears in her eyes.

"Do you think he made it home to see her?"

They were close enough to kiss. "Yes," Pasquale whispered. "He see her again."

Stooped over in the tight pillbox, Dee blew out the match, stepped forward, and hugged him. In the dark, she whispered, "God, I hope so."

At four in the morning, Pasquale was still thinking about the moment in the dark bunker. Should he have kissed her? He had kissed only one other woman in his life, Amedea, and technically she had kissed him first. He might have tried, if not for the humiliation he still felt about the tennis court. Why hadn't it occurred to him that the balls would fly off the cliff? Maybe because in the pictures he'd seen there were no photos of the balls getting past the players. Still, he felt foolish. He had imagined tennis as something purely aesthetic; he hadn't wanted a tennis court, he'd wanted a painting of a tennis court. Obviously, without a fence, the players themselves could run right off the court and fall over the cliff into the sea. Dee Moray was right. A high fence could be erected easily enough. And yet he knew that a high fence would ruin the vision he'd always had, of a flat court hovering over the sea, rising from the cliff-side boulders, a perfect cantilevered shelf covered with players in white clothes, women sipping drinks under parasols. If they were behind fences, you wouldn't see them from the approaching boats. Chain fences would be better, but would cloud the players' view of the sea and would be ugly, like a prison. Who wanted a *brutto* tennis court?

That night, the man Dee Moray was waiting for didn't come, and Pasquale felt somehow responsible, as if his little wish that the man would drown had been upgraded to a prayer and had come true. Dee Moray had retreated to her room at dusk and in the early morning had gotten violently ill again, and could only get out of bed to vomit. When there was nothing left in her stomach, tears rolled from her eyes and her back arched and she sniffed and slumped to the floor. She didn't want Pasquale to see her retch, and so he sat in the hallway and reached his hand around the corner, through the doorway, to hold her hand. Pasquale could hear his aunt stirring downstairs.

Dee took a long breath. "Tell me a story, Pasquale. What happened when the painter returned to the woman?"

"They marry and have fifty children."

"Fifty?"

"Maybe six. He become a famous painter and every time he paint a woman, he paint her."

Dee Moray vomited again, and when she could speak, said, "He's not coming, is he?" It was odd and intimate, their hands connected, their heads in different rooms. They could talk. They could hold hands. But they couldn't see each other's faces.

"He is coming," Pasquale told her.

She whispered: "How do you know, Pasquale?"

"I know."

"But how?"

He closed his eyes and concentrated on the English, whispering back around the corner, "Because if you wait for me . . . I crawl on my knees from Rome to see you."

She squeezed his hand and retched again.

The man didn't come that day, either. And as much as he wanted to keep Dee Moray for himself, Pasquale began to get angry. What kind of man sent a sick woman to a remote fishing village and then left her there? He thought of going to La Spezia and using a phone to call the Grand Hotel, but he wanted to look this bastard in his cold eye.

"I go to Rome today," he told her.

"No, Pasquale. It's okay. I can just go on to Switzerland when I feel better. Maybe he left word for me there."

"I must go to Rome anyway," he lied. "I find this Michael Deane and tell him you wait here."

She stared off for a moment and then smiled. "Thank you, Pasquale."

He gave precise instructions to Valeria for the care of the American: Let her sleep and don't make her eat anything she doesn't want to eat and don't lecture her about her skimpy nightclothes. If she gets sick, send for Dr. Merlonghi. Then he peeked in on his mother, who lay awake waiting for him.

"I'll be back tomorrow, Mamma," he said.

"It will be good for you," she said, "to have children with such a tall, healthy woman with such breasts."

He asked Tommaso the Communist to motor him to La Spezia, so he could take a train to Florence, then on to Rome to scream at Michael Deane, this awful man who would abandon an ailing woman this way.

"I should go to Rome with you," Tommaso said as they cut across a light chop and made their way south. Tommaso's little outboard motor chugged in the water and whined when it came out as he piloted from the back, squinting along the shoreline while Pasquale crouched in front. "These American movie people, they are pigs."

Pasquale agreed. "To send a woman off and then forget about her . . ."

"They mock true art," Tommaso said. "They take the full sorrow of life and make a circus of fat men falling into cream pies. They should leave the Italians alone to make films, but instead their stupidity spreads like a whore's disease among sailors. *Commedia all'italiana!* Bah."

"I like the American Westerns," Pasquale said. "I like the cowboys."

"Bah," Tommaso said again.

Pasquale had been thinking about something else. "Tommaso, Valeria says that no one dies in Porto Vergogna except babies and old people. She says the American won't die as long as she stays here."

"Pasquale—"

"No, I know, Tommaso, it's just old witch talk. But I can't think of a single person who has died young here."

Tommaso adjusted his cap as he thought. "How old was your father?"

"Sixty-three," Pasquale said.

"That's young to me," Tommaso said.

They motored toward La Spezia, weaving among the big canning ships in the bay.

"Have you ever played tennis, Tommaso?" Pasquale asked. He knew Tommaso had been held for a while in a prison camp near Milan during the war and had been exposed to many things.

"Certainly I've watched it."

"Do the players miss the ball often?"

"The better players don't miss so much, but every point ends with someone missing, or hitting it into the net or over the line. There's no way to avoid it."

On the train, Pasquale was still thinking about tennis. Every point ended with someone missing; it seemed both cruel and, in some way, true to life. It was curious what trying to speak English had done lately to his mind; it reminded him of studying poetry in college, words gaining and losing their meaning, overlapping with images, the curious echo of ideas behind the words people used. For instance, when he had asked Dee Moray if the man she loved felt the same way, she had answered quickly that yes, the man loved himself as well. It was such a delightful joke and his pride in understanding it in English had felt so strangely significant. He just wanted to keep repeating the little exchange in his head. And talking about the paintings in the pillbox . . . it was thrilling to see what she imagined—the lonesome young soldier with the photograph of the girl.

In his train car, two young women were sitting next to each other, reading two copies of the same movie magazine, leaning into each other, and chattering about the stories they read. Every few minutes one of them would glance up at him and smile. The rest of the time they read their magazines together; one would point to a picture of a movie star in the magazine and the other would comment on her. *Brigitte Bardot? She is beautiful now but she will be fat.* They spoke loudly, perhaps to be heard over the sound of the train.

Pasquale looked up from his cigarette and surprised himself by asking the women, "Is there anything in there about an actress named Dee Moray?"

The women had been trying to get his attention for an hour. Now they looked at each other and then the taller one answered, "Is she British?"

"American. She is in Italy making the film *Cleopatra*. I don't think she is a big star, but I wondered if there was anything in the magazines about her."

"She is in *Cleopatra*?" the shorter woman asked, and then flipped through her magazine until she found a picture of a stunningly beautiful dark-haired woman—certainly more attractive than Dee Moray—which she held up for Pasquale to see. "With Elizabeth Taylor?" The headline beneath Elizabeth Taylor's photo promised details of the "Shocking American Scandal!"

"She broke up the marriage between Eddie Fisher and Debbie Reynolds," confided the taller woman.

"So sad. Debbie Reynolds," said the other girl. "She has two babies."

"Yes, and now Elizabeth Taylor is leaving Eddie Fisher, too. She and the British actor Richard Burton are having an affair."

"Poor Eddie Fisher."

"Poor Richard Burton, I think. She is a monster."

"Eddie Fisher flew to Rome to try to win her back."

"His wife has two babies! It's shameful."

Pasquale was amazed at how much these women knew about the movie people. It was as if they were talking about their own family, not some American and British movie actors they'd never met. The women were bouncing back and forth, chattering about Elizabeth Taylor and Richard Burton now. Pasquale wished he'd gone on ignoring them. Had he honestly expected them to know

Dee Moray? She'd told Pasquale that *Cleopatra* was her first film; how would these women have heard of her?

"That Richard Burton is a hound. I would not even give him a second look."

"Yes, you would."

She smiled at Pasquale. "Yes, I would."

The women cackled.

"Elizabeth Taylor has been married four times already!" the taller woman said to Pasquale, who would've jumped off the train to get out of this conversation. They went back and forth like a tennis match in which neither player missed.

"Richard Burton's been married, too," the other woman said.

"She is a snake."

"A beautiful snake."

"Her actions make her common. Men see through such things."

"Men see only her eyes."

"Men see tits. She is common!"

"She can't be common with those eyes . . ."

"It is scandalous! They act like children, these Americans."

Pasquale pretended to have a coughing fit. "Excuse me," he said. He stood and left the chattering car, coughing, pausing to glance out the window. They were nearing the station at Lucca and he caught a glimpse of the brick-and-marble Duomo. Pasquale wondered if, when the train got to Florence, he would have enough time before his transfer to take a walk.

In Florence, Pasquale lit a cigarette and leaned on the wrought-iron fence in the piazza Massimo d'Azeglio, down the street and across from Amedea's house. They would have just finished dinner. This was when Amedea's father liked the whole family to go for a walk—Bruno, his wife, and his six beautiful daughters (unless he'd married one off in the ten months that Pasquale had been away from Florence) moving in a cluster down the street, once around the piazza and then back to their house. Bruno took great pride in parading his girls, like horses at auction, Pasquale always thought, the old man's big bald head tilted back, that deep, serious frown on his face.

The sun had broken through at dusk, after a day of clouds, and the whole city seemed to be out strolling. Pasquale smoked, watching the couples and families until, sure enough, after a few minutes, the Montelupo girls rounded the corner—Amedea and the two youngest of her sisters. There were three other girls between the young ones and the oldest, Amedea, but they must have been married off. Pasquale held his breath when he saw Amedea: she was so lovely. Bruno came around the corner next, with Mrs. Montelupo, who pushed the baby stroller. When he saw the stroller, Pasquale let out the breath he'd taken in a deep sigh. So there it was.

He was leaning on the same post he had to lean against when he and Amedea had started seeing one another; he would stand there to signal her. He felt his chest flutter as it used to back then, and that's when she looked up, saw him, stopped suddenly, and reached out for the wall. Pasquale wondered if she looked at their post every day, even now. Unaware of his presence, Amedea's sisters moved on without her; then Amedea resumed walking, too. Pasquale removed his hat—the second part of their old signal. Across the street he saw Amedea shake her head *no*. Pasquale put his hat back on.

The three girls walked in front, Amedea with little Donata and Francesca. Behind them strolled Bruno and his wife and the baby in the carriage. A young couple stopped to gaze in at the baby. Their voices carried across the piazza to Pasquale.

"He is so big, Maria," said the woman.

"He should be. He eats as much as his father."

Bruno laughed proudly. "Our hungry little miracle," he said.

The woman reached into the carriage to pinch the baby's cheek. "You leave some food for your sisters, little Bruno."

Amedea's sisters had turned to watch the couple praise the baby, but Amedea kept her gaze forward, staring across the street as if Pasquale would disappear unless she kept him in her vision.

Pasquale had to look away from Amedea's stare.

The woman admiring little Bruno turned to Amedea's youngest sister, who was twelve. "And do you like having a baby brother, Donata?"

She said she did.

They settled into a more intimate conversation. After that, Pasquale could hear only bits from across the street—about the rains, how warm weather seemed to be lurking around a corner.

Then the couple moved on and the Montelupos finished their lap around the piazza and were devoured, one by one, by the tall wooden door of their narrow house, which Bruno ceremoniously pulled shut behind them. Pasquale stood there smoking. He checked his watch; plenty of time before the last train to Rome.

Ten minutes later, Amedea came striding across the street, her arms crossed as if she were cold. He had never been able to read her lovely brown eyes, beneath their black brows. They were so fluid, so naturally teary that even when she was angry—which was often—her eyes always seemed ready to forgive.

"Bruno?" Pasquale said when Amedea was still several strides away. "You let them name him *Bruno*?"

She walked right up to him. "What are you doing here, Pasquale?"

"I wanted to see you. And him. Can you bring him to me?"

"Don't be stupid." She reached up and took the cigarette from his hand, dragged on it, and blew the smoke from the side of her mouth. He'd almost forgotten how small Amedea was—so wiry and lithe. She was eight years older than him and she carried herself with a mysterious, animal-like sensual ease. He still felt dizzy around her, the matter-of-fact way she used to drag him by the hand to his apartment (his roommate was gone during the day), push him down on the bed, undo his pants, lift her skirt, and settle herself on him. His hands would go to her waist, his eyes would lock hers, and Pasquale would think, This is the whole of the world, here.

"Can't I at least see my boy?" Pasquale said again.

"Maybe in the morning when my father is at his office."

"I'm not going to be here in the morning. I'm taking the train to Rome tonight."

She nodded but didn't say anything.

"So you just . . . pretend he is your brother? And no one thinks it's strange that your mother has another baby . . . twelve years after her last child?"

Amedea answered wearily, "I have no idea what they think. Papa sent me to live with my mother's sister in Ancona and they told people that I was caring for her because she was sick. My mother dressed in pregnancy clothes and then told people she was going to Ancona to deliver. After a month, we came back with my baby brother." She shrugged as if it were all nothing. "Miracle."

Pasquale didn't know what to say. "How was it?"

"Having a baby?" She looked away. "It was like shitting a hen." She looked back and smiled. "Now it's not so bad. He's a sweet baby. When everyone is asleep, I sometimes hold him and tell him quietly: 'I am your mamma, little baby.'" She gave a little shrug of her shoulders. "Other times I almost forget and believe that he's my brother."

Pasquale felt sick again. It was as if they were talking about an idea, an abstraction, and not a child, *their child*. "This is insane. To be acting this way in 1962? It's wrong."

Even as he said this, he knew it must sound ridiculous, since he was taking no part in raising the baby. Amedea said nothing, just stared at him and then removed a bit of tobacco from her tongue. *I tried marrying you*, Pasquale almost said, but thought better of it. She would only have laughed, of course, having been there for his . . . "proposal."

Amedea had been engaged once before, when she was seventeen, to the prosperous but frog-eyed son of her father's partner in his real estate holding firm. When she balked at marrying a man twice her age, her father was furious; she had dishonored the family, and if she would not marry this perfectly good suitor, then she would never marry. She had two choices: go off to a convent or stay in the house and care for her aging parents and whatever children her married sisters bore. Fine, Amedea said, she'd be the family nurse-maid. She didn't need a husband. Later, irritated by her defiant, surly presence around the house, her father allowed her to get a secretarial job at the university. She'd worked there for six years, cutting the loneliness by taking an occasional faculty lover, when, at twenty-seven, she went for a walk and came across nineteen-year-old Pasquale studying on the banks of the Arno. She stood above, and when he looked up, she smiled down at him and said, "Hello, eyes."

From the first, he was wildly attracted to her thin, restless energy, her subversive quick wit. That first day, she asked him for a cigarette but he said he didn't smoke. "I walk by here every Wednesday," she said, "in case you want to start."

A week later, she walked by and Pasquale leaped to his feet and offered her a cigarette, his hands shaking as he pulled the pack from his pocket. He lit her cigarette and she gestured at the open books on the ground—a book of poems and an English dictionary. He explained that he'd been assigned to translate the poem "Amore e morte." "The great Leopardi," she said, and bent to pick up his notebook. She read what he'd translated so far: "'*Fratelli, a un tempo stesso, Amore e Morte/ingenerò la sorte—*' Brothers—the time is same, Love and Death/engendered sorts."

"Good job," she said, "you've cured that song of its music." She handed him back the notebook, said, "Thank you for the cigarette," and walked on.

The next week when Amedea walked by the river, Pasquale was waiting with a cigarette and his notebook, which she took without a word, and read aloud in English: "Brothers of a single breath/born together, Love and Death." She handed him back the notebook, smiled, and asked if he had an apartment nearby. Within ten minutes she was tugging at his pants—the first girl he'd ever kissed, let alone slept with. They met in his apartment two afternoons a week during the next eighteen months. They never spent a night together, and she explained that she would never go out in public with him. She was not his girlfriend, she insisted; she was his tutor. She would help with his studies and train him to be a good lover, give him advice about how to talk to girls, how to approach them, what to avoid saying. (When he insisted he didn't want other girls, he wanted only her, she laughed.) She also laughed at his early, awkward attempts to make conversation. "How can those beautiful eyes have so little to say?" She coached him to make eye contact, to breathe deeply, and to consider his words, not answer so quickly. Of course, his favorite lessons were those she gave on his mattress on the floor—how to use his hands, how to avoid finishing too quickly. After a few successful lessons, she fell off him one day and said, "I'm quite the teacher. How lucky for the woman you're going to marry."

For him, these afternoons were dizzying and liquid, and he'd have continued that way the rest of his life, going to class and knowing that, twice a week, the lovely Amedea was coming to teach him. Once, after an especially intimate encounter, he made the mistake of saying, "*Ti amo*," I love you, and she pushed him away angrily, stood, and began getting dressed.

"You can't just say that, Pasquale. Those words have tremendous power. It's how people end up married." She pulled on her blouse. "Don't ever say that after sex, do you understand? If you feel the urge to say it, go see the girl first thing in the morning, with her night breath and no makeup . . . watch her on the toilet . . . listen to her with her friends . . . go meet her hairy mother and her shrill sisters . . . and if you still feel the need to say such a stupid thing, then God help you."

She told him so often that he didn't really love her, that it was just a reaction to his first sexual experience, that she was too old for him, that they were all wrong for each other, that they were of different classes, that he needed a girl his own age—and she was so assured in her opinions—that Pasquale had no reason to doubt her.

And then, one fateful day, she came to his apartment and said, without preamble, "I'm pregnant." What followed was an awful pause, as Pasquale experienced a moment of misunderstanding (*Did she say pregnant?*) followed by a moment of disbelief (*But*

we almost always took precautions) and another moment when he
waited for her to tell him what to do—as she usually did—so that
by the time he came around to speaking (*I think we should get married*), so much time had passed, the proudly defiant Amedea could
only laugh in his face.

Che ragazzino! Such a boy. Had he learned nothing? Did he
really believe she would let him throw his life away like that? And
even if he really wanted to—which he clearly *didn't*—did he actually think that she would ever marry a penniless boy from a peasant village? Did he really believe that her father would allow such
shame upon his family? And even if her father approved—and he
would never approve—did he really think she would ever make a
husband of such an aimless, unformed boy, a boy she had seduced
out of boredom? The last thing the world needed was another bad
husband. On and on she went, until Pasquale could only mutter,
"Yes, you're right," and believe it. This had always been the me-
chanics of their attraction—her sexual seniority and his childlike
agreeability. She was right, he thought, he couldn't raise a child; he
was a child.

Now, almost a year later, in the piazza across from her family's big house, Amedea smiled wearily and reached for his cigarette
again. "I was sorry to hear about your father. How is your mother?"

"Not good. She wants to die."

Amedea nodded. "It's the hardest thing to be a widow, I would
think. I've thought about coming to visit your *pensione* sometime.
How is it?"

"Good. I'm building a beach. I was going to build a tennis court
but it might not fit." He cleared his throat. "I . . . I have an American guest there. An actress."

"From the cinema?"

"Yes. She is making the film *Cleopatra.*"

"Not Liz Taylor?"

"No, another one."

She took the tone she used to have when she was advising him
about other girls. "And is she beautiful?"

Pasquale acted as if he hadn't thought about it until now. "Not much."

Amedea held out her hands like she was holding cantaloupes. "But big breasts, no? Giant balloons? Pumpkins?" Her hands moved away from her body. "Zeppelins?"

"Amedea," he said simply.

She laughed at him. "I always knew you'd be a big success, Pasquale." Was that mocking, her tone? She tried to hand his cigarette back but he waved it over to her and pulled out a new one for himself. And they stood there smoking their separate cigarettes, not talking, until Amedea's was all ash, and she said she had to get back inside. Pasquale said he had to catch his train anyway.

"Good luck with your actress," Amedea said, and she smiled as if she meant it. Then she darted in her light way across the street, glanced back at him once, and walked off. Pasquale felt an itch in his throat—the urge to yell something after her—but he kept his mouth shut, because he had no idea what those words might be.

7

Eating Human Flesh

1846
Truckee, California

So there's this guy . . . a carriage-maker named William Eddy,
good family man, handsome, honest, but uneducated. It's
1846 and William is married, with two little kids. But he's
dirt-poor, so when the opportunity comes to go to California to make
his fortune, Eddy jumps at it. It's the driving ambition of his time,
his people, to go west. So Eddy signs on with a wagon train leaving Missouri for California. Over credits, this William Eddy and his
pretty young wife are getting ready for the journey, packing up their
meager belongings from their sod-and-log cabin.

The camera makes its way down a long line of wagons, filled with
all of their belongings, herds of cattle moving with them, strung out
for a half-mile leading out of town, kids and dogs running alongside.
On the front of the wagon train we see: CALIFORNIA OR BUST. Swing
around the other side of this wagon and we see: DONNER PARTY.

The trains were always named for the prominent families, but
William Eddy's the closest thing to a decent frontiersman on this
particular train, good hunter and tracker, humble to a fault. The first
night out, the men from the wealthy families meet to discuss the trip
and William steps to the fire to say that he's worried: they've gotten
a late start and he's not sure about this route they're taking. But
he's hushed by the wealthier guys and he just goes back to his ragtag
wagon in the back of the train.

The first act is all action, descent—trouble. Right away the pioneers hit bad weather and wagon wheels breaking. There's a villain in the party, a sturdy German immigrant named Keseberg, who's scammed an old couple into joining his wagon, but when they're out past civilization, Keseberg steals everything from the old people and turns them out, forcing them to walk. Only William Eddy takes the couple in.

The wagon train arrives in Utah, at the halfway point, strung out, weeks behind schedule. At night, the party's cattle are scavenged by Indians. William Eddy is the best hunter, so he kills game along the way. But bad luck and bad weather continue to plague them, and they have to pay for taking this questionable route when everything breaks down on the great salt flats. We pan over this cracked, hard soil, the trail of wagons strung out for miles, cattle starting to fall dead, the settlers forced to stagger across a desert, family by family, horses walking blindly—the foreshadowing of the dissolution of society, everyone turning slightly feral except William Eddy, who retains his human dignity to help the rest of the party get across.

Finally, they make it to Nevada—but it's October, weeks later than any group of pioneers has ever tried to make it through. The snows usually come in mid-November, so they've still got a few weeks to cross the Sierra Nevada Range, and they'll be in California. But they must hurry. They walk and ride all night, hoping to make it.

Now we're up in the clouds. But these aren't fluffy clouds. They are dark and ominous, black masses of foreboding. This is our Jaws *and these clouds are our shark. We're tight on a single snowflake. We follow it down through the sky and see it joined by other flakes. Big. Heavy. We watch that first flake fall, finally coming to rest on the arm of William Eddy, dirty and unshaven. And he knows. His eyes go slowly to the sky.*

They are too late. The snows have come a month early. The Donner Party is already in the mountains, and the snow is blinding—not just flakes . . . curtains of snow fall, making the passage more than difficult. It's impossible. Finally, they enter the mountain valley, and there it is, right before them: the pass, a narrow gap in two rock walls, so tantalizingly close. But the snow here is already ten feet deep and the horses sink to their chests. Wagons bog down. On the other side of that pass is California. Warmth. Safety. But they're too late. The snow makes the mountains impassable. They are in a bowl between two mountain ridges. They can't go forward, can't go back. Doors on both sides have slammed shut.

The ninety people split into two groups. Eddy's larger group is closer to the pass, along a lake, while the second group, with the Donners, is a couple of miles back. Both groups rush to build shelter—three shanty cabins at the lakeside camp and two cabins farther back. At the first camp, near the lake, William Eddy has built a cabin for his wife and his little son and daughter and has allowed other stragglers to take shelter there, too. These cabins are really just lean-tos, covered with hides. Still the snows come. They quickly realize they don't have enough food to last the winter and so they start rationing what cattle they have left. Then a blizzard comes and so much snow falls that the pioneers come out and realize their cows are buried. The pioneers poke sticks in the snow trying to find their dead cows. But they're just . . . gone. And still the snow falls. The fires in their cabins keep the snow melted around them and soon they have to build steps up into the snow around their cabins, twenty-foot walls of white surrounding their shacks so that all you see is the smoke from their fires. Days pass horribly, desperately. For two months they live at the bottom of these snow pits, on starvation rations. They try to hunt but no one can kill any game except . . .

William Eddy. Weakened by hunger, he still goes out every day and manages to shoot some rabbits and even a deer. Earlier, the wealthy families wouldn't share their cattle with him, but Eddy shares his meager game with everyone. But even that food is running out as the game moves down from the snow line. Then, one day, Eddy comes across tracks. He follows the tracks desperately, until he's miles from camp. It's a bear. He catches up to it and raises his rifle weakly . . . shoots . . . and hits it! But the bear turns and charges him. He can't reload, and, nearly starved to death, he has to fight the bear with his rifle stock. He beats the wounded animal to death with his bare hands.

He drags this bear back to the camp, where the people are getting increasingly desperate. William Eddy keeps saying, "We've got to send a team for help," but no one else is strong enough to go, and he's obviously too worried about leaving his family behind to go himself. But now the game has gone down from the mountains, and the snow keeps falling, and finally one night he talks with his wife, who begins the film as a quiet woman, someone who has suffered life more than lived it. Now she takes a deep breath. "Will'm," she says, "you've got to take those who are strong and go. Get help." He protests, but she says, "For our children. Please." What can he do?

What if the only way to save the ones you love . . . is to leave them behind?

By this time the pioneers have eaten all of their horses and mules and even their pets. People are making soup out of saddles and blankets and shoe leather, anything to flavor the snow water. William Eddy's family is down to a few scraps of bear meat. He has no choice. He asks for volunteers. By then, only seventeen people are strong enough to try: twelve men and boys, and five young women. They make crude snowshoes out of harnesses and reins and start out. Right away, two of the boys turn back because the snow is too deep. Even with snowshoes, the rest fall two feet with every step.

Eddy leads his party of fifteen away and they struggle; it takes two days just to make it to the pass. On the first night, they camp and Eddy reaches in his pack and—like a blow to the gut—he realizes his wife has packed the remaining bear meat for him. It's only a few bites, but her selflessness destroys him. She has sacrificed her share for him. He looks back and can just see a curl of smoke from their camp.

What if the only way to save the ones you love . . . is to leave them behind?

They move on. For days and days, the fifteen walk, making slow progress across craggy peaks and snowy valleys. Blizzards blind them and stop them in their tracks. It takes days to go a few thou-

sand yards. With no food except a few bites of Eddy's bear meat, they grow weak. One of the men, Foster, says they must sacrifice one of themselves for food for the others, and they talk of drawing lots. William Eddy says that if someone is going to be sacrificed, then that man must be given a chance. They should pick two men and have them fight to the death. He volunteers to be one of the men. But no one moves. One morning, an old man and a boy are dead of starvation. They have no choice. They build a fire and eat the meat of their companions.

But we don't linger on this aspect. It's just . . . what it is. People hear Donner Party and they think cannibalism, but almost all of the survivors said the cannibalism was nothing . . . it was the cold, the despair, these are the enemy. For days they walk; only William Eddy keeps them from descending into chaos. More men die and the party eats what it can, and still the group walks, until there are only nine left—four of the original ten men and all five women. Two of the surviving men are Indian scouts. The other living white man, Foster, wants to shoot the Indians and eat them. But Eddy won't let him and he warns the Indians, who manage to escape before Foster can kill them. When Foster finds out, he attacks Eddy, but the women break up the fight.

And why do the men die and the women survive? Because women have more body fat to live off of, and are lighter, so they use less energy walking through snow. It is the great irony: muscles kill men.

Eighteen days. That's how long the rescue party walks. For eighteen days they stagger through forty-foot drifts, ice so hard it cracks their skin. They are seven skeletons in tatters when they finally descend below the snow line. In the woods, they see a deer, but William Eddy is too weak to lift his gun. It is wrenching—William Eddy finally sees game, tries to shoulder his rifle, and fails. He just drops the gun. And walks on. For food, they graze on bark and wild grasses, like deer. And then, William Eddy sees a curl of smoke from a small Indian village. But the others are simply too weak to move, so William Eddy leaves them behind and goes on himself.

Remember, this is before the Forty-niners and the real boom in California. The state is virtually empty. San Francisco is a town of a few hundred people, called Yerba Buena. Now we're tight on a cabin at the edge of the mountains. We pull back to see it, idyllic and peaceful, a stream running in front, little patches of snow. We go wider and wider, so that you see this is the only civilization for miles. And there, in the corner of the frame, are two Indians holding up this figure. Now we go closer again, and we see, between the Indians, this gaunt creature, practically a skeleton, wild beard, barefoot, his clothes just tattered rags, staggering to the cabin . . .

. . . is William Eddy! The ranchers get him some water. A bit of flour, which is all his constricted stomach can handle. His eyes well with tears. "There are others . . . in an Indian village near here," he tells them. "Six." A party is sent off. He's done it. Of the fifteen who went for help, William Eddy has brought Foster and the five women to safety and told the ranchers about the others back in the mountains.

But the story's not over. First act, trek into the mountains; second act, descent and escape; third act, the rescue. Eddy has left seventy people up in the mountains, waiting for help. A rescue party is raised, forty men led by a fat, smug cavalryman named Colonel Woodworth. Eddy and Foster are too weak to help, but Eddy wakes momentarily in his bed to see dozens of men riding past the frontier cabin.

When his fever finally breaks, days later, he asks about the rescue party. The ranchers tell him that Woodworth's men are camped only two days away, waiting out a snowstorm. A small rescue party of seven made it back to the Donner Party, but they nearly died crossing the pass and were only able to bring a dozen or so people out because of the deep snow and the weakness of the trapped pioneers. Even being rescued was a great danger; several more died on the way across the mountains. After a long pause, William Eddy speaks. "And my family?"

The rancher shakes his head. "I'm sorry. Your wife and daughter were already dead. Your boy is still alive, but was too young to walk over the pass. They left him in the camp." William Eddy rises from his bed. He must go. His old enemy Foster also left a son behind, and he agrees to go with Eddy, even though they are weak still.

At a camp, miles from the pass, Woodworth tells Eddy a spring snowstorm has made it too dangerous to attempt—but Eddy won't take no for an answer. He offers Woodworth's men twenty dollars for every child they will carry over the pass. A few soldiers agree and they press on—and are nearly killed traversing the pass they've just crossed weeks earlier. Finally, Eddy and Foster and a handful of men stagger back into the Donner camp. It's a scene from hell. Bodies cut up in the snow . . . pieces hanging like sausages in a deli. The smell . . . the despair . . . gaunt survivors unrecognizable as humans. William Eddy can barely muster the strength to walk to the cabin he built months earlier, where he and Foster left their families.

Foster's son is still alive! Foster cries as he holds his boy. But for Eddy . . . he's too late. His son died days earlier. William Eddy has lost his whole family. He goes into a rage and stands above the villain, Keseberg, who may have eaten the children, this man who is nothing more than an animal. Eddy looks down at this beast. He steps forward to kill the man . . . but he can't. He falls down and stares at the sky again, at the very sky that dropped that first snowflake on him. And his head goes to his hands. Foster steps forward to kill Keseberg for him, but a voice comes from the heap that is William Eddy. "Leave him," he tells Foster. Because Eddy knows that this evil lives in all of us, that we are all animals in the end. "Let him be," he says.

William Eddy has simply . . . survived. And as he faces the horizon, we realize that maybe it's all any of us can hope to do. Survive. Caught in the raging crosscurrents of history, of sorrow, and of certain death, a man realizes he is powerless, that all his belief in himself is a vanity . . . a dream. So he does his best, he squirms against the snow and the wind and his own animal hungers, and this is a life. For family, for love, for simple decency, a good man rages against nature, and the brutality of fate, but it is a war he can never win. Every love is the same love, and it is overpowering—the *wrenching grace of what it is to be human. We love. We try. We die alone.*

On-screen, in this snowy field, we see a hundred-fifty years pass in ten seconds, as train tracks come through, then roads are built, then houses, and the first cars begin to ply Truckee Pass on their way to Tahoe, and then an interstate, this once impassable place now just another stretch of freeway—and we are faced with the cruel ease of today's passage, but we pull up and see the forest, and the truth of humanity remains. These trees, this mountain, the inscrutable face of nature, of death.

And as quickly as we saw this freeway, it is gone: a dream, a hallucination, a vision in the destroyed mind of a broken man. It's just a remote mountain pass in the year 1847. The world around him quiet as death. It's dusk. And William Eddy rides out alone.

8

The Grand Hotel

April 1962
Rome, Italy

Pasquale slept uneasily in an expensive little *albergo* near the terminal station. He wondered how guests in these Rome hotels slept with all the noise. He rose early, slipped into his pants, shirt, tie, and jacket, had a *caffè*, and then took a cab to the Grand Hotel, where the American film people were staying. He smoked a cigarette on the Spanish Steps as he prepared himself. Vendors were setting up cut-flower stands and tourists were already flitting about, clutching folded maps, cameras around their necks. Pasquale looked down at the name on the paper that Orenzio had given him and said the name quietly so he wouldn't mess it up.

I am here to see . . . Michael Deane. Michael Deane. Michael Deane.

Pasquale had never been inside the Grand Hotel. The mahogany door opened onto the most ornate lobby he'd ever seen: marble floors, floral frescoes on the ceilings, crystal chandeliers, stained-glass skylights depicting saints and birds and glum lions. It was hard to take it all in and he had to force himself not to gape like a tourist, to appear serious and focused. He had important business with the bastard Michael Deane. People were milling about in the lobby, groups of tourists and Italian businessmen in black suits and eyeglasses. Pasquale didn't see any film stars, but then he wouldn't have known what they looked like, either. He rested for a moment against a white sculpted lion, but its face was so much like a human's that it made Pasquale uncomfortable and he moved on to the front desk.

Pasquale removed his hat and handed the desk clerk the piece of paper with Michael Deane's name on it. He opened his mouth to say his line, but the clerk looked at the paper and pointed to an ornate doorway at the end of the lobby. "End of the hall." A long line of people stretched and winded out the doorway where the clerk pointed.

"I have business with this man, Deane. He's in there?" he asked the clerk.

The man just pointed and looked away. "End of the hall."

Pasquale made his way to the back of the line at the end of the hall. He wondered if these people all had business with Michael Deane. Maybe the man had sick actresses squirreled all over Italy. The woman in line in front of Pasquale was attractive—straight brown hair and long legs, maybe his age, twenty-two or twenty-three, wearing a tight dress and nervously fingering an unlit cigarette.

"Do you have a light?" she asked.

Pasquale struck a match and held it for her. She cupped his hand and breathed in.

"I'm so nervous. If I don't smoke right now I'm going to have to eat a whole cake. Then I'll be as fat as my sister and they'll have no use for me."

He looked past her, along the line of people, into an ornate ballroom, big gold pillars in the corners.

"What is this line?" he asked.

"This is the only way," she answered. "You can try to get in at the studio or wherever they're filming that day, but I think the lines all go to the same place. No, the best way is to do what you did, just come here."

Pasquale said, "I am trying to find this man." He showed her the piece of paper with Deane's name on it.

She glanced at the paper, and then showed him her own piece

of paper, which had the name of a different man on it. "It doesn't matter," she said. "All of the lines lead to the same place eventually."

More people fell in line behind Pasquale. The line led to a small table, where a man and a woman were seated with several stapled sheets of paper in front of them. Perhaps the man was Michael Deane. The man and the woman asked each person in line a question or two and then either sent them back the way they'd come, or to stand in the corner or out another door that seemed to lead outside.

When it was the beautiful girl's turn, they took her paper, asked her age and where she was from, and whether she spoke any English. She said nineteen, Terni, and yes she spoke "English *molto* good." They asked her to say something.

"Baby, baby," she said in something like English. "I love you, baby. You are my baby." She was sent to stand in the corner. Pasquale noticed that all the attractive young girls were sent to this same corner. The other people were sent out the door. When it was his turn, he showed the piece of paper with Michael Deane's name to the man at the small table, who handed it back.

"Are you Michael Deane?" Pasquale asked.

"Identification?" the man said in Italian.

Pasquale handed over his ID card. "I'm looking for this man, Michael Deane."

The man glanced up, then flipped through the pages, and finally wrote Pasquale's name on one of the last pages, which was filled with dozens of names like his, written in the man's handwriting.

"Any experience?" the man asked.

"What?"

"Acting experience."

"No, I am not an actor. I am trying to find Michael Deane."

"Speak English?"

"Yes," Pasquale said in English.

"Say something."

"Hello," he said in English. "How are you?"

The man looked intrigued. "Say something funny," he said.

Pasquale stood a moment and then said, in English, "I ask if she love him and she say yes. I ask if . . . he is in love, too. She say yes, the man love himself."

The man didn't smile but he said, "Okay," and handed Pasquale's ID card back, along with a card that had a number on it. The number was 5410. He pointed to the exit that most everyone else had been taking, except the beautiful girls. "Bus number four."

"No, I am try to find—"

But the man had moved on to the next person in line.

Pasquale followed the snaking line out to a row of buses. He got on the fourth bus, which was nearly full of men between the ages of twenty and forty. After a few more minutes, he saw the lovely women loaded onto a smaller bus. When some more men had gotten on his bus, its door squeaked closed and the engine rumbled to life and the bus started off. They were driven through the city to an area in the *centro* that Pasquale didn't recognize, where the bus stopped. Slowly, the men climbed off the bus. Pasquale could think of nothing to do but follow them.

They walked down an alley and through a gate marked CENTU-RIONS. And sure enough, inside the high fence, costumed Roman centurions were standing everywhere, smoking, eating *panini*, reading newspapers, talking to one another. There were hundreds of these men wearing armor and holding spears. There were no cameras or film crews anywhere, just men in centurion costumes wearing wristwatches and fedoras.

He felt rather foolish doing it, but Pasquale followed the line of men not yet in costume. The line led to a small building, where the men were being measured and fitted. "Is there someone of authority around?" he asked the man in front of him.

"No. That's what's so great." The man opened his jacket and showed Pasquale that he had five of the numbered cards that had been given away at the hotel. "I just keep going through the line. The idiots pay me every time. I don't ever even get a costume. It's almost too easy." The man winked.

"But I'm not supposed to be here," Pasquale said.

The man laughed. "Don't worry. They won't catch you. They won't film today anyway. It'll rain or someone won't like the light or after an hour someone will come out and say, 'Mrs. Taylor is ill again,' and they'll send us home. They film only one of every five days, at most. During the rains, I knew a man who got paid six times each day just to show up. He'd go to all of the extra locations and get paid at each one. They finally caught on and kicked him out. Do you know what he did? He stole a camera and sold it to an Italian film company and do you know what they did? Sold it back to the Americans at twice the price. Ha!"

As they moved forward, a man in a tweed suit was walking toward them, down the line. He was with a woman holding a clipboard. The man was speaking English in quick, furious bursts, telling the woman with the clipboard various things to write down. She nodded and did as he said. Sometimes he sent the people out of line and they left happily. When he got to Pasquale, the man stopped and leaned in extremely close. Pasquale leaned back.

"How old is he?"

Pasquale answered in English before the woman could translate. "I am twenty-two years."

Now the man took Pasquale by the chin and turned his face so that he could look directly in his eyes. "Where'd you get the blue eyes, pal?"

"My mother, she has blue eyes. She is Ligurian. There are many blue eyes."

The man said to the interpreter, "Slave?" and then to Pasquale, "You want to be a slave? I can get you a little more pay. Maybe even more days." Before he could answer, the man said to the woman, "Send him over to be a slave."

"No," Pasquale said. "Wait." He dug out the paper again and spoke to the man in the tweed suit in English. "I am only try to find Michael Deane. In my hotel is an American. Dee Moray."

The man turned his body fully to Pasquale. "What did you say?"

"I am try to find—"

"Did you say Dee Moray?"

"Yes. She is in my hotel. This is why I come to find this Michael Deane. She has wait for him and he doesn't come. She is very sick."

The man looked down at the piece of paper and then made eye contact with the woman. "Jesus, we heard Dee went to Switzerland for treatment."

"No. She come to my hotel."

"Well, goddamn it, man, what are you doing with the extras?"

A car took him back to the Grand Hotel and he sat in the lobby, watching the light glint off a crystal chandelier. There was a staircase behind him, and every few minutes someone would saunter down, as if their appearance would lead to applause. The lifts dinged every few minutes as well, but still no one came for him. Pasquale smoked and waited. He thought of going to the room at the end of the hall and asking someone where he could find Michael Deane but he was afraid they'd just put him on a bus again. Twenty minutes passed. Then another twenty. Finally, an attractive young woman approached. There seemed to be no shortage of these.

"Mr. Tursi?"

"Yes."

"Mr. Deane is so sorry to have kept you waiting. Please, come with me." Pasquale followed her to the lift and the operator took them to the fourth floor. The hallways were well-lit and wide and Pasquale was embarrassed to think of Dee Moray leaving this beautiful hotel for his little *pensione*, with its narrow staircase, where there hadn't been room for the full height of the ceiling and so the builder had simply used the native boulders, blending the wall into the rock ceiling, as if a cave were slowly eating his hotel.

He followed the woman into a suite, the doors connecting several rooms flung open. There appeared to be a great deal of work going on in this suite—people talking on telephones and typing, as if a small business had taken root here. There was a long table of food and lovely Italian girls circulating with coffee. One of them, he saw, was the girl he'd seen in line. But she wouldn't meet his eyes.

Pasquale was rushed through the suite and onto a terrace overlooking the church of Trinità dei Monti. He thought again of Dee Moray, of her saying what a beautiful view she had from her room, and he was embarrassed.

"Please, sit down. Michael will be right with you."

Pasquale sat in a wrought-iron chair on the terrace, the sound of all that typing and talking going on behind him. He smoked. He waited another forty minutes. Then the attractive woman returned. Or was it a different one? "It will be a few more minutes. Would you like some water while you wait?"

"Yes, thank you," Pasquale said.

But the water never arrived. It was after one now. He'd been trying to find Michael Deane for more than three hours. He was thirsty and hungry.

Another twenty minutes passed and the woman returned. "Michael is waiting for you down in the lobby."

Pasquale was shaking—with anger or hunger, he couldn't tell—as he stood and followed her through the suite again and out into the hallway, back down in the lift and to the lobby. And there, sitting on the very couch where he'd been an hour earlier, was a man far younger than Pasquale had imagined—as young as him—a fair, pale American with thin, reddish brown hair. He was chewing his right thumbnail. He was handsome enough, in that washed-out American way, but he lacked some quality that Pasquale would have assigned to the man that Dee Moray was waiting for. Maybe, he thought, there is no man good enough for her.

The man stood. "Mr. Tursi," he said in English. "I'm Michael Deane. I understand you've come to talk about Dee."

What Pasquale did next surprised even him. He hadn't done anything of the kind since a night years ago in La Spezia, when he was seventeen and one of Orenzio's brothers impugned his manhood, but at that very moment he stepped in and punched Michael Deane—in the chest, of all places. He'd never hit anyone in the chest, had never even *seen* anyone hit in the chest. It hurt his whole arm, and made a dull thud, and dropped Deane right back onto the couch, folded over like a garment bag.

Pasquale stood above the folded man, shaking and thinking, Stand up. Stand up and fight; let me hit you again. But slowly Pasquale's anger faded. He looked around. No one had seen the punch. It must've looked as if Michael Deane had simply taken his seat again. Pasquale stepped back a little.

After he caught his breath, Deane unrolled, looked up with a grimace, and said, "Ow! Shit." Then he coughed. "I suppose you think I deserved that."

"Why you leave her alone like this! She is scared. And sick."

"I know. I know. Look, I'm sorry about how things turned out." Deane coughed again and rubbed his chest. He looked around warily. "Can we talk about this outside?"

Pasquale shrugged and they walked toward the door.

"No more hitting, right?"

Pasquale agreed and they left the hotel and walked outside to the Spanish Steps. The piazza was full, merchants yelling out prices for flowers. Pasquale waved them off as they walked deeper into the piazza.

Michael Deane continued to rub his chest. "I think you broke something."

"*Mi dispiace,*" Pasquale muttered, even though he wasn't sorry.

"How is Dee?"

"She is sick. I bring a doctor from La Spezia."

"And your doctor . . . examined her?"

"Yes."

"I see." Michael Deane nodded grimly and started in on his thumbnail again. "Then I don't suppose I need to guess what the doctor told you."

"He ask for her doctor. To talk."

"He wants to talk to Dr. Crane?"

"Yes." Pasquale tried to remember the exact conversation, but he knew the translation would be impossible.

"Look, you should know that none of this was Dr. Crane's idea. It was mine." Michael Deane pulled back, as if Pasquale might hit him again. "All Dr. Crane did was explain to her that her symptoms were *consistent* with cancer. Which they are."

Pasquale wasn't sure he understood. "Are you come to get her now?" he asked.

Michael Deane didn't answer right away, but looked around the piazza. "Do you know what I like about this place, Mr. Tursi?"

Pasquale looked at the Spanish Steps, at the wedding-cake ascension of stairs leading up to the church of Trinità dei Monti. On the steps nearest him, a young woman was leaning forward on her knees, reading a book while her friend drew on a sketch pad. The steps were covered with people like this, reading, taking photographs, and in intimate conversations.

"I like the self-interest of the Italian people. I like that they aren't afraid to ask for exactly what they want. Americans are not like that. We talk around our intentions. Do you know what I mean?"

Pasquale didn't. But he also didn't want to admit it and so he just nodded.

"You and I should explain our positions. I'm obviously in a difficult position and you appear to be someone who can help."

Pasquale was having trouble concentrating on these meaningless words. He couldn't imagine what Dee Moray saw in this man.

They had reached the Fountain of the Old Boat in the center of the piazza—the Fontana della Barcaccia. Michael Deane leaned against it. "Do you know about this fountain, the sinking boat?"

Pasquale looked at the sculpted boat in the center of the fountain, water roiling up through the center of it. "No."

"It's unlike any other sculpture in the city. All of these earnest, serious pieces and this one, it's comic—ridiculous. To my thinking, that makes it the truest piece of art in the city. Do you know what I mean, Mr. Tursi?"

Pasquale didn't know what to say.

"A long time ago, during a flood, the river lifted a boat and dumped it here, where the fountain sits today. The artist was trying to capture the random nature of disaster.

"His point was this: sometimes there is no explanation for the things that happen. Sometimes a boat simply appears on a street. And as odd as it may seem, one has no choice but to deal with the fact that there's suddenly a boat on the street. Well . . . such is the position I find myself in here in Rome, on this movie. Except it's not just one boat. There are fucking boats on every fucking street."

Again, Pasquale had no idea what the man meant.

"You may think what I've done to Dee is cruel. I won't argue that, from a certain vantage, it was. But I just deal with whatever disasters arise, one at a time." With that, Michael Deane produced an envelope from his suit coat. He pressed it into Pasquale's hand. "Half is for her. And half is for you, for what you've done and for what I hope you can do for me now." He put a hand on Pasquale's arm. "Even though you've assaulted me, I'm going to consider you a friend, Mr. Tursi, and I will treat you as a friend. But if I find out that you have given her less than half or that you have talked to anyone about this, I will no longer be your friend. And you don't want that."

Pasquale pulled his arm away. Was this awful man accusing *him* of being dishonest? He remembered Dee's word and he said, "Please! I am frank!"

"Yes, good," Michael Deane said, holding up his hands as if he were afraid Pasquale would hit him again. Then his eyes narrowed and he stepped in close. "You want to be frank? I can be frank. I was sent here to save this dying movie. That's my only job. My job has no moral component. It is not good and it is not bad. It is merely my job to get the boats off the streets."

He looked away. "Obviously your doctor is right. We misled Dee to get her out of here. I'm not proud of myself for that. Please tell her, Dr. Crane shouldn't have chosen stomach cancer. He didn't mean to scare her. You know doctors—almost too analytical. He chose it because the symptoms could match up with those of early pregnancy. But it was only supposed to be for a day or two. That's why she was supposed to go to Switzerland. There's a doctor there who specializes in unwanted pregnancies. He's safe. Discreet."

Pasquale was a few steps behind. So it was true. She *was* pregnant.

Michael Deane reacted to Pasquale's look. "Look, please tell her how sorry I am." Then he patted the envelope in Pasquale's hand. "Tell her . . . it's the way things sometimes are. And I am truly sorry. But she needs to go to Switzerland as Dr. Crane advised her to do. The doctor there will take care of everything. It's all paid for."

Pasquale stared at the envelope in his hands.

"Oh, and I have something else for her." He reached in the same jacket pocket and removed three small, square photographs. They appeared to have been taken on the set of the movie—he could see a camera crew in the background of one—and while the pictures were small, Pasquale could see clearly, in all three of them, Dee Moray. She wore a kind of long, flowing dress and was standing with another woman, both of them flanking a third woman, a beautiful, dark-haired woman who was in the foreground of the pictures. In the best photo, Dee and this dark-haired woman were leaning back, caught by the photographer in a genuine moment, dissolving in laughter. "These are continuity photos," Michael Deane said. "We use these pictures to make sure we get the setup for the next shot right. Costumes, hair . . . make sure no one puts on a wristwatch. I thought Dee might want to have these."

Pasquale looked hard into the top photo. Dee Moray had her hand on the other woman's arm, and they were laughing so hard that Pasquale would have given anything right then to know what was so funny. Maybe it was the same joke she'd shared with him, about this man who loved himself so much.

Deane was looking down at the top photo, too. "She has an interesting look. Honestly, I didn't see it at first. I thought Mankiewicz had lost his mind—casting a blond woman as an Egyptian lady-in-waiting. But she has this quality . . ." Michael Deane leaned in. "And I'm not just talking tits here. There's something else . . . an authenticity. She's a real actress, that one." Deane shook off this thought and looked back at the top photo. "We'll have to reshoot the scenes with Dee in them. There aren't many. What with the delays, the rains, the labor stuff, then Liz got sick, and then Dee got sick. When I sent her away, she told me she was disappointed that no one would ever know she was in this movie. So I thought she would want these." Michael Deane shrugged. "Of course, that was when she thought she was dying."

It hung in the air, the word *dying*.

"You know," Michael Deane said, "I sort of imagined that she'd eventually call me and we'd laugh about this. That it would be a funny story that two people share years later, maybe we'd even . . ." He trailed off, smiled wanly. "But that's not going to happen. She's going to want my balls. But please . . . tell her that once she's over her anger, if she remains cooperative, I'll get her all the film work she wants when we all get back to the States. Could you tell her that? She could be a star if she wants to be."

Pasquale felt like he might be sick. He was trying so hard not to hit Michael Deane again—wondering what kind of man abandons a pregnant woman—when a realization came to him, so obvious that it hit him square in the chest, and he gasped. He'd never had a thought as *physical* as this one, like a kick to his gut: *Here I am, angry at this man for abandoning a pregnant woman . . .*

While my own son is raised believing that his mother is his sister.

Pasquale flushed. He remembered crouching on the machine-gun nest and saying to Dee Moray: *It is not always that simple.* But it was. It was entirely simple. There was one kind of man who ran from such responsibility. He and Michael Deane were such men. He could no more hit this man than he could hit himself. Pasquale felt the sickness of his own hypocrisy and covered his mouth.

When Pasquale said nothing, Michael Deane glanced back at the Fontana della Barcaccia and frowned. "This is the world, I guess."

And then Michael Deane walked away, into the crowd, leaving Pasquale leaning against the fountain. He opened the heavy envelope. It was filled with more money than he'd ever seen—a stack of American currency for Dee and Italian lire for him.

Pasquale put the photos in the envelope and closed it. He looked all around. The day was overcast. People were spread all over the Spanish Steps, resting, but in the piazza and on the street they moved with purpose, at different speeds but in straight lines, like a thousand bullets fired at a thousand different angles from a thousand different guns. All of these people moving in the way they thought right . . . all of these stories, all of these weak, sick people with their betrayals and their dark hearts—*This is the world*—swirling all around him, speaking and smoking and snapping photographs, and Pasquale felt himself turn hard, and he thought he might spend the rest of his life standing here, like the old fountain of the stranded boat. People would point to the statue of the poor villager who had naively come to the city to talk to the American movie people, the man who had been frozen in time when his own weak character was revealed to him.

And Dee! What was he going to tell her? Would he assail the character of this man she loved, this snake Deane, when Pasquale himself was a species of the same snake? Pasquale covered his mouth as a groan came out.

He felt a hand on his shoulder just then. Pasquale turned. It was a woman, the interpreter who had moved down the line of centurion extras earlier in the day. "You're the man who knows where Dee is?" she asked in Italian.

"Yes," Pasquale said.

The woman looked around and then squeezed Pasquale's arm. "Please. Come with me. There is someone who would like very much to talk to you."

9

The Room

Recently
Universal City, California

The Room is everything. When you are in The Room, nothing exists outside. The people hearing your pitch could no more leave The Room than choose to not orgasm. They MUST hear your story. The Room is all there is.

Great fiction tells unknown truths. Great film goes further. Great film improves Truth. After all, what Truth ever made $40 million in its first weekend of wide release? What Truth sold in forty foreign territories in six hours? Who's lining up to see a sequel to Truth?

If your story improves Truth, you will sell it in The Room. Sell it in The Room and you'll get The Deal. Get The Deal and the world awaits like a quivering bride in your bed.

—From chapter 14 of *The Deane's Way: How I Pitched Modern Hollywood to America and How You Can Pitch Success Into Your Life Too*, by Michael Deane

In The Room, Shane Wheeler feels the exhilaration Michael Deane promised. They are going to make *Donner!* He knows it.

Michael Deane is his Mr. Miyagi and he has just waxed the car. Michael Deane is his Yoda and he has just raised the ship from the muck. Shane *did it*. He's never felt so invigorated. He wishes Saundra could've been here to see it, or his parents. He might have been a little nervous in the beginning, but he's never been as sure of anything as he is of this: he killed that pitch.

The Room is suitably quiet. Shane waits. It is old Pasquale who speaks first, pats Shane on the arm, and says, *"Penso è andata molto bene."* I think that went very well.

"Grazie, Mr. Tursi."

Shane glances around the room. Michael Deane is totally inscrutable, but Shane isn't sure that human expression is even possible anymore on his face. He does look to be deep in thought, though, his wrinkly hands crossed in front of his smooth face, his index fingers raised like a steeple before his lips. Shane looks hard at the man: is one of his brows higher than the other? Or is it just fixed that way?

Then Shane glances to Michael Deane's right, where Claire Silver has the strangest look on her face. It could be a smile (she loves it!) or a grimace (God, is it possible she hated it?), but if he had to name it he might go with *pained bemusement*.

Still no one speaks. Shane starts to wonder if maybe he's misread The Room—all of last year's self-doubt creeping back in—when . . . a noise comes from Claire Silver. A humming through her nose, like a low motor starting. "Cannibals," she says, and then she loses it—full, out-of-control, breathless laughter: high, manic, and chirping, and she puts a hand out toward Shane. "I— I'm sorry, it's not— I just— It's—" And then she gives in to the laughter; she dissolves in it.

"I'm sorry," Claire says when she can talk again, "I am. But—" And now the laughter peals again, somehow goes higher. "I wait three years for a good movie pitch . . . and when I get it, what's it about? A cowboy"—she covers her mouth to try to stop the laughter—"whose family gets eaten by a fat German." She doubles over.

"He's not a cowboy," Shane mumbles, feeling himself shrinking, shriveling, dying. "And we wouldn't *show* the cannibalism."

"No, no, I'm sorry," Claire says, breathless now. "I'm sorry." She covers her mouth again and squeezes her eyes shut but she can't stop laughing.

Shane sneaks a peek at Michael Deane, but the old producer is just staring off, deep in thought, as Claire snorts through her nose—

And Shane feels the last of the air leave his body. He's two-dimensional now—a flat drawing of his crushed self. This is how he's felt the last year, during his depression, and he sees now that it was foolish to believe, even for a minute, that he could muster his old ACT confidence—even in its new, humbler form. That Shane is gone now, dead. A veal cutlet. He mutters, "But . . . it's a good story," and looks at Michael Deane for help.

Claire knows the rule: no producer ever admits to *not* liking a pitch, just in case it sells somewhere else and you end up looking like an idiot for passing. You always come up with some other excuse: *The market isn't right for this,* or *It's too close to something else we're doing,* or if the idea is truly awful, *It just isn't right for us.* But after this day, after the last three years, after everything—she just can't help herself. All of her gagged responses to three years of ludicrous ideas and moronic pitches gush out in teary, breathless laughter. An effects-driven period thriller about *cowboy cannibals*? Three hours of sorrow and degradation, all to find out the hero's son is . . . *dessert*?

"I'm sorry," she gasps, but she can't stop laughing.

I'm sorry: the words seem finally to snap Michael Deane out of some trance. He shoots a cross look at his assistant and drops his hands from his chin. "Claire. Please. That's enough." Then he looks at Shane Wheeler and leans forward on his desk. "I love it."

Claire laughs a few more times, dying sounds. She wipes the tears from her eyes and sees that Michael is serious.

"It's perfect," he says. "It's exactly the kind of film I set out to make when I started in this business."

Claire falls back in her chair, stunned—hurt, even, beyond the point she realized was possible anymore.

"It's brilliant," Michael says, warming up to the idea. "An epic, untold story of American hardship." And now he turns to Claire. "Let's option this outright. I want to go to the studio with it."

He turns back to Shane. "If you're amenable, we'll do a short six-month option agreement while I try to set this up with the studio—say, ten thousand dollars? Obviously that's just to secure the rights against a larger purchase price if it's further developed. If that's acceptable, Mr.—"

"Wheeler," Shane says, barely finding the breath to speak his own name. "Yes," he manages, "ten thousand is . . . uh . . . acceptable."

"Well, Mr. Wheeler—that was quite a pitch. You have great energy. Reminds me a bit of myself when I was young."

Shane looks from Michael Deane to Claire, who has gone pale now, and back again to Michael. "Thank you, Mr. Deane. I practically devoured your book."

Michael flinches again at the mention of his book. "Well, it shows," he says, his lips parting to show his gleaming teeth in something like a smile. "Maybe I should have been a teacher, huh, Claire?"

A movie about the Donner Party? Michael as a *teacher*? Language has completely failed Claire now. She thinks of the deal she'd made with herself—*One day, one idea for one film*—and realizes that Fate is truly fucking with her now. It's bad enough trying to live in this vacuous, cynical world, but if Fate is telling her that she doesn't even *understand* the rules of the world—well, that's more than she can bear. People can handle an unjust world; it's when the world becomes arbitrary and inexplicable that order breaks down.

Michael stands and turns again to his dumbstruck development assistant. "Claire, I need you to set up a meeting at the studio next week—Wallace, Julie . . . everyone."

"You're going to take this to the studio?"

"Yes. Monday morning, you, me, Danny, and Mr. Wheeler are going in to pitch *The Donner Party*."

"Uh, it's just called *Donner!*" Shane offers. "With an exclamation point?"

"Even better," Michael says. "Mr. Wheeler, can you give that pitch next week? Just like you did today?"

"Sure," Shane says. "Yeah."

"Okay then." Michael pulls out his cell phone. "And Mr. Wheeler, as long as you're going to be here over the weekend, would it be asking too much for you to help us with Mr. Tursi? We can pay you for translating and put you up at a hotel. Then we'll set about getting you a film deal on Monday. How does all that sound?"

"Good?" Shane suggests. He glances over at Claire, who looks even more shocked than he is.

Michael opens a drawer in his desk and begins searching for something. "Oh, and Mr. Wheeler, before you go . . . I wonder if you could ask Mr. Tursi one more question." Michael smiles at Pasquale again. "Ask him . . ." He takes a deep breath and stammers a bit, as if this is the difficult part for him. "I wonder if he knows if Dee . . . what I'm trying to say is . . . was there a child?"

But Pasquale doesn't need this particular translation. He reaches into an inside pocket of his suit coat and pulls out an envelope. He pulls from it an old, weathered postcard and carefully hands it to Shane. The front of the postcard has a faded blue drawing of a baby. IT'S A BOY! it announces. On the back, the card has been addressed to Pasquale Tursi at the Hotel Adequate View, Porto Vergogna, Italy. Written on the back of the card is a note in careful handwriting:

Dear Pasquale: It seems wrong we didn't get to say good-bye. But I guess some things are meant just for a certain place and time. Anyway, thank you.

Always—Dee.
P.S.: I named him Pat, after you.

The postcard makes the rounds. When it arrives at Michael, he smiles distantly. "My God. A boy." He shakes his head. "Well, not a boy anymore, obviously. A man. He'd be . . . Jesus. What? Forty-something?"

He hands the postcard back to Pasquale, who carefully slides it back in his coat.

Michael stands again and offers his hand to Pasquale. "Mr. Tursi. We're going to make good on this—you and me." Pasquale stands and they shake hands uneasily. "Claire, get these gentlemen settled in a hotel. I'll check in with the private investigator and we'll reconvene tomorrow." Michael adjusts his heavy coat over his pajama pants. "Now I've got to get home to Mrs. Deane."

Michael turns to Shane, extends his hand.

"Mr. Wheeler, welcome to Hollywood."

Michael is already out the door before Claire rises. She tells Shane and Pasquale she'll be right back, and chases her boss, catching him on the pathway outside the bungalow. "Michael!"

He turns, his face clear and glassy beneath the decorative streetlight. "Yes, Claire, what is it?"

She glances back over her shoulder to make sure Shane hasn't followed her outside. "I can find another translator. You don't need to string the poor guy along."

"What are you talking about?"

"The Donner Party?"

"Yes." He narrows his eyes. "What about it, Claire?"

"The *Donner* Party?"

He stares at her.

"Michael, are you telling me you *liked* that pitch?"

"Are you telling me you *didn't*?"

Claire blushes. In fact, Shane's pitch had all the elements: it was compelling, moving, suspenseful. Yeah, it might have even been a great pitch—for a film that *could never be made*: a Western epic with no gunfights and no romance, a three-hour sobfest that ends with the villain eating the hero's child.

Claire cocks her head. "So you're going into the studio Monday morning and pitching a fifty-million-dollar period movie about frontier cannibalism?"

"No," Michael says, and his lips slide over his teeth again in that facsimile of a smile. "I'm going into the studio Monday morning and pitching an *eighty*-million-dollar movie about frontier cannibalism." He turns and starts walking again.

Claire calls after her boss. "And the actress's kid. It was yours, wasn't it?"

Michael turns slowly, measuring her. "You have something rare, you know that, Claire? True insight." He smiles. "Tell me. How did the interview go?"

She's startled. Just when she starts to see Michael as a kind of caricature, a relic, he'll show his old power this way.

She glances down at her heels, looks at the skirt she wore today—interview clothes. "They offered me the job. Curator of a film museum."

"And are you taking it?"

"I haven't decided."

He nods. "Look, I really need your help this weekend. Next week, if you still want to leave, I'll understand. I'll even help. But this weekend I need you to keep an eye on the Italian and his translator. Get me through this pitch Monday morning and help me find the actress and her kid. Can you do that for me, Claire?"

She nods. "Of course, Michael." Then, quietly: "So . . . is it? Your kid?"

Michael Deane laughs, looks to the ground and then back up again. "Do you know the old saying, about success having a thousand fathers and failure only one?"

She nods again.

He wraps the coat around himself again. "In that sense, this little fucker . . . might be the only child I ever had."

10

The UK Tour

August 2008
Edinburgh, Scotland

Some skinny Irish kid knocking into Pat Bender's shoulder in a Portland bar—that's what started it.

Pat turned and saw pale, saw gapped front teeth and Superman hair, saw black glasses, Dandy Warhols T-shirt. "Three weeks in America, know what I hate most?" the kid asked. "Your bloody *sparts*." He nodded toward the muted Mariners game on the bar TV. "Fact, maybe you can explain something about *bess-bowl* that I don't quite get."

Before Pat could speak, the kid yelled, *"Averthing!"* and slid into Pat's booth. "I'm Joe," he said. "Admit it, Americans suck at every *spart* you didn't invent."

"Actually," Pat said, "I suck at American sports, too."

This seemed to amuse and satisfy Joe, and he pointed to Pat's guitar case, perched next to him in the booth like a bored date. "And do you play that Larrivée?"

"Across the street," Pat said, "in an hour."

"Seriously? I'm a bit of a club promoter," Joe said. "What kind of stuff you play?"

"Failed mostly," Pat said. "I used to front this band, the Reticents?" No response, and Pat felt pathetic for trying. And how to describe what he did now, which had begun as a talky acoustic set—like that old show *Storytellers*—but after a year had evolved into a comic-music monologue, Spalding Gray with guitar. "Well," he told Joe, "I sit on a stool and I sing a little. I tell some funny stories, confess to a lot of bullshit; and, once every few months, after the show, I do some amateur gynecology."

And that was how it all started—the whole notion of a UK tour. Like every highlight of Pasquale "Pat" Bender's grubby little career, it wasn't even his idea. It was this Joe, who sat midway back in a half-full club, laughing at "Showerpalooza," Pat's song about the way jam bands stink; howling at Pat's riff about his band's stoned liner notes reading like a Chinese food menu; singing along with the crowd at the chorus on "Why Are Drummers So Ducking Fumb?"

There was something magnetic about this Joe. Any other night, Pat would've focused on this little stab at a front table, white panties strobe-flashing beneath her skirt, but he kept hearing Joe's horse-laugh, which was bigger than the kid himself, and by the time Pat pivoted into the dark, confessional part of the show—the drugs and breakups—Joe was deeply affected, removing his glasses and dabbing his eyes to the chorus of Pat's most heartfelt song, "Lydia."

It's an old line: you're too good for me
Yeah, it's not you it's me
But Lydia, baby . . . what if that's the one true thing
You ever got from me—

Afterward, the kid was crazy with praise. He said it was unlike anything he'd ever seen: funny and honest and smart, the music and comic observations complementing each other perfectly. "And that song 'Lydia'—*Jaysus*, Pat!"

Just as Pat figured, "Lydia" had made Joe wistful about some girl he'd never gotten over—and he was compelled to tell the whole story, most of which Pat ignored. No matter how much they laughed during the rest of the show, young men were always moved by that song, and its description of the end of a relationship, Pat endlessly surprised at the way they mistook its cold, bitter refutation of romantic negation (*Did I ever even exist/Before your brown eyes*) for a love song.

Joe started talking right off about Pat performing in London. It was silly talk at midnight, intriguing at one, plausible at two, and by four thirty—smoking Joe's weed and listening to old Reticents songs in Pat's apartment in Northeast Portland ("This is fuck-me brilliant, Pat! How've I never heard this?")—the idea had clicked into a plan: a whole range of Pat's money-girl-career troubles solved by that simple phrase: *UK Tour.*

Joe said that London and Edinburgh were perfect for Pat's edgy, smart musical comedy—a circuit of intimate clubs and comedy festivals farmed by eager booking agents and TV scouts. Five A.M. in Portland was one P.M. in Edinburgh, so Joe stepped outside to make a call and came back giddy: an organizer at the Fringe Festival there remembered the Reticents and said there was an opening for a last-minute fill-in. It was all set. Pat just had to get from Oregon to London and Joe would take care of the rest: lodging, food, transportation, six weeks of guaranteed paid gigs, with the potential for more. Hands were shaken, backs clapped, and by morning Pat was contacting his students and canceling lessons for the month. Pat hadn't felt so excited since his twenties; here he was, heading back out on the road, some twenty-five years after he started. Of course, old fans were sometimes disappointed to see him now—not just that the old front man of the Reticents was doing musical comedy (ignoring Pat's fine distinction: he was a comic-musical *monologist*), but that Pat Bender was even alive, that he hadn't gone the gorgeous-corpse route. Strange how a musician's very survival made him suspect—as if all the crazy shit of his heyday had been just a pose. Pat had tried writing a song about this strange feeling— "So Sorry to Be Here," he called it—but the song got bogged down in that junkie braggadocio and he never performed it.

But now he wondered if there hadn't been a purpose to all that surviving: the second chance to do something . . . BIG. And yet, as excited as he was, even as he typed e-mails to the few friends he could still ask for money ("amazing opportunity" . . . "break I've been waiting for")

Pat couldn't block out a sobering voice: *You're forty-five, running off like some twenty-year-old with a fantasy of getting famous in Europe?*

Pat used to imagine such cold-water warnings in the voice of his mother, Dee, who had tried to be an actress in her youth and whose every impulse was to tamp down her son's ambition with her own disillusionment. *Just ask yourself,* she'd say when he wanted to join a band or quit a band or kick a guy out of a band or move to New York or leave New York, *Is this about the art . . . or is it really about something else?*

What a stupid question, he finally said to her. *Everything is about something else. The art is about something else! That fucking question is about something else!*

But this time it wasn't his mom's cautionary voice that Pat heard. It was Lydia—the last time he saw her, a few weeks after their fourth breakup. That day he'd gone to her apartment, apologized yet again, and promised to get sober. For the first time in his life, he told her, he was seeing things clearly; he'd already managed to quit doing almost everything she objected to, and he'd finish the job if that's what it took to get her back.

Lydia was unlike anyone he'd ever known—smart, funny, self-aware, and shy. Beautiful, too, although she didn't see it—which was the key to her attraction, that she looked the way she did with no self-consciousness, no embellishment. Other women were like presents he was constantly disappointed in unwrapping, but Lydia was like this secret—so lovely beneath her baggy dresses and low-brimmed Lenin cap. On the last day he saw her, Pat had gently removed that hat. He'd looked into those brown eyes: *Baby,* he said. *More than music, booze, anything, it's you that I need.*

That day Lydia stared at him, her eyes wet with regret. She gently took her cap back. *Jesus, Pat,* she said quietly. *Listen to you. You're like some kind of epiphany addict.*

Irish Joe had a buddy in London named Kurtis, a big, bald hip-hop hooligan, and they stayed in the cramped Southwark flat that

Kurtis shared with his pale girlfriend, Umi. Pat had never been to London before—had been to Europe only once, in fact, on a high school exchange trip his mom arranged because she wanted him to see Italy. He never made it: a girl in Berlin and a pinch of coke got him sent home early for various violations of tour protocol and human decency. There was always talk of a Japanese tour with the Reticents—so much that it became a band joke, Pat and Benny balking at their one real chance, refusing to open for the "Stone Temple Douchebags." So this would be the first time Pat performed outside of North America.

"Portland," said pale Umi upon meeting him, "like the Decemberists." Pat had experienced the same thing in the nineties when he told New Yorkers he was from Seattle: they'd mutter *Nirvana* or *Pearl Jam*, and Pat would grit his teeth and pretend some camaraderie with those ass-smelling latecomer poseur flannel bands. Funny how Portland, Seattle's goofy little brother, had achieved similar alt-cool coin.

The plan in London was for Pat to open in this basement club, Troupe, where Kurtis worked as a bouncer. Once Pat got to London, though, Joe decided that Edinburgh would be a better place to start, that Pat could refine his show there and use the reviews from the Fringe Festival to build momentum in advance of London. So Pat worked up a shorter, funnier version of the show—a thirty-minute monologue interspersed with six songs. ("Hi, I'm Pat Bender, and if I look familiar it's because I used to be the singer for one of those bands your pretentious friends talked about to show what obscure musical taste they had. That or we fucked in the bathroom of a club somewhere. Either way, I'm sorry you never heard from me again.")

He performed the show for Joe and his friends in the flat. He planned to go easy on the darker stuff, and to cut the one serious song, "Lydia," from this shortened show, but Joe insisted he include it. He said it was the "emotional pivot of the whole bloody thing," so Pat kept it, and performed it in the flat—Joe once again removing his glasses and wiping his eyes. After the rehearsal, Umi was as enthusiastic as Joe about the show's prospects. Even quiet, brooding Kurtis admitted it was "quite good."

The London flat had exposed pipes and old rotting carpet, and for the week they stayed there, Pat never felt at home—certainly not the way Joe did, sitting around all day with Kurtis in their dirty gray boxer briefs, getting high. Joe, it turned out, had been a bit broad in describing himself as a club promoter; he was more of a hanger-on/hash dealer, people occasionally stopping by the flat to buy from him. After a few days with these kids, the twenty-year age difference steepened for Pat: the musical references, the sloppy track suits, the way they slept in and never showered and didn't seem to notice it was eleven thirty and they were all still in their underwear.

Pat couldn't sleep more than a few hours at a time, so each morning he cleared out while the others slept. He walked the city, trying to imprint it on his foggy mind—but he was always getting lost on its curving, narrow streets and lanes, with their abruptly changing names, arterials ending in alleys. Pat felt more disoriented each day, not so much by London as by his own inability to absorb it, by his crusty old man's list of complaints: *Why can't I figure out where I am, or which way to look when crossing a street? Why are the coins so counterintuitive? Are all of the sidewalks this crowded? Why is everything so expensive?* Broke, all Pat could do was walk around and look—at free museums, mostly, which gradually overwhelmed him—room after room of paintings at the National Gallery, relics at the British Museum, *everything* at the Victoria and Albert. He was OD'ing on culture.

Then, on their last day in London, Pat wandered into the Tate Modern, into the vast empty hall, and was floored by the audacity of the art, and the sheer scale of the museum; it was like trying to take in the ocean, or the sky. Maybe it was a lack of sleep, but he felt physically shaken, almost nauseated. Upstairs, he wandered among a collection of surrealist paintings and felt undone by the nervy, opaque genius of their expression: Bacon, Magritte, and especially Picabia, who, according to the gallery notes, had divided the world into two simple categories: failures and unknowns. He was a bug beneath a magnifying glass, the art focused to a blinding hot point on his sleepless skull.

By the time he left the museum, Pat was nearly hyperventilating. Outside was no better. The space-age Millennium Bridge fed like a spoon into the mouth of St. Paul's Cathedral, London crashing its tones, eras, and genres recklessly, disorienting Pat even more with these massive, fearless juxtapositions: modernist against neo-classic against Tudor against skyscraper.

At the other end of the bridge, Pat came across a little quartet—cello, two violins, electric piano—kids playing Bach over the Thames for change. He sat and listened, trying to catch his breath but awestruck by their casual proficiency, by their simple brilliance. Christ, if street musicians could do *that*? What was *he* doing here? He'd always felt insecure about his own musicianship; he could chunk along with anyone on the guitar and be dynamic onstage, but Benny was the real musician. They'd written hundreds of songs together, but standing on the street, listening to these four kids matter-of-factly play the canon, Pat suddenly saw his best songs as ironic trifles, smart-ass commentaries on real music, mere jokes. Jesus, had Pat ever made anything . . . *beautiful*? The music these kids played was like a centuries-old cathedral; Pat's lifework had all the lasting power and grace of a trailer. For him, music had always been a pose, a kid's pissed-off reaction to aesthetic grace; he'd spent his whole life giving beauty the finger. Now he felt empty, shrill—a failure *and* an unknown. Nothing.

Then Pat did something he hadn't done in years. Walking back to Kurtis's flat, he saw a funky music store, a big red storefront called Reckless Records, and after pretending to browse awhile, Pat asked the clerk if they had anything by the Reticents.

"Ah right, yeah," the clerk said, his pocked face sliding into recognition. "Late eighties, early nineties . . . sort of a soft-pop punk thing—"

"I wouldn't say soft—"

"Yeah, one of them grunge outfits."

"No, they were before that—"

"Yeah, we wouldn't have anything by them," the clerk said. "We do more—you know—relevant stuff."

Pat thanked him and left the store.

This was probably why Pat slept with Umi when he got back to the flat. Or maybe it was just her being alone in her underwear, Joe and Kurtis having gone to watch a football match at a pub. "Okay if I sit?" Pat asked, and she swung her legs around on the couch and he stared at the little triangle of her panties, and soon they were fumbling, lurching, as awkward as London traffic (Umi: *We mightn't let Kurty know about this*), until they found a rhythm, and eventually, as he'd done so many times before, Pat Bender fucked himself back into existence.

Afterward, with only their legs touching, Umi peppered him with personal questions the way someone might inquire about the fuel economy of a car she's just test-driven. Pat answered honestly, without being forthcoming. *Had he ever been married?* No. *Not even close?* Not really. *But what about that song "Lydia"? Wasn't she the love of his life?* It amazed him, what people heard in that song. *Love of his life?* There was a time when he thought so; he remembered the apartment they'd shared in Alphabet City, barbecuing on the little balcony and doing the crossword puzzle on Sunday mornings. But what had Lydia said after she caught him with another woman? *If you really do love me, then it's even worse, the way you act. It means you're cruel.*

No, Pat told Umi, Lydia wasn't the love of his life. Just another girl.

They moved backward this way, from intimacy to small talk. *Where was he from?* Seattle, though he'd lived in New York for a few years and most recently in Portland. *Siblings?* Nope. Just him and his mother. *What about his father?* Never really knew the man. Owned a car dealership. Wanted to be a writer. Died when Pat was four.

"I'm sorry. You must be awfully close to your mum, then."

"Actually, I haven't talked to her in more than a year."

"Why?"

And suddenly he was back at that bullshit intervention: Lydia and his mom across the room (*We're worried, Pat* and *This has to stop*), refusing to meet his eyes. Lydia had known Pat's mom first, had met her through community theater in Seattle, and unlike most of his girlfriends, whose disappointment was all about the way his behavior affected *them*, Lydia complained on Pat's mother's behalf: how he ignored her for months at a time (until he needed money), how he broke promises to her, how he still hadn't repaid the money he'd taken. You can't keep doing this, Lydia would say, it's killing her—*her*, in Pat's mind, really meaning both of them. To make them happy, Pat quit everything but booze and pot, and he and Lydia lurched along for another year, until his mother got sick. In hindsight, though, their relationship was probably done at that intervention, the minute she stood on his mother's side of the room.

"Where is she now?" Umi asked. "Your mum?"

"Idaho," Pat said wearily, "in this little town called Sandpoint. She runs a theater group there." Then, surprising himself: "She has cancer."

"Oh, I'm sorry." Umi said that her father had non-Hodgkin's lymphoma.

Pat could've asked for details, as she'd done, but he said, simply, "That's tough."

"Just a bit—" Umi stared at the floor. "My brother keeps saying how brave he is. *Dad's so brave. He's battling so bravely.* Bloody misery, actually."

"Yeah." Pat felt squirmy. "Well." He assumed that enough polite post-orgasm conversation had passed, at least it would have in America; he wasn't sure of the British exchange rate. "Well, I guess . . ." He stood.

She watched him get dressed. "You do this a bit," she said, not a question.

"I doubt more than anyone else," Pat said.

She laughed. "That's what I love about you good-lookin' blokes. What, me? Have sex?"

• • •

If London was an alien city, Edinburgh was another planet.

They took the train, Joe falling asleep the minute it pulled out of King's Cross, so that Pat could only guess at the things he saw out the window—clothesline neighborhoods, great ruins in the distance, grain fields and clusters of coastal basalt that made him think of the Columbia River Gorge back home.

"Right, then," Joe said four and a half hours later, sniffing awake and glancing around as they pulled into the Edinburgh station.

They emerged from the station at the bottom of a deep draw—a castle on their left, the stone walls of a Renaissance city on their right. The Fringe Festival was bigger than Pat had expected, every streetlight and pole covered with a flyer for one show or another, the streets swarming with people: tourists, hipsters, middle-aged show-goers, and performers of every imaginable kind—mostly comedians, but actors and musicians, too, acts in singles, pairs, and improv troupes, a whole range of mimes and puppeteers, fire jugglers, unicyclists, magicians, acrobats, and Pat didn't know what—living statues, guys dressed like suits on hangers, break-dancing twins—a medieval festival gone freak.

At the festival office, an arrogant prick with a mustache and an accent even heavier than Joe's—all lilting rhythms and rolling *R*s—explained that Pat was expected to provide his own marketing and that his stipend would be half what Joe had promised—Joe saying someone named Nicole had ensured the rate—Mustache saying Nicole couldn't "ensure her own *arse*"—Joe turning to Pat to say not to worry, he wouldn't take a commission—Pat surprised that he'd ever planned to.

Outside, as they walked toward their accommodations, Pat took everything in. The city walls were like a series of cliff faces, the oldest part—the Royal Mile—leading from the castle and curling like a cobblestone stream down a canyon of smoke-stained stone edifices. The bustling noise of the festival stretched in every direction, the grand houses gutted to make way for stages and microphones, the sheer number of desperate performers sinking Pat's spirits.

Pat and Joe were put up in a boarder's room below street level, in an older couple's flat. "Say somefin' funny!" the cross-eyed husband said when he met Pat.

That night, Joe led Pat to his show—up a street, down an alley, through a crowded bar into another alley, to a narrow, high door with an ornate knob in the middle. An uninterested woman with a clipboard led Pat to his greenroom, a closet of standpipes and mops, Joe explaining that crowds often started slowly but built quickly in Edinburgh, that there were dozens of influential reviewers, and once the reviews came in—"You're a bloody lock for four stars"—the crowds would soon follow. A minute later, the woman with the clipboard announced him, and Pat came around the corner to a smattering of applause, thinking, What's less than a smattering? because there were only six people in the room, scattered out among forty folding chairs, three of the six being Joe and the old couple they were staying with.

But Pat had played his share of empty rooms, and he killed in this one, even riffing a new bit before "Lydia"—"She told our friends she *discovered* me with another woman. Like, what—she'd discovered a cure for polio? She told people she *caught* me having sex, like she'd apprehended Carlos the Jackal. I mean, you could catch bin Laden if you came home and he was fucking someone in your bed."

Pat felt the thing he'd noticed before, that even the appreciation of a small crowd could be profound—he loved how British people hung on the first syllable of that word, *brill*iant, and he stayed up all night with an even-more excited Joe, talking about ways to market the show.

The next day, Joe presented Pat with posters and handbills advertising the show. Across the top was a picture of Pat holding his guitar—under the heading *Pat Bender: I Can't Help Meself!* along with the tagline "One of America's Most Outrageous Comedy Musicians!" and "Four Stars" from something called "The Riot Police." Pat had seen such flyers for other performers at the festival, but . . . "I Can't Help Meself"? And this "One of America's . . ." bullshit?

Every act had to put up such handbills, Joe explained. Pat didn't even like being called a "comedy musician." He wasn't some Weird Al novelty act. Writers were allowed to be irreverent and still be serious. And filmmakers. But musicians were expected to be earnest shit-heels—*I love you, baby* and *Peace is the answer*. Fuck that!

For the first time, Joe was frustrated by Pat, his pale cheeks going pink. "Look. This is just how it's done, Pat. You know who the fuckin' Riot Police are? Me. *I* gave you the four stars." He threw a handbill at Pat. "I paid for this whole bloody thing!"

Pat sighed. He knew it was a different world, a different time— bands expected to blog and flog and twit and fuck-knew-what. Hell, Pat didn't even own a cell phone. Even in the States, no one got away with being a quiet, brooding artist anymore; every musician had to be his own publicist now—bunch of self-promoting twats posting every fart on a computer. A rebel now was some kid who spent all day making YouTube videos of himself putting Legos up his ass.

"Legos in his arse." Joe laughed. "You should use that."

That afternoon they went around handing out flyers on the street. At first it was as demeaning and pathetic as Pat had imagined, but he kept looking over at Joe and being humbled by the fevered energy of his young friend—"See the act what's blown 'em away in the States!"—and so Pat did his best, concentrating on the women. "You should come," he'd say, turning his eyes on, pressing a handbill into a woman's hands. "I think you'll like it." There were eighteen people at his show that night, including the reviewer from something called The Laugh Track, who gave Pat four stars and— Joe read excitedly—wrote on his blog that "the onetime singer for the old American cult band the Reticents delivers a musical monologue that is truly something different: edgy, honest, funny. He is a genuine comic misanthrope."

The next night twenty-nine people came, including a decent-looking girl in black stretch pants, who stuck around after the show to get stoned with him. Pat banged her against the standpipe in his greenroom closet.

* * *

He woke with Joe across from him in a kitchen chair, already dressed, arms crossed. "Ya *fooked* Umi?"

Disoriented, Pat thought he meant the girl after the show. "You *know* her?"

"Back in London, ya daft prick! Did you sleep with Umi?"

"Oh. Yeah." Pat sat up. "Does Kurtis know?"

"Kurtis? She told me! She asked if you'd mentioned her!" Joe tore off his glasses and wiped his eyes. "Do you remember, after you sang 'Lydia' in Portland, I said I was in love with my best mate's girl—Umi. Remember?"

Pat did recall Joe talking about someone, and now that he mentioned it, the name did sound familiar, but he was so excited by the prospect of a UK tour that he hadn't really been listening.

"Kurtis bunks every bird in the East End—just like the daft prick in your song—and I haven't told Umi a *fookin'* thing about it because Kurt's me mate. And the first chance you get . . ." His face went from pink to red and his eyes welled. "I *love* that girl, Pat!"

"Joe, I'm sorry. I had no idea you felt that way."

"Who did you think I was talking about?" Joe snapped his glasses back on and stalked out of the room.

Pat sat there awhile, feeling genuinely awful. Then he dressed and went out in the packed streets to look for Joe. What had he said, *like the daft prick in your song*? Jesus, did Joe think that song was some kind of parody? Then he had a horrible thought: Christ . . . was it? Was he?

All afternoon Pat looked for Joe. He even tried the castle, which buzzed with camera-snapping tourists, but no Joe. He wandered back down into New Town, to the top of Calton Hill, a gentle crest covered with incongruent monuments from different periods in Edinburgh's past. The city's entire history was an attempt to get a better vantage, a piece of high ground on which to build higher—spires and towers and columns, all of them with narrow spiral staircases to the top—and Pat suddenly saw humanity the same way: it was all this scramble to get *higher*, to see enemies and lord it over peasants, sure, but maybe more than that—to build something, to leave a trace of yourself, to have people see . . . that *you were once up there, onstage.* And yet what was the point, really? Those people were gone, nothing left but the crumbling rubble of failures and unknowns.

Forty people at the show that night, his first sellout. But no Joe. "I walked around Edinburgh today and decided that the whole of art and architecture is just some dogs pissing on trees," Pat said. It was early in the show, and he was wandering dangerously off-script. "My whole life . . . I've assumed I was supposed to be famous, that I was supposed to be . . . *big.* What is that? Fame." He leaned over his guitar, looking out on the expectant faces, hoping, along with them, that this was about to get funny. "The whole world is sick . . . we've all got this pathetic need to be seen. We're a bunch of fucking toddlers trying to get attention. And I'm the worst. If life had a theme, you know . . . a philosophy? A motto? Mine would be: *There must be some mistake; I was supposed to be bigger than this.*"

Where did shit shows come from? Pat had no way of knowing if he suffered more bombs than other performers, but shit shows had always come regularly for him. With the Reticents, the consensus was that they'd put out one great album (*The Reticents*), one good one (*Manna*), and one pretentious, unlistenable mess (*Metronome*). And they had a reputation for being unpredictable live, although this was intentional, or at least unavoidable: with him coked up for a few years there, Benny banging smack, and Casey Millar doing a drummer's-fifth at gigs, how could they *not* be uneven? But nobody wanted *even*; the whole point was to put some edge back in the thing—no synth dance mixes, no big hair, no fey makeup, no poseur flannel faux angst bullshit. And if the Reticents had never succeeded beyond cult-club status, they also never became slick self-promoting power-ballad-playing pretenders, either. They stayed true, as people used to say, back when staying true meant something.

But even with the Rets, sometimes, he'd just have a shit show. Not because of drugs or fighting or experimenting with feedback; sometimes they just sucked.

And that's what happened the day he got in a fight with Joe, and the night the reviewer from the *Scotsman* came to see *"Pat Bender: I Can't Help Meself!"* Pat blew the setup for "Why Are Drummers So Ducking Fumb," and then tried to get out of it with some lame eighties comic patter about how it's called scotch in America but just whiskey in Scotland, was scotch tape just . . . tape—people staring at him like, *Yeah, bloody right it's tape, you simple shit.* And he could barely get through "Lydia," imagining everyone saw through him, that everyone but him understood the song.

He felt that odd transference, in which an audience—normally rooting for him to be funny and moving, all of us in this together—started to resent his awkwardness. An untested, apparently unfunny bit about the big asses of Scottish girls (*like sacks of haggis, these girls are—haggis mules, smuggling heart-liver sausage in their pants*) didn't help. Even his guitar sounded shrill to Pat's ear.

Next morning, there was still no sign of Joe. The couple putting Pat up left the *Scotsman* outside his door, open to his one-star review. He read to the words "crass," "rambling," and "angry," and put the paper down. That night, eight people came to his show; after that, things went about the way he imagined. Five people the next night. Still no Joe. Mustache stopped by the stage to tell Pat his weekly contract wasn't being renewed. A ventriloquist would get his theater, his slot, and his boarder's room. Pat's manager had been given his check, Mustache said. Pat actually laughed at this, imagining Joe on his way to London with Pat's five hundred quid.

"So how am I supposed to get home?" Pat asked the man with the mustache.

"To the States?" the guy asked through his nose. "Ehm, I don't know. Does your guitar float?"

The only good thing Pat had gleaned from his dark period was some knowledge about how to survive on the streets. He'd never done more than a few weeks at a time, but he felt oddly calm about what to do. There were several strata of performers in Edinburgh: big acts, smaller paid pros like Pat, hobby guys, and up-and-comers playing what they called "Free Fringe," and finally—below that, and just above beggars and pickpockets—a whole range of buskers, street performers: Jamaican dancers in dirty sneakers and ratty dreadlocks, Chilean street bands, magicians carrying five tricks in a backpack, a Gypsy woman playing a strange flute; and that afternoon, on a street in front of a Costa coffeehouse, Pat Bender, ad-libbing funny lines to American classics: *Desperado, you better come to your senses/With a pound 'n' twenty pences/You ain't never gettin' home.*

There were enough American tourists that, before he knew it, he had thirty-five pounds. He bought a half-pint and some fried fish, then went to the train station, but was stunned to find the cheapest last-minute ticket to London was sixty pounds. Minus food, it might take him three days to raise that much.

Beneath the castle was a long, narrow park, the city walls on either side. Pat walked the length of the park, looking for a place to sleep, but after an hour he decided he was too old to sleep outside with the street kids and went into New Town, bought a pint of vodka, and paid a night hotel clerk five pounds to let him sleep in a toilet stall.

Next morning, he returned to the coffeehouse and resumed playing. He was doing the old Rets song "Gravy Boat," just to prove to himself that he existed, when he looked up to see the girl he'd had sex with against the standpipe in his greenroom. The girl's eyes widened and she grabbed her friend by the arms. "Hey, that's him!"

She turned out to be named Naomi, to be only eighteen, to be vacationing from Manchester, and to be here with her parents, Claude and June, who turned out to be eating in a nearby pub, to be about his age, and to be less than thrilled to meet their daughter's new friend. Naomi almost cried as she told her parents of Pat's troubles, how he'd been "ever so nice," how he'd been ripped off by his manager and stranded here with no way of getting home. Two hours later he was on a train to London, paid for by a father whose true motivation behind helping Pat get out of Scotland was never in doubt.

On the train Pat kept thinking about Edinburgh, about all those desperate entertainers giving out handbills in the streets, about the buskers and spires and churches and castles and cliffs, the scramble to get higher, to be seen, the cycle of creation and rebellion, everyone assuming they were saying something new or doing something new, something profound—when the truth was that it had all been done a million billion times. It was all he'd ever wanted. *To be big. To matter.*

Yeah, well, he could imagine Lydia saying, *you don't get to.*

Kurtis answered the door, iPod earbuds plugged into the holes in his round, dented head. When he saw Pat, his face didn't change—or at least that's what struck Pat when Kurtis shoved him back into the hallway and pinned him against the wall. Pat dropped his pack and guitar and—"Wait—" Kurtis's forearm smashed into Pat's neck, cutting off his breath, a knee coming up into Pat's groin. Bouncer tricks, Pat recognized, until a wide fist mashed his face and knocked even that thought from his head, and Pat slid off the wall to the ground. From the floor he tried to find his breath, got his hand to his bloodied face, and managed to look between Kurtis's legs for Umi or Joe; but the apartment behind Kurtis seemed not only empty . . . but trashed. He imagined the blowout that must have done it, Joe bursting in, all the shit between the three of them finally coming out, Joe telling a stricken Umi that he loved her. He liked imagining Joe and Umi on a train somewhere, the tickets paid for with Pat's five hundred pounds.

Then he noticed Kurtis was in his underwear; *Jesus, these people.* Kurtis stood above him, panting. He kicked the guitar case, Pat thinking: Please, not my guitar. "Ya fucking *coont,*" Kurtis finally said, "ya stupid fucking *coont,*" and he went back inside. Even the air from the slammed door hurt Pat.

It took a few seconds for Pat to get up, and he did so only because he was worried that Kurtis would come back for the guitar.

On the street, people gave him a wide berth, wary of the blood burbling from Pat's nose. At a pub a block away, Pat got a pint, a bar rag, and some ice, cleaned himself in the bathroom, and watched the door of Kurtis's flat. But after two hours, he didn't see anyone: no Joe, no Umi, no Kurtis.

When his beer was gone, Pat pulled the rest of his money from his pocket and laid it on the table: twelve pounds, forty pence. He stared at his sad pile of money until his eyes were bleary and he put his face in his hands and Pat Bender wept. He felt cleansed, somehow, as if he could finally see how this thing he'd identified in Edinburgh—this desperate hunger to get higher—had nearly destroyed him. He felt as if he'd come through some tunnel, made a final passage through the darkness, to the other side.

He was done with all that now. He was ready to stop trying to *matter*; he was ready to simply *live*.

Pat was shaking as he stepped outside into a cool gust, driven with a resolve that bordered on despair. He slipped into the red phone booth outside the pub. It smelled like piss and was papered with faded handbills from rough strip shows and tranny escort services. "Sandpoint, Idaho . . . USA," he told the operator, voice cracking, and he worried that he'd forgotten the number, but as soon as he said the area code—208—it came to him. Four pounds, fifty pence, the operator said, almost half his money, but Pat knew that this could not be a collect call. Not this time. He put the money in.

She answered on the second ring. "Hello?"

But something was wrong. It wasn't his mother . . . and Pat thought, in horror, It's too late. She had died. The house had sold. Christ. He'd come around too late—missed saying good-bye to the one person who had ever cared about him.

Pat Bender stood bleeding and weeping alone in a red phone booth on a busy street in south London. "Hello?" the woman said again, her voice more familiar this time, though still not his mother's. "Is someone there?"

"Hello?" Pat caught his breath, wiped his eyes. "Is . . . Is that— *Lydia*?"

"Pat?"

"Yeah, it's me." He closed his eyes and saw her, ridges of high cheek and those dark bemused eyes beneath her short brown hair, and it felt like a sign. "What are you doing there, Lydia?"

She told him that his mother was undergoing another round of chemo. God—then he wasn't too late. Pat covered his mouth. A few of them were taking turns helping out, Lydia said: first her sisters— Pat's wretched aunts Diane and Darlene—and now Lydia, in from Seattle for a few days. Her voice sounded so clear and intelligent; no wonder he had fallen in love with her. She was crystalline. "Where *are* you, Pat?"

"You won't believe it," Pat said. He was in London, of all places. He'd been talked into doing a UK tour by this kid, but he had some trouble, the kid had ripped him off and . . . Pat could sense the quiet from her end.

"No . . . Lydia," he said, and he laughed—he could imagine how the call must seem from her point of view. How many such calls had she taken from him? And his mom—how many times had she bailed him out? "It's different this time—" But then he stopped. Different? How? This time . . . what? He looked around the phone booth.

What could he say that he hadn't said, what higher ground could he possibly scramble to? *This time, if I promise to never get high-drunk-cheat-steal, can I please come home?* He'd probably said that, too, or would, in a week, or a month, or whenever this thing came back, and it *would* come back—the need to *matter*, to be big, to get higher. *To get high.* And why shouldn't it come back? What else was there? Failures and unknowns. Then Pat laughed. He laughed because he saw this phone call was just another shit show in a long line of them, like the rest of his shit show life, like the shit show intervention of Lydia and his mom, which he'd hated so much because *they didn't really mean it*; they didn't understand that the whole fucking thing was meaningless unless you were truly prepared to cut the person loose.

This time . . . On the other end of the phone, Lydia misread the laugh. "Oh Pat." She spoke in little more than a whisper. "What are you on?"

He tried to answer, *Nothing,* but there was no air to form words. And that's when Pat heard his mother come into the room behind Lydia, her voice faint and pained, "Who is it, dear?" and Pat realized that in Idaho, it was three in the morning.

At three in the morning, he'd called his dying mother to ask her to bail him out of trouble again. Even at the end of her life, she had to suffer this middle-aged shit show of a son, and Pat thought, Do it, Lydia, just do it, please! "Do it," he whispered as a tall red bus rumbled past his phone booth, and he held his breath so no more words could escape.

And she did it. Lydia took a deep breath. "It's no one, Dee," she said, and she hung up the phone.

11

Dee of Troy

April 1962
Rome and Porto Vergogna, Italy

Richard Burton was the worst driver Pasquale had ever seen. He squinted in the direction of the road with one eye and held the wheel lightly between two fingers, elbow cocked. With the other hand he pinched a cigarette out the open window, a cigarette he seemed to have no interest in smoking. From the passenger seat, Pasquale stared at the burning stick in the man's hand, wondering if he should reach over and grab it before the ash got to Richard Burton's fingers. The Alfa's tires chirped and squealed as he cornered his way out of the Roman Centro, some pedestrians yelling and waving their fists as he forced them back onto curbs. "Sorry," he said, or "So sorry," or "Bugger off."

Pasquale hadn't known that Richard Burton was Richard Burton until the woman from the Spanish Steps introduced them. "Pasquale Tursi. This is Richard Burton." Moments before, she had led him away from the steps, still clutching the envelope from Michael Deane, down a couple of streets, up a staircase, through a restaurant and out the back door, until, finally, they'd come across this man in sunglasses, worsted slacks, a sports coat over a sweater and red scarf, leaning against the light blue Alfa in a narrow alley where there were no other cars. Richard Burton had removed his sunglasses and given a wry smile. He was about Pasquale's height, with thick sideburns, tousled brown hair, and a cleft chin. He had the sharpest features Pasquale had ever seen, as if his face had been sculpted in separate pieces and then assembled on-site. He had faint pockmarks on his cheeks and a pair of unblinking, wide-set blue eyes. Most of all, he had the biggest head Pasquale had ever encountered. He'd never seen Richard Burton's movies and knew his name only from the two women on the train the day before, but one look and there could be no doubt: this man was a cinema star.

At the woman's urging, Pasquale explained the whole thing in halting English: Dee Moray coming to his village, waiting there for a mysterious man who didn't come; the doctor's visit and Pasquale's trip to Rome, his mistakenly being sent off with the extras, waiting for Michael Deane and then the bracing meeting with the man, which began with him punching Deane in the chest, quickly led to Deane admitting that Dee was in fact pregnant and not dying, and ended with the envelope of cash that Deane offered as a payoff, an envelope Pasquale still held in his hand.

"God," Richard Burton finally said, "what a heartless mercenary Deane is. I guess they're getting serious about finishing this bloody picture, sending this shit to handle the budgets and the gossip and the rot. Well, he's bollixed it all up. The poor girl. Listen, Pat," and he put a hand on Pasquale's arm, "take me to her, will you, old sport, so I can at least display a whiff of chivalry amid this fuck-all mess?"

"Oh." Pasquale had finally caught up with things, and found himself a bit deflated that this man was his competition and not the sniveling Michael Deane. "Then . . . is your baby."

Richard Burton had barely flinched. "It would appear to be the case, yes." And twenty minutes later, here they were, in Richard Burton's Alfa Romeo, barreling through the outskirts of Rome toward the *autostrada* and, eventually, Dee Moray.

"Brilliant to be out driving again." Richard Burton's hair was rustled by the wind and he spoke above the road noise. The sun glinted off his dark glasses. "I tell you, Pat, I envy the punch you landed on Deane. He's a bloody first-flight ten-year-old cocksuck, that one. I'll likely aim a bit higher when it's my go."

The burning cigarette reached Richard Burton's fingers and he flicked it over the side of his door as if it were a bee that had stung him. "I trust you know I had nothing to do with sending that girl away. And I certainly didn't know she was with child—not that I'm thrilled with that part. You know how these on-set things are." He shrugged and looked out the side window. "But I like Dee. She's . . ." He looked for the word and couldn't find it. "I've missed her." He brought his hand to his mouth and seemed surprised there was no cigarette in it. "Dee and I had a bit of history, and we became friends again when Liz's husband was in town. Then Fox loaned me out to do some bloody stock-work on *The Longest Day*—likely to get rid of me awhile. I was in France when Dee got sick. I talked to her by phone and she said she'd gone to see Dr. Crane . . . that they'd diagnosed her with cancer. She was going to Switzerland for treatment, but we decided to meet once on the coast. I said I'd finish my work on *The Longest Day* and meet her in Portovenere, and I entrusted this blood-blister Deane to set it up. The blighter's a master at insinuating himself. He said she'd taken a bad turn and gone on to Bern for treatment. That she would call me when she returned. What could I do?"

"Portovenere?" Pasquale asked. Then she *had* come to his village by mistake. Or because of Michael Deane's deception.

"It's this goddamn movie." Richard Burton shook his head. "It's Satan's asshole, this bloody film. Flashbulbs everywhere . . . priests with cameras in their cassocks . . . leech fixers coming from the States to keep the girls and booze away . . . gossip columns jumping every time we have a bloody cocktail. I should've walked off months ago. It's insanity. And do you know why it's gone over this way? Do you? Because of her."

"Dee Moray?"

"What?" Richard Burton looked over as if Pasquale hadn't been listening. "Dee? No. No, because of Liz. It's like having a bloody typhoon in your flat. And I didn't come looking for this. Any of it. I was perfectly happy doing *Camelot*. Not that I could get a bloody handshake from Julie Andrews—though, trust me, I was not lacking for female companionship. No, I was done with the bloody moron cinema. Back to the stage for me, regain my promise, the art—all that rot. Then my agent calls, says Fox will buy me out of *Camelot* and pay me four times my price if I'll roll around Liz Taylor in a robe. Four times! And I didn't jump right away, either. Said I'd think about it. Show me the mortal man who has to think about *that*. But I did. And do you know what I was thinking?"

Pasquale could only shrug. It was like standing in a windstorm, listening to this man.

"I was thinking about Larry." Richard Burton looked at Pasquale. "Olivier, lecturing me in that buggering-uncle voice of his." Richard Burton stuck out his lower lip and assumed a nasal voice: " 'Dick, you will, of course, eventually have to make up your mind whether you wish to be a *household word* or an *ac-TOR.*' " He laughed. "Rotten old sotter. Last night of *Camelot*, I raised my glass in a toast to Larry and his bloody stage. Said I'd take the money, thank you, and within a week I'd drive that raven-haired Liz Taylor to her knees . . . or, rather, to mine." He laughed again at the memory. "Olivier . . . Christ. In the end, really what does it matter, whether some Welsh coal miner's son acts on the stage or the screen? Our names are writ in water anyway, as Keats said, so what's it bloody matter? Old sots like Olivier and Gielgud can have their code and shove it up each other's arses, *bugger off, boys, and on with the parade*, right?" Richard Burton glanced over his shoulder, his hair mixed and blended by the wind through the open convertible. "So I'm off to Rome, where I meet Liz, and let me tell you, Pat, I've never seen a woman like this. I mean, I've had a few in my day, but this one? Christ. Do you know what I said first time I met her?" He didn't wait for Pasquale to answer. "I said, 'Don't know if anyone's ever told you this . . . but you're not a bad-looking girl.' "

He smiled. "And when those eyes settle on you? God, the world stops spinning . . . I knew she was married, and more to the point, she's a bloody soul-eater, but I'm not made of steel either. Of course, any right blighter would choose being a great actor over being a household word if the stacks were the same, but that's not really the choice, is it? Because they pile that fuck-all money on the scale, too, and God, man, they put on those tits and that waist . . . and Christ, those eyes—and the thing begins to tip, old sport, till the scale goes right over. No, no, we are definitely writ in water. Or cognac—if we've any luck at all."

He winked and swerved and Pasquale put his hand on the dashboard. "Now, there's an idea. Cognac? Keep an eye out, eh, sport?" He took a deep breath and returned to his story. "Of course, the newspapers get hold of Liz and me and her husband comes to town and I sulked a bit, spent four days pissed, and somewhere in there, sotted and sorry, I went back to Dee again for comfort. Every two weeks, I'd find myself knocking on her door." He shook his head. "She's clear, that one—smart. It's a burden for an attractive woman to be so smart, to see through the curtain. She'd agree with Larry, I'm sure, that I'm wasting my talent making rubbish like this film. And I knew Dee was guns for me. I probably shouldn't have pursued her, but . . . who are we but who we are, am I right?" He patted his chest with his left hand. "You wouldn't happen to have another fag?"

Pasquale pulled out a cigarette and lit it for him. Richard Burton took a long drag and the smoke curled from his nose. "This Crane, the man who diagnosed Dee—Liz's pill-pusher, man rattles when he walks. He and Deane cooked up this cancer rubbish to get Dee out of town." He shook his head. "Goddamn it, what kind of hopeless bastard tells a girl with morning sickness that she's dying of cancer? They'll do anything, these people."

He braked suddenly and the tires seemed to jump, like a scared animal, and the car careened off the road and screeched to a stop at a market on the outskirts of Rome. "You as thirsty as I am, sport?"

"I am hungry," Pasquale said. "I have not eaten."

"Right. Excellent. And you wouldn't have any money, would you? I was so bollixed up when we left, I'm afraid I'm a bit underfunded."

Pasquale opened the envelope and handed him a thousand-lira note. Richard Burton took the money and ran into the market.

He returned a few minutes later with two open bottles of red wine, gave one to Pasquale and settled the other between his legs. "What goddamn kind of place hasn't got a bottle of cognac in it? Are we to write our names in grape piss then? Ah well, in a pinch, I suppose." He took a long pull of the wine and noticed Pasquale watching him. "My father was a twelve-pint-a-day man. Being Welsh, I've got to keep it in control, so I only drink when I'm working." He winked. "Which is why I'm *always* bloody working."

Four hours later, the man responsible for impregnating Dee Moray had drunk all but a few tugs of both bottles of wine and had stopped for a third. Pasquale couldn't believe how much wine the man could handle. Richard Burton parked the Alfa Romeo near the port in La Spezia, and Pasquale asked around in a harbor bar until a fisherman agreed to take them up the coast to Porto Vergogna for two thousand lire. The fisherman walked ten meters ahead of them down to his boat.

"I was born in a tiny village myself," Richard Burton told Pasquale as they settled onto the wooden bench in the stern of the fisherman's dank, ten-meter boat. It was a cold, dark evening and Richard Burton turned up the collar of his jacket against the sharp sea breeze. The boat's captain stood three steps above them, the wheel in his hand as he rode a cross-chop out of the harbor, the froth rising up to the bow, rolling over, and then settling back, the salty air making Pasquale even hungrier.

The captain ignored them. His ears glowed a cold red in the brisk air.

Richard Burton leaned back and sighed. "The stain I'm from is called Pontrhydyfen. Sits in a little glen between two green mountains and is cut by a little river clear as vodka. Little Welsh mining town. And what do you think our river was called?"

Pasquale had no idea what he was talking about.

"Think about it. It'll make perfect sense."

Pasquale shrugged.

"Avon." He waited for Pasquale to react. "Fancy bit of irony, no?"

Pasquale said that it was.

"Right . . . okay then, did someone mention vodka? Right, I did." Richard Burton sighed wearily. Then he called up to the boat's pilot, "Are we truly to have nothing to drink on board? Really? Captain!" The man ignored him. "He's risking outright mutiny, don't you think, Pat?" Then Burton leaned back again, resettled his collar against the cool air, and resumed telling Pasquale about the village where he grew up. "There were thirteen of us little Jenkinses, tit-suckers every last one, till the git after me. I was two when my poor ma finally gave out, sucked dry. We drained the poor woman like deflating a balloon. I got the last of it. My sister Cecilia raised me after that. The old blighter Jenkins was no help. Fifty already when I was born, drunk the minute the sun came up, I barely knew him—his name the only thing he ever gave me. Burton I got from an acting teacher, though I tell people it's for Robert Burton. *Anatomy of Melancholy*? No? Right. Sorry." He ran a hand over his own chest. "No, this is all a thing I invented, this . . . *Burton*. Dickie Jenkins is a petty little tit-pincher, but this Richard Burton chap . . . he bloody well soars."

Pasquale nodded, the chop from the sea and Burton's endless drunk talk conspiring to make him extremely sleepy.

"Jenkins boys all worked in the coalface, except me, and I only escaped by luck and Hitler. The RAF was my way out, and though I turned out too bloody blind to fly, it still got me into Oxford. Tell me, do you know what you say to a kid from my village when you see him at Oxford?"

Pasquale shrugged, worn down by the man's constant chatter.

"You say, 'Get back to cutting that privet!'" When Pasquale didn't laugh, Richard Burton leaned in to explain. "The point being . . . not to blow up my own arse, but just so you know, I wasn't always . . ." He looked for the word. "This. No, I understand what it is to live in the provinces. Oh, I've forgotten a lot, I'll give you that, gotten soft. But I have not forgotten that."

Pasquale had never encountered someone who talked as much as this Richard Burton. When he didn't understand something in English, Pasquale had learned to change the subject, and he tried this now—in part just to hear his own voice again. "Do you play tennis, Richard Burton?"

"More a rugger by training . . . I like the rough and tumble. I'd have played club after Oxford, wing-forward, if not for the ease with which men of the dramatic arts bunk young women." He stared off into space. "My brother Ifor, he was a top rugger. I'd have been his equal if I'd stayed at it, although I'd have been limited to the hockey-playing, big-breasted girls. From my vantage, the stage-jocks got a wider choice." And then he said, to the captain again, "And you're sure you don't have just a nip on board, cap'n? No cognac?" When there was no answer, he fell back against the stern again. "Hope this arsehole goes down with his tub."

Finally, they rounded the breakwater point and the icy wind broke as the boat slowed and they chugged into Porto Vergogna. They bumped against the wooden plug at the end of the pier, seawater lapping over the soggy, sagging boards. In the moonlight, Richard Burton squinted at the dozen or so stone-and-plaster houses, a couple of them lit by lanterns. "Is the rest of the village over the hill, then?"

Pasquale glanced to the top floor of his hotel, where Dee Moray's window was dark. "No. Is only Porto Vergogna, this."

Richard Burton shook his head. "Right. Of course it is. My God, it's barely a crack in the cliffs. And no telephones?"

"No." Pasquale was embarrassed. "Next year, maybe they come."

"This Deane is fucking mad," Richard Burton said, with what sounded to Pasquale almost like admiration. "I'm going to flog that little shit until he bleeds from his nipples. Bastard." He stepped onto the dock as Pasquale paid the Spezia fisherman, who shoved off and chugged away without so much as a word. Pasquale started toward the shore.

Above them, the fishermen were drinking in the piazza, as if they were eagerly awaiting something. They moved around like bees disturbed from their hive. Now they pushed Tommaso the Communist forward and he began making his way down the steps to the shore. Even though Pasquale now understood that Dee Moray wasn't dying after all, he felt certain that something terrible had happened to her.

"Gualfredo and Pelle came this afternoon in the long boat," Tommaso said when he met them on the steps. "They took your American, Pasquale! I tried to stop them. So did your Aunt Valeria. She told them the girl would die if they took her. The American didn't want to go, but that pig Gualfredo told her she was supposed to be in Portovenere, not here . . . that a man had come there for her. And she went with them."

Since the exchange was in Italian, the news didn't register with Richard Burton, who lowered the collar of his jacket again, smoothed himself, and glanced up at the small cluster of white-washed houses. He smiled to Tommaso and said: "I don't suppose you're a bartender, old chap. I could use a shot before telling the poor girl she's been bred."

Pasquale translated what Tommaso had told him. "A man from another hotel has come and take away Dee Moray."

"Taken her where?"

Pasquale pointed down the coast. "Portovenere. He say she supposed to be there and that my hotel can't take care good of Americans."

"That's piracy! We can't allow such a thing to stand, can we?"

They walked up to the piazza and the fishermen shared the rest of their grappa with Richard Burton while they talked about what to do. There was some talk of waiting until morning, but Pasquale and Richard Burton agreed that Dee Moray must know immediately that she wasn't dying of cancer. They would go to Portovenere tonight. There was a buzz of excitement among the men on the cold, sea-lapped shore: Tommaso the Elder talked about slitting Gualfredo's throat; Richard Burton asked in English if anyone knew how late the bars were open in Portovenere; Lugo the War Hero ran back to his house to get his carbine; Tommaso the Communist raised his hand in a kind of salute and volunteered to pilot the assault on Gualfredo's hotel; and it was around this time Pasquale realized that he was the only sober man in Porto Vergogna.

He walked to the hotel and went inside to tell his mother and his Aunt Valeria that they were going down the coast, and to grab a bottle of port for Richard Burton. His aunt was watching from her window and describing what she saw to Pasquale's mother, who was propped up in bed. Pasquale stuck his head in the doorway.

"I tried to stop them," Valeria said. She looked grim. She handed Pasquale a note.

"I know," Pasquale said as he read the note. It was from Dee Moray. "Pasquale, some men came to tell me that my friend was waiting for me in Portovenere and that there had been a mistake. I will make sure you get paid for your trouble. Thank you for everything. Yours—Dee." Pasquale sighed. *Yours.*

"Be careful," his mother said from her bed. "Gualfredo is a hard man."

He put the note in his pocket. "I'll be fine, Mamma."

"Yes, you will be, Pasqo," she said. "You are a good man."

Pasquale wasn't used to this outward affection, especially when his mother was in one of her dark moods. Maybe she was coming out of it. He walked into the room and bent over to kiss her. She had the stale smell she so often got when confined to her bed. But before he could kiss her, she reached out with a clawed hand and squeezed his arm as tightly as she could, her arm shaking.

Pasquale looked down at her shaking hand. "Mamma, I'm coming right back."

He looked at his Aunt Valeria for help, but she wouldn't look up. And his mother wouldn't let go of his arm.

"Mamma. It's okay."

"I told Valeria that such a tall American girl would never stay here. I told her that she would leave."

"Mamma. What are you talking about?"

She leaned back and slowly let go of his arm. "Go get that American girl and marry her, Pasquale. You have my blessing."

He laughed and kissed her again. "I'll go find her, but I love you, Mamma. Only you. There's no one else for me."

Outside, Pasquale found Richard Burton and the fishermen still drinking in the piazza. An embarrassed Lugo said they couldn't borrow his carbine after all, because his wife was using it to stake some tomato plants in their cliff-side garden.

As they walked down toward the shore, Richard Burton nudged Pasquale and pointed to the Hotel Adequate View sign. "Yours?"

Pasquale nodded. "My father's."

Richard Burton yawned. "Bloody brilliant." Then he happily took the bottle of port. "I tell you, Pat, this is one damn strange picture."

The fishermen helped Tommaso the Communist dump his nets and gear and a sleeping cat into the piazza and they used the cart to wheel his outboard motor down to the water. Pasquale and Richard Burton climbed in. The fishermen stood watching from what was left of Pasquale's beach. Tommaso's first yank on the pull start knocked the bottle of port from Richard Burton's hand, but luckily it landed in Pasquale's lap without spilling much. He handed it back to the drunk Welshman. But the little motor refused to catch. They sat rocking in the waves, drifting slowly away, Richard Burton suppressing little belches and apologizing for each one. "Air's a bit stagnant on this yacht," he said.

"Bastard!" Tommaso yelled to the engine. He beat on it and pulled again. Nothing. The other fishermen yelled that it either wasn't getting spark or wasn't getting fuel, then those who'd said spark switched to fuel and fuel to spark.

Something came over Richard Burton then and he stood and, in a deep, resonant voice, addressed the three old fishermen yelling from the shore. "Fear not, Achaean brothers. I swear to you: tonight there will be the weeping of soft tears in Portovenere . . . tears for want of their dead sons . . . upon whom we now go to wage war, for the sake of fair Dee, that woman who so makes the blood run. I give you my word as a gentleman, as an Achaean: we shall return victorious, or not at all!" And while they didn't understand a word of the speech, the fishermen could tell it was epic and they all cheered, even Lugo, who was pissing on the rocks. Then Richard Burton waved his bottle over his two crewmates, in a sort of benediction: Pasquale, huddled against the cold in the back of the boat, and Tommaso the Communist, who was adjusting the choke on the motor. "O you lost sons of Portovenere, prepare to meet the shock of doom borne down upon you by this fearless army of good men." He put his hand on Pasquale's head: "Achilles here and the smelly bloke pulling on the motor, I forget his name, fair men all, pitiless and powerful, and—"

Tommaso pulled, the motor caught, and Richard Burton nearly fell out, but Pasquale caught him and sat him down in the boat. Burton patted Pasquale on the arm and slurred, " . . . more than kin, and less than kind." They chugged away into the grain of the chop. Finally, the rescue party was away.

Onshore, the fishermen were drifting away to their beds. In the boat, Richard Burton sighed. He took a swig and looked once more at the little town disappearing behind the rock wall, as if it had never existed at all.

"Listen, Pat," Richard Burton said, "I take back what I said before about being from a small village like yours." He gestured with the bottle of port. "No, I'm sure it's a fine place, but Christ, man, I've left bigger settlements in my rank trousers."

They walked ashore and straight into Gualfredo's recently remodeled *albergo*, the Hotel de la Mar in Portovenere. The desk clerk required even more of the money from Pasquale's payoff from Michael Deane, but after they'd negotiated his outrageous price, the man gave them the bottle of cognac that Richard Burton wanted and the number of Dee Moray's room. The actor had slept a little in the boat—Pasquale had no idea how—and now he swirled the cognac like mouthwash, swallowed, patted down his hair, and said, "Okay. Good as gold." He and Pasquale climbed the stairs and walked down the hallway to the tall door of Dee's room, Pasquale looking around at Gualfredo's modern hotel and becoming embarrassed again that Dee Moray had ever stayed in his grubby little *pensione*. The smell of this place—clean and something he thought of as vaguely American—made him realize how badly the Adequate View must stink, the old women and rotting, damp sea-smell of the place.

Richard Burton walked in front of Pasquale, weaving on the carpet, righting the ship with each step. He patted down his hair, winked at Pasquale, and rapped lightly, with one knuckle, on the hotel room door. When there was no answer, he knocked louder.

"Who is it?" Dee Moray's voice came from behind the door.

"Ah, it's Richard, love," he said. "Come to rescue you."

A moment later the door flew open and Dee appeared in a robe. They crashed into each other's arms and Pasquale had to look away or risk betraying his deep envy and embarrassment that he'd ever imagined that she could want to be with someone like him. He was a donkey watching two Thoroughbreds prance in a field.

After a few seconds, Dee Moray pushed Richard Burton away. In a voice both chiding and sweet, she asked him, "Where have you been?"

"I was looking for you," Richard Burton said. "It's been something of an odyssey. But, listen, there's something I need to tell you. I'm afraid we've been the subjects of a frightful bit of deception here."

"What are you talking about?"

"Come in. Sit down. I'll explain the whole thing." Richard Burton helped her back into her room and the door closed behind them.

Pasquale stood alone in the hallway then, staring at the door, unsure what to do, listening to the hushed conversation inside and trying to decide whether he should simply stand there, or knock on the door and remind them that he was out here, or just go back down to the boat with Tommaso. He yawned and leaned against the wall. He'd been at it for about twenty hours straight. By now, Richard Burton would have told her that she wasn't dying, that she was in fact pregnant, and yet he heard none of the noises he'd have expected coming from behind the door at the revelation of this news—either a loud expression of anger, or the relief at the truth of her condition, or the shock that she was having a baby. *A baby!* she might yell. Or ask, *A baby?* Yet there was nothing behind the door but hushed voices.

Perhaps five minutes passed. Pasquale had just decided to leave when the door opened and Dee Moray came out alone, her robe pulled tight around her. She had been crying. She said nothing, just walked down the hall, her bare feet padding on the carpet. Pasquale pushed off the wall. She put her arms around his neck and hugged him tightly. He put his arms around her, the tapered notch of her waist; he felt the silk against her skin, and beneath her soft robe, her breasts against his chest. She smelled like roses and soap and Pasquale was suddenly horrified at the way he must smell after the day he'd had—trips on a bus and in a car and in two fishing boats— and only then did the unbelievable nature of this day fully register. Had he actually begun the day in Rome nearly cast as an extra in the movie *Cleopatra?* Then Dee Moray began to shudder like the old motor in Tommaso's boat. He held her for a full minute and tried simply to let the minute be—the firmness of the body beneath the softness of that robe.

Finally, Dee Moray pulled away. She wiped at her eyes and looked into Pasquale's face. "I don't know what to say."

Pasquale shrugged. "Is okay."

"But I want to say something to you, Pasquale, I need to." And then she laughed. "Thank you is not nearly enough."

Pasquale looked down at the floor. Sometimes it was like a deep ache, the simple act of breathing in and out. "No," he said. "Is enough."

He pulled from his coat the envelope of money, much lightened since it had been handed to him on the Spanish Steps. "Michael Deane ask for me give you this." She opened it and shook with revulsion at the bloom of currency. He didn't mention that some of the money was meant for him; it made him feel complicit. "And these," Pasquale said, and handed her the continuity photos of herself. On top was the picture of Dee and the other woman on the set of *Cleopatra*. She covered her mouth when she saw it. Pasquale said, "Michael Deane said I tell you—"

"Don't ever tell me what that bastard said," Dee Moray interrupted, not looking up from the photograph. "Please."

Pasquale nodded.

She still hadn't looked up from the continuity photos. She pointed to the other woman in the photo, the one with the dark hair, whose arm Dee Moray was holding as she laughed. "She's actually quite nice," she said. "It's funny." Dee sighed. She flipped through the other pictures and Pasquale realized now that in one of them she was standing grimly with two men, one of whom was Richard Burton.

Dee Moray looked back toward the open door of her hotel room. And then she wiped her teary eyes again. "I guess we're going to stay here tonight," she said. "Richard's awfully tired. He has to go back to France for one more day of shooting. And then he's going to come with me to Switzerland and . . . we'll see this doctor together and . . . I guess . . . get it taken care of."

"Yes," Pasquale said, the words *taken care of* hanging in the air. "I am glad . . . you are not sick."

"Thank you, Pasquale. Me, too." Her eyes became wet. "I'm going to come back and see you sometime. Is that okay?"

"Yes," he said, but he didn't think for a second that he would ever see her again.

"We can hike back up to the bunker, see the paintings again."

Pasquale just smiled. He concentrated, looking for the words. "The first night, you say something . . . that we don't know when our story is start, yes?"

Dee nodded.

"My friend Alvis Bender, the man who write the book you read, he tell me something like this one time. He say our life is a story. But all stories go in different direction, yes?" He shot a hand out to the left. "You." And the other to the right. "Me." The words didn't match what he'd hoped to say, but she nodded as if she understood.

"But sometimes . . . we are like people in a car on a train, go in same direction. Same story." He put his hands together. "And I think . . . this is nice, yes?"

"Oh, yes," she said, and she put her own hands together to show him. "Thank you, Pasquale." One of her hands fell to Pasquale's chest and they both stared at it. Then she pulled it away and Pasquale turned to leave, summoning every bit of pride in his body to wear on his back like the shield of the centurion he'd almost become that morning.

"Pasquale!" she called after only a few steps. He turned. And she came down the hallway and kissed him again, and although it was on the lips this time, it was not at all like the kiss she'd given him on the patio outside the Hotel Adequate View. That kiss had been the beginning of something, the moment when it felt like his story was beginning. This was an end, the simple departure of a minor character—him.

She wiped her eyes. "Here," she said, and she pressed into his hands one of the Polaroid photographs of herself and the woman with dark hair. "To remember me by."

"No. Is yours."

"I don't want that one," she said. "I have these others."

"One day you will want it."

"I'll tell you what—when I'm old, if I need to convince people that I was in the movies, I'll come get it. Okay?" She squeezed the picture into his hand, then turned and padded back toward her room and disappeared inside. She closed and latched the door slowly and quietly behind her, like a parent sneaking from the room of a sleeping child.

Pasquale stared at the door. He had wished for this world of the glamorous Americans, and like a dream she had come to his hotel, but now the world was back where it belonged, and he wondered if it would have been better to never have glimpsed what lay behind the door.

Pasquale turned and scuffled up the hall, and down the stairs, past the night clerk and outside, to where Tommaso leaned against a wall, smoking. His cap was pulled down on his eyes. He showed Tommaso the photo of Dee and the other woman.

Tommaso looked at it, then shrugged one shoulder. "Bah," he said. And the two men started back toward the marina.

12

The Tenth Pass

Before sunrise, before Guatemalan gardeners, before sharks and Benzes and the gentrification of the American mind— Claire feels a hand on her hip.

"Don't, Daryl," she mutters.

"Who?"

She opens her eyes to a blond-wood desk, a flat-screen television, and the kind of painting they put in hotel rooms . . . because this *is* a hotel room.

She's on her side, and the hand on her hip is coming from behind her. She looks down, sees that she's still dressed; at least they didn't have sex. She rolls over and stares into the big, dewy eyes of Shane Wheeler. She's never awakened in a hotel room next to a man she just met, so she's not quite sure what one says in this situation. "Hi," she says.

"*Daryl.* Is that your boyfriend?"

"He was ten hours ago."

"The strip-club guy?"

Good memory. "Yeah," she says. At some point in their drunken sharing last night, she had explained how Daryl unapologetically watches online porn all day and goes to strip clubs at night and then laughs when she suggests this might be disrespectful to her. (*Hopeless,* she recalls describing her relationship.) Now, as she lies next to Shane, Claire feels a different sort of hopelessness. What's the matter with her, going back to this guy's room? And what to do with her hands now, which not long ago had been running through Shane's hair and over various parts of his body? She reaches for her silenced BlackBerry, takes a data hit: seven A.M., sixty-one degrees, nine new e-mails, two phone calls, and a simple text message from Daryl: *what up*—

She glances back over her shoulder at Shane again. His hair seems even more unruly than it did last night, his sideburns more late-Elvis than alt-hipster. His shirt is off and she can see, on his skinny left forearm, that damned tattoo, ACT, which she half blames for what happened last night. Only in the movies does such a moment require a boozy flashback: how Michael had her book rooms at the W for Shane and Pasquale, how she drove the Italian to the hotel while Shane followed in his rental car, how Pasquale said he was tired and went to his room, and she apologized to Shane for laughing at his pitch, how he shrugged it off, but in the way people shrug off something that genuinely bothers them. How she said, *No, I really am sorry*, and explained that it wasn't him—it was her frustration with the business. How he said he understood and that he felt like celebrating, so they went to the bar and she bought him a drink and gently reminded him that getting a producer interested was only the first step; how he bought the next round of drinks (*I just made ten grand; I can afford two cocktails*) and she the one after; and how, amid all those drinks, they'd told their stories: first the bland, self-serving surface story one tells a stranger—family, college, career—and then the truth, the pain of Shane's failed marriage and the rejection of his book of short stories; Claire's seemingly misguided decision to come out of the cocoon of academia and her anguish over whether to go back in; Shane's painful realization that he was milk-fed veal; Claire's failed quest to make one great film; and then the loud, laugh-until-you-cry sharing—*My boyfriend is a gorgeous zombie who loves strip clubs!* and *I actually live in my parents' basement!*—and more drinks came and the commonplace became revelatory—*I like Wilco* and *I like Wilco*, *too!* and *My favorite pizza is Thai* and *Mine, too!*—and then Shane rolled up the sleeves on his faux-Western shirt, and Claire's eyes fell on that tattoo (*so* weak for ink), that one word, ACT, and she did—leaned over in the bar and kissed him, and his hand rose to her cheek while they kissed, such a simple thing, his hand on her face, but something Daryl never did, and ten minutes later they were in his room, sifting through the minibar for more fuel and making out like college kids, her giggling at the tickle of his bushy sideburns, him pausing to compliment her breasts—a sweet, two-hour, kissing, groping, laughing debate over whether or not to have sex (him: *I'm leaning toward Yes*; her: *I feel like the swing vote*) until . . . they must've fallen asleep.

And now, morning-after, Claire sits up. "This wasn't very professional of me."

"Depends on your profession."

She laughs. "If you paid for that I think you got ripped off."

He puts his hand back on her hip. "There's still time."

She laughs, takes his hand from her hip and sets it on the bed. But she can't say she isn't tempted. The kissing and rolling around were nice enough; she assumes the sex would be good. With Daryl, the sex was the first thing between them, the selling point, the foundation for a whole relationship. But in the last few months, she's felt as if the intimacy has seeped out of it and now there are two distinct phases to sex with Daryl: the first two minutes like an exam from an autistic gynecologist, the next ten a visit from the Roto-Rooter man. At the very least, she imagines, Shane would be . . . present.

Conflicted, confused, she stands, to think, or to buy time.

"Where are you going?"

Claire holds up her phone. "See if I still have a boyfriend."

"I thought you were going to break up with him."

"I haven't decided."

"I'll decide for you."

"I appreciate that, but I should probably take care of it."

"And if the porn-zombie asks where you were all night?"

"Guess I'll tell him."

"Will he break up with you?"

She hears some bit of hopefulness in the question. "I don't know," she says. She pulls the chair out from the desk, sits, and begins thumbing through the calls and e-mails on her phone, to see when Daryl called last.

Shane sits up, too, now, swings his feet over the edge of the bed, and grabs his shirt off the floor. She glances up, can't help but smile at his scrawny attractiveness. He's an aging version of the boys she always fell for in college: in the vicinity of good-looking but a few blocks away. Physically, he's the anti-Daryl (square-jawed Daryl with his five-hundred-push-ups-a-day chest)—Shane all narrow angles and jutting collarbones, just the hint of a roll in his gut. "When, exactly, did you take your shirt off?" she asks.

"I'm not sure. I guess I was hoping to start a trend."

She goes back to her BlackBerry, opens Daryl's "what up" text, and tries to figure out what to type back. Her thumbs hover over the keys. But nothing comes.

"So what did you see in this guy?" Shane asks. "Originally?"

Claire glances up. What did she see? It's too corny to say—but she saw all the clichéd shit: Stars. Flashes of light. Babies. A future. She saw all of this the very first night, as they banged through her apartment door, flinging clothes and chewing each other's lips and reaching and prodding and cupping—and then he lifted her off the ground and all of her college fumblings became as insignificant as bumping into someone on a stairwell. She felt exactly like she'd never been fully alive before the moment Daryl first touched her. And it wasn't just sex; *he was inside her*. She'd never really thought about that phrase until that night, when in the middle of it she looked up and saw herself . . . every bit of herself . . . in *his* eyes.

Claire shakes the memory off. How could she possibly say any of that, especially here? And so she simply says, "Abs. I saw abs." And it's odd; she feels worse for dismissing Daryl as a set of stomach muscles than she does for being in this hotel room with a boy she just met.

Shane nods again at the cell phone in her hands. "So . . . what are you going to tell him?"

"No idea."

"Tell him we're falling in love; that'll end it."

"Yeah?" She looks up. "Are we?"

He smiles as he snaps the buttons on his faux Western shirt. "Maybe. We could be. How will we know if we don't spend the day together."

"Impulsive much?"

"Key to my quirky appeal."

Goddamn it; she thinks that might be the case—his appeal. She recalls Shane saying that he married the harsh, truth-telling waitress after dating for only a few months. She's not surprised—who even *uses* the words *falling in love* fourteen hours after meeting someone? There is something undeniably . . . optimistic about him. And for a moment, she wonders if she ever had such a quality. "Can I ask *you* something?" Claire says. "Why the Donner Party?"

"Oh, no," he says. "You're just looking for a laugh again."

"I told you, I'm sorry about that. It's just that for three years Michael has rejected every idea I bring in as being too dark, too expensive, too period . . . not commercial enough. Then you come in yesterday with—no offense—the darkest, least commercial, most expensive period film I've ever heard about, and he loves it. It's just so . . . *unlikely*. I just wondered where it came from."

Shane shrugs and reaches for one of his socks on the floor. "I have three older sisters. All of my early memories are of them. I loved them; I was their toy, like a doll they dressed up. When I was six or so, my oldest sister, Olivia, developed an eating disorder. Just about destroyed our family.

"It was awful. Olivia was thirteen, and she'd go in the bathroom and throw up. She'd spend her lunch money on diet pills, squirrel food away in her clothes. At first my parents yelled at her, but that did no good. She didn't care. It was like she wanted to waste away. You could see the bones in her arms. Her hair falling out.

"My parents tried everything. Therapists and psychologists, in-patient treatment. My ex thinks that's when they really started becoming so overprotective—I don't know. What I remember is lying in bed one night and hearing my mom weep and my father trying to comfort her, Mom just saying over and over, 'My baby is starving to death.'" Shane still has the sock in his hand, but he doesn't put it on. He just stares at it.

"What happened?" Claire asks quietly.

"Hmm?" He looks up. "Oh, she's fine now. The treatment clicked or something, I guess. Olivia just . . . got over it. She's still got some food hang-ups—she's the sister who never brings food for Thanksgiving, always makes a centerpiece instead. Little pumpkins. Cornucopias. And don't even *mention* the word *brownie* around her. But she came out okay. Married this jackass, but they're happy enough. Have two kids. The funny thing is . . . the rest of my family never talks about that time. Even Olivia shakes off that whole period like it was nothing. 'My skinny years,' she calls them.

"But I never got over it. When I was seven or eight, I'd lie awake at night, praying that if God would make Olivia better, I'd go to church, become a minister . . . something. And so when it didn't happen right away—you know how kids are—I blamed myself, connected my sister's starving to my own lack of faith."

He stares off, rubs the inside of his arm. "By high school, Olivia was fine, and I was over my religious phase. But after that, I was always fascinated by stories of starvation and deprivation. I read everything I could find, did my school reports on the siege of Leningrad and the Potato Famine . . . I especially liked stories of cannibalism: the Uruguayan rugby team, Alfred Packer, the Maori . . . and of course the Donner Party."

Shane looks down and sees the sock in his hands. "I guess I identified with poor William Eddy, who escaped himself, but who could do nothing while his family starved in that awful camp." He absentmindedly puts the sock on. "So when I read in Michael Deane's book how pitching a movie is all about believing in yourself, pitching yourself—it was like a vision: I knew exactly the story I needed to pitch."

A vision? Believing in yourself? Claire looks down, wondering if this *Just-Do-It-Dude* confidence is what Michael was actually responding to yesterday. And what had attracted her last night. Hell, maybe they can make *Donner!* based on nothing more than this kid's passion for it. *Passion*: another word that sticks in her throat.

Claire glances back down at her BlackBerry and sees an e-mail from Michael's producing partner, Danny Roth. The subject line is *Donner!* Michael must have called Danny about Shane's pitch. She wonders if Danny talked some sense into Michael. She opens the e-mail, written in the tortured, hurried, moronic, electronic shorthand that Danny somehow believes is saving him great amounts of time:

> *C—Rbrt says your setting up pitch for Unvsl Mnday on Donner. Has to look gd, re: contract. See if writr has story-bords or bakstory, anthing that looks lk wre furthr down the road. Straigt faces. Danny*

She looks up at Shane, sitting on the edge of the bed, watching her. She looks back down at Danny's e-mail. *Has to look gd . . .* Why would it *look* good and not *be* good? And storyboards to make it look like they're further down the road? *Straight faces?* Then she recalls Michael's boast yesterday: *I'm going to pitch an eighty-million-dollar movie about frontier cannibalism.*

"Ah, shit," she says.

"Another text from your boyfriend?"

Would they really do this? She recalls Danny and Michael talking about the lawyers looking for a way out of Michael's contract with Universal. What a stupid question: of course they would do this. They would never *not* do this. This is what they do. Claire's hand comes to her temple.

"What?" Shane stands and she looks over at him, his big doe eyes and those bushy sideburns framing his face. "Are you okay?"

Claire considers not telling him, letting him have his weekend of triumph. She could just put on blinders and finish out the weekend, help Michael with his doomed pitch and his missing actress, then on Monday accept the cult museum job . . . start stocking up on cat food. But Shane is staring at her with those moon-eyes, and she realizes that she likes him and that if she's ever going to break away it has to be now.

"Shane, Michael has no intention of making your movie."

"What?" He laughs a little. "What are you talking about?"

She sits on the bed next to him and explains the whole thing, as she sees it now, starting with the deal Michael made with the studio—how, at the low point of his career, the studio took on some of Michael's debt in exchange for the rights to some of his old films. "There were two other parts to the deal," she says. "Michael got an office on the lot. And the studio got a first-look deal, meaning that Michael had to show them all of his ideas and he could only go to other studios if they passed. Well, the first-look was a joke. For five years the studio rejected every script Michael brought in. And when he took those scripts and treatments and books out to other studios—if you already know that Universal has rejected an idea, why would you ever want it?

"Then came *Hookbook*. When Michael started developing that idea, he figured a reality show and Web site was beyond the scope of his contract, which he assumed was for *film development* only. But it turned out the contract stipulated the studio got the first shot at all material 'developed in any media.' Here was Michael, with this potentially huge unscripted TV business, and it turned out the studio basically owned it."

"I don't understand what this has to do with—"

Claire holds up her hand. "Ever since then, Michael's lawyers have been looking for a way out of the contract. A few weeks ago they found it. The studio put an escape clause in the contract to protect itself in case Michael wasn't just in a slump, but was totally played out. If Michael brings a certain number of bad ideas over a certain period of time—say, the studio doesn't develop ten straight projects over five years—then either side can opt out. But where the contract stipulates *all material*, the escape clause mentions only *films*. So even though the studio made *Hookbook*, if Michael options and develops ten film ideas in five years and the studio passes on all ten—then either side can walk away with no obligation."

Shane catches up quickly, his brow furrowing. "So you're saying I am—"

"—the tenth pass," Claire says. "An eighty-million-dollar cannibal Western—a movie so dark, expensive, and noncommercial that the studio could never say yes to it. Michael will option your idea for nothing, then send you off to write a spec script he has no intention of making. When the studio passes, he'll be free to sell his TV shows to the highest bidder—for, I don't know, tens of millions."

Shane stares at her. Claire feels awful for telling him, for puncturing the kid's confidence. She puts a hand on his arm. "I'm sorry, Shane," she says.

Then her phone rings. Daryl. Shit. She squeezes Shane's arm, stands, and walks across the room, answering without looking at the screen. "Hey," she says to Daryl.

But it's not Daryl.

It's Michael Deane. "Claire, good, you're up. Where are you?" He doesn't wait for an answer. "Did you drop the Italian and his translator off at the hotel last night?"

She looks over at Shane. "Uh, sort of," she says.

"How soon can you meet me at the hotel?"

"Pretty quickly." She's never heard Michael's voice like this. "Listen, Michael," she says, "we need to talk about Shane's pitch—"

But he interrupts her. "We found her," Michael says.

"Who?"

"Dee Moray! Only her name wasn't Dee Moray. It was *Debra Moore*. She was a high school drama and Italian teacher all these years in Seattle. Can you fucking believe it?" Michael sounds hopped up, high. "And her kid—have you ever heard of a band called the Reticents?" Again, he doesn't wait for her to answer. "Yeah, me neither. Anyway, the investigator worked overnight preparing a file. I'll fill you in on the way to the airport."

"Airport? Michael, what's going on—"

"I have something for you to read on the plane. It will explain it all. Now go get Mr. Tursi and the translator and tell them to get ready. We fly out at noon."

"But Michael—"

He's already hung up, though, before Claire can say, "Wait—fly out where?" She clicks off the call and looks over at Shane, still sitting on the bed, a distant look on his face. "Michael found his actress," she says. "He wants us all to fly off to see her."

Shane doesn't appear to have heard her. He is staring at some point on the wall behind her. She should never have said anything, should have allowed him to go on living in his little bubble.

"Look, I'm sorry, Shane," she says. "You don't have to go. I can find another translator. This business, it's—"

But he interrupts her. "So you're saying he pays me ten thousand dollars to get out of his contract . . ." Shane has the strangest look on his face; it's oddly familiar to Claire. "And then he goes out and makes ten million?"

And now she knows where she recognizes that look from. It's a look she sees every day, the look of someone doing the math, of someone seeing the angles.

"Then maybe my movie is worth more than ten thousand."

Holy shit. The kid's a natural.

"I mean, who wants to go pitch a dead movie idea for ten grand? But for fifty? Or *eighty*?" Shane breaks into a sly smile. "Sign me up."

13

Dee Sees a Movie

April 1978
Seattle, Washington

She called him P.E. Steve, and he was at that very moment driving across town to pick her up for a date. Debra Moore-Bender had grown adept at deflecting the advances of her fellow teachers, but an attractive young widow was apparently too much for the sturdy Steve to abide, and for weeks he circled until he finally made his move—while they sat together at a desk outside a school dance, checking ASB cards beneath a banner that read: EVERLASTING LOVE. SPRING INTO '78!

Debra gave him the usual excuse—she didn't date other teachers—but Steve laughed this off. "What is that, like a lawyer-client thing? Because you know I teach phys ed, right? I'm not a real teacher, Debra."

Her friend Mona had been urging Debra to date Steve ever since word of his divorce reached the teachers' lounge—sweet Mona, whose own romantic life was a series of disasters but who somehow knew what was best for Debra. But what really convinced her was that P.E. Steve asked her to *a movie*. There was this movie she wanted to see—

And now, minutes before he was to pick her up, Debra stood in the bathroom staring into the mirror and running a brush through her feathered blond hair, which ruffled and settled like water in a boat's wake (*Miss Farrah*, some of the students called her, a name

202 • JESS WALTER

she pretended to dislike). She turned to the side. This new hair color was a mistake. She'd spent a decade fighting the awful vanity of her youth and she'd really hoped, at thirty-eight, to be one of those women who were comfortable with middle age, but she just wasn't there yet. Each gray hair still seemed like a weevil in a flower bed.

She glanced at the hairbrush. How many millions of strokes through her hair, how many face washings and sit-ups, how much work had she done—all to hear those words: *beautiful, pretty, foxy.* At one time, Debra accepted her looks without self-consciousness; she didn't need affirmation—no "Miss Farrah" or leering P.E. Steve or even awkward, sweet Mona ("If I looked like you, Debra, I'd masturbate all the time"). But now? Dee set the hairbrush down, staring at it like some kind of talisman. She remembered singing into a brush like that when she was a kid; she still felt like a kid, like a nervous, needy fifteen-year-old getting ready for a date.

Maybe nerves were natural. Her last relationship had ended a year ago: her son Pat's guitar teacher, Bald Marv (Pat nicknamed the men in her life). She'd liked Bald Marv, thought he stood a chance. He was older, in his late forties, had two older daughters from a failed marriage and was keen on "blending the families"—although he was decidedly less keen after he and Debra returned home one night to find Pat already blending, in bed with Marv's fifteen-year-old daughter, Janet.

During Marv's eruption she'd thought about defending Pat— *Why do boys always get blamed in these situations?* After all, Marv's daughter was two years older than him. But this was Pat, and he proudly confessed his elaborate plans like a cornered Bond villain. It had been all his idea, his vodka, his condom. Debra wasn't surprised that Bald Marv ended it. And while she hated breakups—the disingenuous abstractions, *this is just not where I want to be right now,* as if the other person had nothing to do with it—at least Bald Marv stated the case plainly: "I love you, Dee, but I do *not* have the energy to deal with this shit between you and Pat."

You and Pat. Was it really that bad? Maybe. Three boyfriends ago, Coverall Carl, the contractor who worked on her house, had pushed her to get married, but wanted Debra to put Pat in a military school first. "Jesus, Carl," she'd said, "he's nine years old."

And now, up to bat, P.E. Steve. At least his kids lived with their mother; maybe this time no civilians would get hurt.

She walked down the narrow hallway past Pat's school picture—God, that smirk, in every picture, that same cleft-chin, wet-eyed, *see-me* smirk. The only thing that ever changed in his school pictures was his hair (floppy, permed, Zeppelin, spiked); the expression was always there—the dark charisma.

Pat's bedroom door was closed. She knocked lightly, but he must have had headphones on, because he didn't answer. Pat was fifteen now, old enough that she should be able to leave him home alone without some big speech every time she went out, but she couldn't help herself.

Debra knocked again, then opened his bedroom door and saw Pat sitting cross-legged with his guitar across his lap, beneath a Pink Floyd poster of light going through a prism. He was leaning forward, his hand outstretched toward the top drawer of his nightstand, as if he'd just shoved something inside. She pressed into the room, pushing a pile of clothes out of the way. Pat took off the headphones. "Hey, Mom," he said.

"What'd you put in the drawer?" she asked.

"Nothing," Pat said too quickly.

"Pat. Are you going to make me look in there?"

"No one's making you do anything."

On the bottom shelf of his nightstand she saw the rat-eared, loose pages of Alvis's book, at least the one chapter he'd written. She'd given it to Pat a year ago, after a big fight, during which he'd said he wished he had a father to go live with. "This was your father," she said that night, hoping there was something in the yellowed pages to anchor the boy. *Your father.* She'd nearly come to believe it herself. Alvis had always insisted they tell Pat the truth once he got older, when he could understand, but as the years went on Debra had no idea how to do that.

She crossed her arms, like some picture from a parenting guide. "So are you going to open that drawer or am I?"

"Seriously, Mom . . . It's nothing. Trust me."

She moved toward the nightstand and he sighed, set his guitar down, and opened the drawer. He moved some things around and finally removed a small marijuana pipe. "I wasn't smoking. I swear." She felt the pipe, which was cool. No dope in it.

She searched the drawer; there was no marijuana. It was just a drawer full of junk—a couple of wristwatches, some guitar picks, his music composition books, pens and pencils. "I'm keeping the pipe," she said.

"Sure." He nodded as if that were obvious. "I shouldn't have had it in there." When he got in trouble, he always became strangely calm and reasonable. He'd break into this *we're-in-this-together* mode that had always disarmed her; it was as if he were helping her deal with a particularly difficult child. He'd had the same quality at six. One time she'd stepped outside to get the mail, talked to her neighbor, and came back in to find Pat pouring a pan of water on the smoldering couch. "Wow," he said, as if he'd just discovered the fire rather than set it. "Thank God I got to it early."

Now he held up the headphones. Subject change: "You'd like this song."

She looked down at the pipe in her hand. "Maybe I shouldn't go out."

"Come on, Mom. I'm sorry. Sometimes I fiddle around with things when I'm writing. But I haven't gotten high in a month—I swear. Now go on your date."

She stared at him, looking for some sign that he was lying, but his eye contact was as unwavering as ever.

"Maybe you're just looking for an excuse to not go out," Pat said.

That was like him, too, to turn it around on her, and to peg it on some real insight; it was true, she probably *was* looking for an excuse to not go out.

"Loosen up," he said. "Go have fun. I'll tell you what: you can borrow my P.E. clothes. Steve especially likes tight gray shorts."

She smiled in spite of herself. "I think I'll just go with what I'm wearing, thanks."

"He's gonna make you shower afterward, you know."

"You think?"

"Yep: roll call, stretching, floor hockey, shower. That's P.E. Steve's dream date."

"Is that so?"

"Yep. The guy's fatuous."

"Fatuous?" That was Pat, too, showing off his vocabulary while calling her date a moron.

"But don't ask him if he's fatuous, 'cause he'll say, 'Boy I hope so. I paid a lot for this vasectomy.' "

She laughed again in spite of herself—and wished, as always, that she hadn't. How much trouble had Pat squirmed out of at school this way? Female teachers were especially helpless. He got As without books, talked other kids into doing his work, convinced principals to waive rules for him, ditched school and invented fabulist reasons for his absence. Debra would cringe during school conferences when the teacher asked about her diagnosis, or about Pat's trip to South America, or about the death of his sister—*Oh, and his poor father*: murdered, disappeared in the Bermuda Triangle, dead of exposure on Everest. Every year, poor Alvis died all over again, of some new cause. Then, around his fourteenth birthday, Pat seemed to realize that he didn't need to lie to get things, that it was more effective, and more fun, to simply look people in the eye and tell them exactly what he wanted.

She wondered sometimes if having a father around would have balanced her indulgence of him; she'd been overly charmed by his precociousness when he was little, and probably too lonely, especially in those dark years.

Pat set his guitar down and stood up. "Hey. I'm kidding about Steve. He seems nice." He walked over. "Go. Have fun. Be happy."

He really had grown in this last year. Anyone could see it. He'd gotten in less trouble at school, hadn't snuck out of the house, had gotten better grades. Yet she was still discomfited by those eyes, not by their structure or color, but some quality in his stare—what people called a glimmer, a spark, a thrilling *watch-this* danger.

"Do you really want to make me happy?" Debra said. "Be here when I get home."

"Deal," he said, and stuck out his hand. "Okay if Benny comes over to practice?"

"Sure." She shook his hand. Benny was the guitar player Pat had recruited for his band. This was the thing turning Pat around: his band, the Garys. She had to admit (after a couple of school events and a battle of the bands in Seattle Center), the Garys weren't bad. In fact they were pretty good—not as punk as she'd feared, but kind of grubby and straightforward (when she'd likened them to *Let It Bleed*–era Stones, Pat rolled his eyes). And her son onstage was a revelation. He sang, preened, growled, joked; he exuded something up there that shouldn't have surprised her but did: an effortless charm. Power. And ever since the band got together, Pat had been the picture of calm. What does it say about a kid that joining a rock band *settles him down*? But it was undeniable: he was focused and engaged. His motivation still worried her—he talked a lot about *hitting it big*, about *becoming famous*—and so she'd tried to explain the dangers of fame, but she couldn't really be specific, could only make flat, bland speeches about the purity of art and the trappings of success. So she worried that her talk was all a waste of time, like warning a starving person about the dangers of obesity.

"I'll be home in three hours," Debra said now. It would be five or six hours, but this was a habit; cutting the time in half so he might get in only half the trouble. "Until then, don't . . . um . . . don't . . . uh . . ."

As she looked for the proper scale of warning, Pat's face broke into a smile, eyes tipping before the corners of his mouth began their slow climb. "Don't do *anything*?"

"Yes. Don't do anything."

He saluted, smiled, put his headphones back on, grabbed his guitar, and plopped back on the bed. "Hey," he said when she turned away. "Don't let Steve talk you into jumping jacks. He likes to watch the jiggly parts."

She eased the door closed and had just started down the hallway when she looked down at the pipe in her hands. *Now, why would he take a pipe out of its hiding place if he didn't have pot for it?* And when she'd asked what he'd been doing, Pat had to dig around in the drawer for the pipe. Wouldn't it be on top if he'd *just* thrown it in there? She turned in the hallway, went back, and threw the door open. Pat was sitting back on the bed with his guitar, the nightstand dresser open again. Now, though, he had open on the bed the thing he'd actually been hiding from her: his songwriting book. He was bent over it with a pencil. He sat up quickly, red-faced and furious: "What the hell, Mom?"

She stalked over and grabbed the notebook from his bed, not really sure what she was looking for, her mind going to that place parents' minds went: Worst-case-scenario-land. *He's writing songs about suicide! About dealing drugs!* She flipped to a random page: song lyrics, a few notations about melody—Pat had only a rudimentary understanding of music—fragments of sweet, pained lyrics, like any fifteen-year-old might write, a love song, "Hot Tanya" (awkwardly rhymed with *I want ya*), some faux-meaningful tripe about *the sun and moon* and *eternity's womb*.

He reached for the notebook. "Put that down!"

She flipped forward, looking for whatever had been so dangerous that he'd give her his pot pipe rather than admit he was writing a song.

"Fucking put it down, Mom!"

She found the last page with writing on it—the song he must have been trying to hide—and her shoulders slumped when she saw the heading: "The Smile of Heaven," the title of Alvis's book. She read the chorus: *I used to believe/He'd come back for me/Why's heaven smiling/When this shit ain't funny—*

Oh. Debra felt awful. "I— I'm sorry, Pat. I thought—"

He reached up and took the notebook back.

She so rarely saw beneath Pat's smooth, sarcastic surface that she sometimes forgot a boy was there—a hurt boy who was still capable of missing his father even though he didn't remember him. "Oh, Pat," she said. "You'd rather I thought you were smoking pot . . . than writing a song?"

He rubbed his eyes. "It's a bad song."

"No, Pat. It's really good."

"It's maudlin crap," he said. "And I knew you'd make me talk about it."

She sat on the bed. "So . . . let's talk about it."

"Ah, Jesus." He looked past her, at a point on the floor. Then he blinked, laughed, and this seemed to snap him out of some trance. "It's no big deal. It's just a song."

"Pat, I know it's been hard on you—"

He winced. "I don't think you understand just how much I *don't* want to talk about this. Please. Can't we talk about it later?"

When she didn't budge, Pat pushed her gently with his foot. "Come on. I have more maudlin crap to write and you're going to be late for your date. And when you're tardy, P.E. Steve makes you run laps."

P.E. Steve drove a Plymouth Duster with deep bucket seats. He had a gone-to-seed-superhero look, with blocky, side-parted hair and a square jaw, and an athletic body just starting to swell with middle age. Men have a half-life, she thought, like uranium.

"What should we see?" Steve asked her in the car.

She felt ridiculous even saying it: *"The Exorcist II."* She shrugged. "I heard some kids in the library talking about it. It sounded good."

"Fine with me. I figured you more for a foreign-film buff, something with subtitles that I'd have to pretend to understand."

Debra laughed. "It has a good cast," she said, "Linda Blair, Louise Fletcher, James Earl Jones." She could barely even say the real name. "Richard Burton."

"Richard Burton? Isn't he dead?"

"Not yet," she said.

"Okay," P.E. Steve said, "but you might have to hold my hand. The first *Exorcist* scared the shit out of me."

She looked out the window. "I didn't see it."

They ate dinner at a seafood place and she noted when he took one of her shrimp without asking. The conversation was easy and casual: Steve asking about Pat, Debra saying that he was doing better. Funny how every conversation about Pat assumed a baseline of trouble.

"You shouldn't worry about him," Steve said, as if reading her mind. "He's a lousy floor-hockey player, but he's a good kid. The talented ones like that? The more trouble they get in, the more successful they are as adults."

"How do you know that?"

" 'Cause I *never* got in trouble and now I'm a P.E. teacher."

No, this wasn't bad at all. They sat early in the theater with a shared box of Dots and a shared armrest, and shared backgrounds (She: widowed a decade earlier, mother dead, dad remarried, younger brother and two sisters; He: divorced, two kids, two brothers, parents in Arizona). Shared gossip, too: the one about some kids discovering a cache of the shop teacher's raunchy porn above the lathe (He: *I guess that's why they call it* wood *shop*) and Mrs. Wylie seducing the gear-head Dave Ames (She: *But Dave Ames is just a boy*; He: *Yeah, not anymore*).

Then the lights went down and they settled into their seats, P.E. Steve leaning over and whispering, "You seem different from how you are at school."

"How am I at school?" she asked.

"Honestly? You're kinda scary."

She laughed. "Kinda scary?"

"No. I didn't mean 'kinda.' Completely scary. Utterly intimidating."

"*I'm* intimidating?"

"Yeah, I mean . . . look at you. You have seen yourself in a mirror, right?"

She was saved from the rest of this conversation by the coming attractions. Afterward, she leaned forward with anticipation, feeling the buzz she always felt when one of HIS films started. This one started with a mash of fire and locusts and devils, and when he finally came on, she felt both exhilaration and sadness: his face was grayer, ruddier, and his eyes, a version of those eyes she saw every day at home, but now like burned-out bulbs, the spark almost gone.

The movie swung from stupid to silly to incomprehensible, and she wondered if it would make more sense to someone who'd seen the first *Exorcist*. (Pat had snuck into a theater to see it and pronounced it "hilarious.") The plot employed some kind of hypnosis machine made of Frankenstein wires and suction cups, which appeared to allow two or three people to have the same dream. When *he* wasn't on-screen, she tried to concentrate on the other actors, to catch bits of business, interesting decisions. Sometimes, when she watched his films, she'd think about how she would've played a particular scene across from him—as she instructed her students: to notice the *choices* the actors made. Louise Fletcher was in this movie, and Debra marveled at her easy proficiency. Now there was an interesting career, Louise Fletcher's. Dee could have had that kind of career—maybe.

"We can leave if you want," P.E. Steve whispered.

"What? No. Why?"

"You keep scoffing."

"Do I? I'm sorry."

The rest of the movie she sat quietly, with her hands in her lap, watching as he struggled through ridiculous scenes, trying to find something to do with this drek. A few times, she did see bits of his old power crack through, the slight trill in that smooth voice overcoming his boozy diction.

They were quiet walking to the car. (Steve: *That was . . . interesting.* Debra: *Mmm.*) On the way home she stared out her window, lost in thought. She replayed her conversation with Pat earlier, wondering if she hadn't missed some important opening. What if she'd just come out and told him: *Oh, by the way, I'm on my way to see a movie starring your real father*—but could she imagine a scenario in which that information helped Pat? What was he going to do? Go play catch with Richard Burton?

"I hope you didn't pick that movie on purpose," said P.E. Steve.

"What?" She squirmed in the seat. "I'm sorry?"

"Well, just that it's hard to ask someone out for a second date after a movie like that. Like asking someone to go on another cruise after the *Titanic*."

She laughed, but it was hollow. She pretended, to herself, that she went to all of his movies and kept an eye on his career because of Pat—in case it made sense to tell him one day. But she could never tell him; she knew that.

So, if it wasn't for Pat, why did she still go to the movies—and sit there like a spy watching him destroy himself, daydreaming herself into supporting roles, never the Liz parts, always Louise Fletcher? Although it was never *her*, of course, not Debra Moore the high school drama and Italian teacher, but the woman she'd tried to create all those years ago, *Dee Moray*—as if she'd cleaved herself in two, Debra coming back to Seattle, Dee waking up in that tiny hotel on the Italian coast and getting sweet, shy Pasquale to take her to Switzerland, where she would do what they'd wanted, trade a baby for a career, and it was that career she still fantasized about— *after twenty-six movies and countless plays, the veteran finally gets a supporting actress nomination*—

In the bucket seat of P.E. Steve's Duster, Debra sighed. God, she was pathetic—a schoolgirl forever singing into hairbrushes.

"You okay?" P.E. Steve said. "It's like you're fifty miles away."

"I'm sorry." She looked over and squeezed his arm. "I had this weird conversation with Pat before I left. I guess I'm still upset about it."

"You want to talk about it?"

She almost laughed at the idea—confessing the whole thing to Pat's P.E. teacher. "Thanks," she said. "But no." Steve went back to driving and Debra wondered if such a man's matter-of-fact ease could still have some effect on the fifteen-year-old Pat, or if it was too late for all of that.

They pulled up to her house and Steve turned off the car. She wouldn't mind going out with him again, but she hated this part of dates—the turn in the driver's seat, the awkward seeking out of eyes, the fitful kiss and request to see her again.

She glanced over at the house to make sure Pat wasn't watching—no way she could stand him teasing her about a good-bye kiss—and that's when she saw something was missing. She got out of the car as if in a trance, started walking toward the house.

"So that's it?"

She glanced over to see that P.E. Steve had gotten out of the car. "What?" she said.

"Look," he said, "this might not be my place, but I'm just gonna say it. I like you." He leaned on the car, his arm propped on his open door. "You asked me what you were like at school . . . and, honestly, you're like you've been the last hour. I said you were intimidating because of the way you look, and you are. But sometimes it's like you're not even in the room with other people. Like no one else even exists."

"Steve—"

But he wasn't done. "I know I'm not your type. That's fine. But I think you might be a happier person if you let people in sometimes."

She opened her mouth to tell him why she'd gotten out of the car, but *you might be a happier person* pissed her off. She might be a happier person? She might be a— Jesus. She stood there silently—broken, seething.

"Well, good night." Steve got in his Duster, closed the door, and drove away. She watched his car turn at the end of the street, taillights blinking once.

Then she looked back at her house, and the empty driveway, where her car should have been parked.

Inside, she opened the drawer where she kept the spare car keys (gone, of course), peeked in Pat's bedroom (empty, of course), looked for a note (none, of course), poured herself a glass of wine, and sat by the window, waiting for him to come home on his own. It was two forty-five in the morning when the phone finally rang.

It was the police. *Was she . . . Was her son . . . Did she own . . . tan Audi . . . license plate . . .* She answered: *Yes, yes, yes,* until she stopped hearing the questions, just kept saying *Yes.* Then she hung up and called Mona, who came over and picked her up, drove her quietly to the police station.

They stopped and Mona put her hand on Debra's. Good Mona—ten years younger and square-shouldered, bob-haired, with sharp green eyes. She'd tried to kiss Debra once after too many glasses of wine. You can always spot the real thing, that affection; why does it always come from the wrong person? "Debra," Mona said, "I know you love that little fucker, but you can't put up with his shit anymore. You hear me? Let him go to jail this time."

"He was doing better," Debra said weakly. "He wrote this song—" But she didn't finish. She thanked Mona, got out of the car, and went into the police station.

A thick, uniformed officer in teardrop glasses came out with a clipboard. He said not to worry, her son was fine, but her car was totaled—it had gone over an abutment in Fremont, "a spectacular crash, amazing no one was hurt."

"No one?"

"There was a girl in the car with him. She's fine, too. Scared, but fine. Her parents already came down."

Of course there was a girl. "Can I see him?"

In a minute, the officer said. But first she needed to know that her son had been intoxicated, that they'd found a vodka bottle and cocaine residue on a hand mirror in the car, that he was being cited for negligent driving, driving without a license, failure to use proper care and caution, driving under the influence, minor in possession. (*Cocaine?* She wasn't sure she'd heard right but she nodded at each charge, what else could she do?) Given the severity of the charges, this matter would be turned over to the juvenile prosecutor, who would make a determination—

Wait. Cocaine? Where would he get cocaine? And what did P.E. Steve mean that she *didn't let people in*? She'd love to let someone in. No, you know what she'd do? Let *herself out!* And Mona? *Don't put up with his shit?* Jesus, did they think she *chose* to be this way? Did they think she had a choice in the way Pat behaved? God, that would be something, just stop putting up with Pat's shit, go back in time and live some other life—

(*Dee Moray reclines on a beach chair on the Riviera with her quiet, handsome Italian companion, Pasquale, reading the trades until Pasquale kisses her and goes off to play tennis on this court jutting out of the cliffs*—)

"Any questions?"

"Hmm. I'm sorry?"

"Any questions about what I've just told you?"

"No." She followed the fat cop down a hallway.

"This might not be the best time," he said, and glanced back at her over his shoulder as they walked. "But I noticed that you're not wearing a wedding ring. I wondered if maybe sometime you might want to have dinner . . . the legal system can be really confusing and it can help to have someone who—"

(*The hotel concierge brings a phone to the beach. Dee Moray removes her sun hat and puts the phone to her ear. It's Dick!* Hello, love, *he says,* I trust you're as beautiful as ever—)

The cop turned and handed her a card with his phone number on it. "I understand this is a tough time, but in case you feel like going out sometime."

She stared at the card.

(*Dee Moray sighs:* I saw *The Exorcist,* Dick. Oh Jesus, *he says,* that shite? You know how to hurt a fellow. No, *she tells him gently,* it's not exactly the Bard. *Dick laughs.* Listen, darling, I've got this play I thought we might do together—)

The cop reached for the door. Debra took a deep, ragged breath and followed him inside.

Pat was sitting on a folding chair in an empty room, head in his hands, fingers lost in those currents of wavy brown hair. He pushed his hair aside and looked up at her; those eyes. No one understood how much they were in this together, Pat and her. We're lost in this thing, Dee thought. There was a small abrasion on his forehead,

almost like a carpet burn. Otherwise, he looked fine. Irresistible—
his father's son.

He leaned back and crossed his arms. "Hey," he said, mouth
rising up in that sly *what-are-you-doing-here* smile. "So how was
your date?"

14

The Witches of Porto Vergogna

April 1962
Porto Vergogna, Italy

Pasquale slept through the next morning. When he finally woke, the sun had already crested the cliffs behind the town. He climbed the stairs to the third floor and the dark room where Dee Moray had stayed. Had she really just been here? Had he really been in Rome just yesterday, driving with the maniac Richard Burton? It felt as if time had shifted, warped. He looked around the small stone-walled room. It was all hers now. Other guests would stay here, but this would always be Dee Moray's room. Pasquale threw open the shutters and light poured in. He took a deep breath, but smelled only sea air. Then he picked up Alvis Bender's unfinished book from the nightstand and thumbed through the pages. Any day now, Alvis would show up to resume writing in that room. But the room would never belong to him again.

Pasquale returned to his room on the second floor and got dressed. On his desk he saw the photograph of Dee Moray and the other laughing woman. He picked it up. The photo didn't begin to capture Dee's sheer presence, not the way he remembered it: her graceful height and the long rise of her neck and deep pools of those eyes, and the quality of movement that seemed so different from other people, lithe and energetic, no wasted action. He held the photo close to his face. He liked the way Dee was laughing in

218 • JESS WALTER

the picture, her hand on the other woman's arm, both of them just
beginning to double over. The photographer had caught them at a
real moment, breaking up in laughter over something no one else
would ever know. Pasquale carried the photo downstairs and slid it
into the corner of a framed painting of olives in the tiny hallway between the hotel and the *trattoria*. He imagined showing his American guests the photo and then feigning nonchalance: sure, he would
say, film stars occasionally stayed at the Adequate View. They liked
the quiet. And the cliff tennis.

He stared into the photo and thought about Richard Burton
again. The man had so many women. Was he even interested in
Dee? He would take her to Switzerland for the abortion, and then
what? He would never marry her.

And suddenly he had a vision of himself going to Portovenere,
knocking on her hotel room door. *Dee, marry me. I will raise your
child as my own.* It was ridiculous—thinking that she would marry
someone she'd just met, that she would ever marry him. And then
he thought of Amedea and was filled with shame. Who was he to
think badly of Richard Burton? This is what happens when you live
in dreams, he thought: you dream this and you dream that and you
sleep right through your life.

He needed coffee. Pasquale went into the small dining room,
which was full of late-morning light, the shutters thrown open. It
was unusual for this time of day; his Aunt Valeria waited for the late
afternoon to open the shutters. She was sitting at one of the tables,
drinking a glass of wine. That was odd for eleven in the morning,
too. She looked up. Her eyes were red. "Pasquale," she said, her voice
cracking. "Last night . . . your mother—" She looked at the floor.

He rushed past her to the hall and pushed open Antonia's door.
The shutters and windows were open in here, too, sea air and sunlight filling the room. She lay on her back, a bouquet of gray hair on
the pillow behind her, mouth twisted slightly open, a bird's hooked
beak. The pillows were fluffed behind her head, the blanket pulled
neatly to her shoulders and folded once, as if already prepared for
the funeral. Her skin was waxy, as if it had been scrubbed.

The room smelled like soap.

Valeria was standing behind him. Had she discovered her sister dead . . . and then cleaned the room? It made no sense. Pasquale turned to his aunt. "Why didn't you tell me this last night, when I got back?"

"It was time, Pasquale," Valeria said. Tears slid through the scablands of her old face. "Now you can go marry the American." Valeria's chin fell to her chest, like an exhausted courier who has delivered some vital message. "It was what she wanted," the old woman rasped.

Pasquale looked at the pillows behind his mother and at the empty cup on her bedside table. "Oh, Zia," he said, "what have you done?"

He lifted her chin and in her eyes he could see the whole thing: *The two women listening at the window while he talked to Dee Moray, understanding none of it; his mother insisting—as she had for months—that it was her time to die, that Pasquale needed to leave Porto Vergogna to find a wife; his Aunt Valeria making one last desperate attempt, when she'd tried to get the sick American woman to stay, with her witch's story about how no one ever died young here; his mother asking Valeria over and over ("Help me, Sister"), begging her, hectoring—*

"No, you didn't—"

Before he could finish, Valeria slumped to the ground. And Pasquale turned with disbelief toward his dead mother. "Oh, Mamma," Pasquale said simply. It was all so pointless, so ignorant; how could they misconstrue so completely what was happening around them? He turned to his sobbing aunt, reached down, and took her face between his hands. He could barely see her dark, wrinkled skin through the blur of his own tears.

"What . . . did you do?"

Then Valeria told him everything: how Pasquale's mother had been asking for release ever since Carlo died and had even tried to suffocate herself with a pillow. Valeria had talked her out of it, but Antonia persisted until Valeria promised her that, when her older sister could stand the pain no more, she would help. This week, she had called in this solemn promise. Again, Valeria said no, but Antonia said that she could never understand because she wasn't a mother, that she wanted to die rather than burden Pasquale any- more, that he would never leave Porto Vergogna so long as she was alive. So Valeria did as she'd asked, baked some lye into a loaf of bread. Then Antonia had Valeria leave the hotel for an hour, so that she would have no part in her sin. Valeria tried once more to talk her out of it, but Antonia said she was at peace, knowing that if she went now, Pasquale could go off with the beautiful American—

"Listen to me," Pasquale said. "The American girl? She loves the other man who was here, the British actor. She doesn't care about me. This was for nothing!" Valeria sobbed again and fell against his leg, and Pasquale stared down at her bucking, thrashing shoulders, until pity overwhelmed him. Pity, and love for his mother, who would have wanted him to do what he did next: he patted Valeria's wiry nest of hair and said, "I'm sorry, Zia." He looked back at his mother, lying against the fluffed pillows, as if in solemn approval.

Valeria spent the day in her room, weeping, while Pasquale sat on the patio smoking and drinking wine. At dusk he went with Vale- ria and wrapped his mother tight in a sheet and a blanket, Pasquale giving one last gentle kiss to her cold forehead before covering her face. *What man ever really knows his mother?* She'd had an entire life before him, including two other sons, the brothers he'd never known. She'd survived losing them in the war, and losing her hus- band. Who was he to decide that she wasn't ready, that she should linger here a bit longer? She was done. Perhaps it was even good that his mother believed he would run off with some beautiful Ameri- can when she was gone.

The next morning, Tommaso the Communist helped Pasquale carry Antonia's body to his boat. Pasquale hadn't noticed how frail his mother had gotten until he had to carry her this way, his hands beneath her bony, birdlike shoulders. Valeria peeked out from her doorway and said a quiet good-bye to her sister. The other fish- ermen and their wives lined the piazza and gave Pasquale their condolences—"She's with Carlo now," and "Sweet Antonia," and "God rest"—and Pasquale gave them a small nod from the boat as Tommaso once again pulled the boat motor to life and chugged them out of the cove.

"It was her time," Tommaso said as he steered through the dark water.

Pasquale faced forward to keep from having to talk anymore, from having to see his mother's shrouded body. He felt grateful at the way the salty chop stung his eyes.

In La Spezia, Tommaso got a cart from the wharf watchman. He pushed Pasquale's mother's body through the street—like a sack of grain, Pasquale thought shamefully—until they finally arrived at the funeral home, and he made arrangements to have her buried next to his father as soon as a funeral mass could be arranged.

Then he went to see the cross-eyed priest who had presided at his father's mass and burial. Already overwhelmed with confirmation season, the priest said he couldn't possibly say a requiem mass until Friday, two days from now. How many people did Pasquale expect at the service? "Not many," he said. The fishermen would come if he asked them; they would spit-flatten their thin hair, put on black coats, and stand with their serious wives while the priest intoned—*Antonia, requiem aeternam dona eis, Domine*—and afterward, the serious wives would bring food to the hotel. But the whole thing seemed to Pasquale so predictable, so earthbound and pointless. Of course it was exactly what she would have wanted, and so he made arrangements for the funeral mass, the priest making a notation on a ledger of some kind and looking up through his bifocals. And did Pasquale also want him to say *trigesimo*, the mass thirty days after the death to give the departed a final nudge into heaven? Fine, Pasquale said.

"*Eccellente*," Father Francisco said, and held out his hand. Pasquale took the hand to shake it, but the priest looked at him sternly—or at least one of his eyes did. Ah, Pasquale said, and he reached in his pocket and paid the man. The money disappeared beneath his cassock and the priest gave him a quick blessing.

Pasquale was in a daze as he walked back to the pier where Tommaso's boat was moored. He climbed back in the grubby wooden shell. Pasquale felt terrible again that he had transported his mother this way. And then he recalled the strangest moment, almost at random: He was probably seven. He woke from an afternoon nap, disoriented about the time, and came downstairs to find his mother crying and his father comforting her. He stood outside their bedroom door and watched this, and for the first time Pasquale understood his parents as beings apart from him—that they had existed before he'd been alive. That's when his father looked up and said, "Your grandmother has died," and he assumed it was his mother's mother; only later did he learn that it was his father's mother. And yet *he* had been comforting *her*. And his mother looked up and said, "She is the lucky one, Pasquale. She's with God now." Something about the memory caused him to tear up, to think again about the unknowable nature of the people we love. He put his face in his hands and Tommaso politely turned away as they motored away from La Spezia.

Back at the Adequate View, Valeria was nowhere to be found. Pasquale looked in her room, which was as cleaned and made up as his mother's had been—as if no one had ever been there. The fishermen hadn't taken her away; she must have hiked out on the steep trails behind the village. That night, the hotel felt like a crypt to Pasquale. He grabbed a bottle of wine from his parents' cellar and sat in the empty *trattoria*. The fishermen all stayed away. Pasquale had always felt confined by his life—by his parents' fearful lifestyle, by the Hotel Adequate View, by Porto Vergogna, by these things that seemed to hold him in place. Now he was chained only to the fact that he was completely alone.

Pasquale finished the wine and got another bottle. He sat at his table in the *trattoria*, staring at the photo of Dee Moray and the other woman, as the night bled out and he became drunk and dizzy, and still his aunt didn't return, and at some point he must have fallen asleep, because he heard a boat and then the voice of God bellowed through his hotel lobby.

"*Buon giorno!*" God called. "Carlo? Antonia? Where are you?" And Pasquale wanted to weep, because shouldn't they be with God, his parents? Why was He asking for them, and in English? But finally Pasquale realized he was asleep and he lurched into consciousness, just as God switched back to Italian: "*Cosa un ragazzo deve fare per ottenere una bevanda qui intorno?*" and Pasquale realized that, of course, it wasn't God. Alvis Bender was in his hotel lobby first thing this morning, here for his yearly writing vacation, and asking in his sketchy Italian, *What's a fella got to do to get a drink around here?*

After the war, Alvis Bender had been lost. He returned to Madison to teach English at Edgewood, a little liberal arts college, but he was sullen and rootless, prone to weeks of drunken depression. He felt none of the passion he'd once had for teaching, for the world of books. The Franciscans who ran the college tired quickly of his heavy drinking and Alvis went back to work for his father. By the early fifties, Bender Chevrolet was the biggest dealership in Wisconsin; Alvis's father had opened new showrooms in Green Bay and Oshkosh, and was about to open a Pontiac dealership in suburban Chicago. Alvis made the most of his family's prosperity, behaving in the auto business as he had at his little college and earning the nickname All Night Bender among the dealership secretaries and bookkeepers. The people around Alvis attributed his mood swings to what was euphemistically called "battle fatigue," but when his father asked Alvis if he was shell-shocked, Alvis said, "I get shelled every day at happy hour, Dad."

Alvis didn't think he had battle fatigue—he'd barely seen combat—so much as *life* fatigue. He supposed it could be some kind of postwar existential funk, but the thing eating him felt smaller than that: he just no longer saw the point of things. He especially couldn't see the angle in working hard, or in doing the right thing. After all, look where that had got Richards. Meanwhile, he'd survived to come back to Wisconsin and—what? Teach sentence diagramming to morons? Sell Bel Airs to dentists?

On his better days he imagined that he could channel this malaise into the book he was writing—except that he wasn't actually writing a book. Oh, he *talked* about the book he was writing, but the pages never came. And the more he talked about the book he wasn't writing, the harder it actually became to write. The first sentence bedeviled him. He had an idea that his war book would be an antiwar book; that he would focus on the drudgery of soldiering and his book would feature only a single battle, the nine-second firefight at Strettoia in which his company had lost two men; that the entire thing would be about the boredom leading up to those nine seconds; that in those nine seconds the protagonist would die, and then the book would go on anyway, with another, more minor character. This structure seemed to him to capture the randomness of what he'd experienced. All the World War II books and movies were so damned earnest and solemn, Audie Murphy stories of bravery. His own callow view, he felt, fit more with books about the *first* world war: Hemingway's stoic detachment, Dos Passos's ironic tragedies, Céline's absurd black-hearted satires.

Then, one day, as he was trying to coax a woman he'd just met into sleeping with him, he happened to mention that he was writing a book, and she became intrigued. "About what?" she asked. "It's about the war," he answered. "Korea?" she asked, innocently enough, and Alvis realized just how pathetic he'd become.

His old friend Richards was right: they'd gone ahead and started another war before Alvis had finished with the last one. And just thinking about his dead friend made Alvis properly ashamed of how he'd wasted the last eight years.

The next day, Alvis marched into the showroom and announced to his father that he needed some time off. He was returning to Italy; he was finally going to write his book about the war. His father wasn't happy, but he made Alvis a deal: he could take three months off, as long as he came back to run the new Pontiac dealership in Kenosha when he was through. Alvis quickly agreed.

And so he went to Italy. From Venice to Florence, from Naples to Rome, he traveled, drank, smoked, and contemplated, and everywhere he went he packed his portable Royal—without ever removing it from the case. Instead, he'd check into a hotel and go straight to the bar. Everywhere he went, people wanted to buy a returning GI a drink, and everywhere he went, Alvis wanted to accept. He told himself he was doing research, but except for an unproductive trip to Strettoia, the site of his tiny firefight, most of his research involved drinking and trying to seduce Italian girls.

In Strettoia, he woke terribly hung over and went for a walk, looking for the clearing where his old unit had gotten into the firefight. There, he came across a landscape painter doing a sketch of an old barn. But the young man was drawing the barn upside down. Alvis thought maybe there was something wrong with the man, some sort of brain damage, and yet there was a quality to his work that drew Alvis in, a disorientation that seemed familiar.

"The eye sees everything upside down," the artist explained, "and then the brain automatically reverses it. I'm just trying to put it back the way the mind sees it."

Alvis stared into the drawing for a long time. He even thought about buying it, but he realized that if he hung it this way, upside down, people would just turn it over. This, he decided, was also the problem with the book he hoped to write. He could never write a standard war book; what he had to say about the war could only be told upside down, and then people would probably just miss the point and try to turn it right side up again.

That night, in La Spezia, he bought a drink for an old partisan, a man with horrible burn scars on his face. The man kissed Alvis's cheeks and smacked his back and called him "comrade" and "*amico!*" He told Alvis the story of how he'd gotten those burns: his partisan unit had been sleeping in a haystack in the hills when, without warning, a German patrol used a flamethrower to roust them. He was the only one to escape alive. Alvis was so moved by the man's story that he bought him several rounds of drinks, and they saluted each other and wept over friends they had lost. Finally, Alvis asked the man if he could use his story in the book he was writing. This caused the Italian to begin weeping. It was all a lie, the

Italian confessed; there had been no partisan unit, no flamethrower, no Germans. The man had been working on a car two years earlier when the engine had suddenly caught fire.

Moved by the man's confession, Alvis Bender drunkenly forgave his new friend. After all, he was a fraud, too; he'd talked about writing a book for ten years and hadn't written a single word. The two drunken liars hugged and cried, and stayed up all night confessing their weak hearts.

In the morning, a dreadfully hungover Alvis Bender sat staring at the port of La Spezia. He only had two weeks left of the three months his father had given him to "figure this shit out." He grabbed his suitcase and his portable typewriter, trudged down to the pier, and started negotiating a boat ride to Portovenere, but the pilot misheard his slurred Italian. Two hours later, the boat bumped into a rocky promontory in a closet-size cove, where he laid eyes on a runt of a town, maybe a dozen houses in all, clinging to the rocky cliffs, surrounding a single sad business, a little *pensione* and *trattoria* named, like everything on that coast, for St. Peter. There were a handful of fishermen tending nets in little skiffs and the owner of the empty hotel sat on his patio reading a newspaper and smoking a pipe, while his handsome, azure-eyed son sat daydreaming on a nearby rock. "What is this place?" Alvis Bender asked, and the pilot said, "This is Porto Vergogna." *Port of Shame.* Wasn't that where he'd wanted to go? And Alvis Bender could think of no better place for himself and said, "Yes, of course."

The proprietor of the hotel, Carlo Tursi, was a sweet, thoughtful man who had left Florence and moved to the tiny village after losing his two older sons in the war. He was honored to have an American writer stay in his *pensione*, and he promised that his son, Pasquale, would be quiet during the day so Alvis could work. And so it was that in the tiny top-floor room, with the gentle wash of waves on the rocks below, Alvis Bender finally unpacked his portable Royal. He put the typewriter on the nightstand beneath the shuttered window. He stared at it. He slipped a sheet of paper in, cranked it through. He put his hands on the keys. He rubbed their smooth-pebbled surfaces, the lightly raised letters. And an hour passed. He went downstairs for some wine and found Carlo sitting on the patio.

"How is the writing?" Carlo asked solemnly.

"Actually, I'm having some trouble," Alvis admitted.

"With which part?" Carlo asked.

"The beginning."

Carlo considered this. "Perhaps you could write first the ending."

Alvis thought about the upside-down painting he'd seen near Strettoia. Yes, of course. The ending first. He laughed.

Thinking the American was laughing at his suggestion, Carlo apologized for being "*stupido.*"

No, no, Alvis said, it was a brilliant suggestion. He'd been talking and thinking about this book for so long—it was as if it already existed, as if he'd already written it in some way, as if it was just *out there*, in the air, and all he had to do was find a place to tap into the story, like a stream flowing by. Why *not* start at the end? He ran back upstairs and typed these words: "Then spring came and with it the end of my war."

Alvis stared at his one sentence, so odd and fragmented, so perfect. Then he wrote another sentence and another, and soon he had a page, at which point he ran down the stairs and had a glass of wine with his muse, the serious, bespectacled Carlo Tursi. This would be his reward and his rhythm: type a page, drink a glass of wine with Carlo. After two weeks of this, he had twelve pages. He was surprised to discover that he was telling the story of a girl he'd met near the end of the war, a girl who had given him a quick hand job. He hadn't planned to even include that story in his book—since it was apropos of nothing—but suddenly it seemed like the only story that mattered.

On his last day in Porto Vergogna, Alvis packed up his few pages and his little Royal and said good-bye to the Tursi family, promising to return next year to work, to spend two weeks each year in the little village until his book was done, even if it took the rest of his life.

Then he had one of the fishermen take him to La Spezia, where he caught a bus to Licciana, the girl's hometown. He watched out the window of the bus, looking for the place where he'd met her, for the barn and the stand of trees, but nothing looked the same and he couldn't get his bearings. The village itself was twice as big as it had been during the war, the crumbly old rock buildings replaced by wood and stone structures. Alvis went to a *trattoria* and gave the proprietor Maria's last name. The man knew the family. He'd gone to school with Maria's brother, Marco, who had fought for the Fascists and was tortured for his efforts, hung by his feet in the town square and bled like a butchered cow. The man didn't know what had become of Maria, but her younger sister, Nina, had married a local boy and lived in the village still. Alvis got directions to Nina's home, a one-story stone house in a clearing below the old rock walls of the village, in a new neighborhood that was spreading down the hill. He knocked. The door opened a crack and a black-haired woman stuck her face out the window next to the door and asked what he wanted.

Alvis explained that he'd known her sister in the war. "Anna?" the girl asked.

"No, Maria," Alvis said.

"Oh," she said, somewhat darkly. After a moment, she invited him into the well-kept living room. "Maria is married to a doctor, living in Genoa."

Alvis asked if she might have an address for Maria.

Nina's face hardened. "She doesn't need another old boyfriend from the war coming back. She is finally happy. Why do you want to make trouble?"

Alvis insisted he didn't want to make any trouble.

"Maria had a hard time in the war. Leave her be. Please." And then one of Nina's children called for her and she went to the kitchen to check on him.

There was a telephone in the living room, and like a lot of people who had only recently gotten a telephone, Maria's sister kept it in a prominent place, on a table covered with figures of saints. Beneath the phone was an address book.

Alvis reached over, opened the book to the *M* section, and there it was: the name *Maria*. No last name. No phone number. Just a street number in Genoa. Alvis memorized the address and closed the book, thanked Nina for her time, and left.

That afternoon, he took a train to Genoa.

The address turned out to be near the harbor. Alvis worried that he'd gotten it wrong; this did not appear to be the neighborhood of a doctor and his wife.

The buildings were brick and stone, built one on top of the other, their heights like a musical scale descending gradually to the harbor. The ground floors were filled with cheap cafés and taverns that catered to fishermen, while above were flop apartments and simple hotels. Maria's street number led to a tavern, a rotted-wood rat-hole of a place with warped tables and a ragged old rug. A rail-thin, smiling barman sat behind the counter, serving fishermen in droopy caps bent over chipped glasses of amber.

Alvis apologized, said he must have the wrong place. "I'm looking for a woman—" he began.

The skinny bartender didn't wait for a name. He just pointed to the stairs behind the bar and held out his hand.

"Ah." Knowing exactly where he was now, Alvis paid the man. As he climbed the stairs, he prayed there was some mistake, that he wouldn't find her here. At the top was a hallway that opened into a foyer with a couch and two chairs. Sitting on the couch, talking in low voices, were three women in nightgowns. Two of the three were young—girls, really, in short nighties, reading magazines. Neither of them looked familiar.

In the other chair, a faded silk robe over her nightgown, smoking the last of a cigarette, sat Maria.

"Hello," Alvis said.

Maria didn't even look up.

One of the younger girls said, in English, "America, yes? You like me, America?"

Alvis ignored the younger girl. "Maria," he said quietly.

She didn't look up.

"Maria?"

Finally, she glanced up. She seemed twenty years older, not ten. A thickening had occurred in her arms and there were lines around her mouth and eyes.

"Who's Maria?" she asked in English.

One of the other girls laughed. "Stop teasing him. Or give him to me."

With no trace of recognition in her voice, Maria gave Alvis the prices, in English, for various amounts of time. Above her was an awful painting of an iris. Alvis fought the urge to turn it upside down. He bought a half hour.

No stranger to this kind of place, he paid Maria half the agreed-upon price, which she folded and took downstairs to the man behind the bar. Then Alvis followed her down the hall to a small room. Inside, there was nothing but a made bed, a nightstand, a coat rack, and a scratched, foggy mirror. A window looked out on the harbor and the street below. She sat down on the bed, its springs creaking, and began to undress.

"You don't remember me?" Alvis asked in Italian.

She stopped undressing and sat on the bed, unmoved, no recognition in her eyes.

Alvis began slowly, telling her in Italian how he'd been stationed in Italy during the war, how he'd met her on a deserted road and walked her home one night, how on the day he met her he'd reached a point where he didn't care if he lived or died, but that after meeting her he had cared again. He said that she'd encouraged him to write a book after the war, to take it seriously, but that he'd gone home to America (*"Ricorda—Wisconsin?"*) and drank away the last decade. His best friend, he said, had died in the war, leaving behind a wife and a son. Alvis had no one, and he'd come home and wasted all of those years.

She listened patiently and then asked if he wanted to have sex.

He told her that he had gone to Licciana to look for her, and he thought he saw something in her eyes when he said the name of the village—shame, perhaps—because he had been so humbled by what she did for him that night: not the part with her hand, but the way she'd comforted him afterward, held his crying face against her beautiful chest. That was, he said, the most humane thing anyone had ever done for him.

"I'm so sorry," Alvis said, "that you became this."

"This?" She startled Alvis by laughing. "I've always been this." She waved at the room around her and said, in a flat Italian, "Friend, I don't know you. And I don't know this village you speak of. I've always lived in Genoa. I get boys like you sometimes, American boys who were in the war and had their first sex with a girl who looked like me. It's fine." She looked patient, but not particularly interested in his story. "But what were you going to do, rescue this Maria? Take her back to America?"

Alvis could think of nothing to say. No, of course he wasn't going to take her back to America. So what *was* he going to do? Why was he here?

"You made me happy, choosing me over the younger girls," the prostitute said, and she reached out for his belt. "But please. Stop calling me Maria."

As her hands expertly undid his belt, Alvis stared at the woman's face. It had to be her, didn't it? And now, suddenly, he wasn't so sure. She did seem older than Maria should. And the thickening he'd attributed to age—could this actually be someone else? Was he confessing to some random whore?

He watched her thick hands unbutton his pants. He felt paralyzed, but he managed to pull himself away. He buttoned his pants and cinched his belt again.

"Would you rather have one of the other girls?" the prostitute asked. "I'll go get her, but you still have to pay me."

Alvis took out his wallet, his hands shaking; he pulled out fifty times the price she'd quoted him. He placed the money on the bed. And then he spoke quietly. "I'm sorry I didn't just walk you home that night."

She just stared at the money. Then Alvis Bender walked out, feeling as if the last of his life had seeped out in that room. In the front room, the other whores were reading their magazines. They didn't even look up. Downstairs, he edged past the skinny, grinning bartender, and by the time he burst outside into the sun Alvis felt crazy with thirst. He hurried across the street, toward another bar, thinking, These bars, thank God, they go on forever. It was a relief, that he would never exhaust all the bars in the world. He could come to Italy once a year to work on this book, and even if it took him the rest of his life to finish it and drink himself to death, that was okay. He knew now what his book would be: an artifact, incomplete and misshapen, a shard of some larger meaning. And if his time with Maria was ultimately pointless—a random encounter, a fleeting moment, perhaps even the wrong whore—then so be it.

In the street, a truck veered around him and he was jolted out of his thoughts long enough to look back over his shoulder, up at the brothel he had just left. There, in the second-story window, stood Maria—at least that's what he would tell himself—leaning against the glass, watching him, her robe open a little, her fingers stroking the place between her breasts where he had once pressed his face and sobbed. She stared at him a second longer, and then she backed away from the window and was gone.

After that burst of prolific writing, Alvis Bender never made much more progress on his novel when he came to Italy. Instead, he'd cat around Rome or Milan or Venice for a week or two, drinking and chasing women, then come and spend a few days in the quiet of Porto Vergogna. He'd rework that first chapter, rewrite it, reorder things, take a word or two out, put a new sentence in—but nothing came of his book. And yet it always restored him in some way, reading and gently reworking his one good chapter, and seeing his old friend Carlo Tursi, his wife, Antonia, and their sea-eyed son, Pasquale. But now—to find both Carlo and Antonia dead like this, to find Pasquale a full-grown man . . . Alvis wasn't sure what to think. He had heard of couples dying in short order like this, the grief just too much for the survivor to bear. But it was hard to get his mind around: a year earlier, Carlo and Antonia had both seemed healthy. And now they were gone?

"When did this happen?" he asked Pasquale.

"My father died last spring, my mother three nights ago," Pasquale said. "Her funeral mass is tomorrow."

Alvis kept searching Pasquale's face. He'd been away at school the last few springs when Alvis had come. He couldn't believe this was little Pasquale, grown into this . . . this man. Even in his grief, Pasquale had the same strange calm about him that he'd had as a boy, those blue eyes steady in their easy assessment of the world. They sat on the patio in the cool morning, Alvis Bender's portable typewriter and suitcase at his feet where Pasquale had once sat. "I'm so sorry, Pasquale," he said. "I can go find a hotel up the coast if you want to be alone."

Pasquale looked up at him. Even though Alvis's Italian was usually pretty clear, the words were taking a moment to register for Pasquale, almost as if they had to be translated. "No. I would like you to stay." He poured them each another glass of wine, and slid Alvis's glass to him.

"*Grazie,*" Alvis said.

They drank their glasses of wine quietly, Pasquale staring at the table.

"It's fairly common, couples passing one after the other that way," said Alvis, whose knowledge sometimes seemed to Pasquale suspiciously broad. "To die of . . ." He tried to think of the Italian word for grief. "*Dolore.*"

"No." Pasquale looked up slowly again. "My aunt killed her."

Alvis wasn't certain he'd heard right. "Your aunt?"

"Yes."

"Why would she do that, Pasquale?" Alvis asked.

Pasquale rubbed his face. "She wanted me to go marry the American actress."

Alvis thought Pasquale might be insane with grief. "What actress?"

Pasquale sleepily handed over the photo of Dee Moray. Alvis

took his reading glasses from his pocket, stared at the photo, then looked up. He said flatly, "Your mother wanted you to marry Elizabeth Taylor?"

"No. The other one," Pasquale said, switching to English, as if such things could only be believed in that language. "She come to the hotel, three days. She make a mistake to come here." He shrugged.

In the eight years Alvis Bender had been coming to Porto Vergogna, he'd seen only three other guests at the hotel, certainly no Americans, and certainly no beautiful actresses, no friends of Elizabeth Taylor. "She's beautiful," Alvis said. "Pasquale, where is your Aunt Valeria now?"

"I don't know. She ran into the hills." Pasquale filled their wineglasses again. He looked up at his old family friend, at his sharp features and thin mustache, fanning himself with his fedora. "Alvis," Pasquale said, "is it okay if we do not talk?"

"Of course, Pasquale," Alvis said. They quietly drank their wine. And in the quiet, the waves lapped at the cliffs below and a light, salty mist rose in the air, as both men stared out at the sea.

"She read your book," Pasquale said after a while.

Alvis cocked his head, wondering if he'd heard right. "What did you say?"

"Dee. The American." He pointed to the blond woman in the photo. "She read your book. She said it was sad, but also very good. She liked it very much."

"Really?" Alvis asked in English. Then, "Well, I'll be damned." Again, it was quiet except for the sea on the rocks, like someone shuffling cards. "I don't suppose she said . . . anything else?" Alvis Bender asked after a time, once again in Italian.

Pasquale said he wasn't sure what Alvis meant.

"Concerning my chapter," he said. "Did the actress say anything else?"

Pasquale said he couldn't think of anything if she had.

Alvis finished his wine and said he was going up to his room, Pasquale asking if Alvis wouldn't mind staying in a second-floor room. The actress had stayed on the third floor, he said, and he hadn't gotten around to cleaning it. Pasquale felt funny lying, but he simply wasn't ready for someone else in that room yet, even Alvis.

"Of course," Alvis said, and he went upstairs to put his things in his room, still smiling at the thought of a beautiful woman reading his book.

And so Pasquale was sitting at the table alone when he heard the high rumble of a larger boat motor and looked up just in time to see a speedboat he didn't recognize round the breakwater into Porto Vergogna's tiny cove. The pilot had come too quickly into the cove and the boat rose indignantly and settled in the backsplash of its own chop. There were three men in the boat, and as the boat rumbled up to the pier he could see them clearly: a man in a black cap piloting the boat, and behind him, sitting together in back, the snake Michael Deane and the drunk Richard Burton.

Pasquale made no move to go down to the water. The black-capped pilot tied to the wooden bollard and then Michael Deane and Richard Burton climbed out of the boat, stepped onto the pier, and began making their way up the narrow trail to the hotel.

Richard Burton seemed to have sobered up, and was impeccably dressed in a wool suit coat, cuffs of his shirtsleeves peeking out, no tie.

"There's my old friend," Richard Burton called to Pasquale as he climbed toward the village. "I don't suppose Dee's returned here, sport?"

Michael Deane was a few steps behind Burton, taking measure of the place.

Pasquale looked behind him, at the sad cluster of his father's village, trying to see it through the American's eyes. The small block-and-stucco houses must look as exhausted as he felt—as if, after three hundred years, they might yet lose their grip on the cliffs and tumble into the sea.

"No," Pasquale said. He remained seated, but as both men reached the patio, Pasquale glared up at Michael Deane, who took a half step back.

"So . . . you haven't seen Dee?" Michael Deane asked.

"No," Pasquale said again.

"See, I told you," Michael Deane said to Richard Burton. "Now let's go to Rome. She'll turn up there. Or maybe she'll go on to Switzerland after all."

Richard Burton ran his hand through his hair, turned, and pointed to the wine bottle on the patio table. "Do you mind terribly, sport?"

Behind him, Michael Deane flinched, but Richard Burton grabbed the bottle, shook it, and showed Deane that it was empty. "Outrageous fortune," he said, and rubbed his mouth as if he were dying of thirst.

"Inside is more wine," Pasquale said, "in the kitchen."

"Bloody decent of you, Pat," Richard Burton said, patting Pasquale on the shoulder and walking past him into the hotel.

When he was gone, Michael Deane shuffled his feet and cleared his throat. "Dick thought she might have come back here."

"You lose her?" Pasquale asked.

"I suppose that's one way to put it." Michael Deane frowned, as if considering whether or not to say any more. "She was supposed to go on to Switzerland, but it looks like she never got on the train." Michael Deane rubbed his temple. "If she does come back here, could you contact me?"

Pasquale said nothing.

"Look," Michael Deane said. "This is all very complicated. You only see this one girl and I'll admit: it's been rough business for her. But there are other people involved, other responsibilities and considerations. Marriages, careers . . . it's not simple."

Pasquale flinched, recalling when he'd said the same thing to Dee Moray about his relationship with Amedea: *It's not simple.*

Michael Deane cleared his throat. "I didn't come here to explain myself. I came here so you could pass on a message if you see her. Tell her I know she's angry. But I also know exactly what she wants. You tell her that. *Michael Deane knows what you want.* And I'm the man who can help her get it." He reached into his jacket and produced another envelope, which he extended to Pasquale. "There's an Italian phrase I've grown fond of in the last few weeks: *con molta discrezione*."

With much discretion. Pasquale waved the money off like it was a hornet.

Michael Deane set the envelope on the table. "Just tell her to contact me if she comes back here, *capisce*?"

Richard Burton appeared in the doorway then. "Where'd you say that wine was, cap'n?"

Pasquale told him where to find the wine and Richard Burton went back inside.

Michael Deane smiled. "Sometimes the good ones are . . . difficult."

"And he is a good one?" Pasquale asked without looking up.

"Best I've ever seen."

As if on cue, Richard Burton emerged with the unlabeled wine bottle. "Right, then. Pay the man for the *vino*, Deane-o."

Michael Deane put more money on the table, twice the cost of the bottle.

Drawn by the voices, Alvis Bender came out of the hotel, but stopped suddenly in the doorway, staring dumbfounded as Richard Burton toasted him with the dark wine bottle. "*Cin cin, amico,*" Richard Burton said, as if Alvis were another Italian. He took a long pull from the bottle and turned to Michael Deane again. "Well, Deaner . . . I suppose we've worlds to conquer." He bowed to Pasquale. "Conductor, you've a lovely orchestra here. Don't change a thing." And with that, he began making his way back to the boat.

Michael Deane reached into his breast pocket and pulled out a business card and a pen. "And this . . ."—with some fanfare, he signed the back of the card and put it on the table in front of Pasquale, as if he were doing a magic trick—" . . . is for you, Mr. Tursi. Maybe someday I can do something for you, too. *Con molta discrezione*," he said again. Then Michael Deane nodded solemnly and turned to follow Richard Burton down the stairs.

Pasquale picked up the signed business card, flipped it over. It read: *Michael Deane, Publicity, 20th Century Fox.*

In the doorway of the hotel, Alvis Bender stood stock-still, staring open-mouthed as the men made their way down toward the shore. "Pasquale?" he said finally. "Was that Richard Burton?"

"Yes," Pasquale sighed. And that might have been the end of the whole episode with the American cinema people had not Pasquale's Aunt Valeria chosen that very moment to reappear, staggering from behind the abandoned chapel like an apparition, mad with grief and guilt and a night spent outside, her eyes vacant, gray hair bursting from her head like blown wire, clothes dirty, her hunger-hollowed face streaked with muddy tears. *"Diavolo!"*

She walked past the hotel, past Alvis Bender, past her nephew, down toward the two men retreating to the water. The feral cats scattered before her. Richard Burton was too far ahead, but she hobbled down the trail toward Michael Deane, yelling at him in Italian. Devil, killer, assassin: *"Omicida!"* she hissed. *"Assassino cruento!"*

Nearly to the boat with his bottle, Richard Burton turned back. "I told you to pay for the wine, Deane!"

Michael Deane stopped and turned, put his hands up to pitch his usual charm, but the old witch kept coming. She raised a knobby finger, pointed it at him, and affixed him with an accusing lamentation, a horrible curse that echoed against the cliff walls: *"Io ti maledico a morire lentamente, tormentato dalla tua anima miserabile!"*

I curse you to a slow death, tormented by your miserable soul.

"Goddamn it, Deane," yelled Richard Burton. "Would you get in the boat?"

15

The Rejected First Chapter of
Michael Deane's Memoir

2006
Los Angeles, California

ACTION.

Now where to start? Birth the man says.

Fine. I was birthed fourth of six to the bride of a savvy lawyer in the city of angels in the year 1939. But I was not truly BORN until the spring of 1962.

When I discovered what I was meant to do.

Before that life was what it must be for regular people. Family dinners and swimming lessons. Tennis. Summers with cousins in Florida. Fumbles with easy girls behind the school-house and movie theater.

Was I the brightest? No. Best-looking? Not that either. I was what they called Trouble. Capital T. Envious boys routinely took swings. Girls slapped. Schools spit me out like a bad oyster.

To my father I was The Traitor. To his name and his plans for me: Study abroad. Law school. Practice at HIS firm. Follow HIS footsteps. HIS life. Instead I lived mine. Pomona College for two years. Studied broads. Dropped out in 1960 to be in pictures. A bad complexion shot pocks in my plans. So I decided to learn the biz from inside. Starting at the bottom. A job in publicity at 20th Century Fox.

We worked in the old Fox Car Barn next to the greasy Teamsters. Talked on the phone all day to reporters and gossip columnists. We tried to get good stories in the papers and keep bad ones out. At night I went to openings and parties and benefits. Did I love it? Who wouldn't? A different lady on my arm every night. The sun and the strip and the sex? Life was electric.

My boss was a fat jug-eared Midwesterner named Dooley. He kept me close because I was fresh. Because I threatened him. But one morning Dooley wasn't in the office. A frantic call came in. Some sharp was at the studio gate with some interesting photos. A well-known cowboy actor at a party. One of our rising stars. What wasn't so well-known was that this fellow was also a first-class puff. And these pictures showed him blowing reveille on another fella's bugle. Most animated performance this particular actor ever gave.

Dooley would be in the next day. But this couldn't wait. First I reached out to a gossip columnist who owed me. Planted the rumor that the cowboy actor was engaged to a young actress. A rising B-girl. How did I know she'd go for it? She was a girl I'd beefed a few times myself. Having her name connected to a bigger star was the fastest way to the front of the skinnys. Sure she went for it. In this town everything flows upstream. Then I strolled to the gate and casually hired the photographer to shoot promo stills for the studio. Burned the negs of the cowboy-hummer myself.

I got the call at noon. Had it taken care of by five. But next day Dooley was furious. Why? Because Skouros had called. And the head of the studio wanted to see ME. Not him.

Dooley prepped me for an hour. Don't look old Skouros in the eye. Don't use profanity. And whatever you do NEVER disagree with the man.

Fine. I waited outside Skouros's office an hour. Then I stepped inside. He was perched on the corner of his desk. Wore a funeral director's suit. A thick man with black glasses and

slick hair. He gestured to a chair. Offered me a Coca-Cola.
"Thank you." The tight Greek bastard opened the bottle. He
poured a third of it into a glass and handed me the glass.
He held the rest of that Coke like I hadn't earned it yet. He
sat there on the corner of that desk and watched me drink my
tiny Coke while he asked me questions. Where was I from? What
did I hope to do? What was my favorite picture? He never even
mentioned the cowboy star. And what does this big studio boss
want from the Deane?

"Michael. Tell me. What do you know about Cleopatra?"

Stupid question. Every last person in town knew every last
thing about that film. Mostly how it was eating Fox alive.
How the idea had kicked around for twenty years before Walter Wanger developed it in '58. But then Wanger caught his
wife blowing her agent and he shot the agent in the balls.
So Rouben Mamoulian took over Cleo. Budgeted the thing for
$2 million with Joan Collins. Who made as much sense as Don
Knotts. So the studio dumped her and went after Liz Taylor.
The biggest star in the world but she was reeling from bad
publicity after she stole Eddie Fisher from Debbie Reynolds.
Not even thirty and already on her fourth marriage. At this
precarious stage of her career and what's she do? Demands a
million bucks and 10 percent of Cleopatra. No one had ever
made half-a-mil on a picture and this dame wants a mil?

But the studio was desperate. Skouros said yes.

Mamoulian took forty people to England to start production on Cleo in 1960. It was hell right off. Bad weather. Bad
luck. Sets built. Sets torn down. Sets rebuilt. Mamoulian
couldn't shoot a single frame. Liz got sick. A cold became
an abscessed tooth became a brain infection became a staph
infection became pneumonia. Woman had a tracheotomy and
nearly died on the table. Cast and crew sat around drinking
and playing cribbage. After sixteen months of production and
seven million bucks he had less than six feet of usable film.
A year and a half and the man hadn't even shot his height in

film. Skouros had no choice. He fired Mamoulian. Brought in Joe Mankiewicz. Mankie moved the whole thing to Italy and dumped the whole cast except Liz. Brought in Dick Burton to be Marc Antony. Hired fifty screenwriters to fix the script. Soon it was five hundred pages. Nine hours of story. The studio was losing seventy grand a day while a thousand extras sat around getting paid for nothing and it rained and rained and people walked off with cameras and Liz drank and Mankie started talking about making it into three pictures. The studio was in so deep by now there was no turning back. Not after two years of production and twenty million already down the shitter and God knows how much more while poor tight Skouros rode that goddamn thing all the way down hoping against hope that what showed up on-screen was the greatest goddamned movie . . . spectacle . . . ever . . . made.

"What do I know about <u>Cleopatra</u>?" I looked up at Skouros perched on his desk holding the rest of my cola. "Guess I know a little."

Right answer. Skouros poured some more Coke in my glass. Then he reached over to his desk. Grabbed a manila envelope. Handed it to me. I will never forget the photo I pulled out of that envelope. It was a work of art. Two people in tight clench. And not any two people. Dick Burton and Liz Taylor. Not Antony and Cleopatra in a publicity shot. Liz and Dick lip-locked on a patio at the Grand Hotel in Rome. Tongues spelunking each other's mouths.

This was disaster. They were both married. The studio was still dealing with the shit publicity from Liz break-ing up the marriage of Debbie and Eddie. Now Liz is getting beefed by the greatest stage actor of his generation? And a top-notch cocksman to boot? What about Eddie Fisher's little kids? And Burton's family? His poor Welsh rotters with their coal-stained eyes crying about their lost daddy? The pub would kill the movie. Kill the studio. The movie's budget was already a guillotine hanging over Skouros's fat Greek head. This would drop the blade.

I stared at the photo.

Skouros did his best to smile and look calm. But his eyes blinked like a metronome. "What do you think Deane?"

What did Deane think? Not so fast.

There was something else I knew. But I didn't really know yet. See? The way you know about sex before you really know about it? I had a gift. But I hadn't figured how to use it. Sometimes I could see through people. Right to their cores. Like an X-ray. Not a human lie detector. A desire detector. It's what got me in trouble too. A girl tells me no. Why? She's got a boyfriend. I hear no but I SEE yes. Ten minutes later the boyfriend walks in to find his girlfriend with a mouthful of Deane. See?

It was like that with Skouros. He was saying one thing but I was seeing something else. So. What now Deane? Your whole career's in front of you. And Dooley's advice is still playing in your head. (Don't look him in the eye. Don't use profanity. Don't challenge him.)

He says it again. "So. What do you think?"

Deep breath. "Well. It looks to me like you're not the only one getting fucked on this picture."

Skouros stared at me. Then he straightened up from the corner of his desk. He walked around and sat down. From that moment on he spoke to me like a man. No more quarter-Cokes. The old man broke it down. Liz? Impossible to deal with. Emotional. Stubborn. Contrary. But Burton was a pro. And this wasn't his first piece of primo tail. Our only chance was to reason with him. When he was sober.

Good luck with that. Your first assignment is to go to Rome and convince a SOBER Dick Burton that if he doesn't lay off Liz Taylor he's out of the picture. Right. I flew out the next day.

In Rome I saw right away it wouldn't be easy. This wasn't some on-set affair. They were in love. Even that old actress-dipper Burton was in deep with this one. First time in his life he isn't slopping extras and hairdressers too. At the

Grand Hotel I laid it out for him. Gave him Skouros's whole message. Played it stern. Dick just laughed at me. I'd kick <u>him</u> off the film? Not likely.

Thirty-six hours into the biggest assignment of my life and my bluff's been called. An A-bomb couldn't keep Dick and Liz apart.

And no wonder. This was the greatest Hollywood romance in history. Not just some set-screw. Love. All those cute couples now with their conjoined names? Pale imitations. Mere children.

Dick and Liz were gods. Pure talent and charisma and like gods they were terrible together. Awful. A gorgeous nightmare. Drunk and narcissistic and cruel to everyone around them. If only the movie had the drama of these two. They'd film a scene as flat as paper and as soon as the cameras cut Burton would make some wry comment and she'd hiss something back and she'd storm off and he'd chase her back to the hotel and the hotel staff would report these ungodly sounds of breaking glass and yelling and balling and you couldn't tell the fighting from the fucking with those two. Empty booze decanters flying over hotel balconies. Every day a car wreck. A ten-car pileup.

And that's when it came to me.

I call it the moment of my birth.

Saints call it epiphany.

Billionaires call it brainstorm.

Artists call it muse.

For me it was when I understood what separated me from other people. A thing I'd always been able to see but never entirely understood. Divination of true nature. Of motivation. Of desirous hearts. I saw the whole world in a flash and I recognized it at once:

<u>We want what we want.</u>

Dick wanted Liz. Liz wanted Dick. And we want car wrecks. We say we don't. But we love them. To look is to love. A thousand people drive past the statue of David. Two hundred look. A thousand people drive past a car wreck. A thousand look.

I suppose it is cliché now. Obvious to the computer gewgaw-counters with their hits and eyeballs and page views. But this was a transformational moment for me. For the town. For the world.

I called Skouros in L.A. "This can't be fixed."

The old man was quiet. "Are you telling me I need to send someone else?"

"No." I was talking to a five-year-old. "I'm saying this . . . can't . . . be fixed. And you don't <u>want</u> to fix it."

He fumed. This wasn't someone used to getting bad news. "What the fuck are you talking about?"

"How much do you have into this picture?"

"The actual cost of a film isn't—"

"How much?"

"Fifteen."

"You have twenty in if you have a dime. Conservatively you'll spend twenty-five or thirty before it's done. And how much will you spend on publicity to recoup thirty mil?"

Skouros couldn't even say the number.

"Commercials and billboards and ads in every magazine in the world. Eight? Let's say ten. Now you're up to forty mil. No picture in history has ever made forty. And let's be clear. This picture's no good. I've had crabs more enjoyable than this picture. This picture gives shit a bad name."

Was I killing Skouros? You bet I was. Only to save him.

"But what if I could get you twenty million in FREE publicity?"

"That's not the kind of publicity we want!"

"Maybe it is." Then I explained what it was like on set. The drinking. Fighting. Sex. When the cameras ran it was death. But with the cameras off? You couldn't take your eyes off them. Marc Antony and Cleo-fucking-patra? Who gave a shit about those old moldered bones? But Liz and Dick? THIS is our movie. I told Skouros that as long as this thing rages between them the movie's got a chance.

Put this fire out? Hell no. What we need to do is stoke it.

It's easy to see now. In this world of fall and redemption and fall again. Of comeback after comeback. Of carefully released home sex tapes. But no one had thought this way before. Not about <u>movie stars</u>! These were Greek gods. Perfect beings. When one of them fell it was forever. Fatty Arbuckle? Dead. Ava Gardner? Done.

I was suggesting burning the whole town down to save this one house. If I pulled this off people would see our picture not <u>in spite of</u> the scandal but <u>because of</u> it. After this you could never go back. Gods would be dead forever.

I could hear Skouros breathing on the other end of the phone. "Do it." Then he hung up.

That afternoon I bribed Liz's driver. When she and Burton came out onto the patio of the villa they'd rented to hide out in camera shutters started popping from balconies in three directions. Photographers I'd tipped. Next day I hired my own shooter to stalk the couple. Made tens of thousands selling those photos. Used that money to bribe more drivers and makeup people for information. I had my own little industry. Liz and Dick were furious. They begged me to find out who was leaking information and I pretended to find out. I fired drivers and extras and caterers and soon Dick and Liz were relying on me to book their remote getaways and still the photographers found them.

And did it work? It broke bigger than any movie story you've ever seen. Liz and Dick in every newspaper in the world.

Dick's wife found out. And Liz's husband. The story got even bigger. I told Skouros to have patience. To ride it out.

Then poor Eddie Fisher flew to Rome to try to win his wife back and suddenly I had a new problem. For this to work Liz and Dick had to be together when the film wrapped. When the picture opened on Sunset I needed Dick to be boning Liz in the dining room of the Chateau Marmont. And I needed Eddie Fisher to go limping away. But the son of a bitch wanted to fight for his doomed marriage.

The other problem with Liz's husband being in Rome was Burton. He sulked. Drank. And he went back to this other woman he'd been seeing on the side off and on since his first day in Italy.

She was tall and blond. Uncommon-looking girl. Camera loved her. All the actresses then were either coupes or sedans. Broads or girls-next-door. But this was something else. Something new. She had no film experience. Came from the stage. Mankie inexplicably cast her as Cleopatra's lady-in-waiting from nothing more than a casting photo. Figured he'd make Liz look more Egyptian by making one of her slaves blond. Little did he know one of Liz's ladies-in-waiting was actually waiting for Dick.

Christ. I couldn't believe it when I saw her. Who puts a tall blond woman in a movie set in ancient Egypt?

I'll call this girl D–.

This D– was what we'd later call a free spirit. One of those moon-eyed easygoing hippie girls I'd get so much joy out of in the sixties and seventies.

Not that I ever beefed this particular one.

Not that I wouldn't have.

But with Eddie Fisher skulking around Rome Dick went running back to his backup. This D–. I didn't figure her to be a problem. Girl like that you just throw a bone. A cherry role. A studio contract. And if she won't play you fire her. What's that cost? So I had Mankiewicz start giving her five A.M. calls to get her on set. Get her away from Burton. But then she got sick.

We had an American doctor on set. This man Crane. His whole job was to prescribe meds for Liz. He examined this girl D–. Pulled me aside the next day.

"We got a problem. The girl is pregnant. Doesn't know it yet. Some quack doc told her she can't have kids. Well she can."

Of course I'd arranged abortions before. I worked in publicity. It was practically on the business card. But this was Italy. Catholic Italy 1962. At that time it would have been easier to get a moon rock.

Shit. Here I'm leaking that the two biggest stars in the biggest picture in the world are together and I've got to deal with this? Disaster Deane. If Cleopatra comes out and everyone's talking about our stars' torrid affair we got a chance. If they're talking about Burton knocking up some extra and Liz going back to her husband? We're dead.

I put together a three-part plan. First: get rid of Burton for a while. I knew Darryl Zanuck was in France filming The Longest Day. And I knew he wanted Burton for a cameo to class up his war picture. I knew Burton wanted to do it. But Skouros hated Zanuck. Skouros had replaced the old man at Fox. And there were people on the board who wanted to replace him with Darryl's dashing young son Dickie. So I went behind Skouros's back. I called Zanuck and rented him Burton for ten days.

Then I called the doctor and told him to bring this girl D— in for more tests. "What kind of tests?" he said.

"You're the goddamned doctor! Whatever might get her out of town for a while."

I was afraid he'd be squirrelly. Hippocratic oath and all that. But this Crane jumped at the chance. Next day he comes up with a big smile. "I told her she had stomach cancer."

"YOU WHAT?"

Crane explained that the early symptoms of pregnancy were consistent with those of stomach cancer. Cramps and nausea and a bunged-up period.

I'd wanted to get rid of her not kill the poor girl.

Doc said not to worry. He'd told her it was treatable. A Swiss doctor with a new procedure. Then he winked. Of course the doctor in Switzerland puts her under. Gives her the short procedure. And when she wakes up her "cancer" is gone. She's never the wiser. We send her back to the States to recuperate. And I get her work in some pictures back home. Everyone wins. Problem solved. Movie saved.

But this D— was a wild card. Her mother had died of cancer and she took the phony diagnosis worse than bad. And I underestimated Dick's feelings for her.

On the other front Eddie Fisher had given up and gone home. I called Dick in France to tell him the good news. Liz was ready to see him again. But he couldn't see Liz right now. This other girl D— had cancer. She was dying. And Dick wanted to be there for her.

"She'll be fine. There's a doctor in Switzerland who—"

Dick interrupted me. This D— didn't want treatment. She wanted to spend the last of her time with him. And the man was narcissistic enough to think this was a good idea. He's got a two-day break on The Longest Day and he wants to meet D— on the coast in Italy. And since I was so helpful with him and Liz he wants me to set it up.

What could I do? Burton wants to meet her in this remote little coastal town. Portovenere. Right between Rome and the south of France where he's shooting The Longest Day. I opened the map and my eye went straight to this flea speck with a similar name. Porto Vergogna. I ask the travel agent to look into it. She says the town is nothing. A cliff-side fishing village. No phones or roads. Can't even get there by train or car. Only by boat. "Is there a hotel?" I asked. Travel agent said there was a tiny one. So I booked a room in Portovenere for Dick but I sent D— to Porto Vergogna. Told her to wait at the little hotel for Burton. I just needed to stow her for a few days until Dick went back to France and I could get her to Switzerland.

At first it worked. She was stuck in this village. No contact with the world. Burton showed up in Portovenere and found me waiting for him instead. I told him D— had decided to go on to Switzerland for treatment. Don't worry about her. The Swiss doctors are the best. Then I drove him back to Rome to be with Liz.

But before I could get them back together another problem arrived. Some kid from the hotel where D— is staying shows up in Rome and walks right up and punches me. I'd been in Rome three weeks and I'd gotten used to these Italians gouging me so I gave him some cash and sent him away. But he double-crossed me. Found Burton and told him the whole story. How D— wasn't dying. How she was pregnant. Then he took Burton back to her. Great. Now Dick is holed up with his pregnant mistress in a hotel in Portovenere. And my movie hangs in the balance.

But did the Deane give up? Not by a long stretch. I called Zanuck and got Burton back to France for a day of phony re-shoots on The Longest Day. And I raced to Portovenere to talk to this D—.

I've never seen someone so angry. She wanted to kill me. And I understood why. I did. I apologized. Explained that I had no idea the doctor would say it was cancer. Told her the whole thing had gotten out of hand. Told her that her career was made. Guaranteed. All she had to do was go to Switzerland and she could be in any Fox picture she wanted.

But this was one tough nut. She didn't want money or act-ing jobs. I couldn't believe it. I'd never met a young actor who didn't want either work or money or both.

This was when I understood the deep responsibility be-hind my ability to divine desire. It's one thing to know what people truly want. It's another to CREATE that want in them. To BUILD that desire.

I pretended to sigh. "Look. This got out of hand. All he wants is for you to get the abortion and stay quiet about it. So you tell me how we can do that."

She flinched. "What do you mean? 'All he wants'?"

I didn't blink. "He feels really bad. Obviously. He couldn't even ask you himself. That's why he left today. He feels awful about how this all turned out."

She looked more hurt than when she'd thought she actually had cancer. "Wait. You don't mean—"

Her eyes closed slowly. It had never occurred to her that Dick might have known all along what I was doing. And frankly it hadn't occurred to me until that moment either. But in a way it was true.

I acted like I'd assumed she'd known I was acting on his behalf. It was a rush play. I had just a day before Dick got back from France. I had to appear to be defending him. I said he cared deeply for her. That what he was offering didn't change that. I said she shouldn't blame him. That his feelings for her were genuine. But he and Liz were under tremendous pressure with this picture—

She interrupted me. She was putting it together. It had been Liz's doctor who diagnosed her. She covered her mouth. "Liz knows about this too?"

I sighed and reached out for her hand. But she recoiled like my hand was a snake.

I told her there were no reshoots in France. I said Dick had left a ticket to Switzerland in her name at the La Spezia train station.

She looked like she might vomit. I gave her my business card. She took it. I told her that back in the States we'd go over the slate of upcoming Fox films. She could pick any part she wanted. The next morning I drove her to the train station. She got out with her bags. Her arms slack at her side. She stood and stared at the station and the green hills behind it. And then she began walking. I watched her disappear inside. And I was never surer of anything. She'd go to Switzerland. Then she'd show up in my office in two months. Six at the most. A year. But she'd come to collect. They all do.

But it never happened. She never went to Switzerland. Never came to see me.

That morning Burton arrived back from France to see D— but found me waiting for him instead.

Dick was mad as hell. We went to the train station in La Spezia but the agent said she had only come inside and dropped off her luggage. Then she'd turned around and started walking back toward the hills. Dick and I drove back to Portovenere but she wasn't there. Dick even made me get a boat to go back to the little fishing town where I'd hid her for a while. But she wasn't there either. She had disappeared.

We were about to leave the fishing village when the strangest thing happened. This old witch came down from the hills. Cursing and yelling. Our driver translated: "Murderer!" and "I curse you to death."

I looked over at Burton. That old witch really gave it to him. Years later I'd think about that witch's curse as I watched poor Dick Burton drink himself under.

In the boat that day he was visibly spooked. It was the perfect time for my come-to-Jesus talk with him.

"Come on Dick. What were you going to do? Have a kid with her? Marry that girl?"

"Fuck off Deane." I could hear it in his voice. He knew I was right.

"This picture needs you. Liz needs you."

He just stared at the sea.

Of course I was right. Liz was the one. They were in love like that. I knew. He knew. And I made it all possible.

I HAD done exactly what he wanted me to do. Even if he hadn't known it yet. This was what people like me did for people like him.

From now on this would be my place in the world. To divine desire and do the things that other people wanted done. The things they didn't even know they wanted yet. The things they could never do themselves. The things they could never admit to themselves.

Dick stared straight ahead in the boat. Did he and I stay

friends? Yep. Go to each other's weddings? You bet we did. Did the Deane bow his head at the great actor's funeral? Sure I did. And neither of us ever spoke again about what happened in Italy that spring. Not about the girl. Not about the village. Not about the witch's curse.

That was that.

Back in Rome Dick and Liz rekindled. Got married. Made movies. Won awards. You know the story. One of the great romances in the world. A romance I built.

And the movie? It came out. And just like I thought we lived on the publicity of those two. People think <u>Cleopatra</u> was a flop. No. That picture broke even. Broke even because of what I did. Without me it loses twenty million. Any jackass can make a hit film. It takes giant balls to defuse a bomb.

This was the Deane's very first assignment. His very first film. And what does he do? Nothing less than keep an entire studio from going under. Nothing less than burn down the old studio system to build a new one.

And when Dickie Zanuck took over Fox that summer you can bet I was rewarded for it. No more Car Barn for me. No more Publicity. But my true reward wasn't the production job I got from my pal Zanuck. My true reward wasn't the fame and money about to come my way. The women and the coke and any table I wanted at any restaurant in town.

My reward was a vision that would define my career:

We want what we want.

And that is how I came to be born a second time. How I came into the world and changed it forever. How in the year 1962 on the coast of Italy I invented celebrity.

[*Ed. note: Some story, Michael.*

Unfortunately, even if we wanted to use this chapter, Legal has some fundamental issues with it, which our attorneys will address in a separate correspondence.

Editorially, though, there's one other thing you should

know: this chapter does not paint you in a very good light. Admitting you broke up two marriages, and faked a young woman's illness, and bribed her to get an abortion—all in the first chapter—may not be the best way to introduce you to readers.

And even if the lawyers would let us use this anecdote, it's terribly incomplete. So much is left hanging. What happened to the young actress? Did she get the abortion? Did she have Burton's baby? Did she go on acting? Is she someone famous? (That would be cool.) Did you try to make it up to her somehow? Track her down? Get her some great film role? Did you at least learn a lesson or have some regret? Do you see where I'm going?

Look, it's your life and I'm not trying to put words in your mouth. But this story really needs closure—some idea of what happened to the girl, some sense that you at least tried to do the right thing.]

16

After the Fall

September 1967
Seattle, Washington

A *DARK STAGE. The sound of waves. Then appears:*

MAGGIE in a rumpled wrap, bottle in her hand, her hair in snags over her face, staggering out to the edge of the pier and standing in the sound of the surf. Now she starts to topple over the edge of the pier, when QUENTIN rushes out of the cottage and takes her in his arms. She slowly turns around and they embrace. Soft jazz is heard from within the cottage.

MAGGIE: You were loved, Quentin; no man was ever loved like you.

QUENTIN: [*releasing her*] My plane couldn't take off all day—

MAGGIE: [*drunk, but aware*] I was going to kill myself just now. Or don't you believe that either?

"Wait, wait, wait."

Onstage, Debra Bender's shoulders slumped as the director rose from the first row, black-rimmed glasses at the end of his nose, pencil behind his ear, script in hand. "Dee, sweetheart, what happened?"

She looked down into the front row. "What's the matter now, Ron?"

"I thought we agreed you were going to take it further. Make it bigger."

She made quick eye contact with the other actor onstage, Aaron, who sighed and cleared his throat. "I like the way she's doing it, Ron." He put his hands out to Debra: *There. That's all I can do.*

But Ron ignored the other actor as he strode to the end of the stage and climbed the stairs. He stalked purposefully between the actors and put his hand in the small of Debra's back, as if leading her in dancing. "Dee, we've only got ten days before we open. I don't want your performance to get lost because it's too subtle."

"Yeah, I don't think subtlety's the problem, Ron." She twisted gently away from his hand. "If Maggie starts out as a lunatic, there's no place for the scene to go."

"She's trying to kill herself, Dee. She *is* a lunatic."

"Right, it's just—"

"She's a drunk, a pill-popper, a user of men—"

"No, I know, but—"

Ron's hand worked slowly down her back. The man was nothing if not consistent. "This is a flashback in which we see that Quentin did everything he could do to keep her from killing herself."

"Yeah—" Debra shot another look over Ron's shoulder, at Aaron, who was miming masturbation.

Ron stepped even closer, in a cloud of aftershave. "Maggie has sucked the life out of Quentin, Dee. She's killing both of them—"

Over Ron's shoulder, Aaron air-humped a pretend partner.

"Uh-huh," Debra said. "Maybe we could talk in private for a second, Ron."

His hand pressed even farther down. "I think that's a great idea."

They stepped offstage and walked up the aisle, Debra sliding into a wood-backed theater seat. Rather than sitting next to her, Ron wedged in between her and the seat-back in front of her, so that their legs were touching. Christ, did this man secrete Aqua Velva? "What's the matter, sweetheart?"

What's the matter? She almost laughed. Where to start? Maybe it was agreeing to be in a play about Arthur Miller and Marilyn Monroe, directed by the married man she'd stupidly slept with six years ago and then bumped into at a Seattle Rep fund-raiser. Or maybe, now that she thought about it, *that* was her first mistake, going to an event she should've known better than to attend. In her first few years back in Seattle, she had avoided the old theater crowd—not wanting to explain either her child or how her "film career" had died. Then she saw an ad for the fund-raiser in the *P-I*, and she admitted to herself how much she missed it. She walked into the party feeling that warm glow of familiarity, like walking the halls of your old high school. And then she saw Ron, fondue fork in his hand, like a tiny devil. Ron had flourished in the local theater scene in the years since she'd been gone and she was genuinely glad to see him, but he looked at Debra and then at the older man with her—she introduced them: *Ron, this is my husband, Alvis*—and he immediately went pale and left the party.

"It just seems like you're taking this play sort of . . . personally," Debra said.

"This play *is* personal," Ron said seriously. He removed his glasses and chewed on the arm. "All plays are personal, Dee. All *art* is personal. Otherwise, what's the point? This is the most personal thing I've ever done."

Ron had called two weeks after the fund-raiser and apologized for leaving; he said he just hadn't been prepared to see her. He asked what she was doing now. She was a housewife, she said. Her husband owned a Chevrolet dealership in Seattle, and she was at home raising their little boy. Ron asked if she missed acting, and she muttered some inanity about how it was nice to take some time off, but Debra thought to herself, I miss it the way I miss love. I'm half a person without it.

A few weeks later, Ron called to say that the Rep was doing
an Arthur Miller play and that he was directing it. Would she be
interested in reading for one of the leads? She felt breathless, dizzy,
twenty again. But, honestly, she probably would have said no if not
for the movie she'd just seen: Dick and Liz's latest film. *The Taming
of the Shrew*, of all things. It was their fifth movie together, and
while Debra hadn't been able to bring herself to see the earlier ones,
last year both Burton and Taylor had been nominated for Oscars
for *Who's Afraid of Virginia Woolf?*, and she'd started to wonder if
she'd been wrong about Dick throwing away his talent. Then she
saw an advertisement for *The Taming of the Shrew* in a magazine—
"The world's most celebrated movie couple . . . in the film they
were made for!"—and she got a babysitter, said she had a doctor's
appointment, and went to a matinee without telling Alvis. And, as
much as she hated to admit it, the film was marvelous. Dick was
wonderful in it, artful and honest, playing drunk Petruchio in the
wedding scene as if he were born for the part—which, of course,
he was. All of it—Shakespeare, Liz, Dick, Italy—fell on her like an
early death, and she mourned the loss of her younger self, of her
dreams, and in the movie theater that day she wept. *You gave all
that up,* a voice said. *No,* she thought, *they took it from me.* She sat
there until the credits were done and the lights came up, and still
she sat there, alone.

Two weeks later, Ron called to offer her the play. Debra hung
up the phone and found herself weeping again—Pat setting down
his Tinker Toys to ask, *Whassamatter, Mama?* And that night,
when Alvis got home from work and they had their predinner martinis, Debra told Alvis about the phone call. He was thrilled for her.
He knew how much she missed acting. She played devil's advocate:
What about Pat? Alvis shrugged; they'd hire a sitter. But maybe
this wasn't a good time. Alvis just scoffed. There *was* one more
thing, Debra explained: the director was a man named Ron Frye,
and before she'd left for Hollywood—and, eventually, Italy—she'd
had a short, stupid affair with him. There was no great passion
behind it, she said; she was motivated almost entirely by boredom,

or maybe just by his attraction to her. And Ron was married at the time. Ah, Alvis said. But there's nothing between us, she assured Alvis. That was her younger self, the one who believed that if she simply ignored rules and conventions, like marriage, they would have no power over her. She felt no connection to that younger self.

Strong, secure Alvis shrugged off her history with Ron and told her to go for the part. So she did—and she got it. But once rehearsals started, Debra realized Ron had made a connection between himself and Miller's protagonist, Quentin. In fact, he saw himself *as* Arthur Miller, the genius waylaid by a shallow, young, villainous actress—the shallow, young, villainous actress being, of course, her.

In the theater, Dee swung her legs until they were no longer touching his. "Look, Ron, about what happened between us—"

"What *happened*?" he interrupted. "You make it sound like a car accident." He put his hand on her leg.

Some memories remain close; you can shut your eyes and find yourself back in them. These are first-person memories—*I memories*. But there are second-person memories, too, distant *you memories*, and these are trickier: you watch yourself in disbelief—like the *Much Ado* wrap party at the old Playhouse in 1961, when you seduced Ron. Even recalling it is like watching a movie; you're up onscreen doing these awful things and you can't quite believe it—this other Debra, so flattered by his attention, Ron the pipe-smoking actor who went to school in New York and acted Off-Broadway, and you corner him at the wrap party, ramble on about your stupid ambition (*I want to do it all: stage and film*), you play it coquettish, then aggressive, then shy again, delivering your lines impeccably (*Just one night*), almost as if testing the limits of your powers—

But now, in the empty theater, she moved his hand. "Ron. I'm married now."

"So when I'm married it's okay. But your relationships are, what . . . sacred?"

"No. We're just . . . older now. We should be smarter, right?"

He chewed his lip and stared at a point in the back of the theater. "Dee, I don't mean this to sound harsh, but . . . a fortysomethingyear-old drunk? A used-car dealer? *This* is the love of your life?"

She flinched. Alvis had picked her up here twice after rehearsal, and both times he'd stopped for a couple of drinks first. She pressed on. "Ron, if you cast me in this play because you think we have some unfinished business, all I can say is: We don't. That's over. We slept together, what, twice? You need to get past that if we're going to do this play together."

"Get *past* it? What do you think this play is *about*, Dee?"

"It's Debra. I go by Debra now. Not Dee. And the play is not about us, Ron. It's about Arthur Miller and Marilyn Monroe."

He took his glasses off, put them back on, and then ran his hand through his hair. He drew a deep, meaningful breath. Actor tics, treating every moment not only as if it had been written for him but as if it were the pivotal scene in the production of his life. "Did it ever occur to you that maybe this is why you never made it as an actress? Because for the great ones, Dee . . . *Debra* . . . it *is* about them! It's *always* about them!"

And the funny thing was, he was right. She knew. She had seen the great ones up close and they lived like Cleopatra and Antony, like Katherina and Petruchio, as if the scene ended when they left it, the world stopped when they closed their eyes.

"You don't even see what you are," Ron said. "You use people. You play with their lives and treat them like they're nothing." The words stung with familiarity and Debra could say nothing back. Then Ron turned and stormed back toward the stage, leaving Debra sitting in the wooden theater seat alone. "That's it for today!" he yelled.

She called home. The sitter, the neighbor girl, Emma, said that Pat had broken the knob off the television again. She could hear him banging on pots in the kitchen. "Pat, I'm on the phone with your mom."

The banging got louder.

"Where's his dad?" Debra asked.

Emma said that Alvis had called from Bender Chevrolet and asked if she could babysit until ten P.M., that he'd made dinner reservations after work and that if Debra called, she was supposed to meet him at Trader Vic's.

Dee checked her watch. It was almost seven. "What time did he call, Emma?"

"About four."

Three hours? He could be at least six cocktails in—four if he didn't go straight to the bar. Even for Alvis, that was some head start. "Thanks, Emma. We'll be home soon."

"Uh, Mrs. Bender, last time you guys got home after midnight, and I had school the next day."

"I know, Emma. I'm sorry. I promise we'll be home earlier this time." Debra hung up, put her coat on, and stepped out into the cool Seattle air, a light rain seeming to come off the sidewalk. Ron's car was still in the parking lot and she hurried to her Corvair, climbed in, and turned the key. Nothing. She tried again. Still nothing.

The first two years of their marriage, Alvis had got her a new Chevy from his dealership every six months. This year, though, she'd said it was unnecessary; she'd just keep the Corvair. And now it had some kind of starter problem: of course. She thought about calling Trader Vic's, but it was only ten or twelve blocks, almost a straight shot down Fifth. She could take the Monorail. But when she got outside, she decided to walk instead. Alvis would be angry— one thing he hated about Seattle was its "scummy downtown," a bit of which she'd have to walk through—but she thought a walk might clear her mind after that awful business with Ron.

She walked briskly, her umbrella pointed forward into the stinging mist. As she walked, she imagined all the things she should have said to Ron (*Yes, Alvis IS the love of my life*). She replayed his cutting words (*You use people . . . treat them like they're nothing*). She'd used similar words, on her first date with Alvis, to describe the film business. She'd returned to Seattle to find it a different city, buzzing with promise. It had seemed so small to her before, but maybe she had been shrunk by all that happened in Italy, returning beaten to a city that basked in the glow of the World's Fair; even her old theater chums enjoyed a new playhouse on the fairgrounds. Dee stayed away from the fair, and from the theater, the way she avoided seeing *Cleopatra* when it came out (reading and reveling, a little shamefully, in its bad reviews); she moved in with her sister to "lick her wounds," as Darlene aptly described it. Dee assumed she'd give the baby up for adoption, but Darlene talked her into keeping it. Dee told her family that the baby's father was an Italian innkeeper, and it was that lie that gave her the idea to name the baby after Pasquale. When Pat was three months old, Debra went back to work at Frederick and Nelson, in the Men's Grill, and she was filling a customer's ginger ale when she looked up one day to see a familiar man, tall, thin, and handsome, a slight stoop to his shoulders, a burst of gray at his temples. It took a minute to recognize him—Alvis Bender, Pasquale's friend. "Dee Moray," he said.

"Your mustache is gone," she said, and then, "It's Debra now. Debra Moore."

"I'm sorry, Debra," Alvis said, and sat down at the counter. He told her that his father was looking at buying a car dealership in Seattle and he'd sent Alvis out west to scout it.

It was strange bumping into Alvis in Seattle. Italy now seemed like a kind of interrupted dream for her; to see someone from that time was like déjà vu, like encountering a fictional character on the street. But he was charming and easy to talk to, and she found it a relief to be with someone who knew her whole story. She realized that lying to everyone about what had happened had been like holding her breath for the last year.

They had dinner, drinks. Alvis was funny and she felt comfortable immediately with him. His father's car dealerships were thriving, and that was nice, too, being with a man who could clearly take care of himself. He kissed her cheek at the door to her apartment.

The next day, Alvis came by the lunch counter again, and said that he needed to admit something: it was no accident that he'd found her. She'd told him about herself in those last days in Italy—

they had taken a boat together to La Spezia and he'd accompanied her on the train to the Rome airport—and that she figured she'd go back to Seattle. To do what? Alvis had asked. She'd shrugged and said that she used to work at a big Seattle department store, thought maybe she'd go back. So when his father mentioned that he was looking at a Seattle Chevy dealership, Alvis jumped at the chance to find her.

He'd tried other department stores—the Bon Marché and Rhodes of Seattle—before someone at the perfume counter at Frederick and Nelson said there was a tall, blond girl named Debra who used to be an actress.

"So, you came all the way to Seattle . . . just to find me?"

"We *are* looking at a dealership here. But, yes, I was hoping to see you." He looked around the lunch counter. "Do you remember, in Italy, you said you liked my book and I said I was having trouble finishing it? Do you remember what you said—'Maybe it's finished. Maybe that's all there is'?"

"Oh, I wasn't saying—"

"No, no," he interrupted her. "It's okay. I hadn't written anything new in five years anyway. I just kept rewriting the same chapter. But you saying that, it was like giving me permission to admit that it's all I had to say—that one chapter—and to go on with my life." He smiled. "I didn't go back to Italy this year. I think I'm done with all that. I'm ready to do something else."

Something in the way he said those words—*ready to do something else*—struck her as intimately familiar; she had said the same thing to herself. "What are you going to do?"

"Well," he said, "that's what I wanted to talk to you about. What I would really like to do, more than anything, is . . . go hear some jazz."

She smiled. "Jazz?"

Yes, he said. The concierge at his hotel had mentioned a club on Cherry Street, at the foot of the hill?

"The Penthouse," she said.

He tapped his nose charades-style. "That's the place."

She laughed. "Are you asking me out, Mr. Bender?"

He gave that sly half-smile. "That depends, Miss Moore, on your answer."

She took a deep, assessing look at him—question-mark posture, thin features, modish swoop of graying brown hair—and thought: Sure, why not.

There you go, Ron: there's the love of her life.

Now, a block from Trader Vic's, she saw Alvis's Biscayne, parked with one tire partly on the curb. Had he been drinking at work? She looked inside the car, but except for a barely smoked cigarette in the ashtray, there was no evidence that this had been one of his binge days.

She walked into Trader Vic's, into a burst of warm air and bamboo, tiki and totem, dugout canoe hung from the ceiling. She looked around the thatch-matted room for him, but the tables were packed with chattering couples and big round chairs and she couldn't see him anywhere. After a minute, the manager, Harry Wong, was at her arm with a mai tai. "I think you need to catch up." He pointed her to a table in the back and there she saw Alvis, a big wicker chair-back surrounding his head like a Renaissance halo. He was doing what Alvis did best: drinking and talking, lecturing some poor waiter who was doing everything he could to edge away. But Alvis had landed one of his big hands on the waiter's arm and the poor kid was stuck.

She took the drink from Harry Wong. "Thanks for keeping him upright for me, Harry." She tilted the glass, and the sweet liqueur and rum hit her throat, and Debra surprised herself by drinking half of it. She stared at the drink through eyes that had become bleary with tears. One day, when she was in high school, someone had slipped a note into her locker that read "You whore." All that day she'd been pissed off until she got home that night and saw her mother, at which point she inexplicably broke into tears. It was how she felt now, the sight of Alvis—even *Drunk Dr. Alvis*, his lecturing alter ego—enough to break her up. She carefully dabbed her eyes, put the glass to her lips, and finished it. Then she gave the dead soldier to Harry. "Harry, could you bring us some water and maybe some food for Mr. Bender?"

Harry nodded.

She walked through the chattering crowd, catching eyes throughout the room, and picked up her husband's lecture, *Bobby-can-beat-LBJ*, right at its apex: ". . . and I'd argue that the only significant accomplishment of the Kennedy administration, integration, actually belongs to Bobby anyway—and would you look at this woman!"

Alvis was beaming at her, his rummy eyes seeming to melt at the corners. His arm freed, the waiter made his escape, nodding his thanks to Debra for her timely arrival. Alvis stood like a parasol opening. He pulled out her chair, ever the gentleman. "Every time I see you, I lose my breath."

She sat. "I guess I forgot that we were going out tonight."

"We always go out on Fridays."

"It's Thursday, Alvis."

"You are so tied to routine."

Harry brought them each a tall glass of water and a plate of egg rolls. Alvis sipped his water. "That is the worst martini I've ever had, Harry."

"Lady's orders, Alvis."

Debra freed the cigarette from Alvis's hand and replaced it with an egg roll, which Alvis pretended to smoke. "Smooth," he said. Debra took a long draw of his cigarette.

As he ate the egg roll, Alvis said, through his nose, "And how are things in the *the-uh-tuh, dah-ling*?"

"Ron's driving me crazy."

"Ah. The frisky director. Shall I dust your ass for fingerprints?"

His joke masked the slightest insecurity, a pretense of faux jealousy. She was glad for both—his twinge of jealousy and the way he joked it away. That's what she should have told Ron, that her husband was a man who had outgrown such petty insecure games. She told Alvis about Ron constantly interrupting her, pushing her to play Maggie like some kind of caricature—breathy and stupid, like a Marilyn impersonation. "I should never have done this," she said, and she planted the cigarette purposefully in the ashtray, bending the butt like a knee joint.

"Aw, come on." He lit another smoke. "You had to take this play, Debra. Who knows how many opportunities you get in life to do this?" He wasn't talking just about her, of course, but himself, too—Alvis the failed writer, wasting his life selling Chevys, forever doomed to be the smartest guy on the lot.

"He said awful things." Debra didn't tell Alvis how Ron copped a feel (she could handle that herself) or that he'd called Alvis an old drunk. But she did tell him the other awful thing he said—*You use people. You play with their lives and then treat them like they're nothing*—and as soon as she said the words, Debra began crying.

"Baby, baby." He moved his chair and put his arm around her. "You'll worry me if you start acting like this jackass is worth crying over."

"I'm not crying over him." Debra wiped her eyes. "But what if he's right?"

"Jesus, Dee." Alvis waved Harry Wong back over. "Harry. Do you see this sad knockout at my table?"

Harry Wong smiled and said that he did.

"Do you feel used by her?"

"Anytime she wants," Harry said.

"That's why you always get a second opinion," Alvis said. "Now, Dr. Wong, is there anything you can prescribe for such delusions? And make them doubles, please."

When Harry was gone, Alvis turned to her. "Listen to me, Mrs. Bender: Jackass Theater Director does not get to tell you who you are. Do you understand?"

She looked up in his calm, whiskey-brown eyes and nodded.

"All we have is the story we tell. Everything we do, every decision we make, our strength, weakness, motivation, history, and character—what we believe—none of it is *real*; it's all part of the story we tell. But here's the thing: *it's our goddamned story!*"

Debra blushed at his boozy agitation; she knew it was mostly rum talking, but like so many of Alvis's drunken rants, it made some kind of sense.

"Your parents don't get to tell your story. Your sisters don't. When he's old enough, even Pat doesn't get to tell your story. I'm your husband and I don't even get to tell it. So I don't care how lovesick this director is, he doesn't tell it. Even fucking Richard Burton doesn't get to tell *your* story!" Debra looked around nervously, a little stunned; they never mentioned that name—even when they were talking about whether they should eventually tell Pat the truth. "No one gets to tell you what your life means! Do you understand me?"

She kissed him hard, grateful but also trying to shut him up, and when she pulled away, another mai tai was waiting for them both. *The love of her life?* If Alvis was right and this was *her* story? Sure. Why not.

Dee stood shivering outside her open car door, staring up at the dark Space Needle, while Alvis slid into the Corvair. "Let's see what the problem is." Of course, the car started right away. He looked up at her and shrugged. "I don't know what to tell you. Are you sure you turned the key all the way?"

She put a finger to her lip and did her Marilyn voice: "Gosh, Mister Mechanic, no one told me you had to *turn* the key."

"Why'n't you climb in the back with me, ma'am, and I'll show you another feature of this fine car."

She leaned over and kissed him—his hand found the buttoned front of her dress and he flicked a button and slid a hand in, across her belly and down her hip, his thumb pushing under the waistband of her pantyhose. She pulled away and reached down to take his hand. "My, you're a fast mechanic."

He climbed out of the car and gave her a long kiss, one hand behind her neck, the other at her waist.

"Come on, ten minutes in the backseat? The kids are all doing it."

"What about the babysitter?"

"Why not? I'm game," he said. "Think we can talk *her* into it?"

She'd known the joke was coming and still it made her laugh. She almost always knew what was coming with Alvis, and still she laughed.

"She's gonna want four bucks an hour for that," Debra said.

Still holding her, Alvis sighed deeply. "Baby, when you're funny, it is the sexiest thing." He closed his eyes, leaned his head back, and smiled as broadly as his thin face would allow. "Sometimes I wish we weren't married so I could ask you again."

"Ask anytime you want."

"And risk you saying no?" He kissed her and then stepped away, swept his arm, and bowed. "Your chariot." She curtsied and climbed into the cold Corvair. He pushed the door closed and stayed there, looking down into the car. She flicked the wipers and a slick of wet goo washed over the edge of the car and nearly hit Alvis.

He jumped away, and she smiled as she watched Alvis walk to his car.

She felt better, but she was still puzzled about why Ron had angered her so much. Was it just because he was a horny prick? Or was there something familiar and cutting in what he'd said—*the love of your life*? Maybe not. But it didn't have to be like that, did it? Couldn't you outgrow the little-girl fantasy? Couldn't love be gentler, smaller, quieter, not quite all-consuming? Was that what Ron made her feel—guilt (*You use people*), perhaps over the suggestion that, at a tough point in her life, she'd traded on her looks for an older man's love, for some security and a brand-new Corvair, given up on love for her own reflection in his lovesick eyes? Maybe she *was* Maggie. This started the crying again.

She followed the Biscayne, mesmerized by the blinking taillights. Denny Street was nearly empty. She really hated Alvis's car; it was such an old person's sedan. He could take any Chevy off the lot and he chose a Biscayne? At the next red light she pulled up alongside him, rolled her window down. He leaned across the seat and rolled the passenger window down.

"You really need a new car," she said. "Why don't you get another Corvette?"

"Can't." He shrugged. "I've got a kid now."

"Kids don't like Corvettes?"

"Kids love Corvettes." He waved his hand behind him, like a magician, or a girl in a showroom. "But there's no backseat."

"We can put him on the roof."

"We're gonna put five kids on the roof?"

"Are we having five?"

"Did I forget to talk to you about that?"

She laughed, and felt the urge to . . . what, apologize? Or just to tell him, for the thousandth time—perhaps reassuring herself—that she loved him?

Alvis put a cigarette in his mouth and capped it with the car lighter, his face lit by the yellow glow. "No more picking on my car," he said. Then he winked one of his bleary brown eyes, stepped on the gas and brake at the same time, the big motor yowling, tires beginning to chirp and spit yellow smoke, and he timed it perfectly, so that just as the light in front of them changed green, he popped the brake and the car seemed to leap forward. And, in Debra Bender's memory, the noise would always precede what happened: the Biscayne firing into the intersection just as an old black pickup truck—headlights off, gunned at the last minute by another drunk trying to make a late-amber light—streaked in from the left, thundered, then crumpled Alvis's car door, T-boned the Biscayne, and drove it through the intersection, an endless screech of steel and glass, Debra screaming at the same terrible pitch, her anguished cry lingering long after the tangled cars came to rest against the faraway curb.

17

The Battle for Porto Vergogna

April 1962
Porto Vergogna, Italy

Pasquale watched Richard Burton and Michael Deane scurry toward their rented speedboat, his Aunt Valeria chasing them, screaming and pointing her crooked finger: "Murderers! Assassins!" Pasquale stood uneasily. The world was fractured, broken in so many ways that Pasquale could barely conceive of which shard to reach for: his father and mother both gone now, Amedea and his son in Florence, his aunt screaming at the cinema people. The pieces of his broken life lay on the ground before him like a mirror that had always stared back, but which had now broken to reveal the life behind it.

Valeria was wading into the water, cursing and crying, spittle on her old gray lips, when Pasquale reached her. The boat had backed away from the pier. Pasquale took his aunt by her thin, bony shoulders. "No, Zia. Let them go. It's okay." Michael Deane was staring back at him from the boat—but Richard Burton was staring straight ahead, rubbing the neck of the wine bottle between his palms as they made their way toward the breakwater. Behind them, the fishermen's wives watched quietly. Did they know what Valeria had done? She fell back into Pasquale's arms, weeping. They stood on the shore together and watched the speedboat putter around the point, its nose rising proudly as the pilot gunned it, and the boat roared, rose, and sped away.

Pasquale helped Valeria back to the hotel and put her in her room, where she lay in her bed weeping and muttering. "I did a terrible thing," she said.

"No," Pasquale said. And even though Valeria *had* done a terrible thing, the worst sin imaginable, Pasquale knew what his mother would want him to say—and so he said it: "You were kind to help her."

Valeria looked up in his eyes, nodded, and looked away. Pasquale tried to feel his mother's presence, but the hotel felt emptied of her, emptied of everything. He left his aunt in her room. Back in the *trattoria*, Alvis Bender was sitting at a wrought-iron table, staring out the window, an open bottle of wine in front of him. He looked up. "Is your aunt okay?"

"Yes," he said, but he was thinking about what Michael Deane had said—*It's not simple*—and about Dee Moray vanishing from the train station in La Spezia that morning. Days earlier, when they had gone for a hike, Pasquale had pointed out to her the trails from the cliffs toward Portovenere and La Spezia. Now he imagined her walking away from La Spezia, looking up into those hills.

"I am going for a walk, Alvis," he said.

Alvis nodded and reached for his wine.

Pasquale walked out the front door, letting the screen bang behind him. He turned and walked past Lugo's house, saw the hero's wife, Bettina, staring out the front door at him. He said nothing to her, but climbed the trail out of the village, tiny rocks bounding down the cliffs as he stepped. He moved quickly up the old donkey path, above the string marking his stupid tennis court, which blew around the boulders below him.

Pasquale wound through the olive groves as he worked his way up the cliff face behind Porto Vergogna, pulled himself up at the orange grove. Finally, he crested the ledge, walked down the next crease, and made his way up. After a few minutes of walking, Pasquale climbed over the line of boulders and came upon the old pillbox bunker—and saw at once that he'd been right. She had hiked from La Spezia. The branches and stones had been moved to reveal the opening that he'd covered back up the day they left here.

With the wind seeming to flick at him, Pasquale stepped across the split rock onto the concrete roof and lowered himself into the pillbox.

It was brighter outside than it had been the last time, and later in the day, so more light shone through the three little turret windows; yet it still took a moment for Pasquale's eyes to adjust. Then he saw her. She was sitting in the corner of the pillbox, against the stone wall, curled up, her jacket wrapped around her shoulders and legs. She looked so frail in the shadows of the concrete dome—so different from the ethereal creature who had arrived in his town just days earlier.

"How did you know I was here?" she asked.

"I did not," he said. "I just hope."

He sat next to her, on the wall opposite the paintings. After a moment, Dee leaned against his shoulder. Pasquale slid his arm around her, pulled her even closer, her face against his chest. When they'd been here before, it had been the morning—indirect sunlight came in through the gun turret windows onto the floor. But now, in the late-afternoon light, the sun had shifted and its direct light climbed the wall until it landed directly on the paintings before them, three narrow rectangles of sunlight illuminating the faded colors of the portraits.

"I was going to walk all the way back to your hotel," she said. "I was just waiting for the light to fall on the paintings this way."

"Is nice," he said.

"At first, it seemed like the saddest thing to me," she said, "that no one would ever see these paintings. But then I got to thinking: What if you tried to take this wall and put it in a gallery somewhere? It would simply be five faded paintings in a gallery. And that's when I realized: perhaps they're only so remarkable because they're here."

"Yes," he said again. "I think so."

They sat quietly, as the day deepened, sunlight from the turrets slowly edging up the wall of paintings. Pasquale's eyes felt heavy and he thought it might be the most intimate thing possible, to fall asleep next to someone in the afternoon.

On the pillbox wall, one of the rectangles of sunlight beamed across the face of the second portrait of the young woman, and it was as if she'd turned her head, ever so slightly, to regard the other lovely blonde, the real one, sitting curled with the young Italian man. It was something Pasquale had noticed before in the late afternoons, the way the moving sunlight had the power to change the paintings, almost animating them.

"Do you really think he saw her again?" Dee whispered. "The painter?"

Pasquale had wondered that very thing: whether the artist ever made it back to Germany, to the girl in the portraits. He knew from the fishermen's stories that most of the German soldiers had been abandoned here, to be captured or killed by Americans as they swept up the countryside. He wondered if the German girl ever knew that someone had loved her so much that he painted her twice on the cold cement wall of a machine-gun pillbox.

"Yes," Pasquale said. "I think."

"And they got married?" Dee said.

Pasquale could see it all laid out before him. "Yes."

"Did they have children?"

"*Un bambino,*" Pasquale said—a boy. He surprised himself by saying this, and his chest ached the way his belly sometimes did after a big meal; it was all just too much.

"You told me the other night that you would have crawled from Rome to see me." Dee squeezed Pasquale's arm. "That was the loveliest thing to say."

"Yes." *It's not simple—*

She settled into his shoulder again. The light from the pillbox turrets was moving up the wall and was almost done with the paintings, just a single rectangle on the upper corner of the last of the girl's portrait—the sun nearly done for the day with its gallery show. She looked up at him. "You really think the painter made it back to see her?"

"Oh, yes," Pasquale said, his voice hoarse with feeling.

"You're not just saying that to make me feel better?"

And because he felt like he might burst open and because he

lacked the dexterity in English to say all that he was thinking—how in his estimation, the more you lived the more regret and longing you suffered, that life was a glorious catastrophe—Pasquale Tursi said, only, "Yes."

It was late in the afternoon when they got back to the village and Pasquale introduced Dee Moray to Alvis Bender. Alvis was reading on the patio of the Hotel Adequate View and he leaped to his feet, his book falling back onto his chair. Dee and Alvis shook hands awkwardly, the usually talkative Bender seeming tongue-tied—perhaps by her beauty, perhaps by the strange events of the day.

"So nice to meet you," she said. "I hope you will understand if I excuse myself to take a nap. I've had a long walk and I'm terribly exhausted."

"No, of course," Alvis said, and only then did he think to remove his hat, which he held at his chest.

And then Dee connected the name. "Oh, Mr. Bender," she said, turning back. "The author?"

He looked at the ground, embarrassed by the very word. "Oh, no—not a real author."

"You certainly are," she said. "I liked your book very much."

"Thank you," Alvis Bender said, and he flushed in a way that Pasquale had never seen before, had never imagined from the tall, sophisticated American. "I mean . . . it's not finished, obviously. There's more to tell."

"Of course."

Alvis glanced over at Pasquale, then back at the pretty actress. He laughed. "Although, truth be told, that's most of what I've been able to write."

She smiled warmly, and said, "Well . . . maybe that's all there is. If so, I think it's wonderful." And with that she excused herself again and disappeared inside the hotel.

Pasquale and Alvis Bender stood on the patio next to each other and stared at the closed hotel door.

"Jesus. That's Burton's girl?" Alvis asked. "Not what I expected."

"No," was all Pasquale could say.

Valeria was back in the little kitchen, cooking. Pasquale stood by while she finished another pot of soup. When it was done, Pasquale took a bowl of it to Dee's room, but she was already asleep. He looked down on her, making sure she was breathing. Then he left the soup on her nightstand and went back out into the *trattoria*, where Alvis Bender was eating some of Valeria's soup and staring out the window.

"This place has gone crazy, Pasquale. The whole world has flooded in."

Pasquale felt too tired to speak, and he walked past Alvis and to the door, looking out at the greenish sea. Down at the shore, the fishermen were finishing their work for the day—smoking and laughing as they hung their nets and washed down their boats.

Pasquale pushed open the door, stepped onto the wooden patio, and smoked. The fishermen came up the hill one at a time with what was left of their catches, and each one waved or nodded. Tommaso the Elder approached with a string of small fish and told Pasquale he'd saved some anchovies from his sale to the tourist restaurants. Did he think Valeria would want them? Yes, Pasquale said. Tommaso went inside and came out a few minutes later without his fish.

Alvis Bender was right. Someone had opened the taps and the world was pouring in. Pasquale had wanted this sleepy town to wake up, and now . . . look at it.

Perhaps that's why he wasn't even particularly surprised when, a few minutes later, he heard the sound of another boat motor and Gualfredo's ten-meter churned into the cove—this time without Orenzio at the wheel but with Gualfredo piloting it, the brute Pelle at his side.

Pasquale thought he might bite through his own jaw. This was a final indignity, the last thing he could bear. And in his confusion, in his grief, Gualfredo suddenly seemed like some awful thorn in his side. He opened the screen door, went inside, and grabbed his mother's old cane from the coatrack. Alvis Bender looked up from his wine, asked, "What is it, Pasquale?" But Pasquale didn't answer, just turned around and went outside, walking purposefully down the steep *strada* toward the two men, who were climbing out of the boat, the cobblestones falling away as Pasquale marched with purpose, clouds racing through the violet overhead—last sunlight strobing the shoreline, waves drumming on smooth rocks.

The men were out of the boat, coming up the path, Gualfredo smiling: "Three nights the American woman stayed here when she was supposed to be at my hotel, Pasquale. You owe me for those nights."

Still forty meters apart, with the fading sun right behind them now, Pasquale couldn't make out the looks on the men's faces, just their silhouettes. He said nothing, simply walked, his mind roiling with images of Richard Burton and Michael Deane, of his aunt poisoning his mother, of Amedea and his baby, of his failed tennis court, of his flinching before Gualfredo last time, of the truth revealed about himself: his core weakness as a man.

"The Brit skipped out on his bar bill," Gualfredo said, now twenty meters away. "You might as well pay me for that, too."

"No," Pasquale said simply.

"No?" Gualfredo asked.

Behind him, he heard Alvis Bender come out onto the patio. "Everything okay down there, Pasquale?"

Gualfredo looked up at the hotel. "And you have another American guest? What are you running here, Tursi? I'm going to have to double the tax."

Pasquale reached them just at the point where the trailhead met the edge of the piazza, where the dirt of the shore blended into the first cobblestone *strada*. Gualfredo was opening his mouth to say something else, but before he could, Pasquale swung the cane. It cracked against the bull neck of the brute Pelle, who apparently wasn't expecting this, perhaps because of Pasquale's sheepish demeanor the last time. The big man lurched to the side and fell in the dirt like a cut tree, Pasquale lifting the cane to swing it again . . . but finding it broken off against the big man's neck. He threw the handle aside and went after Gualfredo with his fists.

But Gualfredo was an experienced fighter. Ducking Pasquale's haymaker, he landed two straight, compact blows—one to Pasquale's cheek, which burned, and the next to his ear, which caused a dull ringing and sent him reeling backward into the fallen Pelle. Realizing that his own furious adrenaline was a limited resource, Pasquale leaped back at Gualfredo's sausage-packed frame, until he was inside those direct punches, swinging wildly himself, his own blows landing on Gualfredo's head with deep melon *thunk*s and light slaps: wrists, fists, elbows—everything he had.

But then the big lamb-shank hand of Pelle landed on his hair and a second meaty hand fell on his back and he was dragged away, and for the first time it occurred to Pasquale that this might not go his way, that he'd likely need more than adrenaline and a broken cane to pull this off. Then even the adrenaline was gone, and Pasquale made a soft, whimpering noise like a crying child who has exhausted himself. And, like a steam shovel out of nowhere, Pelle slammed a fist into Pasquale's gut, lifting him and dropping him flat to the ground, slumped over, not a molecule of air left anywhere in the world to breathe.

Big Pelle stood over him, a deep frown on his face, framed with the specks of Pasquale's vision as he gasped and waited for the steam shovel to finish him off. Pasquale bent forward and scratched at the dirt below him, wondering why he couldn't smell the sea air but knowing there would be no smelling as long as there was no air. Pelle made the slightest move toward him and then a shadow flashed across the sun and Pasquale looked up to see Alvis Bender fly from the rock wall onto the massive back of Pelle, who hesitated for a moment (he looked like a student with a guitar case strung over his shoulder) before reaching behind himself and tossing off the tall, thin American like a wet rag, sending him skittering across the rocky shore.

Pasquale tried to get to his feet now, but there was still no breath. Then Pelle took a step toward him, and three fantastic things occurred at once: there was an intimate *THUP* in front of him, and a big crack behind, and the big left foot of the giant Pelle burst forth in a red spout, the big man crying out and doubling over to grab his foot.

Wheezing for breath, Pasquale looked back over his left shoulder. Old Lugo was walking down the narrow trail toward them, still in his fish-cleaning slicks, pushing the bolt to send another cartridge into his rifle, a green branch hanging from the dirty barrel of his weapon, which he must have pulled from his wife's garden. The rifle was raised to Gualfredo.

"I'd shoot your tiny pecker, Gualfredo, but my aim is not what it once was," Lugo said. "But a blind man could hit that gut of yours."

"The old man has shot me in my foot, Gualfredo," said the giant Pelle matter-of-factly, formally.

In the next minute there was a fair bit of groaning and shuffling, and then someone let the air back in for Pasquale to breathe. Like children cleaning up a mess, the men seemed to fall back into a simple and rational order, of the sort that emerges when one person in a group is pointing a gun at some number of the others. Alvis Bender sat up, a large knot above his eye; Pasquale's ear was still ringing; and Gualfredo was rubbing his sore head; but Pelle had gotten the worst of it, the bullet tearing through his foot.

Lugo looked at Pelle's wound with some disappointment. "I shot at your feet to stop you," he said. "I did not intend to hit you."

"It was a difficult shot," the giant said with some admiration.

The sun was just a smear on the horizon now and Valeria had come down from the hotel with a lantern. She told Pasquale that the American girl had slept through everything, that she must be exhausted. Then, as Lugo stood by with the rifle, Valeria cleaned Pelle's wound and bandaged his foot tightly with a torn pillowcase and fishing twine, the big man wincing as she tied the wound off.

Alvis Bender seemed especially interested in Pelle's injured foot, and he kept asking questions. Did it hurt? Did he think he could walk? What had it felt like?

"I saw many wounds in the war," Valeria said, with strange tenderness for the giant who had come to muscle her nephew. "This one passed right through." She readjusted the lantern and wiped the sweat from Pelle's beer keg of a head. "You'll be fine."

"Thank you," said Pelle.

Pasquale went to check on Dee Moray. As his aunt had said, she was still asleep, oblivious even to the gunshot that had ended the little skirmish.

When Pasquale came back down, Gualfredo was leaning against the piazza wall. He spoke softly to Pasquale, his eyes still on Lugo's gun. "This is a big mistake you've made, Tursi. You understand this, no? A very big mistake."

Pasquale said nothing.

"You understand I will come back. And my guns will not be fired by old fishermen."

Pasquale could do nothing but give the bastard Gualfredo his coolest stare until, finally, Gualfredo looked away.

A few minutes later, Gualfredo and the limping Pelle started back down the hill for their boat, Lugo accompanying them as if they were old friends, holding the rifle in his arms like a long, skinny baby. At the water, old Lugo turned to Gualfredo, spoke a few sentences, pointed to the village, gestured with the rifle, and then walked back up the trail to the piazza, to where Pasquale and Alvis Bender sat recuperating. The boat fired up and Gualfredo and Pelle disappeared into the darkness.

On the hotel balcony, Pasquale poured the old man a glass of wine.

Lugo the Promiscuous War Hero drank the wine in one long gulp and then looked over at Alvis Bender, whose contribution to the fight had been so minimal. *"Liberatore,"* he said with a whiff of sarcasm—Liberator. Alvis Bender simply nodded. It had never before occurred to Pasquale, but an entire generation of men had been defined by the war, his father, too, and yet they rarely talked about it with one another. Pasquale had always thought of the war as one big thing, but he'd heard Alvis talk about *his war* as if everyone served in a separate war, a million different wars for a million people.

"What did you say to Gualfredo?" Pasquale asked Lugo.

Lugo looked back from Alvis Bender over his shoulder, toward the shore. "I told Gualfredo that I knew he had a reputation as a hard man, but the next time he came to Porto Vergogna I would shoot out his legs and while he lay squirming on the beach I would pull down his pants, shove my garden stick up his fat asshole, and pull the trigger. I told him the last second of his miserable life would be spent feeling his own shit come out the top of his head."

Neither Pasquale nor Alvis Bender could think of a thing to say. They watched old Lugo finish his wine, set the glass on the table, and walk back to his wife. She gently took the rifle from him and he disappeared into his little house.

18

Front Man

At 11:14 A.M., the doomed Deane Party departs LAX on the first leg of its epic journey, taking up an entire first-class row on the Virgin Airlines direct flight to Seattle. In 2A, Michael Deane stares out his window and fantasizes this actress looking exactly as she did fifty years ago (and himself, too), imagines her forgiving him instantly (*Water under the bridge, darling*). In 2B, Claire Silver glances up occasionally from the excised opening chapter of Michael Deane's memoir in whispered awe (*No way . . . Richard Burton's kid?*). The story is so matter-of-factly disturbing that it should instantly seal her decision to take the cult museum job, but her repulsion gives way to compulsion, then curiosity, and she flips the typewritten pages faster and faster, oblivious to the fact that Shane Wheeler is casually tossing unsubtle negotiating gambits across the aisle from 2C (*I don't know; maybe I should shop* Donner! *around . . .*). Seeing Claire immersed in whatever document Michael Deane gave her, Shane begins to worry that it's another script, perhaps one even more outlandish than his *Donner!* pitch, and quickly abandons his coy negotiating tactics. He turns away, to old Pasquale Tursi in 2D, makes polite conversation (*"È sposato?"* Are you married? *"Sì, ma mia moglie è morta."* Yes, but my wife is dead. *"Ah. Mi dispiace. Figli?"* I'm sorry. Any children? *"Sì, tre figli e sei nipoti."* Three children, six grandchildren). Talking about his family makes

Pasquale feel embarrassed about the silly, old-man sentimentality of this late-life indulgence: acting like a lovesick boy off chasing some woman he knew for all of three days. Such folly.

But aren't all great quests folly? El Dorado and the Fountain of Youth and the search for intelligent life in the cosmos—we know what's out there. It's what *isn't* that truly compels us. Technology may have shrunk the epic journey to a couple of short car rides and regional jet legs—four states and twelve hundred miles traversed in an afternoon—but true quests aren't measured in time or distance anyway, so much as in hope. There are only two good outcomes for a quest like this, the hope of the serendipitous savant—sail for Asia and stumble on America—and the hope of scarecrows and tin men: that you find out you had the thing you sought all along.

In the Emerald City the tragic Deane Party changes planes, Shane ever so casually mentioning that the ground they've covered so far in just over two hours would've taken William Eddy months to travel.

"And we haven't even had to eat anyone," Michael Deane says, and then adds, more ominously than he intends, "yet."

For the final leg they pack into a commuter prop-job, a tooth-paste tube of returning college freshmen and regional sales associates. It's a mercifully brief flight: ten minutes taxiing, ten minutes climbing over a bread-knife set of mountains, ten more over a grooved desert, another ten over patchwork farmland, then a curtain of clouds parts and they bank over a stubby, pine-ringed city. At three thousand feet, the pilot sleepily and prematurely welcomes them to Spokane, Washington, ground temperature fifty-four.

Wheels on the ground, Claire notes that six of her eight cell-phone calls and text messages are from Daryl, who has now gone thirty-six hours without talking to his girlfriend and finally suspects something is amiss. The first text reads *R U mad*. The second, *Is it the strippers*. Claire puts her phone away without reading the rest.

They straggle from the Jetway through a tidy, bright airport that looks like a clean bus station, past electronic ads for Indian

casinos, photos of streams and old brick buildings, and signs wel-
coming them to something called "the Inland Northwest." They
make a strange group: old Pasquale in a dark suit and hat, with a
cane, like he's slipped from a black-and-white movie; Michael
Deane looking like a different time-travel experiment, a shuffling,
baby-faced grandpa; Shane, now worried that he's overplayed his
hand, constantly riffling his hair, muttering apropos of nothing:
"I've got other ideas, too." Only Claire has weathered the journey
well, and this reminds Shane of William Eddy's Forlorn Hope: it
was those women, too, who made the passage with some of their
strength intact.

Outside, the afternoon sky is chalky, air crackling. No sign of
the city they flew over, just trees and basalt stumps surrounding
airport parking garages.

Michael's man Emmett has a private investigator waiting for
them, a thin balding man in his fifties leaning on a dirty Ford Ex-
pedition. He's wearing a heavy coat over a suit jacket and holding a
sign that doesn't inspire much confidence: MICHAEL DUNN.

They approach and Claire asks, "Michael *Deane*?"

"About the old actress, yeah?" The investigator barely looks at
Michael's strange face—as if he's been warned not to stare. He introduces himself as Alan, retired cop and private investigator. He
opens the doors for them and loads their bags. Claire slides in back
between Michael and Pasquale and Shane jumps in front next to the
investigator.

Inside the SUV, Alan hands them a file. "I was told this was
top-priority stuff. It's pretty solid work for twenty-four hours, if I
do say so myself."

The file goes to the back and Claire takes charge of it, quickly
flipping past a birth certificate and newspaper birth notice from Cle
Elum, Washington. "You said she was about twenty in 1962," the
investigator says to Michael, whom he eyes in the rearview, "but
her actual DOB is late '39. No surprise there. Two kinds of people
always lie about their ages: actresses and Latin American pitchers."

Claire flips to the second page of the file—Michael looking over one shoulder, Pasquale the other—a photocopy of a 1956 yearbook page from Cle Elum High School. She's easy to spot: the striking blonde with the oversized features of a born actress. Beside her, the two pages of senior class photos are a festival of black-rims and cowlicks, of beady eyes, jug ears, crew cuts, acne, and beehives. Even in black-and-white, Debra Moore fairly jumps, her eyes simply too big and too deep for this little school and little town. Beneath her photo: "DEBRA 'DEE' MOORE: Warrior Cheer Squad—3 years, Kittitas County Fair Princess, Musical Theater—3 years, Senior Showcase, Honors—2 years." Each student has also chosen a famous quote (Lincoln, Whitman, Nightingale, Jesus), but Debra Moore's quote is from Émile Zola: *I am here to live out loud.*

"She's in Sandpoint now," the investigator is saying. "Hour and a half away. Pretty drive. She runs a little theater up there. There's a play tonight. I got you four tickets at will-call and four hotel rooms. I'll drive you back tomorrow afternoon." The SUV merges onto a freeway, descends a steep hill into Spokane: a downtown of low brick, stone, and glass buildings, pocked with billboards and surface parking lots, all of it loosely bisected by this freeway overpass.

They read as they ride, much of the file consisting of playbills and cast lists: *A Midsummer Night's Dream*, put on by the University of Washington drama department in 1959, listing "Dee Anne Moore" as Helena. She pops in every photograph, as if everyone else is frozen flat in the 1950s and here, suddenly, is a modern, animated woman.

"She's beautiful," Claire says.

"Yes," says Michael Deane over her right shoulder.

"*Sì,*" says Pasquale over her left.

Theater reviews clipped from the *Seattle Times* and the *Post-Intelligencer* praise "Debra Moore" briefly in various stage roles in 1960 and 1961, the investigator's yellow-highlighter pen framing "talented newcomer" and "the show-stopping Dee Moore." Next come two photocopied *Seattle Times* articles from 1967, the first about a single-fatality car accident, the second an obituary for the driver, Alvis James Bender.

Before Claire can figure out the connection to Dee Moray, Pasquale takes the page, leans forward, and presses it into the hands of Shane Wheeler in the front seat. "This one? What is it?"

Shane reads the small obituary. Bender was a World War II army veteran and owner of a Chevrolet car dealership in North Seattle. He moved to Seattle in 1963, just four years before his death. He was survived by his parents in Madison, Wisconsin, a brother and sister, several nieces and nephews, his wife, Debra Bender, and their son, Pat Bender of Seattle.

"They were married," Shane tells Pasquale. "*Sposati*. This was Dee Moray's husband—*il marito. Morto, incidente di macchina.*"

Claire looks over. Pasquale has gone white. He asks when. "*Quando?*"

"*Nel sessantasette.*"

"*Tutto questo è pazzesco,*" Pasquale mutters. This is all crazy. He says nothing more, just slumps back in his seat, hand rising slowly to his mouth. He seems to have no more interest in the file and he stares out the window at the strip-mall sprawl, much the way he stared out the window on the plane earlier.

Claire looks from Shane to Pasquale and back. "Did he expect her never to get married? Fifty years . . . that's asking a lot." Pasquale says nothing.

"Have you ever thought about a TV show where you fix people up with their old high school flames?" Shane asks Michael Deane, who ignores the question.

The next pages in the file are a 1970 graduation announcement from Seattle University (a bachelor's degree in education and Italian), obituaries for Debra Moore's parents, probate documents, tax forms for a house she sold in 1987. A much newer high school yearbook shows a 1976 black-and-white staff photo from Garfield High identifying her as "Mrs. Moore-Bender: Drama, Italian." She seems to get more attractive in every photo, her face sharpening—or perhaps it's just in comparison with other teachers, all those dull-eyed men in fat ties and uneven sideburns, lumpy women with close haircuts and cat's-eye glasses. In the Drama Club photo she poses at the center of a mugging, expressive group of shaggy-haired students—a tulip in a field of weeds.

The next page in the file is another photocopied newspaper story, from the *Sandpoint Daily Bee*, circa 1999, saying that "Debra Moore, a respected drama teacher and community theater director from Seattle, is taking over as artistic director of Theater Arts Group of Northern Idaho," that she "hopes to augment the usual slate of comedies and musicals with some original plays."

The file concludes with a few pages about her son, Pasquale "Pat" Bender; these pages are broken into two categories—traffic and criminal charges (DUIs and possession charges, mostly) and newspaper and magazine stories about the various bands he fronted. Claire counts at least five—the Garys, Filigree Handpipe, Go with Dog, the Oncelers, and the Reticents, this last outfit the most successful, signed by the Seattle record label Sub Pop, for whom they produced three albums in the 1990s. Most of the stories are from small alternative newspapers, concert and album reviews, stories about the band having a CD release party or canceling a show, but there is also a capsule review from *Spin*, of a CD called *Manna*, a record the magazine gives two stars, alongside this description: "... *when Pat Bender's intense command of the stage translates to the studio, this Seattle trio can sound rich and playful. But too often on this effort, he sounds uninterested, as if he showed up to the recording session wasted, or—worse for this cult favorite—sober.*"

The last pages of the file are listings in the *Willamette Week* and *The Mercury* for Pat Bender's solo shows in several clubs in the Portland area in 2007 and 2008, and a short piece from the *Scotsman*, a newspaper in Scotland, with a scathing review of something called *Pat Bender: I Can't Help Meself!*

And that's it. They read different sheets from the file, trade them, and finally look up to find that they're on the expanding edge of the city now, clusters of new houses cut into the slabs of basalt and heavy timber. To have a life reduced like that to some loose sheets of paper: it feels a little profane, a little exhilarating. The investigator is tapping a song on the steering wheel that only he hears. "Almost to the state line."

The Deane Party's epic trek is nearing its completion now, a single border left to cross—four unlikely travelers compelled along in a vehicle sparked on the gaseous fuel of spent life. They can cover sixty-seven miles in an hour, fifty years in a day, and the speed feels unnatural, untoward, and they look out their separate windows at the blurring sprawl of time, as for two miles, for nearly two minutes, they are quiet, until Shane Wheeler says, "Or what about a show about girls with anorexia?"

Michael Deane ignores the translator, leans forward toward the front seat, and says, "Driver, anything you can tell us about this play we're going to see?"

FRONT MAN

Part IV of the Seattle Cycle
A Play in Three Acts
by Lydia Parker

DRAMATIS PERSONAE:
PAT, an aging musician
LYDIA, a playwright and Pat's girlfriend
MARLA, a young waitress
LYLE, Lydia's stepfather
JOE, a British music promoter
UMI, a British club girl
LONDONER, a passing businessman

CAST:
PAT: Pat Bender
LYDIA: Bryn Pace
LYLE: Kevin Guest
MARLA/UMI: Shannon Curtis
JOE/LONDONER: Benny Giddons

The action takes place between 2005 and 2008, in Seattle, London, and Sandpoint, Idaho.

ACT I
Scene I

[*A bed in a cramped apartment. Two figures are
entangled in the sheets, Pat, 43, and Marla, 22. It's
dimly lit; the audience can see the figures but can't
quite make out their faces.*]

Marla: Huh.
Pat: Mm. That was great. Thanks.
Marla: Oh. Yeah. Sure.
Pat: Look, I don't mean to be an ass, but do you
       think we could get dressed and get out of
       here?
Marla: Oh. Then . . . that's it?
Pat: What do you mean?
Marla: Nothing. It's just—
Pat: [laughing] What?
Marla: Nothing.
Pat: Tell me.
Marla: It's just . . . so many girls in the bar have
       talked about sleeping with you. I started
       to think there was something wrong with me
       that I hadn't done it with the great Pat
       Bender. Then, when you came in alone tonight,
       I thought, well, here's my chance. I guess
       I just expected it to be . . . I don't
       know . . . different.
Pat: Different . . . than what?
Marla: I don't know.
Pat: 'Cause that's pretty much the way I've always
       done it.
Marla: No, it was fine.
Pat: Fine? This just gets better and better.
Marla: No, I guess I just bought into the whole
       womanizer thing. I assumed you knew things.

Pat: What . . . things?

Marla: I don't know. Like . . . techniques.

Pat: Techniques? Like what? Levitation? Hypnosis?

Marla: No, it's just that after all the talk I figured
      that I'd have . . . you know . . . four or five.

Pat: Four or five what?

Marla: [becomes shy] You know.

Pat: Oh. Well. How many did you have?

Marla: So far, none.

Pat: Well, I'll tell you what: I owe you a couple.
      But for now, do you think we could get dressed
      before—

[*A door closes offstage. The whole scene has taken
place in near darkness, the only light coming from an
open doorway. Now, still in silhouette, Pat pulls the
covers over Marla's head.*]

Pat: Oh shit.

[*Lydia, 30s, short hair, army cargo pants, Lenin cap,
ENTERS. She pauses in the doorway, her face lit by
the light from the other room.*]

Pat: I thought you were at rehearsal.

Lydia: I left early. Pat, we need to talk.

[*She comes in, reaches toward the nightstand to turn
on the light.*]

Pat: Uh, maybe leave the light off?

Lydia: Another migraine?

Pat: Bad one.

Lydia: Okay. Well, I just wanted to apologize for
      storming out of the restaurant tonight. You're
      right. I do still try to change you sometimes.

Pat: Lydia—

Lydia: No, let me finish, Pat. This is important.

[*Lydia walks to the window, stares out, a streetlight casting a glow on her face.*]

Lydia: I've spent so long trying to "fix" you that I
      don't always give you credit for how far we've
      come. Here you are, clean almost two years,
      and I'm so alert for trouble it's all I see
      sometimes. Even when it isn't there.

Pat: Lydia—

Lydia: [turning back] Please, Pat. Just listen. I've
      been thinking. We should move away. Get out of
      Seattle for good. Go to Idaho. Be near your
      mom. I know I said we can't keep running from
      our problems, but maybe it makes sense now.
      Start fresh. Get away from our pasts . . .
      all this shit with your bands, my mom, and my
      stepdad.

Pat: Lydia—

Lydia: I know what you're gonna say.

Pat: I'm not sure you do—

Lydia: You're gonna say, what about New York? I know
      we screwed that up. But we were younger then,
      Pat. And you were still using. What chance did
      we have? That day I came back to the apartment
      and saw that you'd pawned all of our stuff it
      was almost a relief. Here I'd been waiting for
      the bottom to fall out. And finally it did.

[*Lydia turns to the window again.*]

Lydia: After that, I told your mom that if you
      could've controlled your addictions, you'd have

been famous. She said something I'll never
forget: "But dear. That IS his addiction."

Pat: Jesus, Lydia—

Lydia: Pat, I left rehearsal early tonight because
your mom called from Idaho. I don't know how
to say this, so I'm just going to say it. Her
cancer is back.

[*Lydia walks over to the bed, sits on Pat's side.*]

Lydia: They don't think it's operable. She might
have months, or years, but they can't stop it.
She's going to try chemo again, but they've
exhausted the radiation possibilities, so all
they can do is manage it. But she sounded
good, Pat. She wanted me to tell you. She
couldn't bear to tell you herself. She's
afraid you'll start using again. I told her
you were stronger now—

Pat: [whispering] Lydia, please . . .

Lydia: So let's move, Pat. What do you say, just go?
Please? I mean . . . we assume these cycles
are endless . . . we fight, break up, make up,
our lives circle around and around, but what
if it's not a circle. What if it's a drain
we're going down? What if we look back and
realize we never even tried to break out of
it?

[*On the bedside, Lydia reaches into the tangle of
covers for Pat's hand. But she feels something,
recoils, jumps from the bed, and turns on the light,
throwing a harsh light across Pat and the other lump
in the bed. She pulls the covers back. Only now do we
see the actors in full light. Marla holds the sheet*]

294 • JESS WALTER

to her chest, gives a little wave. Lydia backs across
the room. Pat just stares off.]

Lydia: Oh.

[Pat climbs slowly out of bed to get his clothes.
But he stops. He stands there naked, as if noticing
himself for the first time. He looks down, surprised
that he's grown so thick and middle-aged. Finally he
turns to Lydia, standing in the doorway. The quiet
seems to go on forever.]

Pat: So . . . I guess a threesome's out of the question.

CURTAIN

In the half-empty theater there is a collective gasp, followed by
bursts of agitated, uncomfortable laughter. As the stage goes dark,
Claire realizes she's been holding her breath throughout the play's
short opening scene. Now she's breathed out, and the whole audience with her, a sudden release of tense, guilty laughter at the sight
of this cad standing naked on a stage—his crotch subtly and artfully covered by a blanket over the bed's footboard.

In the darkness of a set change, ghosts linger in Claire's eyes.
She becomes aware of the scene's clever staging: played mostly in
half-light, forcing the audience to search the near-darkness for
the figures, so that when the harsh lights finally come up, Lydia's
tortured face and Pat's white softness are boned into their retinas
like X-rays—that poor girl staring at her naked boyfriend, another
woman in their bed, a strobe of betrayal and regret.

This wasn't what Claire was expecting (community theater? in
Idaho?) when they arrived in Sandpoint, a funky Old West ski town
on the shores of this huge mountain lake. With no time to check
into their hotel, the investigator took them straight to the Panida
Theater, its lovely vertical descending sign marking a quaint store-

front in the small L-shaped downtown, classic old box office opening into a Deco theater—too big for this small, personal play, but
an impressive room nonetheless, carefully restored to its old 1920s
movie-house past. The back of the theater was empty, but the front
seats had a good spread of black-clad small-town hipsters, older
Birkenstockers, and fake blondes in ski outfits, even older moneyed
couples, which—if Claire knew her small-town theater—would be
this theater group's *patrons*. Settled in her hard-backed seat, Claire
glanced at the photocopied cover of the playbill: FRONT MAN • PRE-
VIEW PERFORMANCE • THEATER ARTS GROUP OF NORTHERN IDAHO.
Here we go, she'd thought: amateur hour.

But then the thing starts and Claire is shocked. Shane, too:
"Wow," he whispers. Claire sneaks a glance at Pasquale Tursi, and
he appears rapt, although it's hard to read the look on his face—
whether it's admiration for the play or simple confusion about what
that naked man is doing onstage.

Claire glances to her right, at Michael, and his waxen face seems
somehow stricken, his hand on his chest. "My God, Claire. Did you
see that? Did you see *him*?"

Yes. There is that, too. It's undeniable. Pat Bender is some kind
of force onstage. She's not sure if it's because she knows who his
father is, or perhaps because he's playing himself—but for one
quick, delusional moment, she wonders if this might be the greatest
actor she's ever seen.

Then the lights come up again.

It's a simple play. From that opening scene, the story follows Pat
and Lydia out on their parallel journeys. In his, Pat spends three
drunken years in the wilderness, trying to tame his demons. He
performs a musical-comedy monologue about the bands he used
to be in, and about failing Lydia—a show that eventually gets him
dragged to London and Scotland by an exuberant young Irish music
producer. For Pat the trip smacks of desperation, a misguided final
attempt at becoming famous. And it all blows up when Pat betrays

Joe by sleeping with Umi, the girl his young friend loves. Joe runs off with Pat's money and he ends up stranded in London.

In Lydia's parallel story, her mother dies suddenly and Lydia finds herself stuck caring for her senile stepfather, Lyle, a man she's never gotten along with. Lyle provides daft comic relief, constantly forgetting that his wife has died, asking the thirty-five-year-old Lydia why she isn't at school. Lydia wants to move him into a nursing home, but Lyle fights to stay with her, and Lydia can't quite do it. In a storytelling device that works better than Claire expects, Lydia fills in the gaps and marks the passage of time by talking on the phone to Pat's mother, Debra, in Idaho. She never appears onstage but is an unseen, unheard presence on the other end of the phone. "Lyle wet the bed today," Lydia says, pausing for a response from the unseen Debra (or Dee, as she sometimes calls her). "Yes, Dee, it *would* be natural . . . except it was *my* bed! I looked up and he was standing on my bed, pissing a hot streak and shouting, 'Where are the hand towels?'"

Finally, Lyle burns himself on the oven while Lydia is at work, and she has no choice but to move him into a nursing home. Lyle cries when she tells him about it. "You'll be fine," she insists. "I promise."

"I'm not worried about me," Lyle says. "It's just . . . I promised your mother. I don't know who will take care of you now."

In the wake of that realization—that Lyle believes he has been caring for *her*—Lydia understands that she's most alive when she's caring for someone else, and goes to Idaho to take care of Pat's ailing mother. Then, one night, she's asleep in Debra's living room when the phone rings. The lights come up on the other side of the stage—revealing Pat, standing in a red phone booth, calling his mother for help. At first Lydia is excited to hear from him. But all Pat seems to care about is that he's run out of money and needs help to get home from London. He doesn't even ask about his mother.

Lydia goes quiet on the other end of the call. "Wait. What time is it there?" he asks. "Three," Lydia says quietly. And Pat's head falls to his chest exactly as it did in the first scene.

"Who is it, dear?" comes a voice from offstage—the first words Pat's mother has spoken in the entire play. In his London phone booth, Pat whispers, "Do it, Lydia." Lydia takes a deep breath, says, "Nobody," and hangs up, the light going out in the phone booth.

Pat is reduced to being a vagrant in London—ragged, sitting drunk on a street corner playing his guitar cross-legged. He's busking, panhandling to make enough money to get home. A passing Londoner stops and offers Pat a twenty-euro note if he'll play a love song. Pat starts to play the song "Lydia," but he stops. He can't do it.

Back in Idaho, with snow on the cabin window marking the passage of time, Lydia gets another phone call. Her stepfather has died in the nursing home. She thanks the caller and goes back to making tea for Pat's mother, but she can't. She just stares at her hands. She seems entirely alone in the scene, in the world. And that's when a knock comes at the door. She answers. It is Pat Bender, framed in the same doorway Lydia stood in at the beginning of the play. Lydia stares at her long-lost boyfriend, this derelict Odysseus who's been wandering the world trying to get home. It's the first time they've been onstage together since that awful moment when he stood before her, naked, at the start of the play. Another long silence between them follows, echoing the first, extends as long as an audience can possibly bear (*Somebody say something!*), until Pat Bender gives just the slightest shudder onstage, and whispers, "Am I too late?"—somehow conveying even more nakedness than in the first scene.

Lydia shakes her head no: his mother is alive still. Pat's shoulders slump, in relief and exhaustion and humility, and he holds out his hands—an act of surrender. Dee's voice comes again from offstage: "Who is it, dear?" Lydia glances over her shoulder and somehow the moment stretches even longer. "Nobody," Pat replies, his voice a broken husk. Then Lydia reaches out for his hand, and in the instant their hands touch, the lights go down. The play is over.

Claire gasps, releasing what feels like ninety minutes of air. All the travelers feel it—some kind of completion—and in the rush of applause they feel, too, the explorer's serendipity: the accidental, cathartic discovery of oneself. In the midst of this release, Michael leans over to Claire and whispers again, "Did you *see* that?"

On her other side, Pasquale Tursi holds his hand to his heart as if suffering an attack. "*Bravo,*" he says, and then, "*È troppo tardi?*" Claire has to guess at his meaning, for their erstwhile Italian translator seems unreachable, his head in his hands. "Fuck me," Shane says. "I think I've wasted my whole life."

Claire, too, finds herself drawn inward by what she's just seen. Earlier, she told Shane that her relationship with Daryl was "hopeless." Now she realizes that throughout the play she was thinking of Daryl, hopeless, irredeemable Daryl, the boyfriend she can't seem to let go of. *Maybe all love is hopeless.* Maybe Michael Deane's rule is wiser than he knows: We want what we want—*we love who we love.* Claire pulls her phone out and turns it on. She sees the latest text from Daryl: *Pls just let me know U R OK.*

She types back: *I'm okay.*

Next to her, Michael Deane puts his hand on her arm. "I'm buying it," he says.

Claire glances up from her phone, thinking for a moment that Michael is talking about Daryl. Then she understands. She wonders if her deal with Fate is still in play. Is *Front Man* the great movie that will allow her to stay in the business? "You want to buy the play?" she asks.

"I want to buy everything," Michael Deane says. "The play, his songs—all of it." He stands up and looks around the little theater. "I'm buying the whole goddamn thing."

By flashing her business card (*Hollywood? No shit?*) Claire gets an enthusiastic invitation to the after-party from a goateed and liberally pierced doorman named Keith. On his directions, they walk a block from the theater toward a brick storefront, which opens to a wide set of stairs, the building intentionally unfinished, all exposed pipes and half-exposed brick. It reminds Claire of climbing to countless parties in college. But there's something off in the scale, in the width of hallways and the heights of ceilings—all the extravagant, wasted space in these old Western towns.

Pasquale pauses at the door. "*È qui, lei?*" Is she here?

Maybe, says Shane, looking up from his phone. "*C'è una festa, per gli attori.*" It is a party for the actors. Shane returns to his phone and sends a text message to Saundra: "Can we talk? Please? I realize now what an ass I've been."

Pasquale looks up at the building where Dee might be, removes his hat, smooths his hair, and starts up the stairs. At the top of the landing, Claire helps the winded Michael Deane up the last steps. There are three doors to three apartments on the second floor and they walk to the back of the building, to the only open door, propped open with a jug of wine.

This back apartment is big and lovely in the same primitive way as the rest of the building. It takes a moment for them to adjust to the candlelight—it's a huge two-story open loft with high ceilings. The room itself is a work of art, or a junk pile—filled with old school lockers, hockey sticks, and newspaper boxes—all of this surrounding a curved staircase made of old timbers, which seems to float in thin air. Upon further inspection, they can see that the staircase is held with three lines of coiled cable.

"This whole apartment is furnished with found art," says Keith, the theater doorman, who arrives right behind them. He has spiky, thin hair and painful-looking studs in his lips, neck, upper ears, and nose, as well as pirate hoops in his ears. He has acted in TAGNI productions himself, he tells them, but he's also a poet, painter, and video artist. (*That's all?* Claire wonders. *Interpretive dancer? Sand sculptor?*)

"A video artist?" Michael is intrigued. "And is your camera nearby?"

"I always have my camera," Keith says, and he produces a small, simple digital from his pocket. "My life is my documentary."

Pasquale scans the party, but there's no sign of Dee. He leans over to ask Shane for help, but his translator is staring helplessly at Saundra's return text: *You just NOW realized you're an ass? Leave me alone.*

Keith sees Pasquale and Michael looking around, mistakes this for curiosity, and steps in to explain. The apartment's designer, he says, is a former Vietnam vet, featured last month in *Dwell* magazine. "His general concept is that every design form has an innate maturity alongside its youthful nature, that too often we cast aside the more interesting forms just when they're starting to grow into this older, more interesting second nature. Two old hockey sticks—who cares. But hockey sticks made into a chair? Now, that's something."

"It's all wonderful," Michael says earnestly, gazing around at the room.

The cast and crew aren't at the party yet; so far it's just fifteen or twenty black-glasses-and-hippie-sandaled audience members, with their low talk, little squalls of laughter, all of them taking turns inspecting the strange travelers of the lost Deane Party. The crowd is familiar, Claire thinks: smaller, a little rougher around the edges, but not much different from an after-party anywhere. Wine and snacks are lined up on a metallic table made from the door of an old freight elevator; a small backhoe bucket is filled with ice and beer. Claire is relieved, when she goes to the bathroom, to find that the toilet is an actual toilet, and not an old boat motor.

Finally, the cast and crew begin arriving. Word of the great Michael Deane's presence seems to be spreading throughout the crowd, and the ambitious make their way over, casually mentioning their appearance in the straight-to-video movies shot in Spokane, appearing alongside Cuba Gooding Jr., Antonio Banderas, John Travolta's sister. Everyone Claire meets seems to be an artist of some kind—actors and musicians and painters and graphic artists and ballet instructors and writers and sculptors and more potters than a town this size could possibly support. Even the teachers and attorneys also act, or play in bands, or sculpt blocks of ice—Michael fascinated by all of them. Claire is amazed at his energy and genuine curiosity. He's also on his third glass of wine—more than she's ever seen him drink.

An attractive older woman in a sundress, her deep sun-worshipping wrinkles the opposite of Michael's smooth skin, leans in close and actually touches his forehead. "Jesus," she says, "I love your face," as if it's a piece of art he's created.

"Thank you," Michael says, because it is—his work of art.

The woman introduces herself as Fantom "with an F," and explains that she makes tiny sculptures out of soap, which she sells at craft shows and barter fairs.

"I'd love to see them," Michael says. "Is everyone here an artist?"

"I know," Fantom says as she digs through her bag. "It gets old, huh?"

While Michael looks at tiny soap art, the rest of the Deane Party is growing anxious. Pasquale watches the door nervously as his lovesick translator, still stinging over Saundra's texted rejection, pours a tall glass from a bottle of Canadian whiskey and Claire asks Keith about the play.

"Some intense shit, huh?" says Keith. "Debra mostly puts on kiddie plays, musicals, holiday farces—whatever gets the skiers off the mountain for a couple hours. But once a year she and Lydia do something original like this. She gets crap from the board sometimes, from the cranky Christians especially, but that was the trade-off for her. Come keep the tourists happy, and once a year you can bust out something like that."

By this time, all of the cast and crew have made it to the party—except for Pat and Lydia. Claire finds herself in conversation with Shannon, the actress who played the girl in bed with Pat at the start of the play. "I understand you're from"—Shannon swallows, can barely say the word—"Hollywood?" She blinks quickly, twice. "What's *that* like?"

Two glasses of wine in, Claire feels the strain of the last forty-eight hours, and smiles, stops to think about the question. Yes, what *is* it like? Certainly not like she dreamed. But maybe that's okay. We want what we want. At home, she works herself into a frenzy worrying about what she isn't—and perhaps loses track of just where she is. She takes a moment to look around—at this apartment built of garbage on some crazy island of artists in the mountains, where Michael is happily giving out business cards to soap-makers and actors, telling them he "might have something" for them, where Pasquale is nervously watching the door for a woman he hasn't seen in nearly fifty years, where a quickly drunk Shane has rolled up his sleeve to explain the origin of his tattoo to an impressed Keith—and that's when Claire realizes that Pat Bender and his mother and his girlfriend are not coming to this after-party.

"What? Oh yeah," Keith says, confirming her suspicion. "They never come to the after-party. It'd kill Pat to be around all this booze and weed."

"Where are they?" Michael asks.

"Probably up at the cabin," Keith says. "Chilling with Dee."

Michael Deane grabs Keith by the arm. "Will you take us there?"

Claire jumps in. "Maybe we should wait until morning, Michael."

"No," says the leader of the hope-drunk Deane Party. He glances over at old, patient Pasquale and makes one last fateful decision: "It's been almost fifty years. No more waiting."

19

The Requiem

April 1962
Porto Vergogna, Italy

Pasquale woke in darkness. He sat up and reached for his watch. Four thirty. He heard the fishermen's low voices and the sound of boats skidding down to the shore. He rose, dressed quickly, and hurried down through the dusky predawn to the shore, where Tommaso the Communist was fixing his gear in his boat.

"What are you doing here?" Tommaso asked.

Pasquale asked Tommaso if he would motor him to La Spezia later for his mother's requiem mass.

Tommaso touched his chest. "Of course," he said. He would fish for a few hours and then come back to take Pasquale before lunch. Would that work?

"Yes, perfect," Pasquale said. "Thank you."

His old friend tipped his cap, climbed back in the boat, and pulled the starter rope, the motor clearing its throat. Pasquale watched Tommaso join the other fishermen, their shells bobbing on the soft-rocking sea.

Pasquale went back to the hotel and went to bed, but sleep wouldn't come. He lay on his back and thought of Dee Moray in bed just above him.

In the summers sometimes, his parents used to take him to the beach at Chiavari. Once he was digging in the sand when he saw a beautiful woman sunning herself on a blanket. Her skin glistened.

Pasquale couldn't stop staring. When she finally packed up her blanket and left, she'd waved at him, but young Pasquale was far too mesmerized to wave back. Then he saw something fall from her bag. He ran over and picked it from the sand. It was a ring, set with some kind of reddish stone. Pasquale held it in his hand for a moment as the woman walked away. Then he looked up to see that his mother was watching him, waiting to see what he would do. *"Signora!"* he called after the woman, and chased her down the beach. The woman stopped, took the ring back, thanked him, patted him on the head, and gave him a fifty-lira coin. When he returned, Pasquale's mother said, "I hope that is what you would have done even if I wasn't watching you." Pasquale wasn't sure what she meant. "Sometimes," she said, "what we want to do and what we must do are not the same." She put a hand on his shoulder. "Pasqo, the smaller the space between your desire and what is right, the happier you will be."

He couldn't tell his mother why he hadn't returned the ring right away: he imagined that if he gave a girl a ring, they would be married and he would have to leave his parents. And while his mother's lecture had gone over his seven-year-old head, Pasquale saw now what she meant—how much easier life would be if our intentions and our desires could always be aligned.

When the sun finally crested the cliffs, Pasquale washed at the basin in his room and put on his old, stiff suit. Downstairs, he found his Aunt Valeria awake in the kitchen, sitting in her favorite chair. She glanced sideways at his suit.

"I can't go to the funeral mass," his aunt sighed. "I can't face the priest."

Pasquale said he understood. And he went outside to smoke on the patio. With the fishermen away, the town felt empty, only the wharf cats moving around the piazza. There was a light haze; the sun had not yet burned off the morning fog, and the waves were falling lifelessly on the shallow rocks.

He heard footsteps on the stairs. How long had he waited for an American guest? And now he had two. The footsteps were heavy on the wooden patio and soon Alvis Bender joined him. Alvis lit his pipe, bent his neck one way and then the other. He rubbed the light bruise over his eye. "My fighting days are over, Pasquale."

"Are you hurt?" Pasquale asked.

"My pride." Alvis took a pull from his pipe. "It's funny," he said in smoke. "I used to come here because it was quiet and I thought I could avoid the world long enough to write. No more, I guess, eh, Pasquale?"

Pasquale considered his friend's face. It had such an open quality, was such a clearly American face, like Dee's face, like Michael Deane's face. He believed he could spot an American anywhere by that quality—that openness, that stubborn belief in *possibility*, a quality that, in his estimation, even the youngest Italians lacked. Perhaps it was the difference in age between the countries—America with its expansive youth, building all those drive-in movie theaters and cowboy restaurants; Italians living in endless contraction, in the artifacts of generations, in the bones of empires.

This reminded him of Alvis Bender's contention that stories were like nations—Italy a great epic poem, Britain a thick novel, America a brash motion picture in Technicolor—and he remembered, too, Dee Moray saying she'd spent years "waiting for her movie to start," and that she'd almost missed out on her life waiting for it.

Alvis lit his pipe again. *"Lei è molto bella,"* he said. She is very beautiful.

Pasquale turned to Alvis. He'd meant Dee Moray, of course, but at that moment Pasquale had been thinking of Amedea. *"Sì,"* Pasquale said. Then he said, in English, "Alvis, today is the requiem mass for my mother."

So gracious were these two men, so fond of each other, that they sometimes had conversations speaking entirely in the other's language. *"Sì, Pasquale. Dispiace. Devo venire?"*

"No. Thank you. I am go this alone."

"Posso fare qualcosa?"

Yes. There was one thing he could do, Pasquale said. He looked up to see Tommaso the Communist puttering back into the cove.

Almost time. Pasquale turned to Alvis and switched back to Italian to make sure he said it right. "If I do not come back tonight, I need you to do something for me."

Of course, Alvis said.

"Can you take care of Dee Moray? Make sure she gets back safely to America?"

"Why? Are you going somewhere, Pasquale?"

Pasquale reached in his pocket and handed Alvis the money that Michael Deane had given him. "And give this to her."

"Of course," Alvis said, and again, "but where are you going?"

"Thank you," Pasquale said, again choosing not to answer that question, afraid that if he said aloud what he intended, he might lose the strength to do it.

Tommaso's boat was nearly at the pier. Pasquale patted his American friend on the arm, looked around the small village, and, without another word, went into the hotel. In the kitchen, Valeria was making breakfast. His aunt never made breakfast, even though Carlo had insisted for years that a hotel hoping to cater to French and Americans must offer breakfast. (*It's a lazy man's meal,* she always said. *What laggard expects to eat before doing any work?*) But this morning she was making a French brioche and brewing espresso.

"Is the American whore coming down to eat?" Valeria asked.

Here it was, the moment he figured out who he was to be. Pasquale took a breath and climbed the stairs to see if Dee Moray was hungry. He could tell by the light coming from beneath the door that her window shutters were open. He took a deep breath to steel himself, and tapped lightly on the door.

"Come in."

She was sitting up in bed, pulling her long hair into a ponytail. "I can't believe how long I slept," she said. "You don't realize how tired you are until you sleep for twelve hours." She smiled at him, and in that moment, Pasquale doubted that he could ever bridge the gap between his intentions and his desires.

"You look handsome, Pasquale," she said. And she looked down at her own clothes, the same outfit she'd worn to the train station:

tight black pants, a blouse, and a wool sweater. She laughed. "I guess all of my things are still at the station in La Spezia."

Pasquale looked down at his feet, trying not to meet her eyes.

"Is everything okay, Pasquale?"

"Yes," he said, and he looked up, catching her eyes. When he wasn't in the room with her, he had one sense of what was right, but the minute he saw those eyes . . . "You come down for breakfast now? Is a brioche. And *caffè*."

"Yes," she said. "I'll be right down."

He couldn't say the rest. Pasquale nodded slightly and turned to leave.

"Thank you, Pasquale," she said.

Hearing his name caused him to turn back again. Looking in her eyes was like standing by a door slightly ajar. How could you *not* push open the door, see what lay inside?

She smiled at him. "Do you remember my first night here, when we agreed that we could say anything to each other? That we wouldn't hold back?"

"Yes," Pasquale managed to say.

She laughed uneasily. "Well, it's strange. I woke up this morning and I realized I had no idea what to do now. If I'm going to have this baby . . . If I'm going to keep acting . . . If I'm going to go to Switzerland . . . or back to the States. I honestly don't have any idea. But when I woke up, I felt okay. Do you know why?"

Pasquale gripped the doorknob. He shook his head no.

"I was glad that I'd get to see you again."

"Yes," he said. "Me, too," and that door seemed to open a little— and the glimpse he had beyond the door tortured him. He wanted to say more, to say everything on his mind—but he couldn't. It wasn't a question of language; he doubted the words existed at all, in any language.

"Well," Dee said. "I'll be right down." And then, just as he was turning away, she added quietly—the words seeming just to tip from her beautiful lips, spilling like water: "Then maybe we can talk about what happens next."

Next. Yes. Pasquale wasn't sure how he managed to back out of the room, but he did. He pulled her door closed behind him and stood with his hand outstretched against it, breathing deeply. Finally, he pushed off the door, made it to the stairs, and eventually to his room. Pasquale grabbed his coat, his hat, and his packed bag off his bed. He came out of his room and down the stairs. At the bottom, Valeria was waiting for him.

"Pasqo," she said. "Will you ask the priest to say a prayer for me?"

He said he would. Then he kissed his aunt on the cheek and went outside.

Alvis Bender was standing on the patio, smoking his pipe. Pasquale patted his American friend on the arm and started down the path to the pier, to where Tommaso the Communist was waiting for him. Tommaso dropped his cigarette and ground it into the rock. "You look good, Pasquale. Your mother would be proud."

Pasquale climbed in the fish-gut-stained boat and sat in the bow, his knees together like a schoolboy at a desk. He was unable to stop his eyes from sweeping the front of the hotel, where Dee Moray had just stepped onto the porch and was standing next to Alvis Bender. She shielded the sun from her eyes and looked down on him curiously.

Again, Pasquale felt the separate pulls of his mind and body— and right then, he honestly didn't know which way it would go. Would he stay in the boat? Or would he run up the path to the hotel and take her in his arms? And what would she do if he did? There was nothing explicit between them, nothing more than that slightly open door. And yet . . . what could be more alluring?

In that moment, Pasquale Tursi finally felt wrenched in two. His life was two lives now: the life he would have and the life he would forever wonder about.

"Please," Pasquale rasped to Tommaso. "Go."

The old fisherman tugged on the pull-start, but the motor didn't catch. And Dee Moray called from the hotel patio. "Pasquale! Where are you going?"

"Please," Pasquale whispered to Tommaso, his legs shaking now.

Finally, the motor caught. Tommaso sat down in back, took the tiller, and started puttering them away from the pier, out of the cove. On the patio, Dee Moray turned to Alvis Bender for an explanation. Alvis must have told her that Pasquale's mother had died, because her hand went to her mouth.

And Pasquale forced himself to look away then. It was like prying a magnet off steel, but he did it: turned forward in the boat, closed his eyes, still seeing her standing there in his memory. He shook with the strain of not looking back until they rounded the breakwater into the open sea and Pasquale exhaled, his head falling to his chest.

"You are a strange young man," Tommaso the Communist said.

In La Spezia, Pasquale thanked his old friend and watched Tommaso steer his little fishing boat away from the harbor, back toward the channel between Portovenere and Isola Palmaria.

Then he went to the little chapel near the cemetery, where the priest was waiting, his thin hair run with comb lines. Two old funeral-attending women and a feral-looking altar boy were on hand for the occasion, the chapel dark, moldy, and empty, candlelit. The requiem mass seemed to have nothing to do with his mother, and Pasquale was momentarily shocked when he heard her name in the priest's Latin drone (*Antonia, requiem aeternam dona eis, Domine*). Right, he thought, she's gone, and in that realization he broke down. After the funeral, the priest agreed to say a prayer for Pasquale's aunt, and to say the *trigesimo* in a few weeks, and Pasquale paid the man again. The priest raised his hand to bless him, but Pasquale had already turned to go.

Exhausted, Pasquale went to the train station to check on Dee Moray's luggage. It was waiting for her. Pasquale paid the agent and told him she would be coming for her bags the next day. Then he arranged for a water taxi to collect Dee Moray and Alvis Bender. And he bought himself a train ticket to Florence.

Pasquale settled into his seat and went right to sleep, jerking awake as the train pulled into the Florence station. He got a room three blocks from the piazza Massimo d'Azeglio, took a bath, and dressed again in his suit. In the dusky last light of that endless day, Pasquale stood smoking in the shade of the trees across the court-yard until he saw Amedea's family return from their evening walk, strung out like a family of quail.

And when beautiful Amedea lifted Bruno from the stroller, Pasquale thought again of his mother on the beach that day—her fear that, when she was gone, Pasquale wouldn't be able to bridge the gap between what he wanted and what was right. He wished he could reassure his mother: a man wants many things in life, but when one of them is also the right thing, he would be a fool not to choose it.

Pasquale waited until the Montelupos disappeared inside their house. Then he ground his cigarette into the gravel, crossed the piazza, and stepped up to the huge black door. He rang the bell.

There were footfalls on the other side and then Amedea's father answered, his thick, bald head tilted back, fierce eyes taking in Pasquale as if he were surveying an unacceptable meal in a café. Behind her father, Amedea's sister Donata saw Pasquale, and cov-ered her mouth with her hand. She turned and squealed up the stairs: "Amedea!" Bruno looked back at his daughter and then sternly again at Pasquale, who carefully removed his hat.

"Yes?" asked Bruno Montelupo. "What is it?"

Behind her father, on the stairs, lithe, lovely Amedea appeared, shaking her head slightly, as if still trying to dissuade him . . . but Pasquale also thought he saw, beneath the hand that covered her mouth, a smile.

"Sir," he said, "I am Pasquale Tursi of Porto Vergogna. I am here to ask for the hand of your daughter, Amedea." He cleared his throat. "I am here for my son."

20

The Infinite Blaze

Recently
Sandpoint, Idaho

Debra wakes in the dark, on the back deck of her cabin, on the tree side, where she likes to watch the stars. The air is cool, sky clear, pinpricks of light fierce tonight. Insistent. They don't twinkle, they burn. The front deck of the cabin overlooks the mountain-rimmed glacial lake, and this is the view that causes most visitors to gasp. But she doesn't like the front deck as much at night, when light from the docks, the boats, and the other cabins compete for attention. She prefers it back here, in the shade of the house, in a tight, round clearing of pine and fir trees, where it's just her and the sky, where she can see for fifty trillion miles, for a billion years. She'd never really been a sky-watcher until she married Alvis, who liked to drive into the Cascades and look for clear spots away from the light pollution. He considered it a shame when people couldn't grasp the infinite—a failure not just of imagination but of simple vision.

She hears the crunch of gravel; that must have been what woke her—Pat's Jeep coming down the long driveway. They're home from the play. How long was she asleep? She reaches out for her cold teacup. A while. She feels toasty-warm, except for one of her feet, which has slipped out of the blanket. Pat has rigged up two fireplace-shaped space heaters on either side of her favorite chaise, so that she can sleep out here. She balked at first at the waste of electricity; she could just wait until summer. But Pat promised to turn off every light every time he left a room "for the rest of my life," if she would only indulge him this one thing. And she has to admit, it is lovely sleeping out here; it's her favorite thing, waking outside in the cold, nestled in the little incubator her son built for her. She turns off the heaters, checks the horrible pad she sleeps on now—it's dry, thank God—pulls her big cardigan around herself, and starts for the house, a little wobbly still. Inside, she hears the garage door close below.

The cabin sits on a jutting point, two hundred feet above a bay on this deep mountain lake. The house is mostly vertical, designed by her and built with the money she got from selling their home in Seattle: four stories, with an open floor plan and a two-car garage below. Pat and Lydia have the second floor to themselves, the third is common living space—an open living room/kitchen/dining area—and the top floor belongs to Dee: bedroom, bathroom with Jacuzzi tub, and her sitting room. When she was having it built, of course, she had no idea she would spend virtually her entire time here as a cancer patient, and then—after the treatments had all been exhausted and she decided to let the disease run its course—in this weakened end-time. If she had, she might have gone with a rancher, with fewer stairs.

"Mom? We're home!"

He yells up the stairs every time he comes in the house and she pretends she doesn't know why. "Still alive," she's tempted to say, but it would sound harsh. She doesn't feel bitter that way, but it's funny to her, the way people treat the dying—like aliens.

She starts down the staircase. "How'd it go tonight? Good crowd?"

"Small but happy," Lydia calls up the stairs. "The ending worked better tonight."

"Are you hungry?" Debra asks. Pat is always hungry after a performance, and he's been especially famished while doing this play. As soon as Lydia finished writing it, she showed it to Debra, who was torn. It was the best thing Lydia had ever written, a perfect capstone to the cycle of autobiographical pieces Lydia started years earlier with a play about her parents' divorce. And Debra fully believed that she couldn't finish the cycle without writing about Pat. The real problem with *Front Man* was that there was only one person she could imagine playing Pat—and that was Pat. She and Lydia both worried that he might backslide if he had to relive those days—but Debra told Lydia she should let him read it. He took the pages downstairs and came back up three hours later, kissed Lydia, and insisted they do it—and that he play himself. It would be harder, he thought, to watch someone else play him at the peak of his self-absorption than it would be to play it all out again himself. He's been acting with the TAGNI group for more than a year now; it gives him a healthy outlet for performing—not in the narcissistic way he used to with his bands, but in a tighter, disciplined, collaborative spirit. And he's a natural, of course.

Debra is beating eggs when Pat swings around the kitchen pillar and kisses her cheek. Kid still fills a room. "Ted and Isola said to say hi."

"Yeah?" She pours the eggs in the pan. "And how are they?"

"Crazy right-wing nut jobs."

She slices cheese for his omelet, Pat eating every other piece. "I hope you told them that," she says, "because I'm getting awfully tired of them constantly writing checks to support the theater."

"They want us to do *Thoroughly Modern Millie*. Ted wants to be in it. Said I'd be great in it, too. Can you imagine? Me and Ted in a play together."

"Yeah, I'm not sure you have the chops to act with Ted."

"That's because I had such a bad teacher," he says. Then: "How are you feeling?"

"I'm good," she says.

"Did you take a Dilaudid?"

"No." She hates pain medication, doesn't want to miss a thing. "I feel fine."

Pat puts his hand on her forehead. "You're warm."

"I'm fine. You just came from outside."

"So did you."

"I was in that oven you built me. I'm probably cooked."

He reaches for the cutting board. "Let me finish. I can make an omelet."

"Since when?"

"I'll have Lydia do it. She's good at that woman's work."

Debra stops cutting onions and slashes in his direction with the knife.

"Unkindest cut of all," he says.

It's like a little gift, the way he surprises her sometimes with the things he remembers. "I used to teach that play," she says. Without thinking, she quotes her own favorite line: "Cowards die many times before their deaths. The valiant never taste of death but once."

Pat sits at the counter. "That hurts more than the knife."

Lydia comes up the stairs then, towel-drying her hair after her shower. She tells Debra all over again that Ted and Isola were at the play, and that they asked after her.

Debra knows by heart the inflection of their concern, *How IS she?*

Still alive. Oh, the things she would say if she could—but it's a minefield of courtesies and manners, this dying business. She's constantly being offered homeopathic remedies by the funky people up here: magnets and herbs and horse liniments. Some people give her books—self-help books, tomes on grieving, pamphlets on dying. *I'm beyond help, self- or otherwise,* she wants to say, and *Aren't the grieving books more for the survivors?* and *Thanks for the book on dying, but that's the one part I have covered.* They'll ask Pat, *How IS she?* and they'll ask her, *How ARE you?* But they don't want to hear that she's tired all the time, that her bladder is leaky, that she's on the watch for her systems shutting down. They want to hear that she's at peace, that she's led a great life, that she's happy her son has returned—and so that's what she gives them. And the truth is, most of the time, she IS at peace, HAS led a great life, IS happy her son has returned. She knows which drawer the phone number for hospice is in; and the company with the hospital bed; and the provider of the morphine drip dispenser.

Some days she wakes slowly from her nap and thinks it would be okay to just go on sleeping—that it would not be scary at all. Pat and Lydia are as solid as she could hope, and the board has agreed to let Lydia take over the theater. The cabin is paid for, with enough left in the bank for taxes and other expenses, so Pat can spend the rest of his life puttering around outside in the early mornings, which he loves—gardening, painting and staining, pruning trees, working on the driveway and the retaining walls, anything to keep his hands moving. Sometimes, now, when she sees how content Pat and Lydia are, she feels like a spent salmon: her work here is done. But other times, honestly, the whole idea of being at peace just pisses her off. At peace? Who but the insane would ever be at peace? What person who has enjoyed life could possibly think one is enough? Who could live even a day and not feel the sweet ache of regret?

Sometimes, during her various rounds of chemo, she had wanted the pain and discomfort to be over so badly that she could imagine being comforted by her own death. That was one of the reasons she'd decided—after all of the chemicals and radiations and surgeries, after the double mastectomy, after the doctors tried every measure of conventional and nuclear weaponry against her diminishing frame, and after they still found traces of cancer in her pelvic bones—to just let the thing run its course. Let it have her. The doctors said there might still be something to be done, depending on whether it was a primary or secondary cancer, but she told them it didn't matter anymore. Pat had come home, and she preferred six months of peace to another three years of needles and nausea. And she's gotten lucky: she's made it almost two years, and has felt good throughout most of it, although it still stuns her to catch a glimpse in the mirror: *Who is this relic, this tall, thin, flat-chested old woman with her white porcupine hair?*

Debra pulls her sweater around herself, warms her tea. She leans against the sink and smiles as she watches her son eat his second helping of eggs, Lydia reaching over to take a cheesy mushroom from the top. Pat looks up at his mother, to see if she's caught the blatant thievery. "You're not going to stab *her*?"

And that's when a car announces itself on the gravel outside. Pat hears it, too, and checks his watch. He shrugs. "No idea."

Pat goes to the window, puts his hand to the glass, and peers down toward the driveway, the faint glow of headlights down there. "That's Keith's Bronco." He steps away from the window. "The after-party. He's probably wasted. I'll go take care of it."

He skips down the stairs like a boy.

"How was he tonight?" Debra asks quietly when he's gone.

Lydia picks at the leftover onions and mushrooms on Pat's plate. "Great. You couldn't take your eyes off him. God, I'll be glad when this play is over, though. Some nights, he just sits there afterward and stares out, with . . . these distant eyes. For fifteen minutes, he's just done. I feel like I've been holding my breath since I finished this goddamned play."

"You've been holding your breath a lot longer than that," Debra says, and they both smile. "It's a wonderful play, Lydia. You should just let go and enjoy it."

Lydia drinks from Pat's orange juice. "I don't know."

Debra reaches across the table for Lydia's hand. "You had to write it, and he had to play it, and I'm just so grateful I got to see it."

Lydia cocks her head and her brow wrinkles, fighting off tears. "Goddamn it, Dee. Why do you do that?"

Then, through three layers of floor, they hear voices on the stairs, Pat and Keith, and someone else, and then a rumbling up the steps, five, maybe six sets of feet.

Pat comes up first, shrugging. "I guess there were some old friends of yours at the show tonight, Mom. Keith brought them—I hope it's all right . . ."

Pat is followed by Keith. He doesn't seem drunk, but he is carrying his little video camera, which he sometimes uses to chronicle—hell, Debra isn't sure what Keith chronicles, exactly. "Hey, Dee. Sorry to bother you so late, but these people really wanted to see you . . ."

"It's okay, Keith," she says, and then the other people come up the stairs, one at a time: an attractive young woman with curly red hair, and then a thin, mop-headed young man who *does* look drunk—neither of whom Debra recognizes—and then a strange creature, a slightly hunched older man in a suit coat, as skinny as she is, at once vaguely familiar and not; he has the strangest, lineless face, like one of those computer renderings of a face aging, only done in reverse, a boy's face grafted onto the neck of an old man— and finally, another old gentleman, in a charcoal-gray suit. This last man catches her attention as he steps away from the others, to the counter separating the kitchen from the living room. He removes his fedora and looks at her with a set of eyes so pale blue they seem nearly transparent—eyes that take her in with a mixture of warmth and pity, eyes that sweep Dee Moray back fifty years, to another life—

He says, "Hello, Dee."

Debra's teacup drops to the counter. "Pasquale?"

There were times, of course, years ago, when she thought she might see him again. That last day in Italy, as she watched him motor away from the hotel, she couldn't have imagined *not* seeing him again. Not that there was any spoken agreement between them, but there was something implicit, the hum of attraction and anticipation. When Alvis told her that Pasquale's mother had died, that he was going to the funeral and might not come back, Dee was stunned; why hadn't Pasquale told her? And when a boat arrived with her luggage, and Alvis said Pasquale wanted him to get her back to the States safely, she thought that Pasquale must have needed some time alone. So she went home to have the baby. She'd sent him a postcard, thinking, *maybe* . . . but there was no answer. After that, she thought about Pasquale sometimes, although not as often as the years passed; she and Alvis did talk about going to Italy on vacation, going back to Porto Vergogna, but they never made it. Then, after Alvis died and she got her degree in teaching, with a minor in Italian, she'd thought about taking Pat; she even called a travel agent, who said that not only was there "no listing for a Hotel Adequate View," but that she couldn't even find this town, Porto Vergogna. Did she perhaps mean Portovenere?

By then, Debra could almost wonder if the whole thing—Pasquale, the fishermen, the paintings in the bunker, the little village on the cliffs—hadn't been some trick of the mind, another of her fantasies, a scene from some movie she'd watched.

But no—here he is, Pasquale Tursi, older, of course, his black hair gone slate-gray, those deep lines in his face, his jaw falling into a slight jowl, but with the eyes, still the eyes. It is him. And he edges forward a step, until the only thing separating them is the kitchen counter.

She feels a flash of self-consciousness and her twenty-two-year-old's vanity rises: God, what a fright she must look. For several seconds, they stand there, a gimpy old man and a sick old woman, just four feet apart now, but separated by a thick granite counter, by fifty years and two fully lived lives. No one speaks. No one breathes.

Finally, it is Dee Moray who breaks the silence, smiling at her old friend: *"Perché ci hai messo così tanto tempo?"* What took you so long?

That smile is still too large for her lovely face. But what really gets to him is this: she has learned Italian. Pasquale smiles back and says, quietly, *"Mi dispiace. Avevo qualcosa di importante da fare."* I'm sorry. There was something important I had to do.

Of the six other people fanned out around them in this room, only one understands what they've said: Shane Wheeler, who, even after four quick, desperate glasses of whiskey, is still moved by the bond translators often develop with their subjects. It's been quite a day for him, waking up with Claire, finding out his movie pitch was nothing but a distraction, trying unsuccessfully to negotiate better terms during the long trip, then the catharsis of that play, identifying with the ruined life of Pat Bender, reaching out to and getting shut down by his ex; after all of that, and the whiskeys, the emotion of Pasquale's reunion with Dee is almost more than Shane can bear. He sighs deeply, a little whoosh of air that brings the others back into the room . . .

They all watch Pasquale and Dee intently. Michael Deane grips Claire's arm; she covers her mouth with her other hand;

Lydia glances over at Pat (even now, she can't help worrying). Pat looks from his mother to this kindly old man—*Did she call him Pasquale?*—and then his vision swings over to Keith, standing at the top of the stairs, moving to the side with that goddamned camera he carries everywhere, framing the scene, inexplicably filming this moment. "What are you doing?" he asks. "Put that camera away." Keith shrugs and nods his head toward Michael Deane, the man paying him to do this.

Debra becomes aware, too, of the other people in the room. She looks around at the expectant faces until her eyes fall on the other old man, the one with the strange plastic, impish face. Jesus. She knows him, too—

"Michael Deane."

He draws his lips back over his brash, white teeth. "Hello, Dee."

Even now, she feels dread just saying his name, and hearing him say hers; Deane senses this, because he looks away. She's read stories about him over the years, of course. She knows about his long trail of success. For a time she even stopped watching credits for fear of simply seeing his name: A Michael Deane Production.

"Mom?" Pat takes another step toward her. "Are you okay?"

"I'm fine," she says. But she stares at Michael, every eye following hers.

Michael Deane feels their stares and he knows: this is his room now. And *The Room is everything. When you are in The Room, nothing exists outside. The people hearing your pitch could no more leave The Room than—*

Michael begins, turning to Lydia first, and smiling, all charm. "And you must be the author of the masterpiece we just saw." He holds out his hand. "Truly. It was a wonderful play. So moving."

"Thank you," Lydia says, shaking his hand.

Now Deane turns back to Debra: *Always speak first to the toughest person in The Room.* "Dee, as I told your son downstairs, his performance was remarkable. A chip off the old block, as they say."

Pat shrinks from the praise, looks down, and scratches his head uncomfortably, like a kid who has just broken a lamp with a football.

A chip off the old block—Debra shudders at the description, at the threat she senses but can't quite make out yet (*What* exactly *does he want?*), and at the way Michael Deane is taking over this room, watching her son with that old dead-gazed purposefulness, that hunger, a half-smirk on his surgically implacable face.

Pasquale senses her discomfort. *"Mi dispiace,"* he says, and he reaches a hand over the counter between them. *"Era l'unico modo."* It was the only way to find her.

Debra feels herself tense, like a bear protecting a cub. She concentrates on Michael Deane, addressing him as evenly as she can, trying to take the edge out of her voice, not entirely successfully. "Why are you here, Michael?"

Michael Deane treats this as if it were an honest question about his intentions, an invitation to unpack his traveling salesman bag. "Yes, I should get right to that, after disturbing you so late in the evening. Thank you, Dee." Having transformed Dee's accusation into an invitation, he turns now to Lydia and Pat. "I don't know if your mother's ever mentioned me, but I am a film producer"—he smiles with humble understatement—"of some repute, I suppose."

Claire reaches out to take his arm—"Michael . . ." (*Not now, don't ruin this good thing you're doing by trying to produce it*)— but Michael can no more be stopped than a tornado now. He uses Claire's gesture to pull her in, patting her hand as if she's just reminded him of his manners. "Of course. Forgive me. This is Claire Silver, my chief development executive."

Development *executive*? He can't possibly mean that. Still, she's speechless—long enough to look up silently, to see them all staring at her, Lydia especially, sitting on the edge of the counter. Claire has no choice but to echo what Michael said: "It really was a great play."

"Thank you," Lydia says again, blushing with gratitude.

"Yes," Michael Deane says, "great," and The Room is all his now, this rustic cabin no different than any conference room he's ever pitched. "Which is why Claire and I were wondering . . . if you might be interested in selling the film rights—"

Lydia laughs nervously, almost giddily. She shoots a quick

glance to Pat, then back to Michael Deane. "You want to buy my play?"

"The play, maybe the whole cycle, perhaps everything—" Michael Deane lets this hang a moment. "I'd like to option all of it," working hard to sound casual, "your whole story," subtly turning to include Pat, "both of you," avoiding Dee's gaze. "I'd like to buy your . . ." and he trails off, as if what comes next is mere afterthought, "life rights."

We want what we want.

"Life rights?" Pat asks. He's happy for his girlfriend, but he's suspicious of this old man. "What's that *mean*?"

Claire knows. Book, movie, reality show, whatever they can sell about Richard Burton's train wreck of a son. Dee knows, too. She covers her mouth and manages just a single word, "Wait—" before her knees give and she has to grab the counter for support.

"Mom?" Pat runs around the counter, arriving just as Pasquale gets to her, too. They reach for her at the same time, as she buckles, each taking an arm. "Give her some space!" Pat yells.

Pasquale doesn't understand this phrase (*Give her space?*), and he looks across the counter at his translator, but Shane is a little drunk and a little desperate and he chooses instead to translate Michael Deane's offer for Lydia. "Be careful," he leans forward and says quietly. "Sometimes he only *pretends* to like your shit."

Still shocked by her recent promotion, Claire takes her boss by the arm and pulls him toward the living room. "Michael, what are you doing?" she asks under her breath.

He looks past her, to Dee and the boy. "I'm doing what I came to do."

"I thought you came to make amends."

"Amends?" Michael Deane looks at Claire without understanding. "For what?"

"Jesus, Michael. You completely fucked with these people's lives. Why did you come here if it wasn't to apologize?"

"Apologize?" Again, Michael doesn't quite understand what she's saying. "I came here for the story, Claire. For *my story*."

322 • JESS WALTER

Behind the counter, Dee has regained her balance. She looks across the living room at Michael Deane and his assistant; they seem to be arguing about something. Pat has come around the counter, and is supporting her weight. She squeezes his hand. "I'm okay now," she says. Pasquale is holding her other hand. She smiles at him again.

There are only three people in the world who know the secret she's carried for the last forty-eight years, a secret that has defined her since she left Italy, this thing that grew each year until now it fills the room—a room that contains the other two people who know. There were so many reasons for the secret back then—Dick and Liz, and her family's judgment, and the fear of a tabloid scandal, and most of all (she can admit it now) her own pride, her desire to not let a prick like Michael Deane win—but those reasons fell away over the years, and the only reason she has continued to keep the secret is . . . Pat. She thought it would simply be too much for him. What movie star's kid ever stood a chance? Especially one with Pat's appetites? When he was using he was so breakable, and when he was clean his salvation seemed so fragile. She was protecting him, and now she knows what she was protecting him from: this man she has loathed for almost fifty years, who has come into her house and threatened all of it by trying to buy their very lives.

Yet she knows she won't be around to protect Pat forever. And there is the very real guilt of having kept from him something so important, and her fear that he will now hate her for it. Dee looks at Lydia. This affects her, too. Then she looks at Pasquale, and finally at her son, who stares at her with such deep concern that she knows she has no choice anymore. "Pat, I should— You need to— There's something—"

And then, even on the cusp of telling him, she feels the first rush of freedom, hope, the weight of this thing already beginning to fall away—

"About your father—"

Pat's eyes slide from her to Pasquale, but Dee shakes her head. "No," she says simply. She looks at Michael Deane in the living room and wishes to exert one more, tiny bit of rebellion. She will not let the old vulture see this. "Can we go upstairs?"

"Sure," Pat says.

Debra looks at Lydia. "You should come, too."

And so, the doomed Deane Party will not get to see the completion of their journey; they can only watch as Lydia, Dee, and Pat make their way slowly toward the kitchen staircase. Michael Deane gives a small nod to Keith, who starts to follow with his little camera. The leaps in technology and miniaturization are confounding—this little device, the size of a cigarette pack, can do more than the eighty-pound cameras Dee Moray once acted for—and in the camera's tiny screen Lydia is helping Debra toward the stairs. At first Pat walks behind them—but then he stops and turns, sensing people staring at him—as if waiting for him to do something crazy—and all at once a familiar sensation comes over him, like he used to feel onstage. Pat burns from it, and he spins on Keith.

"I told you to put the fucking camera away," Pat says, and he grabs it—the screen now recording the last little digital film it will ever make, the deep lines of a man's palm as Pat stalks through the living room, past the creepy old producer and the red-haired girl, and the drunk dude with the hair. He opens the slider, steps out onto the front porch, and throws the camera as far as he can—grunting as it leaves his hand, toppling over itself—Pat waiting, waiting, until they hear a distant splash in the lake below. He walks back through the room satisfied—"You are my fucking hero," says the kid with the hair as he passes—and Pat shrugs a slight apology to Keith, then makes his way upstairs to find out that his whole life to this point has been a sweet lie.

21

Beautiful Ruins

There would seem to be nothing more obvious,
more tangible and palpable than the present moment.
And yet it eludes us completely.
All the sadness of life lies in that fact.
—*Milan Kundera*

This is a love story, Michael Deane says.

But, really, what isn't? Doesn't the detective love the mystery, or the chase, or the nosy female reporter, who is even now being held against her wishes at an empty warehouse on the waterfront? Surely the serial murderer loves his victims, and the spy loves his gadgets or his country or the exotic counterspy. The ice trucker is torn between his love for ice and truck, and the competing chefs go crazy for scallops, and the pawnshop guys adore their junk, just as the Housewives live for catching glimpses of their own Botoxed brows in gilded hall mirrors, and the rocked-out dude on 'roids totally wants to shred the ass of the tramp-tatted girl on Hookbook, and because this is reality, they are all in love—madly, truly—with the body mic clipped to their back buckle, and the producer casually suggesting just one more angle, one more Jell-O shot. And the robot loves his master, alien loves his saucer, Superman loves Lois, Lex, and Lana, Luke loves Leia (till he finds out she's his sister), and the exorcist loves the demon even as he leaps out the window with it, in full soulful embrace, as Leo loves Kate and they both love the sinking ship, and the shark—God, the shark loves to eat, which is what the mafioso loves, too—eating and money and Paulie

and *omertà*—the way the cowboy loves his horse, loves the corseted
girl behind the piano bar, and sometimes loves the other cowboy,
as the vampire loves night and neck, and the zombie—don't even
start with the zombie, sentimental fool; has anyone ever been more
lovesick than a zombie, that pale, dull metaphor for love, all animal
craving and lurching, outstretched arms, his very existence a sonnet
about how much he wants those brains? This, too, is a love story.

And in the room, the Dutch financiers with the forty mil to kill
wait for Michael Deane to elaborate, but he just sits with his index
fingers steepled in front of his mouth. A love story. He'll speak
when he's ready. This is his room, after all; he's only sorry he won't
be able to attend his own funeral, because he'd leave that fucking
room with a deal for a network pilot and a reality show set in hell.
After the *Donner!* pitch (for thirty grand, that kid really sold it),
Michael got out of his constraining deal with the studio. Now he's
producing on his own again—six unscripted shows already in some
stage of production—surviving the post-studio world just fine,
thank you, raking in more money than he ever thought possible.
Now the money guys come *to him*. He feels thirty again. So the
Dutch financiers wait, and they wait, until finally the index fingers
fall away from Michael Deane's preternaturally smooth mouth and
he speaks:

"This is a secondary cable immersion reality show called *Rich
MILF/Poor MILF*. And as I say, it is, above all, a love story—"

Sure it is. And in Genoa, Italy, an old prostitute waits for the
door to close and then grabs the money the American has left on
the gray sheets—half afraid it will disappear. She looks around,
holds her breath, and listens for his footsteps to recede down the
hallway. She leans back against the wrought-iron bed frame and
counts it—fifty times the price she normally gets for slopping dong;
she can't believe her good goddamn fortune. She folds the bills and
puts them under her garter so that Enzo won't ask for his cut, walks
to the window and looks down, and there he is, standing on the
sidewalk, looking lost: Wisconsin. Wanted to write a book. And
in that flash, the two moments they've shared are perfect, and she

loves him more than any man she's ever known—which is maybe why she pretended not to know him, to not ruin it, to save him the embarrassment of having cried. But no—there was something else, something she hasn't got a name for, and when he glances up from the street below, whatever it is causes Maria to touch the place on her chest where he laid his head that night. Then she steps back from the window—

In California, William Eddy stands on the porch of his little clapboard house, luxuriating in the smoke from his pipe and the weight of breakfast in his gut. It's such a decadent, guilty meal. William Eddy likes every meal, but he goddamn *loves* breakfast. For a year, he kicks around Yerba Buena, gets plenty of work, but then he makes the mistake of telling his story to the broadsheet journalists and the dime-book authors—all of whom embellish in both language and deed, vultures picking through the bones of his life for scandal. When some of the others accuse him of exaggerating to make himself look better, Eddy says to hell with them all and moves south, to Gilroy. *Look better*—Christ in heaven, who looks *better* after such a thing? With the Rush of '49 there's no shortage of work for a carriage builder, and William does well for a while, remarries and has three kids, but soon he's adrift again, alone, and he leaves his second family and runs off to Petaluma; he feels sometimes like a shirt blown off a drying line. His second wife says there's something wrong with him, "something I fear is both unwell and unreachable in you"; his third wife, a schoolteacher from St. Louis, is just now discovering the same thing. He hears occasional word on the fate of the others: surviving Donners and Reeds, the kids he rescued; his old foe and friend Foster runs a saloon somewhere. He wonders if they are unmoored, too. Maybe only Keseburg would understand—Keseburg, who, he's heard, accepted his infamy and has opened a restaurant in Sacramento City. This morning, Eddy feels a bit feverish and weak, and while he won't know it for a few more days, he is dying, at just forty-three, and only thirteen years after his hard passage through the mountains. Of course, such a passage is only temporary. On his porch, William coughs, and the porch boards beneath him creak as he looks east, as he does each morning, feels an ache for the bruised sun on the horizon and his family, ever up there in the cold—

All night, the painter walks north through dark foothills, toward rumors of the Swiss border. He avoids main roads, scouring the rubble of another Italian village for the remnants of his old unit, or for some Americans to surrender to—anything. He thinks of abandoning his uniform, but he still fears being shot as a deserter. At dawn, with the deep *pup-pup* of distant shelling at his back, he takes refuge in the husk of an old burned-out printer's office, leans pack and rifle on the sturdiest wall, and curls up beneath an old drafting table with some grain bags for a pillow. Before he drifts off, the painter goes through his nightly ritual, picturing the man he loves back in Stuttgart, his old piano instructor. *Come home safely,* the pianist begs, and the painter assures him that he will. Nothing more than that, as chaste a friendship as two men can have, but the very possibility has kept him alive—the imagined moment when he does return safely—and so the painter thinks of the piano instructor every night before sleep, as he does now, drifting off in the glow before sunrise, and sleeping peacefully until a couple of partisans come across him and bash in his skull with a shovel. After the first swing, it is done: the painter will not make it home to Germany, to his piano instructor or his sister—killed anyway, a week ago, in a fire at the munitions plant where she worked, his spoiled sister whose photograph he carried to war and whose portrait he painted twice on the wall of a pillbox bunker on the Italian coast. One of the partisans laughs as the German painter lurches and burbles about like some kind of walking dead, but the more decent of the two steps in to finish him off—

Joe and Umi move to West Cork and get married; childless, they divorce four years later, blaming each other for their sad, aging selves. After a few years apart, they see each other at a concert and are more understanding; they share a glass of wine, laugh at the perspective they lacked, and fall back into bed together. This reconciliation only lasts a few months before they go their own ways, happy at least to be forgiven in the other's eyes. It's the same with Dick and Liz: a turbulent ten-year marriage and one truly great film together, *Who's Afraid of Virginia Woolf?* (she gets the Oscar, ironically), then a divorce and a short reprise (more disastrous than Joe and Umi's) before they drift their own ways, Liz into more marriages, Dick into more cocktails, until, at fifty-eight, he can't be awakened in his hotel and he dies that day of cerebral hemorrhage, a line from *The Tempest* apocryphally left on his bed-stand: "Our Revels now are ended—" Orenzio gets drunk one winter and drowns, and Valeria spends the last years of her life living happily with Tommaso the Widower, and the brute Pelle recovers from his gunshot foot, but, having lost his taste for the goon business, works at his brother's butcher shop and marries a mute girl, and Gualfredo gets a just case of syphilis that blinds him, and the son of Alvis's friend Richards is wounded in Vietnam, returns home to work as a benefits advocate for veterans, and is eventually elected to the Iowa State Senate, and young Bruno Tursi graduates with degrees in art history and restoration, works for a private firm in Rome cataloguing artifacts and finds a perfect medication to balance his quiet, low-level depression, and P.E. Steve remarries—the sweet, pretty mother of one of his daughter's softball teammates—and on and on it goes, in a thousand directions, everything occurring at once, in a great storm of the present, of the now—

—all those lovely wrecked lives—

—and in Universal City, California, Claire Silver threatens to quit unless Michael Deane leaves Debra "Dee" Moore and her son alone, and agrees to produce just one project from their trip to Sandpoint: a film based solely on Lydia Parker's play *Front Man*, the poignant story of a drug-addicted musician who wanders off into the wilderness and eventually returns to his long-suffering mother and girlfriend. The budget is just $4 million, and after every financier and studio in Hollywood passes, it is funded entirely by Michael Deane himself, although he doesn't tell Claire that. The film is directed by a young Serbian comic-book artist and auteur, who writes the script himself, based loosely on Lydia's

330 • JESS WALTER

play, or at least the part of the play he read. The auteur makes the musician younger and, generally, more likeable. And, rather than having issues with his mother, in this version the musician has issues with his dad—so the young director can explore his own feelings for his distant, disapproving father. And, rather than having his girlfriend be a playwright in the Northwest, who takes care of her stepfather, the girlfriend in the film becomes an art teacher who works with poor black kids in Detroit, so that they can get some better music on the sound track and also take advantage of the big "Film in Michigan" tax break. In the final script, the Pat character—whose name is changed to Slade—doesn't steal from his mother or cheat repeatedly on his girlfriend, but harms only himself with his addiction, itself changed from cocaine to alcohol. (He's got to be relatable and likeable, Michael and the director agree.) These changes come slowly, one at a time, like adding hot water to a bath, and with each step Claire convinces herself that they're sticking to the important parts of the story— "to its essence"—and in the end she's proud of the film, and of her first coproducer credit. Her dad says, "It made me cry." But the person most moved by *Front Man* is Daryl, who is still on relationship-probation when Claire brings him to an early screening. Late in the film (after Slade's girlfriend Penny has confronted the gangbangers threatening the school where she teaches) Slade sends Penny a text message from London: *Just let me know you're okay.* Daryl gasps and leans over to Claire, tells her, "I sent you that message." Claire nods: she'd suggested it to the director. The film ends with Slade being rediscovered by a record executive vacationing in the UK, and headed for success—but on *his* terms. As Slade's unpacking his guitar after a show he hears a woman's voice. "I *am* okay," she says, and Slade turns to see Penny, finally answering his text. In the theater, Daryl begins crying, for the film is clearly a harsh love letter from his girlfriend about his porn addiction, for which he agrees to seek treatment. And, in fact, Daryl's treatment is an unqualified success; his not waking every day at noon to surf Internet porn and sneaking out to strip clubs at night has given him newfound energy and passion for life—which he channels into his relationship with Claire, and into a shop he opens in Brentwood with another former set designer, making custom furniture for industry people. *Front Man* plays at several festivals, wins the audience award in Toronto, and is generously reviewed. With the foreign box office, it even ends up earning Michael a decent profit—"Sometimes it's like I shit money," he tells a profiler for *The New Yorker*. Claire knows the movie is far from perfect, but with its success, Michael allows her to buy two other scripts for development, Claire happy to no longer expect the dead perfection of museum art, but embrace the sweet lovely mess that is real life. After some initial buzz, *Front Man* is passed over by the Academy Awards, but it does garner three Independent Spirit nominations. Michael can't go to the ceremony (he's off in Mexico recovering from his divorce and receiving a controversial human-growth hormone treatment), but Claire is happy to represent the film's producers, Daryl accompanying her in an eggplant-colored tuxedo she finds for him in a thrift store. He looks great, of course. Unfortunately, *Front Man* doesn't win any Indie Spirit awards, either, but afterward Claire feels buoyant with achievement (and with the two bottles of '88 Dom Perignon that Michael generously reserved for her table) and she and Daryl have sex in the limo, after which she convinces the driver to veer through a KFC drive-through for a bucket of Extra Crispy, Daryl nervously fingering the engagement ring in his purple pants pocket—

Shane Wheeler uses the option money from *Donner!* to rent a small apartment in the Silver Lake area of Los Angeles. Michael Deane gets him a job on a reality show he sells to the Biography Channel based on Shane's suggestion, called *Hunger*, about a houseful of bulimics and anorexics. But the show is too sad for even Shane, let alone viewers, and he gets a job as a writer for another show, called *Battle Royale*, in which famous battles are re-created through computer graphics, so that history is like watching *Call of Duty*, all accompanied by a fast-moving narration by William

Shatner, the scripts written by Shane and two other writers in modern vernacular ("Restricted by their own code of honor, the Spartans were about to get totally stomped . . ."). He continues to work on *Donner!* in his spare time, until a competing Donner Party project makes it to the screen first—William Eddy portrayed as a lying coward—and this is when Shane finally gives up on cannibals. He also tries once more with Claire, but she seems pretty happy with her boyfriend, and once Shane meets the guy he understands: the dude is way better-looking than Shane. He pays Saundra back for the car, and throws in a little more for her ruined credit, but she remains cool to him. One night after work, though, he hooks up with a production assistant named Wylie, who is twenty-two and thinks he's brilliant and eventually wins his heart by getting an ACT tattoo on her lower back—

In Sandpoint, Idaho, Pat Bender wakes at four, makes the first of three pots of coffee, and fills the predawn hours with chores around the cabin. He likes starting work before he's had a chance to really wake up; it gives the day some momentum, keeps him moving forward. As long as he has something to do, he feels good, so he clears brush or he splits wood or he strips, sands, and stains the front deck, or the back deck, or the outbuildings, or he starts the whole process again on the front deck: strip, sand, stain. Ten years ago, he would've thought this some kind of Sisyphean torture, but now he can't wait to slide into his work boots, make coffee, and step into the dark morning; he likes the world best when he's alone in it, that dark, predawn quiet. Later, he goes into town with Lydia to work on sets for the theater's summer-stock children's production. Dee passed on to Lydia the community-theater fund-raising trick: cast as many cute kids as you can and watch their rich ski parents and the flip-flopped lake-folk buy up all the tickets, then use the proceeds to pay for the arty stuff. Capitalism aside, the plays are what another person might call "adorable," and Pat secretly likes them better than the too-serious adult fare. He takes one big role a year, usually in something Lydia picks for him; he and Keith are doing *True West* next. He's never seen Lydia happier. After he tells the crazy zombie producer that he isn't interested in selling his "life rights," and—as politely as he can—to "leave us the fuck alone," the guy still steps up and buys the rights to Lydia's play. When *Front Man* comes out, Pat has no interest in seeing it, but when people tell him that the story was drastically changed, that it bears almost no resemblance to his own life, he is profoundly grateful. He'll take *unknown* over *failure* at this point. With some of the option money, Lydia wants to take a trip—and maybe they will, but Pat can also imagine never leaving North Idaho again. He's got his coffee and he's got his ritual, his work around the cabin, and with the new satellite dish Lydia buys him for his birthday, he's got nine hundred channels and he's got Netflix, which he uses to work his way chronologically through his father's movies—he's in 1967 now, *The Comedians*—and he gets a perverse thrill out of seeing bits of himself in his father, although he's not looking forward to the inevitable decline. Lydia likes watching these movies, too—she teases him about having his father's build (*Last time I saw legs like that, there was a message tied to them*)—sweet Lydia who makes all of the rest of the odd bits come together as a life. And on those days when Lydia, the lake, his coffee, his woodworking, and the Richard Burton film library aren't nearly enough, on those evenings when he craves—*fucking craves*—the old noise and a girl on his lap and a line on the table, when he recalls the way the barista smiled at him in the coffee shop across from the theater, or even thinks of Michael Deane's business card in that drawer in the kitchen, of calling and asking, "How would this work exactly?"—on those days when he imagines getting just a wee bit higher (*See: every day*), Pat Bender concentrates on the steps. He recalls his mother's faith in him, and what she told him that night he found out about his father (*Don't let this change anything*), the night he forgave her and thanked her—and Pat works: he strips, he sands, he stains—strips, sands, and stains, strip-sand-stains, as if his life depended on it, which, of course, it does. And in the dark morning he always rises clear again, resolute; the only thing he really misses is—

—Dee Moray, who sits with one leg crossed over the other on

the back bench seat of a water taxi, the sun warming her forearms as her boat shadows the rough Ligurian coastline of the Riviera di Levante. She wears a cream-colored dress, and when the wind gusts she reaches up and presses her matching hat against her head. This causes Pasquale Tursi, next to her, in his usual suit jacket despite the heat (after all, they have dinner reservations later), to nearly double over with nostalgic longing. He has one of his wistful, fanciful thoughts—that he's somehow summoned from his mind not a fifty-year-old memory of the moment in which he first saw this woman but the actual moment itself. After all, isn't it the same sea, same sun, same cliffs, same *them*? And if a moment exists only in one's perception anyway, then perhaps the rush of feeling he has now is THE MOMENT, and not merely its shadow. Maybe every moment occurs at once, and they will always be twenty-two, their lives always before them. Dee sees Pasquale lost in this reverie and she touches his arm, asks, "*Cosa c'è?*," and while her years of teaching Italian have allowed them to communicate fairly well, the sentiment he feels is, once again, beyond language, so Pasquale says nothing, just smiles at her, rises, and moves to the front of the boat. He points out the cove to the pilot, who looks dubious but nonetheless negotiates the waves and rounds a rocky point into an abandoned inlet, the single pier long gone, just a few rubbled bits of foundation left, like humps of bone in the grass, all that remains of an unlikely village that once sat in a crease in these cliffs. Pasquale explains to her how he closed the Adequate View and moved to Florence, how the last fisherman died in 1973, how the old village was abandoned and absorbed by the Cinque Terre National Park, the families given a small settlement for their little specks of land. Over dinner in Portovenere, on a patio overlooking the sea, Pasquale explains other things, too, the gentle pull of events after he leaves her that day in his hotel, the sweet contented rhythm of his life after that. No, it is not the foreign excitement of his imagined life with her; instead, Pasquale leads what feels like *his* life: he marries lovely Amedea, and she is a wonderful wife to him, playful and adoring, as good a friend as he could ever have wanted. They raise sweet little Bruno, and soon after, their daughters Francesca and

Anna, and Pasquale takes a good job with his father-in-law's holding company, managing and renovating old Bruno's apartment buildings, and he eventually takes over as the patriarch to the Montelupo clan and business, doling out jobs, inheritance, and advice for his children and an army of nieces and nephews, never imagining that one man could ever feel so needed, so full. And it's a life with no shortage of moments to recommend it, a life that picks up speed like a boulder rolling down a hill, easy and natural and comfortable, and yet beyond control somehow; it all happens so fast, you wake a young man and at lunch are middle-aged and by dinner you can imagine your death. *And you were happy?* Dee asks, and he answers, *Oh, yes,* without hesitation, then thinks about it and adds, *Not always, of course, but I think more than most people.* He truly loved his wife, and if he sometimes daydreams other lives, and other women—her, mostly—he also never doubts that he made the right decision. His biggest regret is that they never got to travel together once the children were gone, before Amedea got sick, before her behavior turned erratic—fits of temper and disorientation that led to a diagnosis of early-onset Alzheimer's. Even then, they have some good years, but her last decade is lost, disappearing out from under them both like sand giving way beneath their feet.

At first Amedea simply forgets to shop, or to lock the door, then she loses their car, and then she starts forgetting numbers and names and the uses for common things. He comes inside to see her holding the telephone—with no idea whom she meant to call, or, later, how the thing even works. He locks her in for a while, and then they simply stop leaving the house—and the worst is how he feels himself slipping away in her eyes, and he feels lost in the shimmery mist of identity (*would he cease to exist when his wife stops knowing him?*). Her last year is nearly unbearable. Caring for someone who has no idea who you are is a ripe hell—the weight of responsibility, bathing and feeding and . . . *everything,* that weight growing as her cognition fades, until she is like *a thing* he cares for, *a heavy thing* he pulls through the last uphill part of their life together; and when his children finally talk him into moving her into a nursing facility near their home, Pasquale weeps with sorrow and guilt, but also with relief, and guilt for his relief, sorrow for his guilt, and when the nurse asks what measures they should take to sustain his wife's life, Pasquale can't even speak. So it is Bruno, lovely Bruno, who takes his father's hand and says to the nurse, *We are ready to let her go now.* And she does, go, Pasquale visiting every day and talking to that blank face until one day a nurse calls the house as Pasquale is preparing for a visit and says that his wife has passed. He is more distraught by this than he imagined he would be, her final absence like a cruel trick, as if, somehow after she died, the old Amedea would be allowed to return; instead, there is only the hole in him. A year passes and Pasquale finally understands his mother's sorrow after Carlo died—so long has he existed in the perception of his wife and his family that now he feels like nothing. And it is brave Bruno who recognizes in his father his own battles with depression, and he urges the old man to remember the last moment he felt his being without its relation to beloved Amedea, his last moment of individual happiness or longing—and Pasquale answers without hesitation, *Dee Moray*, and Bruno asks *Who?*, the son having never heard the story, of course. Pasquale tells his son everything, then, and it is Bruno again who insists that his father go to Hollywood and find out what happened to the woman in the old photograph, and to thank her—

Thank me? Debra Bender asks, and in his answer, Pasquale chooses his words carefully, mulling them over for some time, hoping she will understand: *I was living in dreams when I met you. And when I met the man you loved, I saw my own weakness in him. Such irony, how could I be a man worthy of your love when I had walked away from my own child? That is why I went back. And it was the best thing I ever did.*

She understands: she began teaching as a kind of self-sacrifice, subverting her own desires and ambitions for the ambitions of her students. *But then you find there's actually more joy and that it really does lessen the loneliness,* and this is why her last years, running the theater in Idaho, have felt so rich to her. And what she loved about Lydia's play: that it gets at this idea that true sacrifice is painless.

They linger and talk this way for three more hours after dinner, until she feels weak and they walk back to the hotel. They sleep in separate rooms, neither of them sure yet what this is—if it's anything, or if such a thing is even possible at this hour of their lives—and in the morning they have coffee and talk about Alvis (Pasquale: *He was right that tourists would ruin this place*; Dee: *He was like this island where I lived for a while*). And on the deck in Portovenere they decide to go on a hike, but first they plan the rest of Dee's three-week vacation: next they'll go south, to Rome, then to Naples and Calabria, then north again to Venice and Lake Como, as long as her strength holds—before returning at the end to Florence, where Pasquale shows her his big house and introduces her to his children and his grandchildren and his nieces and nephews. Dee is envious at first, but as they keep coming in the door, she is overtaken with joy—*there are so many*—and she accepts a warm blush of responsibility for all of this, if Pasquale is to be believed, holds a baby and blinks away tears as she watches Pasquale pull a coin from the ear of his grandson (*He's the beautiful one now*) and perhaps it's another day, or maybe two—what business does memory have with time?—before she feels the dark dizziness come and another before she is too weak to rise, another before the sharp tug in her stomach is more than Dilaudid can handle, and then—

They finish their breakfast in Portovenere, go back to the hotel, and put on hiking boots. Dee assures Pasquale that she's up for this, and they take a taxi to the end of the road, crowded now with cars and walkers and the bicycles of tourists. At a turnaround, he helps her out of the cab, pays the driver, and they set off once more on a trail along a vineyard leading into the park, up into the striated foothills that serve as backdrop to the sea-scraped cliffs. They have no idea if the paintings have faded away, or have been spray-painted with graffiti, or if the bunker still exists—or, for that matter, if it ever existed at all—but they are young and the trail is wide and easily traveled. And even if they don't find what they're looking for, isn't it enough to be out walking together in the sunlight?

Acknowledgments

My deepest thanks: to Natasha De Bernardi, Monica Mereghetti, and Olga Gardner Galvin for help with my *brutto Italiano*; to Sam Ligon, Jim Lynch, Mary Windishar, Anne Walter, and Dan Butterworth for giving the book reads at various stages; to Anne and Dan for enduring hikes in the Cinque Terre; to Jonathan Burnham, Michael Morrison, and everyone at HarperCollins; and most of all, to my editor, Cal Morgan, and my agent, Warren Frazier, for their generous work, support, and guidance.

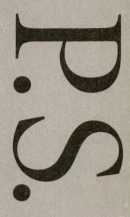

About the author

About the book

Read on

Insights,
Interviews
& More . . .

A Brief Interview with Jess Walter

By Weston Cutter

Originally ran in the Kenyon Review *on July 16, 2012*

First, in the broadest possible sketchings, who are folks who've been influential on you or your work (in any context: if you were deeply influenced by, say, Kirk Gibson's homer in the '88 World Series, that'd be awesome; this one's almost always more fun when it's not exclusively re: books)?

Outside books, I'm inspired by the Coen Brothers, whose genre collisions thrill me. I listen to music as I write, and my playlist swings from old funk and R&B (William DeVaughn and the Delfonics), Bowie, Dylan, Steely Dan, lots of lyric-heavy alt-stuff (Beck, Jeff Tweedy, Richmond Fontaine, John Wesley Harding) . . . But mostly, honestly, I'm influenced by boring old writers; my holy trinity might be Vonnegut, Didion, and DeLillo, but there would be a thousand saints: Laurence Sterne, James Cain, Fitzgerald, some Richards (Heller, Price, Powers, Russo), some metafictionists (Barthelme, Coover, and Millhauser), some story writers (Gaitskill, Wolfe, Carver), Cormac McCarthy, Elmore Leonard, William Kennedy, my friend Sherman Alexie, Gabriel García Márquez, David Mitchell, Edward P. Jones, and on and on I'd go if you'd let me . . .

This is as much a personal question as a polite one for public consumption: how much work do you do torquing your plots, getting things in order? One of the delicious aspects of your work is the unique thrill offered by a narrative that's been carefully planned by someone, an aspect I don't necessarily believe is super common at present, at least in some of the literary fiction I read. Is it a ton of work? Are there charts and graphs? Are there surprises en route?

Charts and graphs: that's funny. I don't ever think of plot that way, certainly not as some separate element from . . . writing. The story is just the story, all tied up in voice and language and characters. I think about what's happening as I'm writing the sentences, I guess; it's got to go somewhere or I'm bored. I sharpen the story as I'm sharpening the language and characters. *Beautiful Ruins* was written and rewritten and rewritten over parts of fifteen years; it was something of a puzzle to put together. There were plenty of false starts and bits that fell away (including a badly executed po-mo chapter in which I came into my own novel pitching a film). I don't really plan ahead, except in the sense that I try to write toward something happening every day (today, a guy accidentally shot his brother with a crossbow). I like to surprise myself. I don't write drafts. I write until I'm stuck, then I move on to something else, and when I go back to it, I start at the very beginning to make it feel like a smooth, seamless surface. If I have any organizational secret, it's not rushing things, and keeping a writing journal in which I try to comment on what I'm doing, make suggestions to myself, chide and encourage, try to float above the thing, see the shape and the themes as they're emerging. I try not to be timid about what "happens" in a novel. One good thing about my journalism career was that I saw amazing, outrageous, unlikely things happen all the time. I covered cults and shootouts and congressional campaigns and murders and mob hits. Sometimes we equate "realism" with some kind of daily grind. Presumably, I'm writing about these characters at this time because something happens to them that is remarkable . . . worth remarking upon. I remember reading *One Hundred Years of Solitude* and marveling at all that happened just in the first sentence. ("Many years later, as he faced the firing squad, Colonel Aureliano Buendía was to remember that distant afternoon when his father took him to discover ice.") There's a whole novel in that sentence. ▶

A Brief Interview with Jess Walter *(continued)*

What's the difference, for you as you're writing each, between embarking on short stories or novels?

The embarking is always the same. Early to the desk. Fingers on the home keys. Coffee and a giant cookie. I don't usually know where I'm going until I've got some pages. I have a thousand ideas for stories but I tend not to know much about them when I start, even whether it's a story or a novel. The ideas tend to be pretty specific, but also open-ended (what if an air force survival instructor went to Las Vegas to rescue his stepsister from a life of prostitution?). Then I just write, figure out who these people are, why they're doing what they're doing. I think character is elemental; if you pay attention to the people, you'll get the action right. I usually have three or four things going at once, a story or two, sometimes even two novels, and if I get stuck I just jump over to the next one. I do this so I won't leave the desk, and I've found, over the years, that it makes me both more productive and less worried if something hits a wall (and everything always hits a wall). I grew up in a very blue-collar family and came at fiction through newspapers, so that daily work ethic is how I still approach writing. This doesn't work, move to that, that doesn't work, move to this. My dad worked for forty years in an aluminum plant. I don't think he ever got "aluminum block." One grandfather was killed when a crane fell on him, the other when he was stretching fence on our family cattle ranch, so I'm not likely to ever complain that writing is hard work.

This one's going to be mildly harder to articulate: you seem to be very intentional in your novels in addressing topical concerns. Beautiful Ruins *is, as you wrote in the press packet, ". . . a story about fame and how we all endeavor now to live our lives like movie stars, like celebrities, each of us an eager inner publicist managing our careers and our romances and our fragile self-images (our Facebook pages and LinkedIn profiles)." I know* The Financial Lives of the Poets *dealt with the implosion of the economy. In the broadest possible way: how do you balance the demands of a novel between the impulse to make it specifically address some larger social thing versus letting it find its own way, become its own beast, regardless of what it ends up addressing? Is the duality false? I've not written anywhere near enough to know, but I'm curious.*

I suppose my journalism background has something to do with that impulse to capture what's going on around me. But I also just love books that strike a thematic chord, books that are *about something* in that larger sense. It doesn't have to be current, though; a book like *The Known World* blows up what we thought we knew about slavery, while using real facts in a kind of documentary overlay to what is a beautifully structured and written narrative. That kind of work just thrills me as a reader, and makes me want to go write something. I remember reading *Resistance, Rebellion, and Death* by Camus and his exhortation to seek out "the wager of our generation," and this seems to be a good thing for a novelist to attempt. As for balancing those impulses against the demands of character and narrative . . . yes, I do try to let it become its own beast, but then, when I see the beast, I go back in to make it the hairiest damn beast I can. I think my writing journal again comes in handy there. I usually find the thematic strains when I go back and rewrite and then record them in my journal (with *Beautiful Ruins*, I wrote once, "Oh my god, this book is really about regret . . .") and then in the revision, I sharpen those things, too. I probably fall back on those old writer tropes: that each book tells you what it needs and that writing is the process of discovery. But I find those things to be generally true, so it's easy to cling to them.

Do you ever write poetry?

I write everything, short fiction, novels, nonfiction, scripts, essays, book reviews, journalism, humor, and yes, least successfully, poetry. I decided the protagonist of *The Financial Lives of the Poets* would be a bad poet (he's actually a newspaper business writer) in part because I had no choice. The only two poems of his that I like were mine and existed before the book did: "A Brief Political Manifesto" and "Dry Falls." The rest of that shit is all his. The writers I'm most intimidated by are the poets I'm friends with or have worked with: Robert Wrigley, Chris Howell, Nance Van Winckel, Dan Butterworth, Tod Marshall, Fleda Brown, Joseph Millar, Kwame Dawes, Dorianne Laux, David St. John (again, on and on and . . .).

What's the view out your window?

I work above my garage behind our house and I can see across our lawn to the back of our house (it's a brick 1906 Tudor-ish thing) and beyond to the Spokane River gorge, which is right out our front door, and across to the silhouette of Mt. Spokane. I get to work at dawn most mornings and see the sun rise. We live in a city, ten minutes by bike from downtown, but because the river gorge is there, we're on a kind of wildlife freeway, so at least once a week I see some animal come up into our lawn—deer and coyotes and skunks and turkeys and eagles and, once, a scrawny, bedraggled moose that looked like he'd been on a six-week meth bender. ⟍

In the Time of Galley Slaves

I HATE WHEN AUTHORS say things like, *This novel took me fifteen years to write.* Or *It was as if my characters took over the story.*

These seem like blatant attempts to make mysterious what is a fairly mundane activity—writing—to fill it with magical, superhuman suffering, or worse, to dissuade civilians from trying to do it. After all, who wants to suffer for a decade and a half hoping for some strange fictional alchemic reaction? Who wants to spend *fifteen years* on a book?

Now, after writing several of these things, I can safely say that when a writer claims to have spent fifteen years on a novel, there's a good chance that what he means is that he managed to squeeze in two or three years of writing during fifteen years of drinking and self-loathing.

As for the characters taking over a story, I tried that. As a young writer I waited for my carefully crafted people to take over my stories, to do something, do *anything.* Instead, they tended to do what my brother and I did then: sit around, watch TV, drink beer. Toss a Nerf football around. Good way to spend a Saturday. Bad narrative strategy.

In 1967, in an interview in the *Paris Review,* Herbert Gold ran this "characters-take-over-the-story" trope past Vladimir Nabokov, who replied: "[T]hat trite little whimsy about characters getting out of hand . . . is as old as the quills. . . . My characters are galley slaves."

In the same interview, Nabokov, the most magical of stylists, described his writing process in less than magical terms: "The pattern of the thing precedes the thing. I fill in the gaps of the crossword at any spot I happen to choose. These bits I write on index cards until the novel is done."

Exactly: galley slaves, crossword puzzles, index cards. An author uses language to find a voice and create a narrative pattern that he applies to fictional creations whose seeming actions are in fact the author's artful depiction of human behavior channeled through a process that is more clerical than magical. Writers write. Characters row.

And that's how I tried to write for the last twenty years, with blue-collar get-over-yourself hard work—less a mystic than a coal miner.

Which is why it pains me to admit a couple of things about *Beautiful Ruins*.

This book took me fifteen years to write.

And I only finished it when the characters took over the story.

I think all novels are, in some way, about time.

I don't mean in the way that they are about World War II or marital discord or a string of rodeo clown murders. I mean there's something in the way time moves through and around a novel, and through us and around us when we are reading it, that is singular to books, that is transcendent, that causes us to *rise above the highway,* to contemplate time's passage and its meaning, and to feel its wistful power and wrenching distortions. I think this is truer and more pronounced with novels than with any other form.

Fiction has the power to slow time, to speed it up, to dilate it, to flash it forward and back, to make it as precise as today's date or as wispy as a distant memory. We read about a woman arriving by boat in a small Italian village in 1962, where a hotel owner in the sea watches her while three hundred years of the village's history wash over us, and we flash back eight months to the death of the man's father and then to the day the man took over this hotel, then forward again to the exact moment we started, ten pages and thirty minutes and fifty years ago—the woman still climbing out of the boat, the man still watching her from the water. Back and forth time goes in fiction, as we contemplate lifetimes in a few hundred pages.

Even a reader's enjoyment of a book is tied to time. Most of the nicest e-mails and notes I get include some connection to the time spent reading it: "I tore through it in two days." Or "I lingered over the pages because I didn't want it to end."

Indeed, if you are the type of person who loves reading (objectively speaking: the *best* kind of ▶

person), then your favorite books flag your memory like Post-it notes, calling back specific moments in your own life: epiphanies, tragedies, instances in which the world seemed to open up. I can still close my eyes and recall the afternoons I spent reading *One Hundred Years of Solitude* for the first time, my infant daughter napping on my chest while I flipped the last pages to that glorious, timeless end.

A great film plays before you in a couple of hours while you sit there passively. It's the same with a great play or a great TV show or even a great album. Everyone sees the same movie, but every reader experiences a different book, because reading involves you in hours of active, creative work, the characters, their movements and thoughts re-created in your own mind, their struggles and triumphs connecting to your own until a book becomes like a piece of music you've played—and sometimes mastered—over a period of days, or weeks. *Time* is one of the reasons we go so deep into books, one of the reasons we love them, one of the reasons novels remain, to my mind, the most immersive and compelling art form.

For the author, too, time becomes increasingly important, especially when more of it begins to slip into the rearview. You start to realize that these things are finite, these stories you're writing, and you're so grateful when one of them . . . finishes.

Of course I didn't WANT *Beautiful Ruins* to take fifteen years. Every time I abandoned the book, it was like ending a relationship: that tug of regret, of wasted time and opportunity, the self-blame, feeling foolish and demoralized, wondering if any of this is worth it. During fourteen of those fifteen years the novel existed in my mind as my favorite failure, a hot mess of half-finished sentences and half-formed characters and incomplete stories that I somehow *loved* beyond all reason since I was pretty certain that, as a book, it would never amount to anything.

I would work on it, then abandon it, stop and start and pick it up and put it down, try to find another way into the story, until I realized that these different paths into the story *were the story*. From 1997 until 2012, while I failed over and over at this book, I wrote and published five other novels, along with twenty or so short stories and a thousand other things: essays, reviews, poems, plays, and scripts. I started four or five other novels that also failed—at the time, anyway—half-written wrecks that sit in files, their characters waiting for me to come give them one more chance.

Now, in the gauzy veil of bullshit that we call hindsight, I can see that this particular novel needed all fifteen of those years to be any good, that it needed, more than rewriting, more than organization or index cards or galley slaves . . . time. That I needed time as a writer and a human being, a father and a failure, to finally understand the themes of the novel, to really get to know its people.

I first went to Italy with my wife in early 1997. She had relatives up and down the boot, and I was enchanted by all of it. My favorite place was the quaint villages of the Cinque Terre. We arrived in the first town, Monterosso al Mare, in February, in the off season, after a heavy rain, and we seemed to be the only tourists there. In the morning, the sun came out and we threw open the wooden shutters of our hotel room to see the Ligurian Sea below our window. We hiked the cliff-side trails and took pictures of each other, ate fish and bread, drank wine. We stayed in a place called Albergo Pasquale, and I took a business card from the owner and put it in my wallet. I loved the sound of that name, *Pasquale*, and the double meaning of his name: Passover, a man passed over by life. That card's still in my wallet.

Not long after we got back, my mother was diagnosed with stomach cancer. While I was helping my family nurse her, I started working on a story about a sick young woman who comes to a town in Italy where cancer can't kill you. The first sentence I wrote was this: "She arrived in the village by boat, the only way one could arrive directly." I invented an earnest young man named Pasquale who fell in love with her, and I called his hotel the Hotel Adequate View, because—the reason for about half of my authorial decisions—it struck me as funny. That summer, after my mom died and I couldn't figure out what to do with Dee and Pasquale, I quit working on my Italian novel and jumped to something else.

But I kept finding my way back to it over the next few years, usually when I was stuck on one of the other novels I was writing. I worked a little on movie scripts, and so Dee became an actress. Pasquale was a college student who couldn't leave home because his father had just died. The book had maybe a dozen different titles during that time: *The Beautiful American*, *The Smile of Heaven*, *The Port of Shame*, and, for the longest time, *The Hotel Adequate View*. I probably rewrote that first sentence alone three hundred times, moving words around obsessively: "The *actress* arrived in his village by boat, the only way you could come . . . The actress *came to Porto Vergogna* by boat . . . She came by boat to his town . . . *The first time he saw* the actress she was in a boat . . ."

The story itself was pretty simple, reflecting a question I had asked myself: what might cause a man to go looking for a woman he hasn't seen in years? I wondered if the truth we know from physics—that an object has the most stored energy in the moment right *before* it acts (think of a drawn bow)—was true of romance, too, if *potential* wasn't, in some way, love's most powerful form. As I worked on the story, it slowly became about storytelling, too, spreading out broadly among these diverse characters and forms. But always in the center were Dee and Pasquale. In some versions, they slept together. In one, he fathered her baby. In another, she moved back to America and became a lesbian. In still others, by the time Pasquale decided to go find her Dee was already dead. ("Seems a little nihilistic," a writer friend suggested.) When I got stuck, I created a character named Alvis Bender, who was stuck on the first chapter of *his* novel. When I sat in meetings in Hollywood, instead of taking notes on whatever bad idea we were making worse, I made notes for my novel. I found myself at the Tate Modern in London and the Edinburgh Fringe Festival and in Sandpoint, Idaho, and my characters went there too. I kept finding things that amused me. Every time I went back to the novel I started ▶

at the beginning: "The actress arrived . . ." Most of it I ended up throwing away, including an entire draft and several misguided chapters. In one ending, the whole story turned out to have been a pitch for a film; in another even more postmodern version, the writer who came in to pitch a film in Michael Deane's office was me; the story I was pitching, my novel *The Zero.* (I turned out to be the least realistic and sympathetic character I've ever written.) Over the years characters came and went, changed gender and age, gained and lost pounds and years and children, but always, in the center, Dee and Pasquale remained strangely the same, their desire for connection the only constant in this puzzle I was building without any idea what the final picture should look like.

I keep a series of writing journals in which I track my ideas and progress and write notes on stories I start, abandon, restart, and sometimes even finish. *Beautiful Ruins* (or, as it was called during most of that time, the Italian Novel or *The Hotel Adequate View*) appears over the years in those twenty-some journals like a recurring dream, usually showing up a few days after I had finished or abandoned another novel or short story and was looking for something else to work on. From February 2001: *Back to Italian novel: What if I set part of it in early '90s, grunge . . . I just need the right title and backstory.* And from March 2007: *Pasquale wants to be a better man. . . . Can art be a lie? Can it be anything else . . .*

Over and over, I wrote in my journal: *Gave up on the Italian novel . . .* and *Italian novel hit another wall.* But—and I apologize in advance for this—no matter how many times I quit writing that book, it was as if Dee and Pasquale wouldn't take no for an answer.

Readers often ask some version of "How long does it take to write a novel?" It's a great question, but when I give the most honest answer—"A novel takes as long as it takes"—I feel like a Buddhist. Or an asshole.

In 2007, I had stalled on a comic story about a suburban family raising cattle and went back to the Italian Novel. My good friend and fellow writer Dan Butterworth invited me to come to Florence to speak to his students there, so I decided to go and immerse myself again and see if I could find some way to finish it. This was it: if, after a decade, I couldn't get it right this time, I'd walk away. I took pages and pages of notes as Dan and I hiked Cinque Terre and hung out in Florence and did our best to support the local wine economy.

On my last night in Italy, I went to bed and started writing in my journal, ideas and insights and sketches. I'd just start to fall sleep and then wake up with another thought and jot it down ("Paintings inside the machine gun turrets?"). I had all sorts of small epiphanies about the way we saw our lives as movies and novels. Characters burst forth with fresh details about themselves ("Deane's assistant went to film school!"). That night, I wrote thirty pages in my journal. The final entry: "Oh wow. Birds chirping. I wrote all night."

Fired up by my trip, I spent much of the next year and a half researching and rewriting *The Hotel Adequate View*, starting again from the very beginning ("The *dying* actress came to his village . . ."). I realized I had the hardest time explaining the novel. Once I did an event with another author, and when the audience asked what we were working on I said I'd just abandoned a suburban cattle-ranching novel for a multigenerational, multi-genre, multi-point-of-view book about 1960s Italy, present-day Hollywood, World War II, and the Donner Party. It was quiet for a moment, and then the other writer said, "I think you should go back to the cattle-ranching book."

Finally, in the summer of 2008, I finished *The Hotel Adequate View*. After more than a decade, I had finally done it. I was ecstatic. For forty-eight hours. Then I realized it wasn't really done. I had most of the pieces, but the puzzle still hadn't come together. Exhausted, I set the book aside and started another novel, hoping to write something very different, something linear, straightforward, and first-person. Eight months later, when I finished *The Financial Lives of the Poets* (the other asshole answer to "How long does a novel take?" is *somewhere between eight months and fifteen years*), I recalled something my hero Kurt Vonnegut had written in a copy of *The Sirens of Titan* he'd generously sent me six years earlier: "To my fellow novelist Jess Walter: This is the one book of mine that wrote itself. All the others refused."

I knew exactly what he meant.

So in 2009, I went back to the novel that kept refusing to write itself. And there, waiting for me, were Dee and Pasquale. They'd been waiting patiently for more than a decade (or since 1962, depending on how you counted), and I almost felt like I owed it to them to see if there wasn't some way I could finally reunite them. I went back to the first scene, to the first sentence, and started yet another rewrite ("The dying actress *arrived* in his village . . ."). I threw out more than half of what I'd done, reworked every sentence, and set out once more to do right by two characters I had now "known" for almost a third of my life.

I dove back into my research and came across two pieces that helped me finish. The first involved Richard Burton. In each draft of the novel, he exerted more influence (he had first climbed into a car with Pasquale sometime around 2005). In 2010, I was reading a piece by Louis Menand in *The New Yorker* about Dick Cavett, in which he referenced Burton's four interviews with Cavett in 1980 and described the fifty-four-year-old Welsh actor as "already a beautiful ruin . . ."

It was as if that phrase *beautiful ruin* rose off the page. I immediately went back through the novel, stunned at how many times I had used words like *ruins* and *rubble* to describe the people and places, the remnants of the Hollywood system, the shards of our culture; the very novel itself was constructed of artifacts, bits of movies and books and plays. I had my title.

Later, I was reading *The Art of the Novel* by Milan Kundera and I came across this: "There would seem to be nothing more obvious, more tangible and palpable than the present moment. And yet it eludes us completely. All the sadness of life lies in that fact."

This, I saw, could be the ending of the book, a way of acknowledging the power of certain moments in our lives. These are the ruins of our memories, ▶

About the book

which loom in our minds like the Parthenon, even as they are decayed and weathered by time and regret. I hoped to convey the significance of such isolated moments in our lives, to show that Pasquale and Dee's first meeting—which had kicked around in my own head since 1997— might indeed be powerful enough to drive him to find her almost fifty years later. I felt almost as if I'd been carrying these characters around in my hands for fifteen years and now I could let all their stories go, like a handful of dandelion seeds, all those tangible, palpable moments—whether they occurred in 1962 or 2008 or 1945 or 1847— in one glorious ruined present-tense . . . moment.

So I wrote toward that ending, and went back and forth, and one day I looked up and I was done.

Of course, there was much more to it than that: another rewrite, *molto* Italian translations, a few continuity fixes—more patterns, index cards, crossword puzzles—but really, it seemed like I'd finished this time. And the sense of accomplishment seemed to correspond in some way to the number of years I'd spent on it. There are so many elements an author thinks about while writing every day—big things like story and characters, language and voice, and small, technical things like point of view and verb tense—but one element I don't think I'd ever considered before was . . . time. And now, time seemed like the most important piece of all.

I was thirty-one when I started this book, when Dee first got out of that boat and Pasquale sloshed over to meet her. I was forty-six when I finally finished it, when this old couple walked away once more into the hills above Cinque Terre. As crazy as it sounds, whenever I read that last scene, I imagine my old galley slaves turning and nodding, and I feel genuinely happy for them. ⌒

Have You Read?
More by Jess Walter

THE FINANCIAL LIVES OF THE POETS

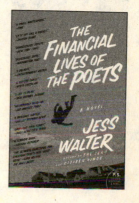

A few years ago, small-time finance journalist Matthew Prior quit his day job to gamble everything on a quixotic notion: a website devoted to financial journalism in the form of blank verse. When his big idea—and his wife's eBay resale business—ends with a whimper (and a garage full of figurines), they borrow and borrow, whistling past the graveyard of their uncertain dreams. One morning Matt wakes up to find himself jobless, hobbled with debt, spying on his wife's online flirtation, and six days away from losing his home. On a desperate two a.m. run to 7-Eleven for milk he falls in with some local stoners and is inspired to hatch the biggest and most misbegotten plan yet.

Following Matt in his weeklong quest to save his marriage, his sanity, and his dreams, *The Financial Lives of the Poets* is a hysterical, heartfelt novel about how we can reach the edge of ruin—and how we can begin to make our way back.

"A deliciously antic tale of an American dream gone very sour . . . part noir gumshoe, part average Joe, [Matt Prior] is a sharp, wide-eyed, soulful observer with a keen eye for the layers of bureaucracy and doublespeak. . . . The novel delivers a scathing indictment of our country's character and the 'ruined systems' we labor under." —*Washington Post*

"The novel has warmth, and its protagonist emerges as a bourgeois Everyman of the downturn." —*The New Yorker*

"A real find. . . . The ultimate something-for-everyone-don't-skip-must-read." —Sara Nelson, *Daily Beast*

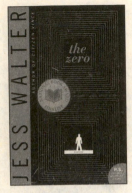

Have You Read? *(continued)*

THE ZERO

- National Book Award Finalist
- Winner of the Pacific Northwest Booksellers Award
- *Los Angeles Times* Book Prize Finalist
- PEN USA Literary Fiction Award Finalist
- A *Washington Post*, *Seattle Times*, and *Kirkus Reviews* Best Book of the Year

Hero cop Brian Remy wakes up to find he's shot himself in the head—so begins a harrowing tour of a city and a country shuddering through the aftershocks of a devastating terrorist attack. As the smoke clears, Remy finds himself lurching between moments of lucidity and days when he doesn't seem to be living his own life at all. The landscape around him is at once fractured and oddly familiar: a world dominated by a Machiavellian mayor known as "The Boss." With a new girlfriend he doesn't know and a son who pretends he's dead, Remy chases a trail of paper scraps for a shadowy intelligence agency known as the Department of Documentation. Whether that trail will lead Remy to an elusive terror cell—or send him circling back to himself—is only one of the questions posed by this provocative yet deeply human novel.

Likened to the works of Franz Kafka and Joseph Heller, *The Zero* is an extraordinary story of how our trials become our transgressions, of how we forgive ourselves and whether or not we should.

"Walter is an immensely talented writer. . . . He's written a new thriller not only with a conscience but also full of dead-on insights into our culture and its parasitic response to a national tragedy."
—*Washington Post*

"This is political satire at its best: scathing, funny, dark. Grade: A." —*Entertainment Weekly*

CITIZEN VINCE

- Winner of the Edgar Allan Poe Award for Best Novel
- Finalist for the ITW Thriller of the Year Award
- An NPR's *Fresh Air* Top Ten Book
- A Best Book of the Year (the *Washington Post*, the *Atlanta Journal-Constitution*, and *Milwaukee Sentinel*

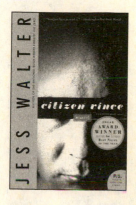

Darkly hilarious and unexpectedly profound, *Citizen Vince* is an irresistible tale about the price of freedom and the mystery of salvation by an emerging writer of boundless talent.

Eight days before the 1980 presidential election, Vince Camden wakes up at 1:59 a.m. in a quiet house in Spokane, Washington. Pocketing his stash of stolen credit cards, he drops by an all-night poker game before heading to his witness-protection job dusting crullers at Donut Make You Hungry. This is the sum of Vince's new life: donuts and forged credit cards—not to mention a neurotic hooker girlfriend.

But when a familiar face shows up in town, Vince realizes that his sordid past is still close behind him. During the next unforgettable week, on the run from Spokane to New York, Vince Camden will negotiate a maze of obsessive cops, eager politicians, and assorted mobsters, only to find that redemption might just exist—of all places—in the voting booth. Sharp and refreshing, *Citizen Vince* is the story of a charming crook chasing the biggest score of his life: a second chance.

"Refreshing. . . . entertaining. . . . For readers who appreciate wry precision and expert timing, it may be enough to know that *Citizen Vince* arrives with sky-high praise from both Ken Bruen and Richard Russo, with whom Mr. Walter shares these qualities. For others, the book's fusion of humor, crime, and politics may be recommendation enough."

—Janet Maslin, *New York Times*

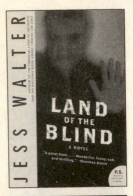

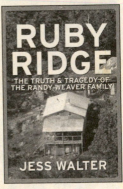

Have You Read? *(continued)*

LAND OF THE BLIND

In this fiendishly clever and darkly funny novel, Jess Walter speaks deeply to the bonds and compromises we make as children—and the fatal errors we can make at any moment in our lives.

"Intelligently written, bittersweet, and thoroughly absorbing . . . an affecting meditation on friendship and the price of betrayal."
—*Seattle Times*

OVER TUMBLED GRAVES

• A *New York Times* Notable Book

During a routine drug bust, Spokane detective Caroline Mabry finds herself on a narrow bridge over white-water falls in the center of town, face-to-face with a brutal murderer. As Caroline and her cynical partner, Alan Dupree, are thrown headlong into the search for a serial murderer who communicates by killing women, they uncover some hard truths about their profession . . . and each other.

"Riveting. . . . Without ever taking the easy way out, the book explores the battle of good versus evil on very human terms."
—*Washington Post Book World*

RUBY RIDGE

On the last hot day of summer in 1992, gunfire cracked over a rocky knob in northern Idaho, just south of the Canadian border. This is the true story of what happened on Ruby Ridge: the tragic and unlikely series of events that destroyed a family, brought down the number-two man in the FBI, and left in its wake a nation increasingly attuned to the dangers of unchecked federal power.

"A stunning job of reporting."
—*New York Times Book Review*

"The definitive account of Ruby Ridge."
—*New York Post*

Don't miss the next book by your favorite author. Sign up now for AuthorTracker by visiting www.AuthorTracker.com.